SMALL COMPUTER
THEORY
AND
APPLICATIONS

McGraw-Hill Publications in Electronic Computer Technology

Gordon Silverman, Project Editor

Books in This Series:

SMALL COMPUTER THEORY AND APPLICATIONS by Denton J. Dailey

MATHEMATICS FOR COMPUTERS by Arthur D. Kramer

INTEGRATED CIRCUITS FOR COMPUTERS: PRINCIPLES AND APPLICATIONS by William L. Schweber

COMPUTERS AND COMPUTER LANGUAGES by Gordon Silverman and David Turkiew

DIGITAL TECHNOLOGY WITH MOS INTEGRATED CIRCUITS by Ronald J. Webb

SMALL COMPUTER THEORY AND APPLICATIONS

DENTON J. DAILEY
Butler County Community College
Butler, Pennsylvania

McGRAW-HILL BOOK COMPANY

New York   Atlanta   Dallas   St. Louis   San Francisco   Auckland   Bogotá   Guatemala
Hamburg   Lisbon   London   Madrid   Mexico   Milan   Montreal   New Delhi   Panama
Paris   San Juan   São Paulo   Singapore   Sydney   Tokyo   Toronto

Sponsoring Editor: John J. Beck
Editing Supervisor: Vivian Koenig
Design and Art Supervisor: Nancy Axelrod
Production Supervisor: Mirabel Flores

Cover Photography: James Nazz

The manuscript for this book was processed electronically.

Library of Congress Cataloging-in-Publication Data

Dailey, Denton J.
  Small computer theory and applications.

  Includes index.
  1. Microcomputers. I. Title.
QA76.5.D244   1987   004.16   87-4035
ISBN 0-07-050409-1

Small Computer Theory and Applications

1234567890 DOCDOC 8943210987

ISBN 0-07-050409-1

CONTENTS

PREFACE

Small Computer Theory and Applications is designed for use by students of technology who will have careers in electronics, computers, and related technical fields. All technically trained individuals should understand the general nature of the small computer, its peripherals, architecture, and various operating systems, and how to troubleshoot it. While this book stresses hardware, the author has used an integrated approach that covers software and applications as well.

To use this text to its utmost advantage, students should have a basic understanding of dc and ac circuit theory, linear and digital electronics, and the use of electronic test equipment. Some knowledge of high-level languages, such as BASIC, or assembly language programming will enhance the students' appreciation of the material, although this is not an essential requirement.

With the proliferation of the computer many new technical, as well as nontechnical, employment opportunities have developed. A broad range of skills is required in order to take advantage of emerging computer career possibilities. These skills vary from knowledge of the physical elements of the computer (the hardware) to the ability to design the information needed to initiate operational commands or instructions (the software). The topics included in this book provide technically oriented students a foundation in both the hardware and the software elements of the computer. The topics will also provide educational support for many technical curriculums whose programs include study of the small digital computer. While emphasis is primarily on the small computer, which is also known as the microcomputer, the personal computer, or the PC, the material is arranged so that it can be applied to the study of other, larger computer systems.

The central theme of this text is the important architectural elements of a small computer, and an 8088 microprocessor is used as the model. The student becomes familiar with the technical knowledge that underlies the important skills of interfacing other electronic systems to the computer and troubleshooting. Topics which are highlighted include operation of the memory, input/output (I/O) techniques, interrupts, interfacing applications such as data acquisition and control—digital-to-analog (D/A) and analog-to-digital (A/D) conversion—and data communication including coverage of major communications standards and error detection and correction techniques. Study of programmed, polled, and interrupt-driven data acquisition methods provides an important background for the many real-time applications of the PC. A study of the PC would not be complete without discussion of the hardware associated with its graphics system.

In order to develop a full understanding of the computer, the student is introduced to machine and assembly language programming. Emphasis is placed on the use of a "user-friendly" assembler/debugger, which avoids the technical difficulties associated with more complex macro assemblers. Programming examples emphasize engineering-related applications, particularly those which career-oriented individuals are likely to encounter in the workplace. These examples are carefully stated and include detailed solutions. The power of a high-level language programming capability is not overlooked as many BASIC examples are included to supplement discussion of software material.

An accompanying laboratory manual that contains various activities and experiments is available. This manual is designed to reinforce the concepts and material presented in the text and to provide important opportunities for the student to practice what is discussed in the classroom.

The author wishes to acknowledge the constructive recommendations provided by Frank T. Duda, Jr., of Grove City College, Grove City, Pennsylvania; Frank T. Gergelyi of Metropolitan Technical Institute, Fairfield, New Jersey; and Richard L. Rouse, DeVry Institute of Technology, Kansas City, Missouri, as well as the assistance of Dr. Gordon Silverman.

Denton J. Dailey

AN OVERVIEW OF MICROCOMPUTER SYSTEMS

1

This chapter serves as a broad introduction to microprocessors and microcomputers. Topics to be discussed include background information regarding the development of microprocessors and modern microcomputer systems. Some comparisons between early microcomputer technology and current microcomputer technology will be made. Also, some general information regarding system options, such as input and output devices that are now available, will be presented.

1-1 HISTORICAL BACKGROUND

Microprocessor and microcomputer technologies have evolved rapidly over the last few years. The first microprocessors developed were used primarily to provide for low-cost, flexible automatic control in industrial applications. The use of the microprocessor in such applications allowed much greater flexibility of operation when compared to conventional hard-wired digital logic. Hard wiring is the term applied to circuits (usually digital) that are designed (wired) to perform one specific function. If modifications in the operation of the circuit are required or the intended application environment is changed, often a complete redesign of the hard-wired circuit is necessary. The programmability of the microprocessor allows most such changes in operational requirements to be made through programming, eliminating the need for costly hardware redesigns. This was one of the main driving forces behind the development of early microprocessors.

1-1.1 Microprocessor Development

The first commercially available microprocessor to be developed was the Intel 4004. The 4004 was a 4-bit central processing unit (CPU) that combined the equivalent of about 5 ft³ of discrete circuitry (resistors, transistors, diodes, and interconnecting wiring) onto a silicon chip about ¼ in square. The 4004 had a rather limited instruction set, and although it is now largely obsolete, it did open the door for the widespread acceptance of microprocessors. The successor to the 4004 was the Intel 8008. The 8008 was essentially an 8-bit version of the 4004 with an expanded instruction set. The 8008 is also obsolete today. The next major microprocessor to be released was the Intel 8080. The 8080 had a much larger and more powerful instruction set than the 8008, operated at higher speeds, and was quickly implemented in the design of new equipment. At about the same time that the 8080 was released, several other manufacturers released microprocessors of their own. Two of these, the Motorola 6800 and the MOS 6502, are still very popular and widely used today.

1-1.2 Microcomputer Development

If there is one field of electronics that was pioneered by experimenters, it is that of the microcomputer for personal use (what are now called personal computers). The first microcomputers to become commercially available were introduced in the mid-1970s. A typical example of these early microcomputers was the Altair 8800 produced by MITS. The Altair 8800 was designed around the Intel 8080 CPU. In 1975 this microcomputer sold for $621 assembled, with no on-board memory, keyboard, or display (other than light-emitting diodes, or LEDs, for reading the binary contents of various registers and memory locations). At that time, a circuit board housing 1K byte of random access memory (RAM) sold for $97 and a 4K byte memory board cost $246. Programming was done in machine language via toggle switches on the front panel of the machine, although a BASIC interpreter was available at extra cost. In all, owning a personal computer was a fairly expensive proposition at that time, and it helped a lot if one was also an experienced electronics experimenter, engineer, or programmer, armed with some test equipment.

One of the reasons for the high cost of these early microcomputers was the relatively low volume of units that were being produced and sold. In order for a complex piece of equipment such as a microcomputer to be offered at low prices, a large number of units must be produced and sold. This helps to offset the cost of design, development, labor, marketing, and manufacturing. Large-volume production and sales are one reason why very sophisticated personal computers are available today at reasonable prices. Another factor accounting for the high cost of early microcomputers was the cost of the electronic components that were available at that time. In 1975 an Intel 8080A could be purchased for about $38. In 1985 the same 8080A sold for about $4. The cost of memory has also been decreasing rapidly. Again, in 1975 a cost of about 2 cents/bit was typical for dynamic RAM as compared to 1985, when memory costs were about 0.005 cents/bit and decreasing. The comparisons could go on, but the point is that the microcomputer field has changed dramatically over a very short time and is still evolving rapidly.

The typical personal computer in use today is actually a relatively complex electronic system. From a system standpoint, the computer may be broken down into several functional blocks as shown in Fig. 1-1. The

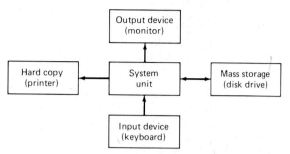

Fig. 1-1 Block diagram of a typical small computer.

central block may be referred to by any of several different names. For example, this block is called the *system unit* by most microcomputer manufacturers. For consistency, this textbook will refer to the central block as the system unit also. The system unit is essentially the actual computer itself. All the other blocks connected externally to the system unit allow for communication between it and the outside world, and for the long-term or mass storage of data and programs. These external devices are referred to as peripheral devices, or just peripherals.

Review Questions for Section 1-1

1. What was the first microprocessor that was produced?
2. What was the main use for the earliest microprocessor?
3. Name two microprocessors that were competitors of the Intel 8080.
4. State two reasons for the decrease in the cost of microcomputers since their inception.
5. What term is applied to an external device that is connected to a computer?

1-2 THE SYSTEM UNIT

The system unit may be considered the heart of the personal computer. This section usually contains the CPU, the memory, the input/output (I/O) ports, the operating system read-only memory (ROM), the facilities for high-level language usage, and the power supply. In some cases, disk drives are also built into the system unit housing, and as such they might possibly be considered a part of it. Even though this is sometimes the case, in this text, disk drives will be treated as peripheral devices. The main sections that make up a typical system unit are shown in the block diagram of Fig. 1-2. Each major section depicted will now be discussed.

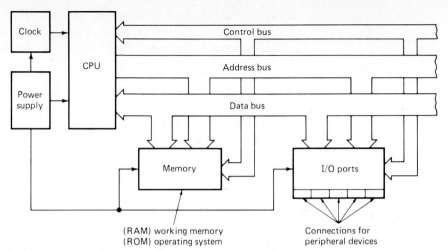

Fig. 1-2 Simplified block diagram of a typical system unit.

1-2.1 The CPU

In most microcomputers, the CPU is responsible for the performance of all logical and arithmetic operations. It also may provide all of the timing and control signals required for system operation. In some cases, however, other devices aside from the CPU may be required to generate some control and timing signals and may even be responsible for the performance of many arithmetic operations. The exact details of how these various tasks are accomplished vary from one system to the next.

A microprocessor is not the same thing as a microcomputer. A microcomputer is a complete system containing memory, input and output devices, various support circuitry, and a microprocessor. The microprocessor, or CPU, is just one of the many basic building blocks (albeit an extremely important one) of the microcomputer as a whole.

In general, most CPUs will consist of the following subsections: an arithmetic logic unit, general purpose registers, special purpose registers, and control logic circuits. Brief descriptions of each of these sections are presented below.

1. **The arithmetic logic unit (ALU).** This is the part of the CPU that is responsible for the computational and logical abilities of the CPU. The ALU performs these various operations on what are referred to as operands. Any data that is manipulated in some way is an operand.

2. **General purpose registers.** Usually two or more general purpose registers are integrated into the CPU. They are used for short-term (temporary) storage of data that is to be or has been acted upon by the CPU. One of the most frequently used general purpose registers is called the accumulator.

3. **Special purpose registers.** These registers are used by the CPU to keep track of what it is doing. Three commonly implemented special purpose registers are the instruction pointer (often called a program counter), the flag or status register, and the stack pointer. Often, other special

purpose registers are also included on the CPU chip for addressing purposes. These are often referred to as index registers or base pointers.

4. Control logic. This section coordinates the movement of data to and from the internal registers, the ALU, and the external connections to the CPU. Generally, an external clock provides the basic timing signal from which all processor actions are referenced. The control logic section produces additional signals at specific times and of specific duration based on the clock signal, for the purposes of reading and writing to and from memory and peripheral devices.

1-2.2 Memory

The memory of the typical microcomputer consists of two sections: the working or program memory, which is composed of random access memory (RAM), and a section of read-only memory (ROM). The contents of the ROM are preprogrammed, and are normally unalterable. The contents of RAM may be altered, and this forms the area of memory in which data and programs are stored.

In most microcomputer applications, the ROM is used for the permanent storage of the operating system and high-level language facilities. The operating system is a very important part of the overall microcomputer system, and is discussed later in this chapter. High level languages are programming languages that allow programs to be created in a form other than the native machine code or mnemonic format for the CPU used in a given machine.

Random access memory is that portion of memory in which data or programs that are written by the user are stored. The size of the memory is generally measured in kilobytes (K byte). In computer parlance, 1K byte = 1024 bytes. For example, a computer that has 2K byte of RAM has storage space for 2048 bytes of instructions and data. A computer with 64K byte of memory actually has 65,536 different byte-length memory locations. As microcomputers become more powerful, memory sizes are specified in megabytes (Mbyte). A 1 Mbyte memory would have 1,048,576 different byte-length memory locations. An example of a microprocessor that can directly address very large amounts of memory is the Motorola 68000. This chip can directly address 16 Mbyte of memory. In general, the more memory that a CPU can address, the more potentially powerful it is, although this is not always the most important feature to consider in a given application.

1-2.3 The Buses

The CPU transfers data to and from memory and other external devices via a group of lines that constitute what is called the data bus. As shown in the block diagram of Fig. 1-2, the data bus is bidirectional. That is, each line of the data bus can serve to carry data either to the CPU or from the CPU. Currently, most microprocessors have data buses that are either 8 or 16 bits wide. The general trend is toward wider data buses, because of the higher data transfer rates that can be achieved. Manufacturers are now producing microprocessors with data buses that are 32 bits wide.

The specific memory location or external device to be accessed is represented by a unique pattern of bits on another group of conductors called the address bus. The address bus is unidirectional, and is driven by the CPU. As in the case of the data bus, address bus widths have been increasing. Older CPUs, such as the Intel 8080 and the Motorola 6800, have 16-bit address buses. The Intel 8088 has a 20-bit address bus, while the Motorola 68000 has a 23-bit address bus.

In order to provide the CPU with information regarding the status of the various devices which it controls and vice versa, the CPU must also be able to send and receive control signals. For example, the system RAM must have read and write signals sent to it for proper operation. An assortment of other various control signals must also be used to allow proper system operation. The lines over which these signals are sent are often called the control bus. The individual lines that make up the control bus are not usually bidirectional. Some of them carry signals from the CPU to other devices, while some carry signals from external devices to the CPU. The data bus is generally the only group of bidirectional lines.

1-2.4 Input/Output (I/O) Ports

The system unit may communicate with peripheral devices via the I/O ports. A port may be unidirectional, as in the case of a video display port, or bidirectional, as in the case of the port that interfaces with the secondary or mass storage device, such as a disk drive. There are many different ways in which a port may be implemented by the computer designer. Often it is possible to program a port to act as either an input or an output, depending upon the requirements of the particular application. In general, ports provide the computer with a means of interfacing with the outside world. The concepts and techniques related to ports and interfacing will be covered in greater detail in later chapters.

1-2.5 The Operating System

The operating system is basically a program that takes care of the many details that are necessary for proper operation of the computer. Some of the tasks performed by the operating system include initializing the computer, reading the keyboard, sending video data to the monitor, performing system self-tests, allocating sections of memory for certain uses, and providing an interface between secondary storage devices, such as disk drives and magnetic tape units. Generally, in smaller systems, the operating system program is stored in the ROM and is activated when the computer is powered-up. Most operating systems are designed to be transparent to the user. This means that the operating system goes about its business without the user being aware of its presence.

Review Questions for Section 1-2

1. What is the function of the ALU?
2. Explain the difference between a microprocessor and a microcomputer.

3. What is the general term given to a group of conductors that carry data and control signals to or from the CPU?
4. What software is responsible for giving the microcomputer the ability to interpret input from a device such as a keyboard?
5. What sections of the microcomputer provide physical connections to which input or output devices may be connected?
6. Internally, what section of the CPU is used for short-term storage of data?

1-3 PERIPHERAL DEVICES

The computer is of little use without provisions for it to communicate with the outside world. Peripheral devices provide this communication ability. This section will provide a general overview of some commonly available peripheral devices.

1-3.1 Input Devices

The keyboard is the most commonly used and one of the most versatile of all microcomputer input devices. There are, however, several other input device options available that may be used in place of or in addition to the keyboard. One input device that is very popular is called a *mouse*. A mouse is a small boxlike device that contains a transducer which converts the relative movement of the mouse on a surface into a digital signal that is sent to the computer over a cable. This signal is interpreted by the computer and is used to position the cursor on the CRT screen. This device was given this name because it does bear some resemblance to a rather strange looking rodent. The mouse is a very handy input device for menu-driven software applications. Most programs that are designed to work with a mouse represent different menu selections in a symbolic form called an icon. An icon is a picture or symbol that represents a certain task that may be performed by the program. Normally, a mouse will also include a push-button switch that is pressed when the cursor has been positioned correctly. This signal causes the program to perform the function that is being pointed to by the cursor.

Some other input devices available include light pens, bar code readers, touch-sensitive screens, digitizers, and even audiomicrophones for voice recognition. The uses for most of these input devices are essentially self-explanatory, with the possible exception of the digitizer. Digitizers are used frequently in computer-aided drafting applications. Basically, a digitizer is a device that converts the position of a pointer or sighting cross hairs over a drawing into data that a computer can manipulate or store for future use. Such positional information can be used to locate corners, centers, and other elements of a mechanical drawing. Three-dimensional digitizers are also available. These devices translate the location of a pointer in space into three coordinate values. These values can be used to create 2D projection drawings of objects whose outlines have been digitized.

Touch-sensitive screens are constructed much like any other CRT, except that the screen has a matrix of very fine wires running vertically and horizontally across its face. Again, a menu-driven program designed to work with this type of screen will usually print a name or an icon beneath the point where two of the wires on the CRT face intersect. The user then chooses the desired operation by pressing on the appropriate point of the screen. This causes the wires to short together and perform just like a push-button switch. The wire matrix may be decoded as would a normal keyboard matrix.

A light pen may consist of nothing more than a phototransistor or photodiode connected to a resistor (connected to the computer, of course). The schematic for a possible light pen circuit is shown in Fig. 1-3. The

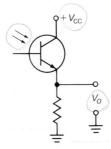

Fig. 1-3 Phototransistor light sensor.

output signal is taken from the junction of the resistor and the phototransistor. The circuit might be used this way: A program could be written that causes a small bright spot to be moved very rapidly across the screen and down one line at a time. By placing the pen against the screen, the phototransistor could be triggered into conduction whenever the bright spot passes beneath it. This causes the pen to generate a lower voltage at its output, which could be used to signal the program to perform some action, based upon the location of the spot when the pen was triggered. Obviously, there could be quite a bit of programming involved to accomplish this task, but the actual light pen circuitry is relatively simple.

There are many other input devices available, and new ones are coming out every day. A look through a few of the computer-oriented magazines will show that many such devices are being developed.

1-3.2 Video Displays

The video display is definitely the most popular output device in use with microcomputers today, and there are several different kinds of video displays available. Probably the least expensive method of producing a video display involves the use of a television receiver and a modulator. A modulator is a device that accepts a video signal from the computer and, with it, modulates the amplitude of a radio frequency (RF) carrier to produce a signal that is compatible with the receiver. Modulation is a process whereby two signals are mixed in a nonlinear manner. Examples of other devices that use modulation are radio transmitters and television transmitters. In fact, the modulator that is used to interface a television to a computer could be thought of as a miniature low-power television transmitter. This video display interfacing method is used very often in lower-cost systems. The problem with this method is that the bandwidth of a standard television is too low to produce a very high resolution display, hence the picture quality tends to be rather poor.

A substantial improvement in picture resolution can be achieved through the use of a monitor. The different types of video display monitors commonly used are shown in Fig. 1-4. Raster scanning is by far the most

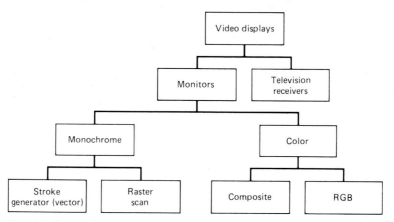

Fig. 1-4 Categories of computer video displays.

popular video technique in use today. Raster scanning is the same method used to generate pictures on a conventional television receiver, where an electron beam is constantly scanned back and forth and down the CRT screen at a rapid rate. In the case of a raster scan monochrome monitor, the video signal is taken directly from the computer and is used to produce the image without going through the intermediate steps of modulation and subsequent demodulation that are necessary with a standard television set. This video display technique will be discussed in more detail in Chap. 9.

Another method of producing video output involves the use of a vector display monitor. A vector-type monitor does not constantly scan the CRT face a line at a time with the electron beam as in raster scanning. Instead, the beam is deflected from point to point on the screen as required to produce various line segments and points, much as the display on an oscilloscope is generated. Such displays are well suited for engineering drawing and computer-aided drafting applications, where high resolution is a major consideration.

Color displays are also almost exclusively of the raster scan variety. Currently, there are two popular types of color monitors in use (other than color televisions). They are composite monitors and red-green-blue (RGB) monitors. A composite monitor is designed in such a way that a single line may carry a signal that contains all of the required video information— such as color, luminance (intensity), and synchronization—to the monitor in composite form. This is very similar to the method used with monochrome monitors. In fact, the only difference is that color information has been added to the signal.

RGB monitors normally have a separate input line for each video attribute. This means that there are input lines for each of the primary colors—red, green, and blue—and one line each for intensity (brightness), vertical sync, and horizontal sync. Although most RGB monitors have a single intensity control line that is used to vary the brightness of all colors identically, there are some that allow independent control of each color's intensity. That is, the intensity signal for each different color (electron gun) is carried on a separate line. This allows many more color and shading variations than are possible with a single intensity control signal. RGB monitors generally produce a higher resolution display than composite color monitors, but most of them (the single intensity control line types, in particular) are limited in their ability to display many different colors. Also, RGB monitors are usually more expensive than similar composite monitors. Most microcomputers produced today have provisions for both composite and RGB type monitors.

Liquid crystal displays (LCDs) are used on most battery-powered, portable, or "notebook" computers. Small portable computers that are about the same size as a typical notebook are often referred to as notebook computers. LCDs have very low power requirements, which makes them just about the only video display choice practical in battery powered applications. Aside from having very low power requirements, LCDs are also very thin and lightweight. Once again, this makes them the ideal choice in portable applications. A few of the problems associated with LCDs are relatively narrow viewing angles and slow response times for rapidly changing displays, although both characteristics are constantly being improved upon. Also, ambient light is required for viewing an LCD.

A relatively recent development in display technology is the color LCD. Previously, LCDs were limited to black and white (silver-gray, actually). This new technology has already been put to use in miniature portable television receivers, and will no doubt be put to good use in microcomputer applications.

Other display types have been produced, such as plasma discharge displays and LED displays; however, they are not as popular as the conventional CRT-type video displays. The main problem with LED-based displays in portable computer applications is that they require relatively high power levels for reasonably large display areas, while in normal microcomputer applications, the CRT display provides higher resolution and better viewing characteristics. Plasma displays show promise in high resolution graphics applications, but are still relatively expensive in comparison to CRT types.

1-3.3 Printers

Whenever hard copy is required in a computer application, a printer is called for. Printers can be categorized in several different ways. One possible categorization is illustrated in Fig. 1-5.

Dot matrix printers are the workhorses of the microcomputer world. A dot matrix printer produces an image or a part of an image by rapidly

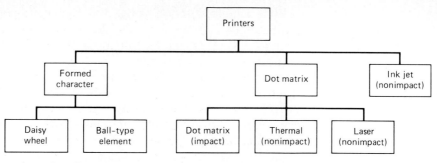

Fig. 1-5 Possible categorization of computer printers.

extending a combination of pins or print wires from its print head as the head is moved across the platen. The platen is the surface on which the paper rests during printing. The extended pins strike an ink-covered ribbon which in turn transfers the pattern formed by the extended pins onto the paper. The quality of print produced with dot matrix printers may vary greatly from one model to another. In general, though, the more pins that are available to produce dots, the better the print quality. Many dot matrix printers do not print an entire character at one time. This is because the print head has only one column of print wires to work with. This print head layout is illustrated in Fig. 1-6. A character is formed one column of

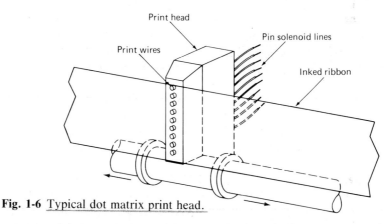

Fig. 1-6 Typical dot matrix print head.

dots at a time. Most dot matrix printers are very fast, printing anywhere from about 80 to 200 characters/s, and many also have some graphics capability. This is one of the more desirable aspects of dot-matrix-type printers; that is, often they allow the creation of custom characters and good quality graphics.

Daisy wheel printers are similar to normal typewriters in that they form a character image when a solenoid-driven hammer strikes a spoke on a round wheel-like character element. Figure 1-7 shows a daisy wheel print element. The impact causes that particular character to be transferred to paper via an inked ribbon. When different characters are to be printed, the daisy wheel is rotated to the correct character position prior to each hammer strike. The print quality of daisy wheel printers is very good, and

Fig. 1-7 Daisy wheel print element.

is considered to be of letter quality. Daisy wheel printing speeds are relatively low when compared to a good dot matrix printer, with a speed of about 30 characters/s being typical. Also, the characters that may be printed with a daisy wheel are limited to those that are present on the wheel itself. Daisy wheel printers are generally more expensive than dot matrix printers.

The thermal, ink jet, and laser printers each differ from the standard dot matrix printers and daisy wheel printers in that they are nonimpact-type printers; that is, they don't rely upon the force of a pin or hammer of some sort to physically pound the ink onto a piece of paper. As might be expected, most nonimpact printers are much quieter in operation than their impact counterparts.

Ink jet printers work by directing a very thin, well defined stream of ink onto the paper. The ink jet is fired from a nozzle that moves back and forth across the paper like the print head of a dot matrix printer. One common method of forming the characters with the ink jet is to use electrostatic deflection. The ink may be charged to a high potential, and deflected in the desired direction by electrodes surrounding the ejection nozzle. The principle is the same as that behind the deflection of the electron beam in a CRT. Another common ink jet printer approach uses a grid of nozzles, each of which may be activated independently of the others. Typically, a small piezoelectric device is used to force ink out of a given nozzle to form an image. Ink jet printers are typically about as fast as good dot matrix printers and produce characters that are at least as good in quality.

Thermal printers form an image by selectively heating small wires in a matrix (similar to a dot matrix printer) in the print head. The heated areas form dots on specially treated heat sensitive paper. Print quality can be quite good, and the thermal printer speed can also be about the same as that of a dot matrix printer. Also, thermal printers are very quiet. The main problem with most thermal printers is the requirement for special heat sensitive paper. This makes them more expensive to operate than an equivalent dot matrix printer. Thermal printers are very quiet and very reliable because they have few moving parts when compared to dot matrix or other impact printers.

For the microcomputer user with few budget restrictions, there are the laser printers. Laser printers produce an image by focusing a pulsed semiconductor laser source across an electrically charged rotating drum. The portion of the drum that is illuminated by the laser electrostatically attracts a powdered toner. The toner is a pigment that is baked onto the paper after it has been exposed to the laser. The operation is very much like that of a photocopying machine. To form an image, the laser beam is scanned across the charged drum, through the use of mirrors and prisms. As the laser beam is scanned, it is pulsed in accordance with the image that is to be formed on the drum. The toner powder will adhere to the areas of the drum that were exposed to the laser. As the drum rotates, it transfers the toner onto the paper. Once the toner is transferred to the paper, it is quickly baked on to form a permanent image. The quality of images produced is very good (letter quality), and print speeds are extremely high (around 10 pages/min, typically). The main drawback to using laser printers is their relatively high cost. This puts them beyond the means of many microcomputer users. However, many business applications that require high print speeds, quality, and quantities more than justify the cost of laser printers.

Another useful device for producing hard copy is the *X-Y* plotter. When an application calls for good printed graphics—such as map making, mechanical drawing, or integrated circuit layout—the *X-Y* plotter is the way to go. The main idea behind the *X-Y* plotter is to give the computer the ability to make drawings the way that a drafter might. As the name implies, *X-Y* plotters have two axes of movement; that is, a pen can be moved east or west along one axis and north or south along the other axis. Pen movement can be accomplished using conventional analog servo-mechanisms, or digitally, using stepper motors. The stepper motor method is used almost exclusively today. Figure 1-8 shows a small *X-Y* plotter for

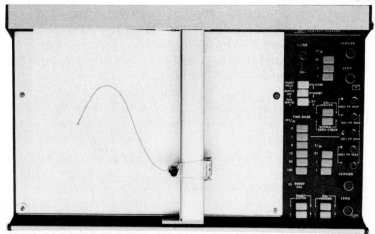

Fig. 1-8 Typical small *X-Y* plotter.

general use. Figure 1-9 shows a large *X-Y* plotter used for producing mechanical drawings. In the case of the plotter shown in Fig. 1-9, the pen is actually moved left and right only. The paper is moved beneath the pen on a rotating drum instead of having the pen move along the other axis. This allows very large drawings to be produced without taking up excessive floor space.

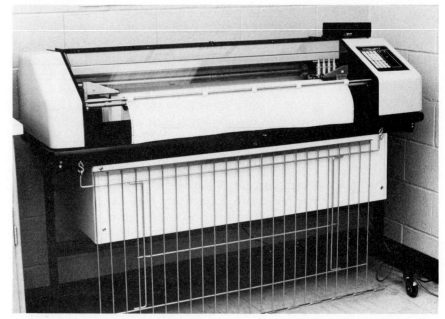

Fig. 1-9 Large *X-Y* plotter used for computer-aided drafting applications.

Review Questions for Section 1-3

1. What is meant by the term *video attribute*?
2. What is an icon?
3. What is the function of a modulator?
4. What is the name of the part of a dot matrix printer that actually produces the image dots?
5. What are the advantages of nonimpact printers over impact types?
6. What type of pen-drive mechanisms are used on *X-Y* plotters?

1-4 SECONDARY STORAGE DEVICES

Secondary storage devices (also called mass storage or external storage devices) allow the microcomputer to store and retrieve large amounts of information for extended periods of time. Although secondary storage devices are considered peripheral devices, they do not provide a communication link with the outside world, and therefore have not been grouped in with the input and output devices.

1-4.1 Disk Storage

The standard secondary storage medium for most microcomputer systems in use today is the floppy disk. There are currently two standard floppy disk sizes in use: 5.25-in and 8-in. The 5.25-in floppy disk is often referred to as a diskette or minidiskette, although in this text it will just be referred to as a disk. A partially dissected floppy disk is shown in Fig. 1-10. The

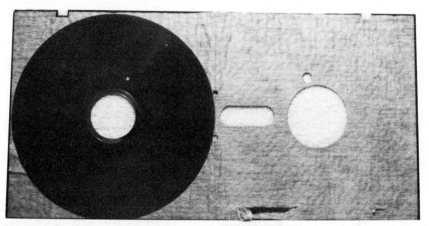

Fig. 1-10 Partially dissected floppy disk.

disk itself is a thin piece of Mylar, coated with a thin layer of ferrous oxide. The disk is rotated inside the plastic jacket, and the read-write head of the disk drive contacts the disk through the oblong opening. The notch seen at the right side of the disk is used for write protection purposes. For most drives, if the notch is covered, the disk is protected from being written on. The white lining inside the disk jacket cleans off any dust particles or loose oxide that may be present on the Mylar disk surface. The smaller round opening in the disk jacket is used to locate an index hole in the disk. An index hole is used by the disk drive as a reference to mark the beginning of storage blocks on the disk.

Another disk storage device that has recently appeared on the scene is the 3.5-in disk. These disks are sometimes referred to as *microfloppies*. The 3.5-in disk is not actually a floppy (synonymous with flexible) disk because it is housed in a rigid plastic case. The actual disk inside the case is very similar to that of a regular floppy disk. The 3.5-in disk has recently been gaining in popularity. This is because the 3.5-in floppies have high storage densities, are proving to be more reliable than 5.25-in floppy disks (since they are mechanically more rugged and therefore less prone to mechanical damage), and are physically smaller.

When choosing a floppy disk, one must also be aware of several other specifications. Some computers require soft-sectored disks, while others require hard-sectored disks. A soft-sectored disk has no particular required size of blocks in which data is stored. Hard-sectored disks have fixed, predefined areas allocated for storage. A soft-sectored disk must always be formatted before it can be used. Formatting is the process whereby markers that designate the size of the data storage blocks or sectors are written onto the disk. The size of the sectors may often be determined by the programmer, based upon the options available with the particular computer being used. This is where the index hole comes into use. It is used as a master reference point to mark the beginning of all the sectors. After that, the rest is up to the user or the system designer. A hard-sectored disk has index holes that mark the beginning of each sector on the disk. The number of sectors is fixed and cannot be altered. Most microcomputer systems use soft-sectored disks.

Disks are also specified as either single-sided or double-sided. A single-sided disk is guaranteed to store data on only one side of the disk, even though both sides of the disk may be coated with oxide. Appropriately enough, double-sided disks can have data stored on either or both sides.

Storage density must also be considered when disks are being chosen. Since it is currently the most widely used in microcomputer applications, the 5.25-in floppy format will be referred to here. There are three popular disk storage densities available: single density, double density, and quad density. The storage density of a disk or a disk drive refers to how many tracks/in the disk will contain. A single-density disk or disk drive is capable of having 24 tracks/in, double density means 48 tracks/in, and quad density is 96 tracks/in. The layout of the tracks and sectors on a disk is shown in Fig. 1-11. Notice that the tracks are represented by concentric rings around

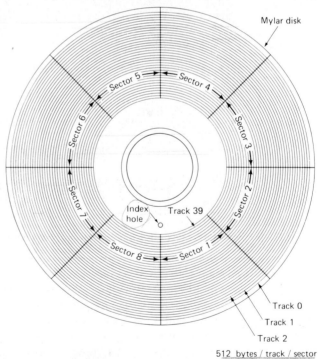

Fig. 1-11 Typical disk track and sector organization.

the center of the disk. The tracks are divided radially into sectors. What this all means is that in most systems, in order to use a disk in a particular drive, the disk must have the correct format (soft or hard) and the correct storage density. Normally, higher-density disks can be used with a drive that is designed to work with a lower-density disk. For example, a double-sided double-density (DS/DD) disk can be written to with a single-sided, single-density (SS/SD) or a double-sided single-density (DS/SD) drive without any problems.

Fixed or hard disk drives (sometimes called *Winchester drives*) are also available for many microcomputers. A hard disk operates along the same lines as a floppy disk, but with tremendously higher storage and access speed capability. As a comparison, consider that the storage capability of a DS/DD disk on an IBM PC is advertised as 360K byte, while typical hard disks can store anywhere from around 2 Mbyte to over 25 Mbyte. This extremely high storage capacity makes hard disks ideal for holding large data bases, such as mailing lists and accounts. A data base is a program that is used to access and maintain a collection or collections of data items. A large size hard disk is shown in Fig. 1-12. In this case, the

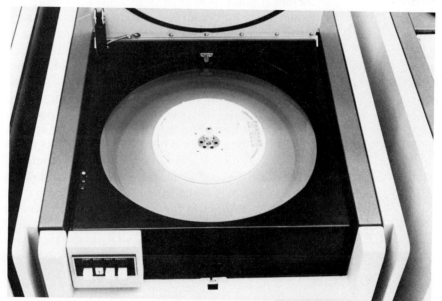

Fig. 1-12 Hard disk and disk drive used with a minicomputer.

disk is an aluminum ring about 1 ft in diameter by about $\frac{1}{16}$ in thick. The ferrous oxide coating is applied to the disk, which is enclosed in a plastic housing. There are many different sizes of hard disks available for use with microcomputers, ranging from the size shown in Fig. 1-12 to 3.5-in-diameter units that mount on a circuit board.

Whether the hard disk is in use or not, the read-write head never comes in contact with the disk itself, as occurs in the operation of a floppy disk. In this case, the head actually floats on a cushion of air produced by the rapidly spinning disk. The distance that separates the head from the disk (flying height) is on the order of 10^{-6} in. With such close spacing between the head and the disk, it is very important that the disk environment be kept as clean as possible. Even a particle of smoke or a fingerprint can impair the operation of a hard disk. To this end, a filtered supply of air may be provided to the disk drive, or it may be totally sealed from the outside.

1-4.2 Tape Storage

At one time, audiocassette tape was a very popular microcomputer storage medium. This was due mainly to the fact that inexpensive disk drives and disk-based operating systems were not available. Standard audiocassette recorders were the usual mass storage device for most microcomputer systems before the development of floppy disk drives. Cassette tape recorders still provide a low-cost method of data storage, but not without some major drawbacks. The main disadvantage associated with cassette data storage is its poor access time. Reading data from a tape can be a very time-consuming process because magnetic tape drives are sequential access devices. In order to get to a desired block of data, all data stored before it must be read through. This is in sharp contrast to disk storage, where access to blocks of data is essentially random. The comparison is analogous to looking for a song you want to hear on a cassette versus doing the same on a record album.

Even though cassette tape access is slow, it does have some practical uses. One of the good things about cassette storage is that a cassette can store an enormous amount of data. A 30-min cassette can hold about 1 Mbyte of data. This means that cassettes can be useful for long-term storage of information that is required rather infrequently but that may be needed at some future date. This application is known as archival storage. When the data is required, it may be loaded onto a disk and processed as necessary. Since disk access is much faster than that of the cassette, the information may be called up from the disk very quickly.

A close relative to the standard cassette recorder is a device called a streaming tape drive. Streaming tape drives share the advantages of the high storage capacity of the hard disk and the lower cost associated with audiotape recording, although access speeds are much higher than are possible with standard cassettes. Streaming tape drives are used in many microcomputer systems as the primary mass storage medium and for providing backup of important disk-based information, such as operating systems, data bases, and other critical programs and data. Streaming tape drives allow very high data transfer rates, with greater than 50,000 bits/s being common. A streaming tape cassette is shown with a standard audiocassette for comparison in Fig. 1-13.

Review Questions for Section 1-4

1. What are the three standard floppy disk sizes?
2. What is the term given to the process whereby a disk is made ready for use with a disk drive?

Fig. 1-13 Standard audiocassette and a streaming tape cassette.

3. What is the purpose of an index hole?
4. What are the names of the storage areas on a disk?
5. What is meant by the term *archival storage?*
6. Why is retrieval of information from a sequential access device generally slower than that from a random access device?

1-5 MODEMS

Since they are such commonly used devices, modems will be discussed briefly in this chapter. Chapter 10 will present further details concerning modems and data communication applications in general.

Computers are often used in data communications applications. Such applications generally require the use of a device called a modem (short for modulator-demodulator). Most modems provide an interface that allows a computer to communicate with other devices via the telephone system. The modem converts the computer's digital output into an audio signal (modulation) that can be transmitted over the telephone lines. Likewise, the modem also provides conversion of the received audio signal into a digital format suitable for computer use (demodulation). There are two ways in which a modem may be connected to the telephone system: with a direct connection to the line via a standard telephone jack or through an acoustic coupler. In the first approach, the electrical signals generated by the modem are driven directly onto the lines. An acoustic coupler converts the modem's output into an audio signal that is picked up by the telephone handset. The direct connection method is used much more often today.

Modems are often classified in terms of the speed with which they can transmit and receive data. The units used to express the rate of transmission are usually either bits/s or baud rate (Bd). The baud rate is the reciprocal of the time that a given bit of data (the representation of a 1 or 0) is present at the output of the modem. Typical baud rates used today are 75, 100, 150, 300, 600, 1200, 2400, 4800, 9600, and 19,200 Bd. Modems that operate at rates up to 300 Bd are considered to be low speed modems. Because of bandwidth limitations, modems that are used to communicate over standard telephone lines are limited to about 1200 Bd. For higher data transmission rates, specially conditioned lines may be leased. Modems are also classified as either full duplex or half duplex. A full duplex modem will allow simultaneous transmission and reception of data. Half duplex modems must receive and transmit data at different times.

Modems are available for almost all personal computers produced today. The use of a modem allows access to several large data bases, such as CompuServe and The Source, and enables the user to communicate with other modem-equipped computers. CompuServe and The Source are data bases that are accessed by a computer via the telephone system. In order to gain access to the data base, the customer must have a valid access code or password. In order to receive an access code, a user's fee must be paid to the company that controls the data base.

Review Questions for Section 1-5

1. Would most modems be classified as serial or parallel devices? Explain your reasoning.
2. When a modem is in the transmit mode (the computer is sending data out), would the modem be functioning as a modulator or a demodulator?
3. What function is performed by a modem when it is used to convert a received audio signal into a digital signal?
4. What is the main limiting factor for data transmission speeds using the telephone system?
5. What device converts the output of a modem into an audio signal?

SUMMARY

The rapid advancement of integrated circuit technology has allowed the microcomputer to become a very useful and powerful business, educational, scientific, and entertainment tool. The costs of microprocessors and related devices have declined rapidly over the past few years, while the power of systems based on such devices has increased.

The microcomputer system is composed of several building blocks: the system unit and various peripheral devices. The system unit communicates with the peripheral devices via I/O ports. Some commonly used peripheral devices include keyboards, monitors, disk drives, printers, plotters, tape drives, and modems. Disk and tape drives are considered mass storage devices.

The disk drive is the most commonly used of all mass storage devices, with floppy disks currently being the most popular disk storage medium. Floppy disks are available in various sizes, and are divided into tracks and sectors. Magnetic tape is usually used for archival storage.

The operating system is a program that is contained in ROM, and provides the instructions that allow for automatic initialization of the system. Peripheral device I/O routines are normally included in the operating system program. A high-level language interpreter is also usually contained in the system's ROM.

Some data communications applications may be realized using a modem to interface the computer to the telephone system. A modem converts the digital output of the computer into an audio form that is compatible with the standard telephone system. When a modem receives a signal, it converts the audio into the digital format required by the computer.

CHAPTER QUESTIONS

1-1. What part of a computer provides a channel through which peripheral devices may communicate with the computer?

1-2. Name two types of color monitors and explain their differences.

1-3. Explain one problem with using a television receiver as a monitor.

1-4. How many index holes does a soft sectored floppy disk have?

1-5. In what manner is data written to and read from a magnetic tape storage device?

1-6. What is the name given to a symbol that is used to represent a task or function to be performed by a program?

1-7. Would a dot matrix printer be considered a formed character printer? Would an IBM Selectric typewriter?

1-8. What type of magnetic tape storage device has a very high rate of data transfer?

1-9. Which of the microprocessor buses is bidirectional?

1-10. In what method of video display generation is an electron beam repeatedly scanned back and forth and down the face of a CRT?

CHAPTER PROBLEMS

1-11. If a modem has a bit time of 1.11 ms, what is its baud rate?

1-12. Based on the circuit shown in Fig. 1-3, draw the schematic for a light pen circuit using a photodiode as the detector that will produce a low logic output when no illumination is present and a high logic level when illumination is present.

1-13. If a modem has a bit time of 104.17 μs, what is its baud rate?

1-14. Another modem has a baud rate of 1200 Bd. For what length of time will a given bit be represented?

1-15. A certain single-sided floppy disk can store 327,680 bytes of data. If this disk has 40 tracks and 8 sectors/track, how many bytes can be stored in a single sector?

INTRODUCTION TO THE 8088 CPU ARCHITECTURE AND INSTRUCTION SET

Monolithic microprocessors are the integrated circuits that make today's personal computers possible. In this chapter you will be introduced to one of the most widely used microprocessors on the market today, the Intel 8088 (iAPX 88/10).

The 8088 was closely modeled after its immediate predecessor, the Intel 8086. The 8086 (iAPX 86/10) is a high-density 16-bit CPU, with a 16-bit data bus multiplexed onto a 20-bit address bus. The 8086 can directly address up to 1 Mbyte of memory (actually 1,048,576 bytes). From the preceding brief overview, it is clear that the 8086 is quite a powerful CPU in comparison to the older 8080 and 6800 chips. But there is one slight problem to applying it in a personal computer, and that is the 16-bit data bus. There are literally hundreds of different peripheral devices and integrated circuits on the market that are designed for use with 8-bit computers. Such 8-bit devices are relatively inexpensive and readily available. This may be part of the reason that many manufacturers have chosen the 8088, the 8-bit data bus version of the 8086, as the CPU for their personal computers.

Both the 8086 and 8088 are packaged in 40-pin ceramic dual in-line pins (DIPs); and internally, both have the same size and number of registers. The 8088 also has the same instruction set as the 8086, so the two devices are software compatible. The main difference between the two microprocessors is in the size of their external data buses. The 8088 has an 8-bit data bus, while that of the 8086 is 16 bits wide. Although this chapter is written specifically for the 8088, the material presented also applies to the 8086, in most cases.

2-1 8088 ARCHITECTURE

In order to retain much of the power of a true 16-bit CPU, the 8088 has essentially the same internal structure as the 8086. That is, internally the

8088 can handle data in 16-bit groups. Such 16-bit groups are called words, when applied to the 8088. The 8088 can also process data 1 byte at a time, as would a conventional 8-bit CPU. Functionally, the 8088 CPU is divided into two sections: the bus interface unit (BIU) and the execution unit (EU). The block diagram in Fig. 2-1 illustrates this structure.

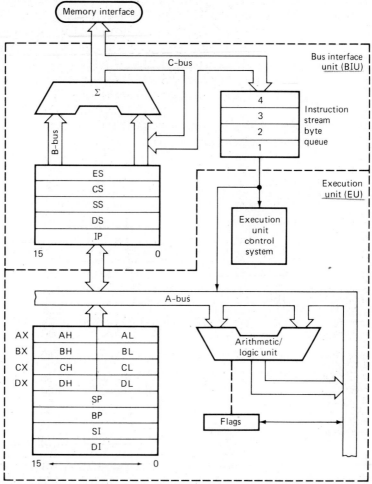

Fig. 2-1 Internal organization of the 8088 CPU. (Courtesy of Intel Corporation.)

2-1.1 The Bus Interface Unit

The major parts of the BIU are the segment registers, the instruction stream byte queue (pronounced "Q"), and the address summing block. Connections between these blocks are made via internal buses labeled B and C. The BIU handles all transfers of data to and from the CPU over the external 20-bit address/data bus.

The Instruction Queue The function of the instruction queue is to increase processor throughput. Throughput is a general term that refers to the average speed with which program tasks are performed. When executing a program, a microprocessor (such as the Intel 8080 or the Motorola 6800) fetches an instruction from memory, decodes it, executes it, and then fetches the next instruction, decodes it, executes it, and so on. Only one of these operations (fetch or execute) can be performed at a time, and often the CPU spends as much time on fetching instructions as it does on executing them. The time spent fetching instructions from memory is essentially wasted time. The 8088 BIU is able to fetch up to 4 additional bytes and load them into the instruction queue while a given instruction is being decoded and executed. In other words, the 8088 can do two things at one time. This enhances execution speed because access to the queue is much faster than access to memory.

Segment Registers and Address Summer The 8088 CPU contains four 16-bit wide registers called segment registers. The segment registers are used by the address summer to form a 20-bit address code. The names of the individual segment registers are the extra segment (ES), code segment (CS), stack segment (SS), and data segment (DS). The segment registers are programmable and are used to form base addresses from which specific areas of program memory are addressed. The term *base address* refers to a particular address location to which an offset (or offsets) quantity is added. The sum of the base address and the offset address yields the absolute address of the memory location accessed.

2-1.2 The Execution Unit

The execution unit section of the 8088 is exactly the same as that of the 8086. This is the part of the CPU where the instructions are decoded, control signals are generated, and data is manipulated. The main sections of the EU are the arithmetic logic unit (ALU), the general purpose registers, the special purpose registers, and the control logic.

The Arithmetic Logic Unit The arithmetic logic unit is the part of the EU that is responsible for all of the computational and logical abilities of the CPU. The ALU is designed to work with both 8- and 16-bit operands, and interfaces with memory and input/output (I/O) devices over an 8-bit data bus that is time multiplexed onto the 20-bit external bus along with the addresses. Time multiplexing means that during some time intervals, eight of the CPU pins are used for data transfer (as a data bus), while during other times those same lines are used for addressing purposes. This multiplexing technique reduces the number of pins required on the integrated circuit (IC) package, which in turn reduces the cost of the CPU.

The General Purpose Registers There are four general purpose 16-bit registers available within the EU. They are labeled AX, BX, CX, and DX, and are shown in Fig. 2-1. These registers may also be used to form eight independent 8-bit registers. When used as 8-bit registers, the low order bytes of the 16-bit registers are designated as AL, BL, CL, and DL; while the high-order bytes of the registers are designated as AH, BH, CH, and DH. Most of these registers (both 8- and 16-bit) can be used in any arithmetic or logical operations that the 8088 can perform. However, a few of them are used for specific purposes by certain instructions. Such specialized uses of the general purpose registers were implemented to produce a more powerful instruction set. That is, certain registers are implied by a given instruction as containing specific information, such as the number of times a loop is to be executed. The details of the instructions that use the general purpose registers in this way will be presented later in this chapter.

Special Purpose Registers   The 8088 EU contains four other 16-bit registers which serve as pointers and indexes. These registers are called the stack pointer (SP), base pointer (BP), source index (SI), and destination index (DI). The main purpose of these registers is to hold offset or displacement addresses for operand sources and destinations located in memory. The terms *offset* and *displacement* are used synonymously, and refer to memory addresses located relative to a predetermined base location. You will recall that a given segment register will contain the base location to which an offset is added in order to specify an absolute address. The index and pointer registers may also be used to hold instruction operands as well as offset quantities. An operand is an entity (a number or register) that is to be operated upon or manipulated in some way by an instruction. Arithmetic operations can be performed directly on the contents of the SP, BP, SI, and DI registers to allow the computation of operand offset addresses.

The Flags   The last register in the EU is the 16-bit flag or status register. Nine of the 16 bits in this register are used to indicate processor status and the occurrence (or lack of occurrence) of specific events that may take place during the execution of certain instructions. The occurrence of a particular event will set its corresponding flag; otherwise the flag will be cleared. For example, if two 1-byte numbers are added and a carry out of the most significant bit (MSB) of the result is generated, the carry flag will be set (CF = 1). However, if the addition did not produce a carry out of the MSB, the carry flag will be cleared (CF = 0). Several of the flags are used to control the operation of the CPU. These control flags are the TF, IF, and DF. The details of the flag register are presented in Fig. 2-2.

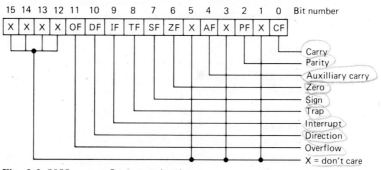

Fig. 2-2 8088 status flag organization.

Review Questions for Section 2-1

1. What is the function of an instruction queue?
2. What is meant by the term *multiplexed bus*?
3. Which registers are considered to be general purpose registers?
4. Which registers are used as bases to which offset addresses are added?
5. What term is given to a quantity that is acted upon in an arithmetic or logic operation?
6. How would a given flag indicate that a specific event did not occur during the execution of an instruction?

2-2 SEGMENTED ADDRESSING

It was stated earlier that the 8088 has a 20-bit address bus, but a quick look back at Fig. 2-1 shows that the largest registers available within the CPU are 16 bits wide. How is it possible to produce a 20-bit address using such registers? The engineers at Intel have devised a method called segmented addressing to produce the required 20-bit addresses. Basically, segmented addressing works this way: A given segment register is used to point to the beginning of a block of memory that is 64K byte (65,536 bytes) long. Since there are four segment registers, there will be four such 64K byte blocks. Any individual location within one of these blocks of memory is addressed relative (in the positive direction, or toward higher memory) to the contents of the segment registers. The 64K byte blocks that are formed this way are referred to as the current data segment, current code segment, current stack segment, or current extra segment, depending on which segment register is being referenced during a memory access.

Internally, the CPU treats the contents of the segment registers as if they were multiplied by 16_{10} when accessing memory. This has the same effect as shifting the binary contents of the segment registers left by four places, which is also the same as shifting the hexadecimal equivalent of the register's contents left by one place. The end result is that the contents of a given segment register represent a 20-bit binary number with zeros in the four least significant bit positions, or a 5-digit hex number with a 0 in the least significant digit. This shifted number is used as a base upon which a 64K byte block or segment of memory may be addressed. The instruction being executed specifies where within a particular segment of memory the operand is located, by providing an offset or displacement address that is added to the contents of the shifted segment register contents. This summation occurs in the summing block of the BIU. Figure 2-3 shows how the absolute address of a memory location is determined by the CPU. Notice that a segment address alone can point to only every 16th byte of memory because the four least significant bits are always effectively 0. This means that segment boundaries can occur only at 16-byte intervals.

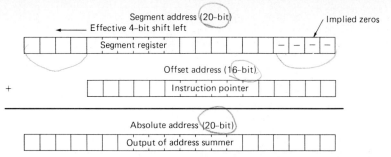

Fig. 2-3 Formation of the absolute address from segment and offset words.

Example 2-1

The DS register contains $A300_{16}$. A certain instruction specifies that its operand is located at an offset address of $950F_{16}$ into the current data segment. What is the absolute address of the operand in hex?

Solution

The absolute address may be found by first shifting the contents of the DS register left one place, producing DS = $A3000_{16}$. Next, the offset is added to the shifted DS contents, producing $A3000_{16} + 950F_{16} = AC50F_{16}$. This is the absolute address of the operand.

As stated before, the 64K byte blocks of memory that are based on the segment register contents may begin on any 16-byte interval within the total memory address space. The various segments that are created may be totally isolated from one another, or they may overlap. Figure 2-4*a* illustrates nonoverlapping segments based on the contents of the segment registers given as CS = 0000_{16}, DS = 1000_{16}, SS = 2000_{16} and ES = 3000_{16}.

Figure 2-4*b* shows how segments could overlap with the segment register contents CS = 0100_{16}, DS = 0200_{16}, SS = 0300_{16} and ES = 0400_{16}. In the case of Fig. 2-4*b*, each segment overlaps the previous one by 61,337 bytes. There may be certain times when it is desirable to have overlapping segments, and even segments that start at the same address (100 percent overlap).

Example 2-2

A certain operation requires the contents of absolute memory location $07DB2_{16}$ to be examined. The instruction used to examine this location specifies that its operands must be located within the current data segment. If the DS register contains $020A_{16}$, what offset address must be supplied to the instruction?

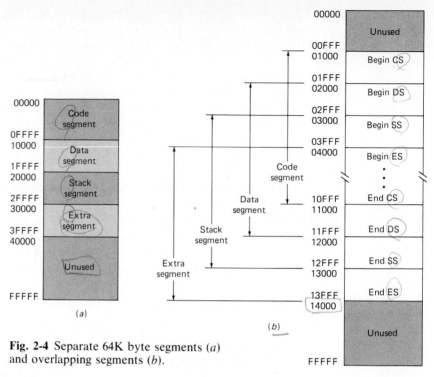

Fig. 2-4 Separate 64K byte segments (*a*) and overlapping segments (*b*).

Solution

The correct offset may be found by subtracting the shifted contents of the segment register from the absolute address of the destination: $07DB2_{16} - 02A00_{16} = 5D12_{16}$. The offset address of the operand within the current data segment is $5D12_{16}$.

2-2.1 Segment Designations

The segment registers are involved in every transfer between the CPU and memory. Each of the 64K byte memory segments referenced with the segment registers may be used by the CPU for specific purposes, depending on which instruction is being executed.

Normally, all instructions are fetched from the current code segment. The offset that specifies where in the current code segment a given instruction is to be fetched from is supplied by the instruction pointer (IP). While an instruction is being executed, the IP increments to the offset (within the current code segment) of the next available instruction.

The data segment is used in the addressing of instruction operands. There are many different ways that operand locations may be specified when using the 8088. Most of these methods base the location of operands within the current data segment. That is, the offset that points to an operand will usually use the DS register as its base or reference point.

There are exceptions, but in general, operands are located within the data segment.

The stack segment is used, appropriately enough, to define the location of the beginning of the stack. Like most modern CPUs, the 8088 has a memory-based stack. The stack is used as a last-in first-out (LIFO) register for storing critical data that must be preserved when a subroutine is called or an interrupt is initiated. Data is placed in the stack with the PUSH instructions, and retrieved from the stack by POP instructions. The SP register is used to specify what is called the top of the stack. The top of the stack is pointed to by the SP. The SP register contains the offset of the last word that was stored in the stack.

The ES register is used to locate the block of memory to which a sequence or string of bytes is to be moved. Contiguous blocks of data (strings) can be moved easily from one place to another using a powerful class of instructions called string manipulation instructions. The ES register may also be used for other purposes under program control; however, for the time being, it will be considered a special purpose register.

Review Questions for Section 2-2

1. Define the term *segmented addressing*.
2. How long are the 8088 memory segments?
3. Explain the difference between an absolute address and an offset address.
4. In a certain 8088-based microcomputer, the data segment register contains $A010_{16}$. It is desired to access a byte of data that is located at absolute address $AA000_{16}$. What hex displacement must be added to the DS contents to address this byte?
5. How many 64K byte long segments is it possible to have in an 8088-based system that has 1 Mbyte of memory?
6. The contents of the CS register are $500F_{16}$. A certain machine language program begins at an offset of $100B_{16}$ relative to the beginning of the code segment. What is the absolute address of the beginning of this program?

2-3 OPERAND ADDRESSING

You will recall that an operand is the quantity upon which an instruction operates. For example, in the addition problem $X = 2 + 5$, the numbers 2 and 5 are the operands. Likewise, in an operation such as occurs when the contents of a register are shifted, complemented, or manipulated in some way, the register that was specified is generally considered to be the operand (although actually, the register's contents are manipulated).

The 8088 provides 25 different ways by which the location of an operand may be specified. In general, though, operands may be located through either register references or memory references. In register-referenced addressing, the operand is located in a particular register that is implied by the instruction opcode. For example, the instruction INC AX (INCrement the AX register) implies that the operand to be incremented is contained in the AX register. In such cases, no offset is required because a register has no address. Register addressing is the simplest addressing method to use.

Memory-referenced addressing may require up to four quantities to be added to specify the location of a given operand. In such a case, the contents of various registers and perhaps an immediate offset may have to be added in order to specify the memory location of an operand. The term *immediate* refers to a quantity (8- or 16-bit) that is located immediately following an instruction in memory. The base and index registers are often used as operand pointers (they contain offsets) by instructions that use the memory-referenced addressing mode.

2-3.1   Register Mode Addressing

To reiterate, register mode addressing is the term used when an instruction's operand is located within a register. One of the forms of the increment (INC rEGISTER) instruction would be an example of an instruction that uses register mode addressing. INC is also a single operand instruction. The idea is that the location of only one operand needs to be explicitly identified in the instruction. That operand is the particular register that is being referenced. The second operand is implied by the nature of the operation. This is sometimes referred to as implied addressing, as well as register mode addressing. For example, INCrement implies the operation "add 1," while DECrement implies "subtract 1." The form of the INC rEGISTER instruction is shown in Fig. 2-5a. The 3 least significant bits of the opcode (the **reg** field) are used to specify which register is to be incremented. Any of the 8-bit and 16-bit registers may be INCremented, with the exception of the segment registers, the flags, and the instruction pointer. The register codes are shown in Fig. 2-5b. A given code is entered into the **reg** field of the instruction opcode to specify which register is the operand to be incremented.

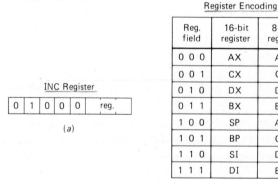

Register Encoding

Reg. field	16-bit register	8-bit register
0 0 0	AX	AL
0 0 1	CX	CL
0 1 0	DX	DL
0 1 1	BX	BL
1 0 0	SP	AH
1 0 1	BP	CH
1 1 0	SI	DH
1 1 1	DI	BH

(b)

INC Register

| 0 | 1 | 0 | 0 | 0 | reg. |

(a)

Fig. 2-5 8088 INCrement register opcode format (Courtesy of Intel Corporation) (a) and encoding of the opcode register (**reg**) field (b).

Register addressed instructions can also have two operands. The 8088's ADD reg/memory with register to either instruction, for example, may be used to add the contents of any two of the general purpose registers and store the result in either one. This instruction can also reference an operand that is located in memory.

Example 2-3

Write the opcode for the instruction that will increment the CX register.

Solution

Using the opcode format of Fig. 2-5a and the register codes of Fig. 2-5b, the final form of the opcode is shown below in binary and hexadecimal notation. The mnemonic for the instruction is also presented to the right of the opcode.

0100 0001   (41_{16})   INC CX

The various opcode/operand combinations that will be discussed in this chapter will generally be presented in both numerical (machine) form and mnemonic form. More detailed explanations of the mnemonics will be presented when assembly language is discussed.

The INCrement and DECrement instructions can also be used to modify the contents of memory locations, although the addressing methods used are more complex and will be discussed in detail later in this chapter.

2-3.2 Immediate Operand Addressing

Along with register mode (or implied) addressing, immediate addressing is one of the simplest addressing modes available. In immediate addressing, the operand always immediately follows the instruction in memory. Since the 8088 can operate on either 8- or 16-bit operands, the size of the operand must be specified in the instruction. As an example, consider the ADD immediate to accumulator instruction. The form of this instruction is shown in Fig. 2-6a. This instruction may be either 2 or 3 bytes long, depending on the size of the immediate operand. The least significant bit (LSB) of the opcode is designated as the w (word) field. If $w = 0$, the operand is 1 byte long and the result of the addition is stored in the AL register, as shown in Fig. 2-6b. If $w = 1$, then the operand occupies the next 2 bytes (a word) immediately following the opcode and the result is stored in the AX register, as shown in Fig. 2-6c.

Intel has designed the 8088 such that when word-length (2-byte) operands are placed in memory, the first byte entered is the least significant byte of the operand. The most significant byte of the operand is located in the next higher address. This is true of all 16-bit-long memory-based operands,

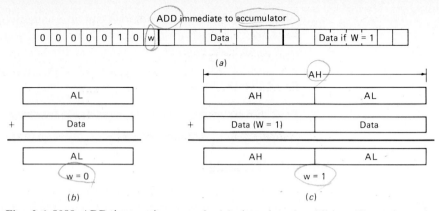

Fig. 2-6 8088 ADD instruction opcode (*a*), byte-length addition (*b*), and word-length addition (*c*). (Courtesy of Intel Corporation.)

including immediate operands. This may be a little confusing at first, so you might want to think of it this way: The byte in the lowest address is the low-order byte of the operand, while the high-order byte of the operand is in the higher memory location. One of the disadvantages of immediate addressing is that often 3 and sometimes 4 bytes of memory within the current code segment (the section of memory in which instructions are stored) are taken up by an instruction using this mode. If immediate operand instructions are used frequently, a long program may exceed the length of the code segment (64K byte). Such an occurrence would require manipulation of the CS register to allow the program to be executed properly. Frequent use of instructions that use other addressing modes saves more room in the code segment for the actual program. For example, most instructions that do not use immediate addressing reference operands that are stored in the current data segment. Since the data segment is 64K bytes long, a large number of operands may be referenced without losing room for instruction opcodes. Of course, this assumes that the code and data segments do not overlap.

Example 2-4

Write the complete opcode and operand sequence that is required to add immediately the number $6EFB_{16}$ to the accumulator (AX). Also, what will be the sum produced by the addition, assuming the contents of the accumulator were $59A6_{16}$ prior to execution of the instruction?

Solution

Using the ADD immediate to AX instruction opcode, the 3 bytes below appear in the order that they would be entered in memory.

Since the operand is a word, **W** = 1 and the opcode is:

0000 0101   (05_{16})

The operand is written as:

1111 1011   (FB₁₆)   low-order byte
0110 1110   (6E₁₆)   high-order byte

The result of the addition is C8A1₁₆. This number would be present in the AX register after execution. The instruction created in Example 2-4 could be represented mnemonically as follows:

```
ADD AX,6EFB
```

2-3.3 Direct Memory Addressing

In direct memory addressing, the word immediately following an instruction opcode is the offset of the operand. The offset address word is entered in memory least significant byte first, just as word-size operands are. The offset is used to specify the displacement of the operand from the beginning of the current data segment.

One of the instructions that can use the direct addressing mode is MOV (move). MOV is used to move a byte or a word from one place to another. The form of the MOV Memory to accumulator instruction is shown in Fig. 2-7a. The **w** field of the opcode is again used to specify whether the operand is a byte or a word in length. The offset of the operand in the current data segment is specified immediately following the opcode, low order byte first. If it is a word move (**w** = 1)—that is, if a 16-bit piece of data is to be moved from memory to the accumulator—the low-order byte of the operand is located at the offset specified in the MOV direct instruction. The high-order byte is located in the next higher memory location. Since the 8088 data bus is 8 bits wide, the operand is obtained by the CPU in two successive fetches and placed in the AX register in the normal format (low-order byte in AL, high-order byte in AH). The word move to accumulator actions are shown in Fig. 2-7b). When a byte move is performed (**w** = 0), the operand is placed in the AL register while AH is unaffected, as shown in Fig. 2-7c.

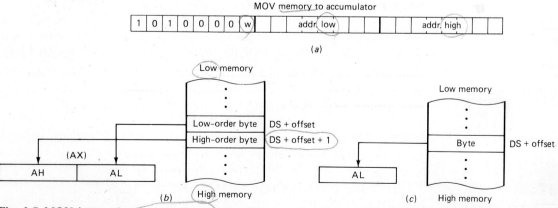

Fig. 2-7 MOV instruction opcode format (a), with word-length operand organization (b), and byte-length operand (c). (Courtesy of Intel Corporation.)

Example 2-5

Assume that CS = DS = $0A00_{16}$. Write the opcode and offset values required to move a byte of data located at absolute address $C050_{16}$ into the accumulator (AL).

Solution

The location of the instruction itself need not be considered because the offset written following the opcode points to the operand relative to the beginning of the current data segment, which is obtained by shifting the contents of the DS register left one place (in hex). This yields $A000_{16}$ as the start of the data segment. The required offset is obtained by subtracting the data segment start address from the absolute address of the operand.

$$C050_{16} - A000_{16} = 2050_{16}$$

Now that the necessary offset has been determined, the opcode is written with the offset following in low-order byte first form.

1010 0000	$(A0_{16})$	opcode
0101 0000	(50_{16})	low offset
0010 0000	(20_{16})	high offset

In mnemonic form, this instruction would appear as:

```
MOV AL,[2050]
```

where the brackets indicate that [2050] is the offset of the operand; that is, [2050] points to the operand. Without the brackets, 2050 is interpreted as an immediate operand to be MOVed into AL. Of course, 2050_{16} is too large to fit into AL anyway, since AL is an 8-bit register.

The direct addressing mode allows the possibility of the entire 64K byte data segment to be used for operand storage. Keep in mind that if any other segments overlap, though, the available space will be somewhat less.

2-3.4 Indirect Memory Addressing

Indirect addressing is the most powerful and flexible addressing mode available with the 8088. Unfortunately, it is also the most complex. Indirect addressing specifies operand addresses through the addition of the contents of one or more registers and possibly a byte or word-length offset appended to the instruction. Normally, an operand will be located within the current data segment, because it is the default reference area for operand addressing. There are, however, a few exceptions, and data segment operand referencing can even be intentionally overridden, if so desired.

An example of a very useful instruction that can be used in the indirect addressing mode is MOV. In its most general form, MOV can transfer either a byte or a word from a register or memory location to another register or memory location. The format for this instruction is shown in Fig. 2-8. Working from left to right, the **d** field is used to specify the

MOV reg./mem. to/from reg.

| 1 | 0 | 0 | 0 | 1 | 0 | d | w | mod | 0 | 0 | 0 | r/m |

Fig. 2-8 The most general MOV instruction opcode format. (Courtesy of Intel Corporation.)

direction of the move. If **d** = 0, then the location (register or memory) specified by the **mod** and **r/m** fields is the destination of the move. If **d** = 1, then the register specified by the **reg** field is the destination of the move. The **w** field indicates whether the operand is a word (**w** = 1) or a byte (**w** = 0). The second byte of the instruction begins with a 2-bit **mod** (mode) field. This field may be used to specify where the offset or displacement of one of the operands is located. Alternatively, the **mod** field can specify that the operand is located by an offset immediately following the opcode, or that there is no offset and the operand is in a register. The **reg** (register) field selects one of the general purpose registers (8- or 16-bit, depending on whether **w** is 0 or 1) to be used as either the destination or the source of the move.

The **r/m** field is used to determine in which general purpose register an operand is located, or which base and index register(s) contains the offset of the operand. The actual function of the **r/m** field is determined by the contents of the **mod** field.

There is no disputing that this is a complex and confusing addressing mode. There are so many different ways in which operands, sources, and destinations can be specified that one may be overwhelmed by the options. However, as the various instructions that use this addressing mode are presented, the operation of the indirect addressing mode should become clear.

2-3.5 Relative Addressing

The final form of addressing to be considered is relative addressing. This method of addressing is used in all conditional jumps. Jumps cause the CPU to begin execution of instructions at a point that is not the next instruction in the linear sequence of a program. In effect, a jump of one type or another increases or decreases the contents of the instruction pointer so that it is possible to jump from one place to another within a program.

The relative address of the conditional jump is a 1-byte two's complement quantity that immediately follows the instruction. The maximum displacement or distance that can be jumped using relative addressing is $+127$ or -128 bytes. This means that at the most, the instruction pointer can be increased by 127_{10} or decreased by 128_{10}.

Two's Complement Arithmetic   When binary numbers are interpreted as being in two's complement form, the MSB represents the sign of the number. Whenever the MSB of a two's complement quantity is 0, the number is positive and equal to the value it would have under normal circumstances. Any time the MSB of the quantity is 1, the number is negative. The easiest way to determine the magnitude of most of the negative two's complement numbers is to follow the steps below.

1. Invert (complement) each bit in the negative number.
2. Add 1 to the inverted number.
3. Calculate the value of the resulting number as a normal unsigned binary quantity.

The result of Step 3 is the absolute magnitude of the original negative number.

Converting a positive two's complement number into a negative number of equal absolute magnitude is also very simple. The method is very similar to that in which negative numbers are converted into magnitudes as shown above. The following steps are used.

1. Write the magnitude of the number in binary form.
2. Invert each bit of the magnitude.
3. Add 1 to the inverted number.

The result of these steps is a negative two's complement number with the same absolute magnitude as the original positive number.

___

Example 2-6

The hexadecimal numbers below represent negative two's complement values. Calculate the absolute value of each of the numbers. Express the answers in hexadecimal form.

a. 8C
b. 80
c. FF
d. A2

Solution

The first number will be converted demonstrating the application of the 3-step method above. The remaining three results may be verified by the reader.

1. Writing the number in binary form:

$$8C = 1000\ 1100$$

2. Complementing:
   0111 0011

3. Adding 1:

$$0\underline{111\ 0100} = 74_{16}$$

The rest are as follows:

b. $80 = 80_{16}$
c. $FF = 1_{16}$
d. $A2 = 5E_{16}$

Notice in the previous example that 80_{16} is equivalent to 128_{10}, which is the largest negative value possible using 1-byte two's complement numbers.

Using Relative Addresses   Now that a review of two's complement arithmetic has been presented, the topic of relative addressing will again be considered. When determining the relative offset or displacement of a destination, it is important to remember that the IP automatically increments after each instruction fetch. To determine the relative address required for a forward conditional jump (a jump to a higher address), you can just count the number of bytes forward to the destination of the jump from the next address following the relative offset byte of the jump instruction. Remember, this is done because the IP increments after the fetch, such that it points to the next instruction. The example below illustrates the computation of a forward jump.

Example 2-7

The opcode for a conditional jump instruction is located at address 0100_{16} within the current code segment. What must the relative displacement byte of the instruction be if the program is to continue execution at address $01A5_{16}$ in the code segment, if the conditions of the jump are met?

Solution

Since the conditional jump instruction is located at address 0100_{16} in the current code segment, the displacement will be located at the next location (0101_{16}). The IP will automatically increment to 0102_{16} after the displacement byte is fetched. The displacement byte required for the instruction may be found by subtracting the IP contents after the displacement fetch from the destination address within the current code segment.

$$01A5_{16} - 0102_{16} = A3_{16}$$

If the required displacement of a conditional jump is greater than $+127_{10}$ ($7F_{16}$), then the destination is too far away for the conditional jump alone to reach. A solution to this problem requires a combination of the conditional jump and one of the unconditional jumps; that is, the destination of the conditional jump must be an unconditional jump. Unconditional jumps can be used to branch to any location within the code segment, whereas conditional jumps are limited to the range of an 8-bit two's complement distance.

In order to cause a conditional jump to go backward in memory, the two's complement of the distance from the destination to the byte immediately following the displacement (the instruction pointer contents) must be determined. To do this, you can simply count the number of bytes between the destination and the relative displacement byte and add 1 to account for the IP increment, and then take the two's complement of the result. Alternatively, the subtraction method given in the following example may be used.

Example 2-8

A certain conditional jump instruction is located at address $B0EE_{16}$ in the current code segment. If the jump is executed, the next instruction to be performed is at address $B09C_{16}$. What hexadecimal value must the displacement byte of the conditional jump have?

Solution

The distance between the destination and the source may be found by subtracting the address of the destination ($B09C_{16}$) from the address of the byte following the displacement ($B0F0_{16}$).

$$B0F0 - B09C = 54_{16}$$

The two's complement of this number is the required displacement. So first the number is written in binary form.

$$54_{16} = 0101\ 0100_2$$

Next, the complement is taken and 1 is added.

$$1010\ 1011 + 1 = 1010\ 1100_2$$

Converted to hexadecimal, the displacement is AC_{16}.

Review Questions for Section 2-3

1. In register indirect addressing, where and how is an operand located?
2. How are word-length operands entered in memory?

3. In which addressing mode is the offset of the operand located immediately following the instruction opcode?
4. In which segment are the instruction opcodes located?
5. How do relative addresses differ from offset addresses?
6. The first byte of a 2-byte conditional jump instruction is located at address 0100_{16} relative to the beginning of the current code segment. The destination of the jump is located at address 0088_{16} relative to the beginning of the current code segment. What relative address must be written as the second byte of the jump instruction?

2-4 THE 8088 INSTRUCTION SET

A few examples of instructions from the 8088 instruction set have been presented in the previous section, although most of the details have been left out for the sake of clarity. The 8088 instruction set is not the easiest thing to interpret, so this section will be full of examples. The instructions will be broken down into six categories: data transfer, arithmetic, logic, string manipulation, control transfer, and processor control. Several examples of instructions within each category will be presented.

To make things a little easier, the entire register set and field encoding tables are presented in Fig. 2-9. These tables are used in constructing instruction opcodes, and will be referred to throughout the following sections of this chapter.

2-4.1 Data Transfer Instructions

Data transfer instructions are used to move data from one place (memory location, register, or port) to another (memory, register, or port). There are several different types of data transfer instructions available. Each subgroup of these instructions will be discussed individually.

The MOV Instructions The sources and destinations of MOVes include registers, memory, and I/O ports. The MOV instruction formats are given in Fig. 2-10. The first instruction presented is MOV register/memory to/ from register. This instruction may use either the indirect memory addressing mode or the register addressing mode and is the most general of all the MOV instructions.

Let us begin by determining how to interpret this instruction. Suppose it was desired to transfer the contents of the AX register into the CX register using this particular instruction. In this case, register addressing is used. First, let us assign the **w** field a value of 1 because this will be a word move (AX and CX are 16-bit registers).

Next, the **reg** field could be defined as representing the AX register. Using the register field encoding chart in Fig. 2-9, we find that the code for the AX register is 000. This will be placed in the **reg** field of the instruction.

Since this is a register to register move, the **r/m** field must now be defined as representing the CX register. Looking at the **mod** encoding table

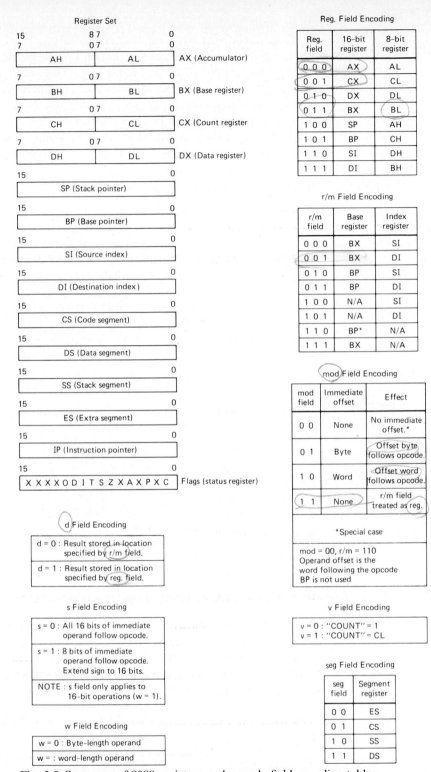

Fig. 2-9 Summary of 8088 registers and opcode field encoding tables.

we find that if **mod** = 11, then the **r/m** field is encoded using the register encoding table. From this we get **mod** = 11 and **r/m** = 001.

Finally, the **d** (direction) field must be filled in. Looking at the **d** field encoding table in Fig. 2-9, we find that if **d** = 0, the **r/m** field specifies the destination of the move. Since it was previously determined that the **r/m** field of the opcode represents CX, the CX register will be the destination of the move if **d** is assigned a value of 0.

All of these codes are entered into the instruction to form the required opcode. The final form for the opcode is shown below in binary and hex forms, along with their mnemonics. These 2 bytes would be located somewhere in the current code segment of memory in the order given.

```
1000 1001   (89₁₆)   MOV CX,AX
1100 0001   (C1₁₆)
```

Example 2-9

Write the binary and hex equivalent for the instruction that will move the contents of the BL register into the CH register using the MOV register/memory to/from register instruction. The **reg** field is to specify the destination register (CH).

Solution

The opcode is constructed using the opcode encoding information presented in Fig. 2-9.

1. It's a byte move, so **w** = 0.
2. The **reg** field is to represent CH, so **reg** = 101.
3. Since it's a register to register move, **mod** = 11.
4. The **r/m** field must specify BL, so **r/m** = 011.
5. Since the **reg** field is to be the destination, **d** = 1.
6. The final opcode appears below.

```
1000 1010   (8A₁₆)   MOV CH,BL
1110 1011   (EB₁₆)
```

So far it has been shown how to use the MOV register/memory to/from register instruction to transfer the contents of one register to another. Let us now use this instruction to transfer the contents of a register to a memory location in the register indirect addressing mode. In this case, the **r/m** field will specify an offset into either the current data segment or the current stack segment. The way to tell which segment will be referenced is by using the **r/m** encoding chart in Fig. 2-9. If the BP register is used in the offset computation, the operand is located within the current stack segment. Otherwise, the operand is located in the current data segment. The **mod** field is used to indicate whether or not an additional offset byte or word is to follow the instruction. The **mod** encoding table in Fig. 2-9 is used to choose the desired format. The following examples should help clarify these points.

Example 2-10

Using the MOV register/memory to/from register instruction, write the complete sequence of bytes that will move the contents of memory location 0A00 within the current data segment into the DH register. The SI register and an offset word that follows the instruction are to be used to compute the total offset; that is, the contents of the SI register and the immediate word-length offset are added to produce the offset of the memory-based operand. Assume that the SI register contains 00F0 when determining the offset word.

Solution

1. It's a byte move, so $w = 0$.
2. The **reg** field must specify the DH register, so **reg** = 110.
3. The **reg** field specifies the destination of the move, so $d = 1$.
4. The **r/m** field itself must represent the SI register, so **r/m** = 100.
5. The **mod** field must indicate that a word-length offset follows the instruction, so **mod** = 10.
6. The offset word is determined and placed immediately following the instruction, low-order byte first.

$$\text{Offset word} = \text{operand offset} - \text{SI}$$
$$= 0A00 - 00F0$$
$$= 0B10 \ (0000 \ 1011, \ 0001 \ 0000_2)$$

7. The final opcode, immediate offset word, and mnemonics for the instruction appear as shown below.

```
1000 1010   (8A₁₆)   MOV DH,[SI+0B10]
1011 0100   (B4₁₆)
0001 0000   (10₁₆)
0000 1011   (0B₁₆)
```

It is worth repeating that the offset word used after the instruction is placed in memory, low-order byte first. There are many more ways that the MOV register/memory to/from register instruction could be implemented. These will be left as exercises at the end of the chapter.

Some of the most commonly used operations involve the transfer of data between the accumulator and memory. The accumulator of the 8088 may be either the AX register or the AL register. If you are MOVing a byte, AL is used; if it's a word, AX is used. Since these are such frequently occurring cases, two specialized MOVes are included in the instruction set; the MOV accumulator to memory and MOV memory to accumulator instructions (see Fig. 2-10). These instructions both use the direct addressing

MOV

Register/memory to/from register: `1 0 0 0 1 0 d w` | mod | reg | r/m

Immediate to register/memory: `1 1 0 0 0 1 1 w` | mod | 0 0 0 | r/m | data | data if w = 1

Immediate to register: `1 0 1 1 w` reg | data | data if w = 1

Memory to accumulator: `1 0 1 0 0 0 0 w` | offset addr. low | offset addr. high

Accumulator to memory: `1 0 1 0 0 0 1 w` | offset addr. low | offset addr. high

Register/memory to segment reg: `1 0 0 0 1 1 1 0` | mod | 0 | seg. | r/m

Segment reg to register/memory: `1 0 0 0 1 1 0 0` | mod | 0 | seg. | r/m

Fig. 2-10 Opcode formats for all variations of the MOV instruction. (Courtesy of Intel Corporation.)

mode. The **w** field specifies whether the operand is a word or a byte. If the operand is a word, the low-order byte must immediately precede the high-order byte in memory in order to be moved into the accumulator properly (low-order byte in AL, high-order byte in AH). Likewise, if a word is moved from AX to memory, it will be placed with the low-order byte in the location pointed to by the offset, while the high-order byte will be placed in the next higher address (offset + 1). The offset word follows the same rule: low-order byte first, high-order byte second.

Example 2-11

The DS register contains $2C00_{16}$, and a certain word-length operand begins at location $0A0F_{16}$ in the current data segment. Write the hex instructions required to move this operand into the accumulator and then move it to location 0010_{16} in the current data segment. The mnemonics for the instructions are as follows.

```
MOV AX,[0A0F]
MOV [0010],AX
```

Solution

Use the instruction MOV memory to accumulator with **w** = 1:

1010 0001	$(A1_{16})$
0000 1111	$(0F_{16})$
0000 1010	$(0A_{16})$

Next, use the MOV accumulator to memory instruction with **w** = 1:

$acc \rightarrow mem$ | 1010 0011 | $(A3_{16})$
| 0001 0000 | (10_{16})
| 0000 0000 | (00_{16})

This is the sequence in which the opcodes and offsets would occur in a program.

The MOV immediate to register instruction (Fig. 2-10) is very simple to use. The operand is placed low-order byte first (of course) following the instruction opcode if **w** = 1. The remaining two MOV instructions are used for the transferal of data to and from the segment registers. They can both use either register direct or register indirect addressing.

The PUSH and POP Instructions PUSH and POP are used to store data in the stack and retrieve data from the stack, respectively. Information POPed from or PUSHed into the stack is done in word form only. A single byte cannot be used. The stack segment register (SS) designates the lowest address that may be used as the stack is filled. The stack pointer (SP) contains the offset into the current stack segment of the last word that was pushed into the stack. As more PUSHes are executed, the stack grows toward lower memory. The PUSH and POP instructions are shown in Fig. 2-11.

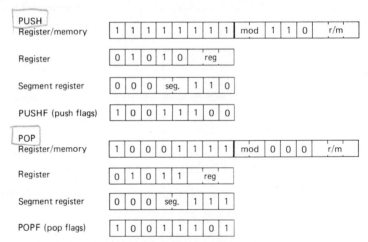

Fig. 2-11 The PUSH and POP instruction opcodes. (Courtesy of Intel Corporation.)

Whenever a PUSH instruction is executed, the CPU first decrements the stack pointer by 2. This makes available 2 bytes of memory for the word being pushed. The CPU then writes the word into the two empty locations in the stack. The SP will now be pointing to the offset of the word that was just pushed. Figure 2-12a and b illustrates the action of the PUSH instructions. The POP instructions work in just the opposite manner. When a POP is executed, the CPU first reads the 2 bytes that were last

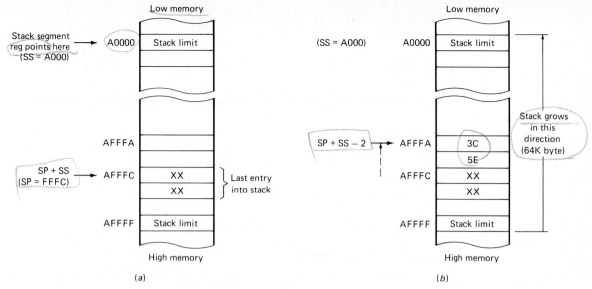

Fig. 2-12 Stack organization before a PUSH (*a*) and after (*b*).

entered into the stack and transfers them into the destination. The CPU then increments the stack pointer by 2. This effectively moves the top of the stack back to the next available word (in higher memory) in the stack. Figure 2-13*a* and *b* illustrates the action of the POP instructions.

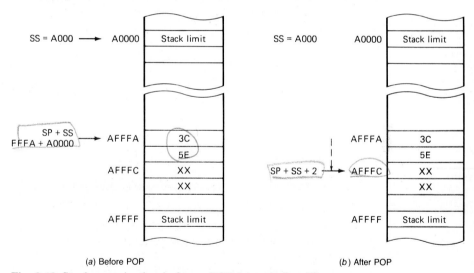

Fig. 2-13 Stack organization before a POP (*a*) and after (*b*).

There are a total of eight different POP and PUSH instructions. If you examine the instruction set, you should notice that each PUSH instruction has a complementary POP instruction. This is rather convenient because once you determine how one instruction is developed, the corresponding PUSH or POP is developed the same way. The most general PUSH instruction is PUSH register/memory. Again, the register encoding tables of Fig. 2-9 are used to specify whether the contents of a register or a memory location are to be the operand. A basic understanding of how to use the MOV instructions should provide enough background to follow the example below.

Example 2-12

The BX register contains $00D0_{16}$, and the SI register contains $BB00_{16}$. Write the opcode in both binary and hex forms for the instruction that will push the contents of location $BBDD_{16}$ in the current data segment onto the stack. Use the BX and SI registers and a single byte following the opcode to form the memory operand offset.

Solution

The PUSH register/memory instruction is used. Refer to the encoding tables in Fig. 2-9 for the determination of the proper field codes.

1. The offset following the instruction is to be a byte, so **mod** = 01.
2. The BX and SI registers contain the operand offset, so **r/m** = 000.
3. The value of the offset byte following the PUSH instruction is determined by subtracting the sum of the BX and SI registers from the offset of the operand to be pushed into the stack, producing offset = $0D_{16}$.
4. The final opcode followed by the offset appears as shown below.

        1111 1111 (FF_{16})
        0111 0000 (70_{16})
        0000 1101 ($0D_{16}$) $\Rightarrow BBDD - (00D0_{16} + BB00_{16}) = 0D$

The mnemonics required for Example 2-12 would appear as shown below.

        PUSH [BX+SI+0D]   BBDD

Remember that the PUSH and POP instructions always work with word-length operands.

Example 2-13

Write the opcode that will POP the word currently at the top of the stack into the DX register. The mnemonics for this instruction are as follows.

        POP DX

Solution

Referring to the instruction formats in Fig. 2-11, the format of the POP register instruction is 01011 **reg**. The **reg** field is 3 bytes wide. The code for the DX register is found in the register encoding table of Fig. 2-9 as

DX = 010. The complete opcode in binary and hex forms is shown below.

0101 1010   ($5A_{16}$)

The XCHG Instructions   The XCHG instructions are used to swap the contents of a general purpose register with the contents of another general purpose register or memory location. The two XCHG instructions are shown in Fig. 2-14. The general form XCHG register/memory with register can be used to swap byte- or word-size data. The XCHG register with accumulator instruction swaps only word-size data between the AX register and any of the other general purpose registers. It is less versatile, but it takes up only 1 byte of memory.

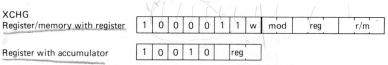

XCHG
Register/memory with register

| 1 | 0 | 0 | 0 | 0 | 1 | 1 | w | mod | reg | r/m |

Register with accumulator

| 1 | 0 | 0 | 1 | 0 | reg |

Fig. 2-14 Opcode structure for the exchange (XCHG) instruction. (Courtesy of Intel Corporation.)

Example 2-14

Write the opcode for the XCHG instruction that will swap the contents of the memory location at an offset address of $10A0_{16}$ in the current data segment with the contents of the AL register. The offset address is to be placed immediately following the XCHG instruction, as indicated by the mnemonics below.

XCHG AL,[10A0]

Solution

This assignment requires the use of the special case of **mod** field encoding that is presented in Fig. 2-9. If **mod** = 00 and **r/m** = 110, then the offset of the operand is contained in the next 2 consecutive bytes following the instruction. This is a byte-size swap, so **w** = 0 and the **reg** encoding for AL is 000. The entire opcode/offset sequence is shown below. Notice that the offset is written low-order byte first.

opcode
1000 0110	(86_{16})
0000 0110	(06_{16})
1010 0000	($A0_{16}$)	— offset
0001 0000	(10_{16})

The IN and OUT Instructions   One of the most important aspects of computer operation is the machine's ability to exchange information with the outside world. The 8088 sends and receives data in byte or word form to and from peripheral devices through ports, via the IN and OUT instructions. Refer to Fig. 2-15 for the IN and OUT instruction formats.

Fig. 2-15 IN and OUT I/O transfer instruction opcode formats. (Courtesy of Intel Corporation.)

It is possible to access up to 2^{16} (65,536) different ports using the IN variable port and OUT variable port instructions. All port input and output operations reference the accumulator (AX if $w = 1$, and AL if $w = 0$). The port number must be loaded into the DX register prior to execution of either instruction. Most systems, however, will not have anywhere near 65,536 ports. In the instances where relatively few ports are required, the IN fixed port and OUT fixed port instructions may be used. These two instructions can access only the first 256 ports. The port number is specified in the byte following the opcode. As usual, the w field in each of the instructions is used to indicate byte- or word-length operand.

Example 2-15

Write the opcode (in binary and hex forms) and the mnemonics for the instruction that will send the contents of AX to port 87_{10}.

Solution

The OUT fixed port instruction will be used. Writing the mnemonic form first, and converting the port number to hex (it is assumed that an assembler interprets all numbers in hex format), the following code is obtained.

OUT 87

The binary and hex equivalent of the mnemonics will now be created. Since the operand is a word, $w = 1$. The port number must be converted into binary and hex forms. The resulting codes are shown below.

1110 0111 $(E7_{16})$
0101 0111 (57_{16})

The XLAT Instruction   The purpose of the XLAT instruction is to transfer a byte from a lookup table into the AL register. A lookup table is a series of ordered data elements stored in memory. The XLAT instruction format is shown in Fig. 2-16. This instruction is useful for translating from one code to another when no simple mathematical relationship exists between the two codes. For example, the conversion of a 4-bit binary coded decimal (BCD) bit pattern into its equivalent 7-segment LED display code could be a candidate for the XLAT instruction.

XLAT
Translate byte to AL

Fig. 2-16 Opcode format for the translate (XLAT) instruction. (Courtesy of Intel Corporation.)

The BX register specifies the offset of the beginning of the translation table in the current data segment. The AL register specifies the index or distance into the table at which the operand is located. Upon execution of the XLAT instruction, the index contained in AL is overwritten, with the contents of the table entry being referenced. The display segment designations are shown in Fig. 2-17a. Figure 2-17b illustrates the action of the

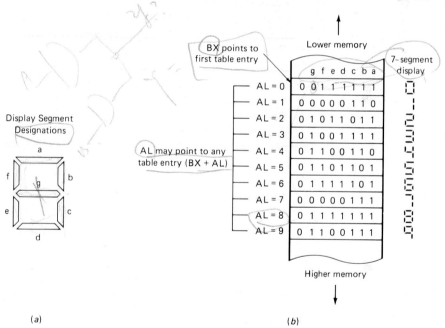

(a)   (b)

Fig. 2-17 Standard 7-segment LED display (a) and translation table contents in memory (b).

XLAT instruction when used for the BCD to 7-segment decoding operation. A logic high (binary 1) represents a lighted segment. Bits 0 through 6 of each of the entries in the translation table correspond to segments a through f of the display, respectively. If, for example, XLAT was executed and BX contained 0100_{16} (the table began at offset 100_{16} in the current data segment) and AL contained 08_{16}, then table entry number 8 (0111 1111) would be loaded into AL. This is the 7-segment code for the digit 8 (all segments on).

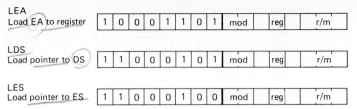

LEA
Load EA to register

| 1 | 0 | 0 | 0 | 1 | 1 | 0 | 1 | mod | reg | r/m |

LDS
Load pointer to DS

| 1 | 1 | 0 | 0 | 0 | 1 | 0 | 1 | mod | reg | r/m |

LES
Load pointer to ES

| 1 | 1 | 0 | 0 | 0 | 1 | 0 | 0 | mod | reg | r/m |

Fig. 2-18 Load effective address opcode variations. (Courtesy of Intel Corporation.)

The LEA, LDS, and LES Instructions   The LEA instruction, shown in Fig. 2-18, transfers the offset address (in the current data segment) of the source operand designated by the **mod** and **r/m** fields into the register specified by the **reg** field (the destination operand). All transferred operands (effective offsets) are 16 bits long. This instruction is useful for passing the address of an operand from one part of the program to another. This is referred to as parameter passing.

The LDS instruction is used to transfer the contents of four consecutive memory locations into a pair of 16-bit registers. The offset address of the first memory location whose contents are to be transferred is specified by the **mod** and **r/m** fields. The first 2 bytes transferred are placed in the register specified by the **reg** field. The first byte is placed in the low side of the register and the second byte is placed in the high side. The next 2 consecutive bytes are automatically transferred into the DS register in the same manner. The LES instruction works the same way, except that the second 2 bytes are transferred into the ES register instead of the DS register.

The LAHF and SAHF Instructions   Both the LAHF and SAHF instruction formats are shown in Fig. 2-19. The LAHF instruction transfers the contents of

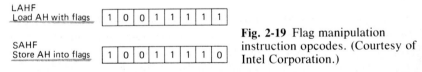

LAHF
Load AH with flags

| 1 | 0 | 0 | 1 | 1 | 1 | 1 | 1 |

SAHF
Store AH into flags

| 1 | 0 | 0 | 1 | 1 | 1 | 1 | 0 |

Fig. 2-19 Flag manipulation instruction opcodes. (Courtesy of Intel Corporation.)

the SF, ZF, AF, PF, and CF (flags) into the AH register. Execution of the SAHF instruction transfers certain bits of AH into those same flags. The flag-AH correspondence is shown in Fig. 2-20. The black lines represent

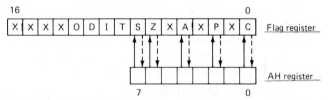

Fig. 2-20 Correspondence between flag register and AL bits during execution of LAHF (colored) and SAHF instructions.

LAHF execution, and the dotted lines represent SAHF execution. These instructions were included to allow for easier conversion of 8085 machine language programs into 8088 machine code. The flag bits that are acted upon by LAHF and SAHF are the flags present in the 8085 CPU.

Review Questions for Section 2-4.1

1. What is the maximum number of I/O ports that the 8088 can access?
2. Explain the term *parameter passing*.
3. When data is pushed into the stack, toward which end of memory does the stack grow?
4. Write the mnemonics and the binary and hex forms for the instruction that will move the contents of the BX register into the CX register. Use the MOV instruction.
5. Repeat the preceding problem using the XCHG instruction.
6. Write the mnemonics and the opcode in binary and hex forms for the instruction that will push the contents of the AX register into the stack.
7. Write the mnemonics and the binary and hex forms for the MOV instruction that will transfer a byte, whose location (in the current code segment) is given by the sum of the contents of the SI register and the immediate operand 20_{16}, into the CX register.
8. Write the hex equivalent for the following instruction mnemonic.

```
MOV BH,[SI]
```

2-4.2 Arithmetic Instructions

Unlike the earlier 8-bit microprocessors, the 8088 provides instructions for all four arithmetic operations (addition, subtraction, multiplication, and division). All arithmetic instructions support both 8- and 16-bit operands. The status flags (OF, CF, AF, SF, ZF, and PF) are affected by the execution of arithmetic instructions.

Signed Arithmetic   At this point, a word about the arithmetic instructions in general is in order. The addition and subtraction instructions perform in exactly the same way on both unsigned and signed numbers. You will recall that signed numbers are represented in two's complement notation. Operands represented in both two's complement and unsigned binary form will yield correct results when added or subtracted. For example, consider the addition of the two unsigned binary numbers shown in Fig. 2-21. The top number (the addend) is equal to 150_{10}, and the second number (the augend) is equal to 82_{10}. The sum of these numbers is equal to 232_{10}. Everything works out just fine. Suppose that we now interpret the operands as being signed two's complement quantities. Is the result still correct? To answer this question, let us first convert the operands into their signed

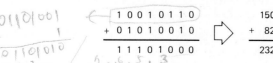

```
  ←─( 1 0 0 1 0 1 1 0        150
  + 0 1 0 1 0 0 1 0    ⇨   + 82      Fig. 2-21  Addition of binary numbers and
    ─────────────────        ───       their decimal equivalents (unsigned binary).
    1 1 1 0 1 0 0 0        232
```

decimal equivalents. The addend is equal to -106_{10} and the augend is still equal to $+82$ because the MSB is 0. Adding these decimal numbers produces -24_{10} as the result. Now, let's express this result as a two's complement binary number. The conversion produces $1110\ 1000_2$, which is the same result obtained when adding the unsigned operands. This will be true for 16-bit and longer operands as well. The only difference between signed and unsigned numbers is in the way that you interpret them.

The Status Flags   The flags are divided into two groups: status flags and control flags. The status flags are used to indicate the occurrence of certain events or conditions during the execution of an instruction. All of the addition and subtraction instructions, and most of the other arithmetic instructions, affect the status flags. The control flags are used to control the actions of the CPU. Right now, we are only interested in the status flags. However, brief descriptions of the control flags will also be presented for completeness. The characteristics of the status flags (1 through 6) and the control flags (7 through 9) are presented below.

1. The carry flag (CF) indicates whether or not a carry from or borrow into the MSB of the resultant of an operation has occurred. The CF is set if a carry or borrow from the MSB occurs; otherwise it is cleared.
2. The parity flag (PF) indicates whether or not an operation has produced a result with an even number of bits set to logic 1 (even parity). The PF is set if the resultant of an operation has even parity, and is cleared if it has odd parity.
3. The auxillary carry flag (AF) indicates the presence of a carry or borrow from bit 3 of a resultant. The AF is set if a borrow from or carry into bit 3 occurs, and is cleared otherwise.
4. The zero flag (ZF) indicates whether or not an operation produced a result of 0. The ZF is set if the result = 0, and is cleared otherwise.
5. The sign flag (SF) indicates whether or not the MSB of a result is 1 or 0. The SF is set if MSB = 1, and is cleared if MSB = 0.
6. The overflow flag (OF) indicates whether or not a signed result that was produced is out of range. If the result is out of range, the OF is set; otherwise it is cleared.
7. The direction flag (DF) controls the direction in which a sequence of data elements (string) is moved. If the DF = 0, a string is moved beginning with the element at the lowest address. If the DF = 1, a string is moved beginning with the element that is located at the highest address.
8. The interrupt flag (IF) enables or disables CPU response to hardware interrupt requests. If the IF = 0, interrupt requests are ignored (masked). If the IF = 1, interrupt requests are honored.
9. The trap flag (TF) allows programs to be executed in single-step manner. If the TF = 0, machine code is executed normally by the CPU. If the TF = 1, the CPU generates an interrupt (type 1) after the execution of each machine language instruction.

The ADD and ADC Instructions   There are three different ADD instructions in the 8088 instruction set. The format for these instructions is shown in Fig. 2-22. The differences among the three instructions are the addressing modes used by each. The ADD reg/memory with register to either instruction is used just like the first MOV instruction that was discussed. The example below will illustrate one way to use this instruction.

ADD
Reg/mem with register to either

| 0 | 0 | 0 | 0 | 0 | 0 | d | w | mod | reg | r/m |

Immediate to reg/mem

| 1 | 0 | 0 | 0 | 0 | 0 | s | w | mod | 0 | 0 | 0 | r/m |

| | | data | | | | | data if s:w = 01 | |

Immediate to accumulator

| 0 | 0 | 0 | 0 | 0 | 1 | 0 | w | | | data | | | | data if w = 1 | |

Fig. 2-22 Variations of the ADD opcode. (Courtesy of Intel Corporation.)

Example 2-16

A certain word-length operand has its location given by the sum of the contents of the BP register and a constant offset of $2F2_{16}$. This operand is to be added to the contents of the AX register. The resultant sum is to be stored in the AX register also. The mnemonic form for this instruction is

    ADD AX,[BP + 02F2]

Write the opcode and offset sequence (in binary and hex forms) that will implement this instruction.

Solution

Using the opcode format in Fig. 2-22, the following steps result in the construction of the instruction opcode.

1. Since this is a word-length operation, **w** = 1.
2. The **reg** field must specify the AX register, so **reg** = 000.
3. There is a word-length offset to follow the ADD, so **mod** = 10.
4. The BP register contains part of the offset, so **r/m** = 110.
5. The AX register is the destination of the sum, so **d** = 1.

The complete instruction and the offset word are shown below.

0000 0011	(03_{16})
1000 0110	(86_{16})
1111 0010	$(F2_{16})$
0000 0010	(02_{16})

Notice that the memory-based operand of the previous example was not located in the data segment but in the stack segment. This occurred because the BP register was used in the computation of the operand offset.

Any instruction that uses the contents of the BP register when computing an offset will reference the current stack segment.

There is a new symbol present in the ADD immediate to register/memory instruction: the s field. Here's the idea behind the s field. An instruction can have only one w field. This means that both operands of an ADD instruction, for example, will be either 8 bits or 16 bits long, as specified in the w field. However, when an immediate operand is used with the ADD instruction (the immediate operand is being added to the contents of a register), the immediate operand may be either 8 or 16 bits long. If the register-based operand being specified is 16 bits long ($w = 1$) and the immediate operand is also 16 bits long, the s field must be set to 0. However, if the immediate operand is only 8 bits long, and the register based operand is 16 bits long, the sign bit of the memory-based operand must be extended to the full 16 bits in order to produce correct two's complement results. The use of the s field is summarized below.

1. $s = 0$: The immediate operand is the same length (8 or 16 bits) as the register specified in the opcode.
2. $s = 1$: The immediate operand is 8 bits long. The sign bit is extended to 16 bits.

Example 2-17

Write the complete opcode and operand sequence required to immediately ADD $2C_{16}$ to the contents of the DX register. The immediate operand is to be sign-extended. The mnemonics for this instruction are

ADD DX,+2C

The plus sign indicates to the assembler program that 2C is to be sign-extended to 16 bits as a positive number. A negative sign would indicate the addition of a negative sign-extended byte.

Solution

1. The register-based operand is 16 bits long, so $w = 1$.
2. The immediate operand is 8 bits long, so $s = 1$.
3. It's a register-based ADD, so the special case of the **mod** and **r/m** field codes is used. Therefore, **mod** = 00, **r/m** = 110.

The final instruction opcode and immediate operand are shown below.

1000 0011	(83_{16})
0000 0110	(06_{16})
0010 1100	($2C_{16}$)

If the immediate operand was 16 bits long, it would be entered following the opcode low-order byte first, and sign extension would not be required.

The ADD immediate to accumulator instruction is the simplest ADD instruction to use. If the immediate operand is 8 bits long ($w = 0$), then the AL register is used as the location of the second operand and as the destination. If the immediate operand is 16 bits long ($w = 1$), then the AX register is used.

The add with carry (ADC) instructions operate in essentially the same ways as the previously covered addition instructions. The only difference is that the carry flag is added to the LSB of the sum. The ADC instructions are shown in Fig. 2-23. These instructions are used to perform multiple precision addition. In the context of the 8088, multiple precision arithmetic refers to the addition and subtraction of operands that are longer than 16 bits.

ADC

Reg/mem with reg to either

0	0	0	1	0	0	d	w	mod	reg	r/m

Immediate to reg/mem

1	0	0	0	0	0	s	w	mod	0	1	0	r/m

data				data if s:w = 01	

Immediate to accumulator

0	0	0	1	0	1	0	w	data		data if w = 1	

Fig. 2-23 Various formats of the ADD with carry (ADC) instruction. (Courtesy of Intel Corporation.)

The SUB and SBB Instructions These two groups of instructions are shown in Fig. 2-24. Both groups follow the same addressing and operand format rules as the ADD and ADC instructions. The rules for the s (sign-extend) field previously presented also apply to the subtraction instructions.

SUB

Reg/mem and reg to either

0	0	1	0	1	0	d	w	mod	reg	r/m

Immed from reg/mem

1	0	0	0	0	0	s	w	mod	1	0	1	r/m

data				data if s:w = 01	

Immed from accumulator

0	0	1	0	1	1	0	w	data		data if w = 1	

SBB

Reg/mem and reg to either

0	0	0	1	1	0	d	w	mod	reg	r/m

Immed from reg/mem

1	0	0	0	0	0	s	w	mod	1	0	1	r/m

data				data if s:w = 01	

Immed from accumulator

0	0	0	1	1	1	0	w	data		data if w = 1	

Fig. 2-24 Formats for the subtract (SUB) and subtract with borrow (SBB) instruction opcodes. (Courtesy of Intel Corporation.)

The INC and DEC Instructions These are two of the simplest instructions available with the 8088. The formats of these instructions are shown in Fig. 2-25. The general forms of the INC and DEC instructions can operate on either byte- or word-length operands in memory or in any of the 8- or

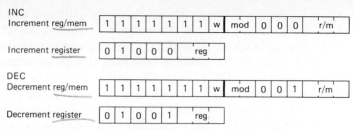

INC
Increment reg/mem | 1 | 1 | 1 | 1 | 1 | 1 | 1 | w | mod | 0 | 0 | 0 | r/m |

Increment register | 0 | 1 | 0 | 0 | 0 | reg |

DEC
Decrement reg/mem | 1 | 1 | 1 | 1 | 1 | 1 | 1 | w | mod | 0 | 0 | 1 | r/m |

Decrement register | 0 | 1 | 0 | 0 | 1 | reg |

Fig. 2-25 Increment (INC) and decrement (DEC) opcode formats. (Courtesy of Intel Corporation.)

16-bit registers that may be specified by the **mod** and **r/m** fields. The short forms of these instructions work only with the 16-bit general purpose registers.

Example 2-18

Write the mnemonics and the binary and hex opcode forms for the instruction that will increment the contents of the BH register.

Solution

The mnemonic for this instruction is as follows.

```
INC BH
```

The construction of the opcode is presented in the steps below.

1. BH is an 8-bit register, so **w** = 0.
2. The **r/m** field is to specify a register, so **mod** = 11.
3. The register being incremented is BH, so **r/m** = 111.

The final opcode is shown below.

1111 1110   (FE₁₆)
1100 0111   (C7₁₆)

The DAA, DAS, AAA, and AAS Instructions   Quite often, the input to a digital system, such as a computer, will be in the form of one or more BCD digits. It is quite convenient from a programmer's point of view if the CPU has the ability to perform arithmetic operations directly on these numbers without having to first convert them to standard binary code. The decimal adjust for add (DAA) and decimal adjust for subtract (DAS) instructions are used to correct arithmetic results following the addition and subtraction of packed BCD numbers. Both of these instructions require that the result of the BCD operation be stored in the AL register. BCD numbers are said to be packed when a single byte contains the BCD codes for two decimal digits. For example, if a certain byte of memory contains the packed BCD code 0100 1001$_{\text{BCD}}$, the decimal value represented by this byte is 49$_{10}$. Let us assume that the AL register contains the packed BCD code 0011 1000$_{\text{BCD}}$ (38$_{10}$). Suppose these two numbers are to be added and the sum placed in the AL register. Will the addition result in the proper BCD representation of the sum? The answer is no. In this case, the sum should be 1000 0111$_{\text{BCD}}$ (87$_{10}$); but the 8088 adds the two numbers as if they were in standard binary form, producing 1000 0001$_2$, which is equivalent to 81$_{10}$ when interpreted as a BCD quantity. The addition of these two BCD numbers is illustrated in Fig. 2-26a. Notice that a carry from bit 3 into bit 4 (a half carry) occurs. The half carry causes the auxiliary carry flag (ACF) to be set. However, if a DAA instruction is executed immediately following the addition, the setting of the AF will cause the bit pattern 0000 0110 to be added to the sum. This will automatically transform the result into proper BCD format. This correction is shown in Fig. 2-26b.

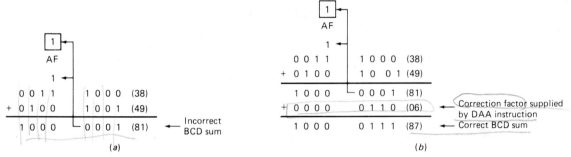

Fig. 2-26 Addition resulting in intermediate carry and an incorrect BCD sum (a) and correction of sum (b).

A similar situation occurs when either of the 4-bit BCD codes in the sum is greater than 1001 (9$_{10}$). In Fig. 2-27a, the numbers added are 1000 0111$_{\text{BCD}}$ (87$_{10}$) and 0011 1000$_{\text{BCD}}$ (38$_{10}$). In this case, no half carry occurs, but the result is still incorrect because both digits are invalid BCD codes. The DAA instruction would correct this result by adding 0110 0110 to the resulting sum. The action of the DAA instruction is shown in Fig. 2-27b.

Fig. 2-27 Incorrect BCD sum (a) and corrective action performed by DAA instruction (b).

Notice that the true BCD result represents the 3-digit number 125$_{10}$. The carry flag (CF) is set by the corrective action, and represents the most significant digit (MSD) of the sum. The DAS instruction works in a similar manner, except that it is used following the subtraction of packed BCD numbers. The formats of the DAA and DAS instructions are shown in Fig. 2-28. The rules that the DAA and DAS instructions follow are summarized below.

DAA
Decimal adjust for add

| 0 | 0 | 1 | 0 | 0 | 1 | 1 | 1 |

DAS
Decimal adjust for subtract

| 0 | 0 | 1 | 0 | 1 | 1 | 1 | 1 |

Fig. 2-28 Opcode construction for decimal adjust for addition (DAA) and decimal adjust for subtraction (DAS) instructions. (Courtesy of Intel Corporation.)

1. If an addition or subtraction instruction sets the AF (flag) or if the least significant digit (LSD) of the sum is greater than 9_{10}, then 0110 is added to the result.
2. If the CF (flag) is set or if the MSD of the sum is greater than 9_{10}, then 0110 0000 is added to the result.
3. If both the AF and CF are set or if both digits of the sum are greater than 9_{10}, then 0110 0110 is added to the result.

The ASCII adjust add (AAA) and ASCII adjust subtract (AAS) instructions work in a manner similar to the DAA and DAS instructions, except that only the LSD of the result is corrected. The formats of these instructions appear in Fig. 2-29. The rationale behind these instructions is that often

AAA
ASCII adjust for add

| 0 | 0 | 1 | 1 | 0 | 1 | 1 | 1 |

AAS
ASCII adjust for subtract

| 0 | 0 | 1 | 1 | 1 | 1 | 1 | 1 |

Fig. 2-29 Opcode formats for the AAA and AAS instructions. (Courtesy of Intel Corporation.)

operands are encountered in ASCII format. The ASCII code representations for the digits 0 through 9 are shown in Fig. 2-30. The three most significant bits (ASCII is a 7-bit code) have no bearing on the value of the digits represented. They are just part of the total ASCII code. These digits are referred to as unpacked BCD because only 1 digit is represented by a single byte. Since ASCII is a 7-bit code, the eighth bit may be used for error detection, as a parity bit, for example. Normally, before arithmetic operations are performed on unpacked BCD numbers such as these, the four MSBs are masked off by ANDing the byte with 0000 1111. The AAA

Digit	ASCII code
0	0 1 1 0 0 0 0
1	0 1 1 0 0 0 1
2	0 1 1 0 0 1 0
3	0 1 1 0 0 1 1
4	0 1 1 0 1 0 0
5	0 1 1 0 1 0 1
6	0 1 1 0 1 1 0
7	0 1 1 0 1 1 1
8	0 1 1 1 0 0 0
9	0 1 1 1 0 0 1

Fig. 2-30 ASCII code representations for digits 0 through 9.

and AAS instructions are used immediately following the addition and subtraction of unpacked BCD numbers, respectively.

The NEG Instruction The purpose of the NEG instruction is to produce the two's complement of a byte or word. As indicated by the NEG instruction format in Fig. 2-31, the contents of any memory location or general purpose register may be converted into the two's complement value of equivalent magnitude.

NEG
Negate register or mem

1	1	1	1	0	1	1	w	mod	0	1	1	r/m

Fig. 2-31 Negate instruction opcode. (Courtesy of Intel Corporation.)

The CMP Instruction Sometimes a decision must be made based on a comparison of the values of two operands. The CMP instruction is used in such cases. The reason that the CMP instruction is included in the Arithmetic Instructions section is because it is essentially the same as the SUB instruction. The main difference between the instructions is that the result of a CMP subtraction is not stored in one of the operands; only the flag settings are retained. The formats for the CMP instruction are shown in Fig. 2-32. The same addressing rules that apply for the SUB instructions apply to the CMP instructions.

CMP
Reg/mem and reg

0	0	1	1	1	0	d	w	mod	reg	r/m

Immed with reg/mem

1	0	0	0	0	0	s	w	mod	1	1	1	r/m

		data				data if s:w = 01	

Immed with accumulator

0	0	1	1	1	1	0	w			data				data if w = 1	

Fig. 2-32 Formats for the compare (CMP) instruction opcodes. (Courtesy of Intel Corporation.)

The MUL, DIV, IMUL and IDIV Instructions The 8088 has instructions that support both multiplication and division operations. These instructions represent a major advance over past 8-bit CPU designs. The opcode formats for the 8088 multiplication and division instructions are shown in Fig. 2-33.

MUL
Unsigned multiply

1	1	1	1	0	1	1	w	mod	1	0	0	r/m

IMUL
Integer multiply

1	1	1	1	0	1	1	w	mod	1	0	1	r/m

DIV
Unsigned divide

1	1	1	1	0	1	1	w	mod	1	1	0	r/m

IDIV
Integer divide

1	1	1	1	0	1	1	w	mod	1	1	1	r/m

Fig. 2-33 The 8088 multiply and divide instruction opcode formats. (Courtesy of Intel Corporation.)

The MUL and DIV instructions are used when the operands are unsigned numbers. As usual, if **w** = 0, the operands are 8 bits long; and if **w** = 1, the operands are 16 bits long. Since these instructions have no **reg** field, one of the operands is assumed to be present in either AL (**w** = 0) or AX (**w** = 1).

When multiplying two 8-bit numbers, the possibility exists that the product may be 16 bits long. Because of this, the 8088 stores the product of such 8-bit operands in the entire AX register. Likewise, the multiplication of two 16-bit operands can produce a 32-bit product. This product is stored with the low-order word in the AX register and the high-order word in the DX register. Both forms of the MUL operand locations are illustrated in Fig. 2-34a and b.

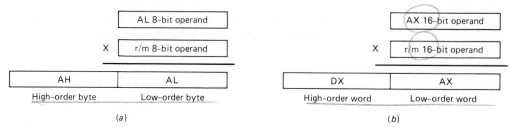

Fig. 2-34 Operand and product locations for byte multiplication (a) and word-length multiplication (b).

The DIV instruction is designed such that if **w** = 0, the contents of the AX register are the dividend and an 8-bit operand whose location is specified by the **mod** and **r/m** fields is the divisor. The quotient is stored back in the AL register, while the remainder is stored in AH. If **w** = 1, the dividend is the DX AX register pair and the divisor is a 16-bit operand specified by the **mod** and **r/m** fields. The quotient is located in the AX register, and the remainder is in DX. The DIV operand locations are illustrated in Fig. 2-35a and b.

The MUL and DIV instructions yield correct results only when their operands are interpreted as unsigned binary numbers. In order to overcome

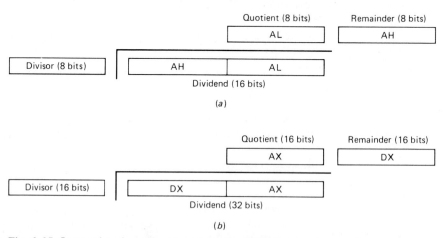

Fig. 2-35 Operand and quotient locations for 8088 division instructions.

this problem, the integer multiply (IMUL) and integer divide (IDIV) instructions are used whenever *signed* operands are being referenced. The operands and results of these instructions have the same format as MUL and DIV (Figs. 2-34 and 2-35). One of the characteristics of the IDIV instruction is that it will always produce a remainder with the same sign as the dividend. For example, if we divide − 15 by 2, two possible correct answers are − 7 with remainder − 1 and − 8 with remainder + 1. Both are correct, but the 8088 will produce a quotient of − 7 with a remainder of − 1 in order to comply with the sign rule.

The CBW and CWD Instructions The purpose of the convert byte to word (CBW) and convert word to double word (CWD) instructions is to prepare the contents of the AX (for CBW) and AX-DX (for CWD) registers for execution of the IDIV instruction. The opcode formats for CBW and CWD are shown in Fig. 2-36. You will recall that the IDIV instruction is designed

CBW
Convert byte to word | 1 | 0 | 0 | 1 | 1 | 0 | 0 | 0 |

CWD
Convert word to double word | 1 | 0 | 0 | 1 | 1 | 0 | 0 | 1 |

Fig. 2-36 Byte to word and word to double word conversion instruction opcodes. (Courtesy of Intel Corporation.)

to work with signed operands. Suppose that you wanted to divide an 8-bit dividend, say 1001 0000 (− 112), by some other 8-bit divisor. The dividend would be loaded into the AL register. You will recall, though, that the IDIV instruction assumes that the entire AX register contains the dividend. Since we're really using only an 8-bit dividend, we must extend the sign bit out to the MSB of AX. To accomplish this task, the CBW instruction is used right after the 8-bit dividend is placed in AL. After CBW is executed, AX will contain 1111 1111 1001 0000, regardless of what the AH section contained before. If our dividend happened to be positive, then all of the higher-order bits (AH) would have been cleared.

CWD performs the same operation on the AX and DX registers that CBW performs on AX. In other words, CWD extends the sign of a 16-bit dividend contained in the AX register all the way out to the MSB of the DX register. This may be done prior to a 32-bit IDIV operation when using a 16-bit dividend.

The AAM and AAD Instructions These are the last of the arithmetic instructions. Their opcode formats are shown in Fig. 2-37. ASCII adjust for multiply

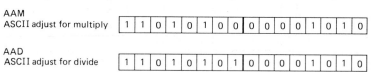

AAM
ASCII adjust for multiply | 1 | 1 | 0 | 1 | 0 | 1 | 0 | 0 | 0 | 0 | 0 | 0 | 1 | 0 | 1 | 0 |

AAD
ASCII adjust for divide | 1 | 1 | 0 | 1 | 0 | 1 | 0 | 1 | 0 | 0 | 0 | 0 | 1 | 0 | 1 | 0 |

Fig. 2-37 ASCII adjust for multiplication and division instruction opcode formats. (Courtesy of Intel Corporation.)

(AAM) is used following the multiplication of two unpacked BCD operands. Packed BCD operands must be unpacked prior to multiplication or division. Remember that unpacked BCD represents a decimal digit with the four least significant bits of a byte. The remaining 4 bits must be masked off (cleared). The product of two unpacked BCD numbers will be corrected or arranged into unpacked BCD form by the use of the AAM instruction. The AAD instruction is different than the previous ASCII adjust instructions in that it is executed immediately before IDIV is executed. The quotient and remainder produced by the IDIV instruction will automatically be written in the proper unpacked BCD form.

Example 2-19

Write the mnemonics and opcodes for the instructions that will perform the following operations. Immediate offsets and operands are not required.

1. Compare the contents of the AX register with a word whose location is specified by the contents of the SI register and an immediate offset byte. Assume that the operands are being tested only for equality.
2. Add the contents of a sign-extended immediate byte to the contents of the BX register.
3. Add with carry the contents of the AL register to the contents of a memory location whose offset immediately follows the opcode.

Solution

1. The CMP register/memory and memory instruction is used with the fields set as follows: $w = 1$, $mod = 01$, $r/m = 100$, $reg = 000$. Since the operands are being tested for equality, the d field may be set arbitrarily. The final opcode is shown below with $d = 0$. The mnemonics are shown to the right of the hex contents of the instruction. XX stands for the hex representation of the immediate offset that is added to the SI pointer. In an actual program, a number would be entered here.

   0011 1001   (39_{16})   CMP [SI + XX],AL
   0100 0100   (44_{16})

2. The ADD immediate to register/memory instruction is used with the following field settings: $s = 1$, $w = 1$, $mod = 11$, $r/m = 011$. The final opcode is shown below.

   1000 0011   (83_{16})   ADD BX,+XX
   1100 0011   ($C3_{16}$)

3. The ADC reg/memory with register to either instruction is used with the fields set as follows: $w = 0$, $mod = 00$, $r/m = 110$, $reg = 000$, $d = 1$. The final opcode is shown below.

   0001 0010   (12_{16})   ADC [XX],AL
   0000 0110   (06_{16})
   XXXX XXXX   ($??_{16}$)

The quantity [XX] represents the 2-digit hex offset pointer. This would be filled in by the programmer according to the offset location of the operand to which AL will be added.

Review Questions for Sections 2-4.2

1. When does the 8088 fetch an instruction operand from the current stack segment instead of from the data segment?
2. When must an operand be sign-extended?
3. Explain the term *masking*.
4. How does the 8088 determine the sign of the remainder of a IDIV operation?
5. Explain the difference between packed and unpacked BCD.
6. The contents of the AX register are $5AC6_{16}$. What will the contents of AX be after the execution of the CBW instruction?

2-4.3   The Logic Instructions

The 8088 logic instructions can be divided into two groups: the boolean instructions and shift/rotate instructions. The boolean instructions include NOT, AND, OR, XOR, and $\overline{TEST}$. All of the boolean instructions require two operands except for NOT, which is a single-operand instruction. All of the shift and rotate instructions are single-operand instructions.

The Boolean Instructions   The opcode formats for the boolean instructions are shown in Fig. 2-38. The NOT instruction inverts each bit in a given register or memory location. The AND instruction logically ANDs the contents of two operands bit for bit, and enters the result in the destination operand. OR and XOR also perform their respective logic operations based on the contents of two operands on a bit for bit basis. The result is stored in the destination operand.

The $\overline{TEST}$ instruction is very similar to the AND instruction. In fact, the execution of $\overline{TEST}$ causes two operands to be ANDed together. The result of the $\overline{TEST}$, however, is not retained following the operation. Only the flag settings are retained. $\overline{TEST}$ is useful for determining whether or not a certain bit in an operand is a 1 or a 0. For example, if you needed to know the contents of bit 2 of a register, without destroying the original contents, you could do the following: Execute $\overline{TEST}$ with 0000 0100 as one of the operands and the register of interest as the other. If bit 2 of the register was 0 prior to the $\overline{TEST}$, the ZF (flag) will be set. If bit 2 was 1 prior to the $\overline{TEST}$, the ZF will be cleared. The mnemonics for this operation would appear as shown below.

```
TEST AL ,04
```

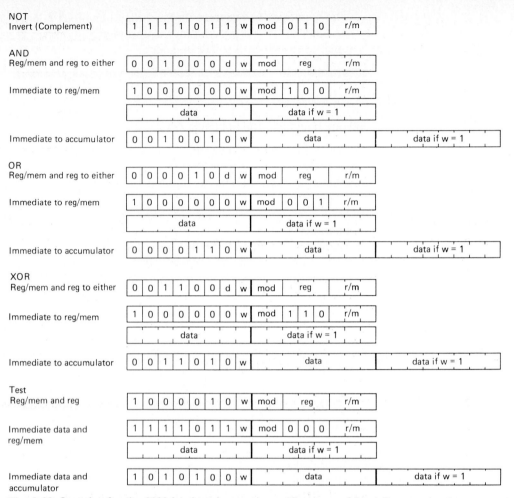

Fig. 2-38 Opcodes for the 8088 boolean instructions. (Courtesy of Intel Corporation.)

The Shift and Rotate Instructions The opcode formats for the shift and rotate instructions are shown in Fig. 2-39. Another new field (**v**) has been added to these instruction opcodes. The **v** field is used to cause multiple shifts or rotates to occur. If **v** = 0, then one shift or rotate is performed by the instruction any time it is executed. If **v** = 1, then the CPU performs the shift or rotate operation a predetermined number of times each time it is executed. The number of times that the operation is to be performed is given by the contents of the CL register. All of the shift and rotate instructions contain the **v** field.

The actions of the shift and rotate instructions are illustrated in Fig. 2-40. Some of the uses for these instructions include the doubling and halving of numbers and the testing of numbers to determine whether they are even or odd. As usual, the low-order byte of a memory-based word is located at the offset specified in the instruction, and the high-order byte follows.

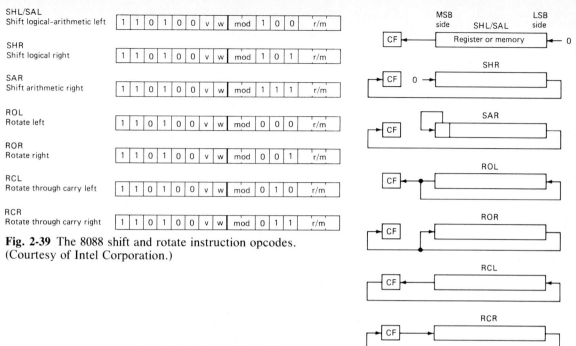

SHL/SAL
Shift logical-arithmetic left

SHR
Shift logical right

SAR
Shift arithmetic right

ROL
Rotate left

ROR
Rotate right

RCL
Rotate through carry left

RCR
Rotate through carry right

Fig. 2-39 The 8088 shift and rotate instruction opcodes.
(Courtesy of Intel Corporation.)

Fig. 2-40 Action of the shift and rotate
instructions on register and memory contents.

Example 2-20

Write the opcodes and mnemonics for the instructions that will perform the following operations.

1. Logically AND the contents of the DL register with the contents of a memory location whose offset is the sum of the BP and DI registers.
2. Rotate right the contents of a word stored in memory. The offset of the word is specified by a byte immediately following the opcode. The number of successive rotations to be performed is contained in the CL register.

Solution

1. The AND reg/memory and register to either instruction is used with fields set as follows: $w = 0$, **mod** = 00, **r/m** = 011, **reg** = 010, **d** = 0. The final opcode and its mnemonic are shown below.

    0010 0000   (20_{16})   AND [BP+DI],DL
    0001 0011   (13_{16})

2. The rotate right (ROR) instruction is used with fields set as follows: $v = 1$, $w = 1$, **mod** = 00, **r/m** = 110. The complete opcode is shown on the following page.

```
1101 0011   (D3₁₆)    ROR WORD PTR [XX],CL
0000 1110   (0E₁₆)
```

An explanation of the mnemonic form of the ROR instruction is now in order. You will recall that memory-based operands may be either byte- or word-length. Since ROR could operate on either size operand, explicit instructions as to the size of the memory-based operand must be included in the mnemonic; in this case, WORD PTR means that the immediate offset points to a word-length operand. If the operand were a byte, then BYTE PTR would have been used. More will be said about this notation later in this chapter.

Review Questions for Section 2-4.3

1. What is the purpose of the **v** field in the shift and rotate instructions?
2. Describe the operation of the $\overline{\text{TEST}}$ instruction.
3. The AL register contains $2F_{16}$. What are the hex contents of AL after two shift arithmetic left (SAL) operations are performed?
4. Write the opcode for the rotate through carry left (RCL) instruction that will shift the contents of the AX register CL times. The mnemonic for this instruction would be written as shown below.

   ```
   RCL AX,CL
   ```

5. The hex contents of the AX register are 3355_{16}. What will the hex contents of AX be if 5533_{16} is XORed with it?
6. Explain how two of the available logic instructions could be used to clear a register.

2-4.4   String Manipulation Instructions

A string is a sequence of data (bytes or words) that resides in a contiguous (uninterrupted) block of memory locations. Some of the string manipulation instructions allow the programmer to move the entire sequence of data from one block of memory to another. Others allow strings to be searched for certain elements. The opcode formats for the string manipulation instructions are shown in Fig. 2-41.

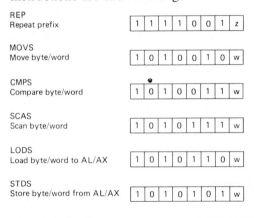

REP
Repeat prefix

MOVS
Move byte/word

CMPS
Compare byte/word

SCAS
Scan byte/word

LODS
Load byte/word to AL/AX

STDS
Store byte/word from AL/AX

Fig. 2-41 Opcode formats for 8088 string manipulation instructions. (Courtesy of Intel Corporation.)

The REP Instruction The repeat (REP) instruction is used as a prefix that allows the string instructions to perform operations on strings that are greater than 1 byte or word in length. Instructions that are referred to as prefixes must be written prior to an instruction that is to be enhanced. The number of elements contained in the string to be referenced by the instruction following REP is contained in the CX register. The **z** field is determined based on the following information:

1. If **z** = 0, then the instruction following REP is executed repeatedly until the ZF (flag) is cleared.
2. If **z** = 1, the instruction following REP is executed repeatedly until the ZF is set.

There is one case in which the **z** field of the repeat prefix is ignored. This case occurs when the repeat prefix is used with the MOVS instruction. MOVS is discussed next.

The MOVS Instruction The move string element (MOVS) instruction is used most often in conjunction with the repeat prefix. As such, this is the only form that will be covered here. The **w** field indicates the size of each string element. If **w** = 0, the elements are bytes; if **w** = 1, the elements are words. The **z** field is ignored by the MOVS instruction. Only the CX count is used. When executing the REP/MOVS instruction, the offset of the start of the string to be moved is assumed to be present in the source index (SI) register. The SI contains the offset into the current data segment. The offset of the destination of the string move is contained in the destination index (DI) register. The DI register specifies the offset into the current extra segment.

The SI and DI registers may be used to represent either the beginning or the end of the string storage block. For example, if the SI and DI registers represent the low-memory end of the string, as the MOVS progresses, the elements from successively higher locations in the data segment are moved to higher locations in the extra segment. If the SI and DI registers represent the high-memory end of the string, the elements are moved from successively lower locations in the data segment to successively lower locations in the extra segment. These operations are illustrated in Fig. 2-42a and b. The state of the direction flag (DF) determines whether or not MOVS is to proceed toward lower or higher memory when executed. If the DF = 0, then the SI and DI registers contain the lowest offset of the string. If the DF = 1, then the SI and DI registers contain the highest offset of the string.

The CMPS Instruction Two strings can be compared using the compare string element (CMPS) instruction. Again, the REP prefix is usually used in conjunction with this instruction. However, in this case, the **z** field is used according to the rules previously given. For example, if REP/CMPS is used with **z** = 1, string comparison will continue as long as the elements being compared are equal (equal elements cause ZF = 1). If two elements are not equal, the comparison is terminated, and the CX register will

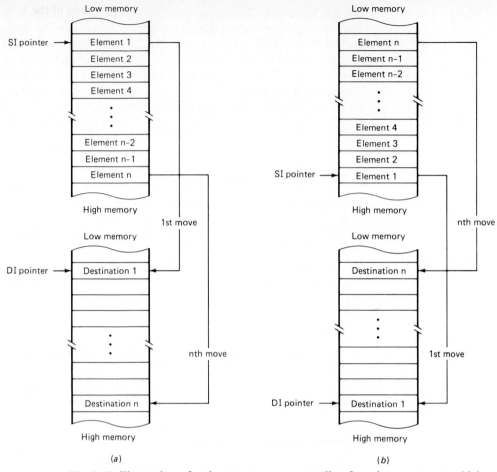

Fig. 2-42 Illustration of string movement proceeding from low memory to high (*a*) and from high memory to low (*b*).

contain the next element number past the point at which inequality was found. The offsets of the strings to be compared are contained in the SI and DI registers, and the direction of progression is determined by the DF (flag).

The SCAS Instruction The scan string instruction (SCAS) is useful for searching a string for an element with some particular value. For example, the first string element equal to 0 could be located using the REP prefix with $z = 0$. As the string is scanned (toward higher memory if the DF $= 0$, lower memory if the DF $= 1$), the occurrence of an element with all bits 0 would be flagged and execution of the REP/SCAS instruction would terminate. The CX register would contain the element number that is one position past the match or mismatch point within the string.

The LODS and STDS Instructions The load string element instruction is used to load the accumulator (AL if $w = 0$, AX if $w = 1$) with the contents of a string element whose offset is given by the contents of the SI register. The SI is automatically incremented (DF = 0) or decremented (DF = 1) following the transfer. If **w** = 0, the SI is incremented or decremented by 1; if **w** = 1, then the SI is incremented or decremented by 2. The store data to string (STDS) instruction causes the contents of AL or AX to be transferred to the location whose offset is contained in the DI register. The DI is automatically incremented or decremented following the transfer. The REP prefix is not normally used with either the LODS or STDS instructions.

Example 2-21

Write the opcodes for the instructions that will move a string of 64_{10} byte-length elements from a starting offset 0050_{16} in the current data segment into a block of memory beginning at offset $0A15_{16}$ in the current extra segment. Assume that these are nonoverlapping segments, and disregard the DF.

Solution

The opcodes for one possible solution are shown below. The instruction mnemonics have also been presented for clarity.

1. The SI register is loaded with 0050_{16}. The MOV immediate to register instruction is used.

```
1011 1110   (BE16)   MOV SI,0050
0101 0000   (5016)
0000 0000   (0016)
```

2. The DI register is loaded with $0A15_{16}$ using MOV as in Step 1.

```
1011 1111   (BF16)   MOV DI,0A15
0001 0101   (1516)
0000 1010   (0A16)
```

3. The CX register is loaded with 40_{16} (64_{10}) in a similar manner.

```
1011 1001   (B916)   MOV CX,0040
0100 0000   (4016)
0000 0000   (0016)
```

4. The repeat prefix is written (the **z** field may be disregarded).

```
1111 0010   (F216)   REP
```

5. The MOVS instruction is written with **w** = 0.

```
1010 0100   (A416)   MOVS
```

Review Questions for Section 2-4.4

1. Describe the function of the repeat prefix.
2. Execution of a MOVS instruction will transfer string elements between which two segments?
3. What is the function of the DF (flag)?
4. When the repeat prefix is used in conjunction with the SCAS instruction, which flag determines whether the scan should be repeated?
5. Referring to Example 2-21, what value must the DF (flag) have if the string source and destination areas overlap such that the beginning of the string source section lies around the middle of the string destination area?

2-4.5 The Control Transfer Instructions

All of the available jumps, calls, and returns used by the 8088 are classified as control transfer instructions. Control transfer refers to the execution of instructions in a nonsequential manner. There are two kinds of control transfers: unconditional and conditional. Most of the 8088 control transfer instructions are of the conditional variety; that is, the jump is executed only if certain conditions, as indicated by the status flags, exist.

Unconditional Transfer Instructions   The opcode formats for the unconditional control transfer instructions are shown in Fig. 2-43. All of the unconditional

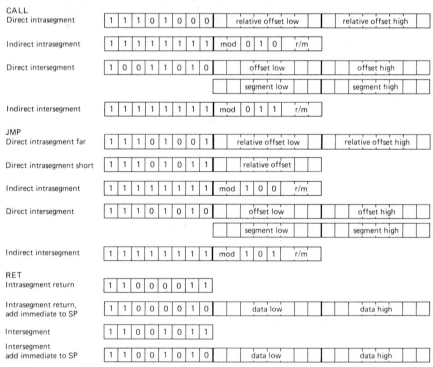

Fig. 2-43 Unconditional control transfer instructions. (Courtesy of Intel Corporation.)

transfers have the ability to cause the CPU to branch to a location that is outside of the current code segment. Such unconditional control transfers are called intersegment calls, jumps, and returns. Control transfers that are limited to within the current code segment will be referred to as intrasegment transfers.

The intrasegment CALL instruction causes the 8088 to begin the execution of a subprogram or subroutine whose offset address within the current code segment may be specified immediately following the opcode (direct mode) in two's complement form, or in the register indirect mode. The intersegment CALL also may use either of these two addressing modes. In the direct mode, the first 2 bytes following the opcode specify the offset (not in two's complement) of the destination (low-order byte first). The beginning of the code segment to which this offset refers is specified in the next 2 consecutive bytes (again, low-order byte first).

An indirect CALL uses the **mod** and **r/m** fields to specify the location of the first byte of the IP and CS values to be referenced in the current data segment. Here is what happens when an intersegment CALL is executed:

1. The IP register is incremented to the offset of the next available instruction.
2. The incremented contents of the IP and CS registers are saved (pushed into the stack).
3. The first word (the offset word) is loaded into the IP.
4. The second consecutive word (the segment word) is loaded into the CS register.
5. Execution of the subroutine begins.

Intrasegment (*intra* means within; therefore intrasegment means within segment) CALLs work the same way, except the CS contents are not saved because they will not be changed.

Upon the completion of the subroutine that was CALLed, the original contents of the IP (and the CS, if it was an intersegment CALL) are popped from the stack by the appropriate return (RET) instruction. Notice that two of the RET instructions have immediate data fields. This data is added to the contents of the stack pointer after the CS and IP values are popped off. Adding the contents of the CALL data field to the SP register effectively pops off any data that may have been pushed into the stack by the subroutine. This restores the stack to the same state that it had immediately before the CALL. Of course, the programmer must know how much data was pushed into the stack during the subroutine in order to fill in the data field correctly.

The JMP instruction is similar to CALL, except that the contents of the IP and CS registers are not pushed into the stack. Since this is the case, it is obvious that the RET instruction cannot be used to return to the next instruction following the JMP. The JMP can be considered to be analogous to the GOTO statement in BASIC. There are two kinds of direct intrasegment jumps: the short JMP and the far JMP. The short JMP has a single-byte offset that represents the relative displacement to the destination in two's complement form. The far JMP uses a word-length relative offset specification. The intersegment JMP instruction is addressed in the same way as the intersegment CALL instruction.

Example 2-22

A JMP instruction is located at address $B300_{16}$ in the current code segment. Write the opcode and relative offset for this JMP such that program execution will continue at address $A000_{16}$ in the current code segment after the JMP is executed. Also, write the mnemonic representation for this jump.

Solution

The far intrasegment JMP (direct) instruction is used. The relative offset required is found by subtracting the address of the destination ($A000_{16}$) from the contents of the IP that exist after the JMP opcode/offset fetch ($B303_{16}$), and then taking the two's complement of the difference (because this is a backward jump). You will recall that the IP is automatically incremented to the next available instruction when an instruction is decoded. The complete instruction sequence is shown below, along with its mnemonic representation. Notice that the mnemonic representation specifies the address of the jump destination in terms of the offset addresses in the left-hand column.

```
1110 1001   (E9₁₆)    JMP  A000
1111 1101   (FD₁₆)
1110 1100   (EC₁₆)
```

Notice that the mnemonic form specifies the destination of the jump based on the offset location that was presented in the example stated. This characteristic of the mnemonic form of various jump and loop instructions will be discussed further in the next section.

Conditional Control Transfer Instructions   The conditional transfer instructions are primarily responsible for the ability of a microprocessor-based system to seem "intelligent." They allow the computer to make logical decisions based on the existence of certain conditions, just as a human would.

All of the conditional transfer instructions are essentially short jumps which may or may not occur, depending on the results of previously executed instructions. The presence or absence of conditions that determine whether a jump should occur or not is indicated by the status flags. All of the conditional jump instructions are short jumps, and, as such, the maximum distance that may be spanned by such a jump is $+127$ or -128 bytes. This may seem quite limiting, but in most cases, short jumps are all that is required. If a greater distance must be covered, the solution mentioned in the section on relative addressing could be used: the destination of a conditional jump may be an unconditional far intrasegment JMP or an intersegment JMP instruction. The opcode formats for the conditional jump instructions are shown in Fig. 2-44.

Some of the conditional JMP instructions are designed to be used when arithmetic operations involving signed numbers determine the flag settings, and some, when operations involving unsigned numbers are performed. Conditional JMP instructions that use the terms *less than* or *greater than*

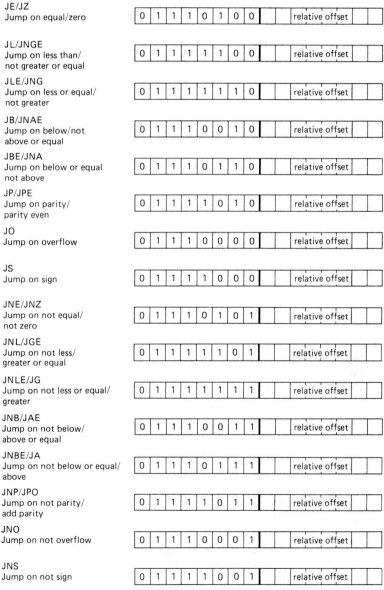

Fig. 2-44 Conditional transfer instructions. (Courtesy of Intel Corporation.)

in their mnemonics are to be used when signed numbers are operated on to determine the jump conditions. The terms *above* and *below* are used when operations involving unsigned numbers are responsible for altering the flags. For example, the jump on less/not greater or equal (JL/JNGE) instruction will cause a jump to occur if a previously executed instruction causes SF + OF = 1 (+ means logical OR). The jump on below/not above or equal (JB/JNAE) instruction, however, will cause a jump to occur if the CF = 1. Both instructions would seem to mean the same thing since *below* and *less than* are similar in meaning. However, the condition codes (flags) used in the determination of each jump are different. The relationships between the flags and the conditional jump instructions are summarized in Fig. 2-45.

Instruction	Jump conditions
JE/JZ	ZF = 1
JL/JNGE	SF $\oplus$ OF = 1
JLE/JNG	(SF $\oplus$ OF) + ZF = 1
JB/JNAE	CF = 1
JBE/JNA	CF + ZF = 1
JP/JPE	PF = 1
JO	OF = 1
JS	SF = 1
JNE/JNZ	ZF = 0
JNL/JGE	SF $\oplus$ OF = 0
JNLE/JG	(SF $\oplus$ OF) + ZF = 0
JNB/JAE	CF = 0
JNBE/JA	CF + ZF = 0
JNP/JPO	PF = 0
JNO	OF = 0
JNS	SF = 0

Note: $\oplus$ = XOR, + = OR

Fig. 2-45 Flag conditions tested by conditional transfer instructions.

The LOOP Instructions   There are three different loop instructions that allow the programmer to specify the number of consecutive times that a certain instruction sequence (loop) is to be performed. In each case, the number of passes to be made through the loop is determined by the count present in the CX register. A loop instruction is normally placed at the end of the sequence of instructions that are to make up the body of the loop. The LOOP instruction formats are shown in Fig. 2-46. The simplest instruction (LOOP) causes looping without regard to the processor status flags (an unconditional loop). As long as CX does not contain 0, the loop will be executed. LOOPZ/LOOPE will cause the instructions within the loop to be performed until the ZF (flag) is cleared during the execution of the loop, or until CX is decremented to 0, whichever occurs first. LOOPNZ/LOOPNE causes the loop to be executed until either the ZF is set or CX

| LOOP
Loop CX times | 1 | 1 | 1 | 0 | 0 | 0 | 1 | 0 | relative addr. of loop start |

| LOOPZ/LOOPE
Loop while zero/equal | 1 | 1 | 1 | 0 | 0 | 0 | 0 | 1 | relative addr. of loop start |

| LOOPNZ/LOOPNE
Loop while not zero/equal | 1 | 1 | 1 | 0 | 0 | 0 | 0 | 0 | relative addr. of loop start |

| JCXZ
Jump on CX = 0 | 1 | 1 | 1 | 0 | 0 | 0 | 1 | 1 | relative addr. |

Fig. 2-46 The LOOP instruction opcodes. (Courtesy of Intel Corporation.)

is decremented to 0. The CX register is automatically decremented each time the LOOP instruction is executed. The relative address of the beginning of the LOOP is expressed as a 1-byte two's complement number immediately following the particular loop opcode.

Example 2-23

Write the instructions necessary to form a delay loop that will repeat unconditionally 100_{10} times. Assume that this loop is to begin at address 4000_{16} in the current code segment.

Solution

Since the purpose of this loop is just to cause a time delay and nothing else, all that must be done is the loading of CX with the proper count (100_{10}) and the calculation of a relative address for the LOOP instruction. The opcode sequence is shown below, with the memory addresses shown in the left-hand column. The instruction mnemonics are given in the right-hand column. You will recall that the IP will always be pointing one instruction ahead of an instruction that is being executed. The relative address of the LOOP instruction is determined based on this fact.

```
4000   1011 1001   (B9₁₆)   MOV CX,0064
4001   0110 0100   (64₁₆)
4002   0000 0000   (00₁₆)
4003   1110 0010   (E2₁₆)   LOOP,4003
4004   1111 1110   (FE₁₆)
```

The program segment in the above example is more similar than any of the previous examples to the segment that would be produced by an assembler program. Notice that the operand for the mnemonic representation of the LOOP instruction bears little resemblance to the actual hex construction of that instruction. This is the way that an assembler would represent the loop destination. That is, in the mnemonic form, the operand (relative address) of the LOOP instruction is written in terms of the offset of the destination (the hex offset addresses in the left-hand column). This is done because it is a form that is easier for the programmer to understand than all of the two's complement notation that actually makes up the instructions. You will recall that the same situation occurred in Example 2-22.

From what has been covered so far, the operation of the LOOP instruction is described by the flowchart in Fig. 2-47. But there is a slight problem

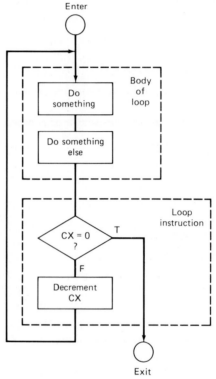

Fig. 2-47 Flowchart of LOOP instruction execution.

here. Notice that even if CX contains 0 at the outset, the instructions that make up the loop will be executed one time, because the CX test (a part of the LOOP instruction) does not occur until the end of the loop. There may be times when the procedure that is performed by the loop should not be executed at all, such as when the loop is encountered while CX = 0000_{16}. The jump on CX zero (JCXZ) instruction is designed to be used on just such occasions. The use of JCXZ requires that the number of times the loop is to be performed be contained by CX prior to the execution of the LOOP instruction. When JCXZ is used at the beginning of the loop, if CX = 0, the loop will be skipped. The destination of JCXZ is usually the next instruction following the LOOP instruction, and is specified with a 1-byte two's complement offset address. The flowchart in Fig. 2-48 illustrates the operation of a LOOP instruction when combined with JCXZ.

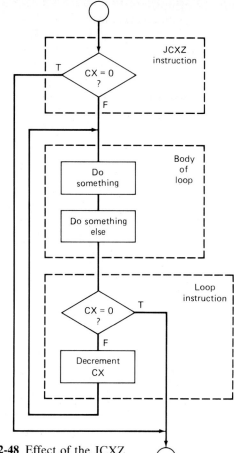

Fig. 2-48 Effect of the JCXZ instruction on LOOP execution.

Review Questions for Section 2-4.5

1. Explain the difference between conditional and unconditional control transfer.
2. Explain the difference between an intersegment CALL and an intrasegment CALL.
3. How does a JMP differ from a CALL?
4. Which jump instructions are used when signed operands are involved in the setting of the status flags?
5. Write the hex opcode for the indirect intersegment CALL that will cause a routine, whose starting address is pointed to by the contents of the AX register to be executed. The mnemonics for this instruction are CALL [AX]
6. Write the hex opcode sequence for the direct intrasegment JMP that will cause a routine that begins at offset address $00A0_{16}$ to be executed. The first byte of the JMP instruction is located at an offset of $015C_{16}$ in the current code segment.

2-4.6 Interrupt Instructions

Interrupts permit the suspension of normal program execution and the performance of some other necessary action. There are two fundamental ways of generating an interrupt: One is through hardware and the other is through software. Peripheral devices that require the services of the CPU may call attention to themselves via hardware interrupts. There are two hardware interrupt pins on the 8088: interrupt request (INTR) and non-maskable interrupt (NMI). The INTR pin is used to signal to the CPU that an external device is requesting service. If the interrupt flag (IF) is cleared, the interrupt request is ignored. If the IF is set, execution of the current program is suspended and the interrupt is acknowledged and serviced. After the interrupt is acknowledged, the interrupting device must specify an interrupt number to the 8088 for a proper response. This number tells the CPU which interrupt service routine to execute. The NMI is always serviced regardless of the state of the IF. The nonmaskable interrupt is reserved for alerting the 8088 to the occurrence of an extreme emergency, such as an impending power failure or a system malfunction.

The 8088 supports services for up to 256 different interrupts. In the case of a software interrupt, the service routine (interrupt type specification) to be performed may be specified immediately following the interrupt opcode, or the opcode itself may imply the interrupt type. The opcode formats for the software interrupt instructions are shown in Fig. 2-49. The first interrupt

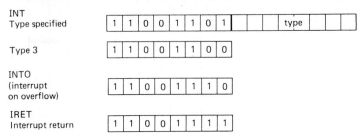

Fig. 2-49 Software interrupt instruction opcodes. (Courtesy of Intel Corporation.)

shown can invoke any of the possible 256 service routines available. The second byte of the instruction specifies the number of the service routine requested. The other two interrupt instructions are type specified inherently.

All 8088 interrupts are vectored interrupts. The idea behind vectored interrupts is that the interrupt number does not represent the actual address of the service routine, but instead, it points to a particular address vector contained in a table in memory. The vectors contain the starting addresses of the service routines. Here is what happens when a software interrupt is executed.

1. The flags, CS, and (IP + 1) are pushed into the stack.
2. The appropriate interrupt vector is located.
3. The IP and CS registers are loaded with the starting address of the service routine (the vector).
4. The service routine is executed.

In order for Step 3 of this procedure to work, a section of memory must be reserved at all times for interrupt vectors. The 8088 has been designed such that absolute addresses 00000_{16} through $003FF_{16}$ serve this purpose. The 8088 interrupt vector memory map is shown in Fig. 2-50. Each vector

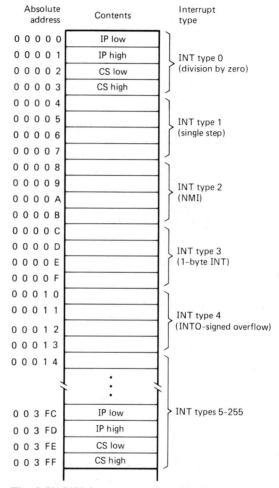

Fig. 2-50 8088 interrupt vector organization.

occupies 4 consecutive bytes of memory. Notice that the lowest address represents the lowest interrupt vector, and that the IP and CS words are placed in memory low-order byte first. Intel has reserved the first five interrupt vectors for special purposes; the remaining vectors may be used for any purpose the computer designer wishes.

Example 2-24

What is the absolute address (in hex) of the start of the vector for the type 32_{10} interrupt? What is the address of the last byte that makes up this vector?

Solution

Since the interrupt vectors are each 4 bytes long, the absolute address of a given vector is found by multiplying the hex interrupt number by 4, as shown below.

$$32_{10} = 20_{16}$$
$$20_{16} \times 4_{16} = 80_{16}$$

The vector is four bytes long, so the final byte is located at address 83_{16}.

There are two 1-byte software interrupts present in the 8088 instruction set: INT type 3 and interrupt on overflow (INTO). The 1-byte INT instruction is always interpreted by the 8088 as a type 3 interrupt. This instruction was designed to allow the insertion of break points in an assembly language program. Break points are just breaks in the execution of a program that allow the contents of the various registers and flags to be examined. The details of why this instruction is required are beyond the scope of this text and will not be covered here.

The INTO (1-byte, type 4) instruction is designed to be used following any arithmetic instruction that uses signed operands. The occurrence of a sign change (overflow) caused by the arithmetic operation will set the OF (flag) and initiate the signed overflow service routine. An overflow into the MSB caused by an unsigned arithmetic operation will also set the OF; but in a case such as this, it makes no difference and the INTO instruction need not be used. Unlike the hardware interrupt request (IRQ), none of the software interrupts are maskable; that is, they are honored by the 8088 even if the IF (flag) is set.

Interrupt service routines are much like any other subroutines in assembly or machine language; and as such, once the interrupt is serviced, control is usually returned to the main program. The interrupt return (IRET) instruction is placed at the end of the service routine to allow execution of the main program to resume. The only difference between IRET and an intersegment RET is that IRET pops the flag register contents from the stack in addition to the contents of the CS and IP. Should an interrupt service routine be executed via a CALL, the IRET will assume that the flag contents have been saved in the stack (which they would not be, using a CALL) and meaningless garbage will be written into the flags upon return.

Review Questions for Section 2-4.6

1. What is an interrupt vector?
2. When should the INTO instruction be used?
3. Where are the 8088 interrupt vectors located?
4. How many bytes are required to store an interrupt vector?

5. What is the absolute address (hex) for the first byte of the type 12 interrupt?

6. What register's contents are automatically saved when an interrupt is processed?

2-4.7 Miscellaneous Instructions

Only a few more 8088 instructions remain to be covered; the processor control instructions, the segment override prefix, and the no operation (NOP) instruction. Although the segment override prefix and the NOP instruction are not really related in operation or use, they have been grouped together for convenience.

Processor Control Instructions The processor control instructions allow the manipulation of the carry (CF), direction (DF), and interrupt (IF) flags and also provide some control over the 8088 itself. All of the processor control instructions are presented in Fig. 2-51. The clear direction flag (CLD) and

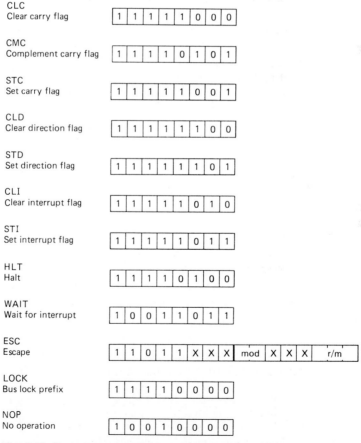

Fig. 2-51 Processor control instruction opcodes. (Courtesy of Intel Corporation.)

set direction flag (STD) instructions are used in conjunction with MOVS to control the direction of string moves. The clear interrupt flag (CLI) and set interrupt flag (STI) instructions may be used to allow the programmer some flexibility in controlling processor response to interrupts. There are no instructions that allow the trap flag (TF) to be modified. The TF must be modified indirectly when the flags are pushed into the stack. In other words, the bit that represents the TF in the stack may be altered before the flags are popped back into the status register. The TF is used to allow single-stepping of machine language programs. If the TF = 1, the 8088 will generate a type 1 interrupt after the execution of each instruction, until the TF is cleared.

The halt (HLT) instruction is used to stop program execution. While HLT is being decoded, the contents of the IP register are incremented to the next instruction address, just as with any other instruction. After execution of HLT, the 8088 will just sit and wait for an external (hardware) interrupt or a reset signal to be applied to the CPU. Initiation of an external interrupt causes the contents of the CS and IP registers to be pushed onto the stack and the execution of the appropriate service routine to begin. When the service routine is finished, normal program execution continues at the instruction immediately following HLT.

The purpose of the wait for test (WAIT) instruction is to provide a means by which the 8088 can be synchronized with another CPU or subordinate processor (coprocessor), or some other external device. The 8087 numeric data processor (NDP) is an example of one such coprocessor. When WAIT is executed, the 8088 goes into an idle or wait state, and remains there until the coprocessor has done its job. Actually, before a subordinate processor can take over, the escape (ESC) instruction must be executed by the 8088. ESC instructs the coprocessor that it is to prepare to perform some operation. The first **x** field designates which coprocessor is to be used (there may be more than one), and the second **x** field specifies which coprocessor instruction is to be executed. The **mod** and **r/m** fields specify the location of the memory-based operand for the coprocessor. Execution of the WAIT instruction following ESC causes the 8088 to remain in a wait state for as long as the coprocessor takes to perform the instruction. When the coprocessor is finished, it informs the 8088 of this by driving the 8088 test pin to logic 0. This causes the 8088 to exit the wait state and resume normal execution.

Today, it is not uncommon for several processors to share a common memory or data bus. Whenever two or more CPUs are used in such a system, the possibility of the occurrence of a bus conflict arises; that is, several processors may try to manipulate the same data in memory at the same time, or transfer data over a common bus, or drive an address onto a common address bus. This could produce some real problems. The 8088 $\overline{\text{LOCK}}$ instruction is used as a prefix to enable several CPUs to share the same memory. Basically, $\overline{\text{LOCK}}$ causes the 8088 to send out a signal that prevents another processor from accessing memory until the instruction following the $\overline{\text{LOCK}}$ prefix is completed. The bus will be locked until the execution of the prefixed instruction is completed.

The Segment Override Prefix and NOP In previous sections, it has been stated that all operands were assumed to reside within the current data segment. The only exception was when the base pointer (BP) was used in the computation of the operand address, in which case the operand was assumed to be located within the current stack segment. Since there are four different segments available at any time, it would seem that for maximum flexibility, one should be able to locate operands in any of the segments at any time. The 8088 does provide this capability in the form of the segment override prefix. The opcode format for the segment override prefix is shown in Fig. 2-51. The **seg** field is used to determine which segment register is to be referenced by the instruction following the prefix. The **seg** field encoding chart is shown in Fig. 2-9. As an example of where the segment override prefix could be used, consider the following situation. Suppose that an operand was located within the current extra segment and that the extra segment did not overlap with any other segment. The operand could be moved into the AL register, for example, by using the segment override prefix with **seg** = 00 prior to a MOV instruction. The example below illustrates this application.

Example 2-25

Write the instruction sequence that will move the contents of a byte-length operand located at offset address $33A0_{16}$ in the current extra segment into the AL register. The offset of the operand is to immediately follow the instruction opcode.

Solution

1. The segment override prefix is entered with **seg** = 00.
2. The MOV register/memory to/from register instruction will be used with the fields set as follows: **w** = 0, **mod** = 00, **r/m** = 110, **reg** = 000, and **d** = 1.

The instruction sequence and mnemonic representations are shown below.

```
0010 0110   (26₁₆)   ES:
1000 1010   (8A₁₆)   MOV AL,[33A0]
0000 0110   (06₁₆)
1010 0000   (A0₁₆)
0011 0011   (33₁₆)
```

The segment override prefix may be used with any instruction and with any other prefix. Any prefix will affect only the instruction immediately following it, and no others. More than one prefix may be used with a given instruction; however, when a string instruction is being prefixed, the repeat prefix must be the last one entered before the instruction.

The last instruction to be covered is no operation (NOP). For all practical purposes, NOP does nothing except take up 1 byte of memory, use up some time, and increment the instruction pointer by 1. The NOP opcode format is shown in Fig. 2-51. NOPs are usually used just to take up space in programs and to satisfy timing requirements.

Review Questions for Section 2-4.7

1. What is the function of the ESC instruction?
2. What is the purpose of the segment override prefix?
3. How does a coprocessor cause the 8088 to exit the wait state?
4. Write the opcode for the instruction that will exchange the contents of the AX register with itself. What instruction have you just written?
5. Write the opcode sequence required to move the contents of the CX register into 2 bytes of memory located at an offset of 0100_{16} in the current code segment. Use the MOV register/memory to/from register instruction, the mnemonics of which are MOV [0100],CX
6. Why might it be unnecessary to use the segment override prefix to move a byte from some location within the current data segment to a location within the current extra segment?

SUMMARY

This chapter has introduced the basic architecture of the 8088 microprocessor and illustrated the methods of constructing 8088 instruction opcodes. The 8088 contains four general purpose 16-bit registers, AX, BX, CX, and DX, which can be accessed as 8-bit registers by referencing either the high- or low-order bytes of the register. The remaining registers are used for specific purposes and are all 16 bits wide. These registers are the instruction pointer, stack pointer, flag register, base pointer, source index, destination index, code segment, stack segment, data segment, and extra segment. The 8088 uses a 20-bit time multiplexed bus, of which 8 lines are used for data and address purposes at various times.

The purposes of the various opcode fields and their encoding procedures have also been demonstrated. The various 8088 instructions are constructed by encoding the various fields that make up a given opcode. The fields that make up the instructions are used to specify the addressing mode and the operand source and destinations. Field encoding tables are used for the purpose of determining the required codes within the opcode.

CHAPTER QUESTIONS

2-1. How wide is the 8088 address bus?

2-2. How does the 8088 differ from the 8086?

2-3. Which 8088 registers are considered general purpose registers?

2-4. What is the maximum positive offset that can be achieved using a word-length relative address?

2-5. How must memory be allocated for the storage of strings in an 8088-based system?

2-6. When would the segment override prefix be used in conjunction with a MOV instruction?

2-7. What instruction performs corrective actions when BCD quantities are added?

2-8. Which 8088 instruction is useful for code conversion operations?

2-9. Which special purpose register will cause an instruction to access an operand in the current stack segment if it is used in the formation of an indirect address?

2-10. Arithmetic operations involving what type of BCD numbers require the masking of the four most significant bits of the operands?

CHAPTER PROBLEMS

2-11. Construct the opcode (in binary and hex forms) for the MOV instruction that will transfer the contents of a byte-length operand, whose location is pointed to by the BP register, into the stack pointer. The mnemonic form for this instruction is MOV SP,[BP]

2-12. Rewrite the opcode of Problem 2-11 such that the source operand is pointed to by the sum of the contents of the BX register and an immediate byte-length offset. The mnemonic form for this instruction is MOV SP,[BP+XX], where XX is the hex representation of the immediate offset.

2-13. Write the binary and hex forms for the instruction that will POP the contents from the top of the stack into a memory location whose address is pointed to by the immediate offset $A5C0_{16}$. POP [A5C0]

2-14. Write the opcode for the instruction that will exchange the contents of the DI register with AX. XCHG AX,DI

2-15. Rewrite the XCHG instruction of Problem 2-14 such that the BP register contents are swapped with the contents of AX.

2-16. Write the opcode and mnemonic forms for the instruction that will add the contents of AL to the contents of CH.

2-17. Write the opcode for the CMP instruction that will compare the contents of an immediate byte-length operand with the contents of the AL register. CMP AL,XX

2-18. The instruction CMP AX,BX is performed. If the AX operand is greater than the BX operand, how will the SF (flag) be affected?

INTRODUCTION TO ASSEMBLY LANGUAGE PROGRAMMING

3

Chapter 2 introduced the mnemonic forms for many of the instructions contained in the 8088's instruction set. This chapter will present some of the main ideas and operational characteristics of assembler programs and assembly language programming. Features that are commonly implemented in many assemblers will be presented, along with some typical programming applications. Some of the more commonly used assembly language debugging utilities will also be discussed.

3-1 ASSEMBLY LANGUAGE FUNDAMENTALS

Because they are essentially machine-independent and easy to understand and develop programs with, high-level languages, such as BASIC and Pascal, are practically ideal for most programming applications. However, there are many things that cannot be done easily or even at all when working with a high-level language. For example, there may be some program execution speed requirements to be considered that could make a high-level language inadequate for a given task. You should be aware that compiled languages are generally much faster in execution than interpretive languages. However, most compilers will produce machine code that could be speeded up and made more efficient if the assembly was done manually. The use of a low-level language, such as machine or assembly language, allows the programmer almost total control over the machine. For example, it is not possible to quickly manipulate the contents of specific registers using BASIC alone, but with the use of machine or assembly language, such tasks are very easily accomplished.

3-1.1 Assembly and Machine Language

The term *machine language programming* is generally applied when instructions are entered into the computer in numerical (binary or hexadecimal) form. This is the instruction format that was studied in Chap. 2, and it is the native language of the CPU. In binary machine language programming, the programmer must enter the proper instructions and data using toggle switches. You can imagine how difficult and time consuming this kind of programming could be when used with the 8088 CPU (especially the toggle switch method). Just learning how to construct the opcodes is difficult enough, let alone forming useful programs in this manner. However, on some older microprocessor-based equipment out in the field, this is exactly what must be done. Another version of machine language program entry is performed in hexadecimal format using a keyboard as the primary input device. An example of a device that requires entry of instructions and data in hexadecimal form is the popular Et-3400 microprocessor trainer from Heath.

Assembly language programming is performed using a program called an assembler or a macro assembler. The main task of either type of program is to allow the programmer to enter instructions in mnemonic form. The mnemonics that are entered are called the source code. The assembler converts the mnemonics into their equivalent binary forms and stores them in memory. The machine language program that is produced is called the object code. This is very similar to what a compiler does, except that in this case, the user has almost total control over the program structure. The differences between assemblers and macro assemblers will be explained in greater detail in later sections.

3-1.2 General Assembler Features

Along with the entry of instructions and data to be used by the CPU, the programmer must also supply the assembler with instructions on what to do when assembling the program. Such instructions may or may not produce machine code and are referred to as pseudo-opcodes (pseudo-ops) or assembler directives. Macro assemblers generally include some predefined instruction sequences that are frequently used, and also allow the programmer to create specific instruction sequences. These instruction sequences are treated by the programmer and the assembler as extensions of the actual CPU instruction set, and are referred to as *macro instructions* or just macros for short. Assemblers that can use macros are referred to as macro assemblers. Macros are assigned names (labels) and are entered by using the label as if it were a normal instruction mnemonic. For example, a routine that calculates the sine of an angle could be written and assigned the label "sine." Whenever the sine macro is to be invoked, the macro label is used just as if sine were an actual 8088 instruction mnemonic.

Another type of program that is frequently used in the testing of assembly language programs is called a debugger. Debuggers have provisions that allow the following tasks to be performed with ease: displaying and modifying the contents of the various registers in the CPU, program single-stepping, breakpoint insertion, movement of blocks of instruction code and data, block filling, and machine code disassembly. These debugging commands, or utilities, will be examined in greater detail later in this chapter.

3-1.3 The Assembly Process

Many assemblers require that the source code be written using an editor program. The job of the editor is to accept the programmer's instructions and create a source code. The source code consists of the instruction mnemonics, macros, labels, and any other parts that describe the structure of the program to be developed. A typical source code file is shown in Listing 3-1.

Listing 3-1

```
                      ORG  06CC:0100H
          INIT        MOV  CX,0005H
          SEND        MOV  DX,00F0H
                      MOV  AL,FFH
                      OUT  DX,AL
                      CMP  CX,0000H
                      JE RECEIVE
                      JMP SEND
          RECEIVE     MOV  DX,00F1H
                      IN AL,DX
                      CMP AL,00H
                      JE SEND
                      END
```

The first instruction encountered, ORG (origin), is a pseudo-op, or assembler directive. ORG tells the assembler to start the program at address 06CC:0100. This is the address format that is most commonly used when 8088 segmented addressing is being used. The first 4 hex digits represent the segment register contents, while the second 4 hex digits represent the offset within the segment that was just specified. The absolute address is found by using the shift and add method presented in Chap. 2. The segment:offset format will be used for the remainder of this chapter. Referring back to the editor listing, the H designator tells the assembler that the number is in hex form. The different sections of the program begin with names or labels in the left-hand column. The INIT label denotes a single instruction that initializes the CX register to 0005_{16}. The SEND label denotes the section that sends data to port $00F0_{16}$. You will recall that the OUT instruction can reference ports using an immediate byte or based on the contents of the DX register. The DX register referenced version is used here. AL is cleared, and sent to port $00F0_{16}$ five consecutive times. The CX register is used to hold a count, and it is tested to see if it contains 0 after AL is sent to the port. If CX = 0, then the section labeled RECEIVE is entered; otherwise, CX is decremented, and execution continues at the instruction labeled by SEND.

The next section, RECEIVE, reads port $00F1_{16}$. You will recall that the IN instruction is accumulator-specific; that is, the destination of the port operand is the accumulator. If AL contains 00_{16} after the port is read, then the program branches back to the INIT labeled instruction and the whole process is repeated. If AL contains anything other than 0, the program is terminated by the END pseudo-op.

Notice that no addresses are specified by the programmer, except the origin. The assembler will be responsible for supplying the necessary opcodes and addresses when it generates the object code.

Most of the more sophisticated assemblers are what are referred to as two-pass assemblers. A two-pass assembler reads the source code two times before producing a usable object code file. On the first pass, a symbol table is created. The assembler determines at what addresses the instructions that have labels are located, and makes a table of these values. On the second pass of the assembly, the opcodes are created, with address references that were entered in the symbol table used for branch destinations.

These types of assemblers generally have many different pseudo-ops and other options to choose from. This gives them much flexibility, but also makes them rather difficult to use. For this reason, as the programming process is presented in the following section, a very simple assembly process will be assumed. This will allow more attention to be paid to the actual task to be performed, rather than to the details of an assembler program.

Review Questions for Section 3-1

1. What does the object code of an assembly language program consist of?
2. What is a macro?
3. Most assemblers require the source code to be created using what kind of program?
4. What is the term given to a symbolic name that represents the location of an instruction?
5. What is produced by a two-pass assembler during the first pass of an assembly?
6. What pseudo-op is used to specify to the assembler where a program is to be located in memory?

3-2 ASSEMBLY LANGUAGE PROGRAM DEVELOPMENT

In most cases, the programming process begins with a general statement of the problem or task to be solved. An assembly language solution to the problem is, in general, more easily developed if the desired task is first expressed in flowchart form. The flowchart provides a graphic description of the sequence of events that must take place when the program is executed. Next, the actual instructions that correspond to the flowchart are written.

3-2.1 Assembly Language Structure

Let us now consider the development of a simple program using an assembler. Suppose that we wish to write a program, for hardware testing purposes, that will clear locations 0200_{16} through 0300_{16} in the current data segment. The main idea has just been stated, so now a flowchart will be developed. In most cases, a flowchart should make no references to specific registers or instructions, in order to make it CPU-independent. Figure 3-1 shows one possible flowchart design for the task that was previously stated. Once the flowchart is complete, the actual program must be written.

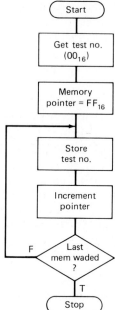

Fig. 3-1 Flowchart for program to load a test value into 256 consecutive memory locations.

   A very simple assembly process will be used to write the program. In order to simplify the programming process, it will be assumed that the assembler automatically initializes the segment registers such that all four segments totally overlap; that is, $\overline{CS} = DS = SS = ES$. The first thing that will be done is the determination of the starting address of the program. Let us assume that all programs written with the assembler will begin at offset 0100_{16} in the current code segment (assembly always occurs in the current code segment). This starting address will be entered by supplying the assembler with the following command.

```
A 0100
```

Now that the starting address has been entered, the program may be written. Working from the top of the flowchart down, the mnemonics are developed as shown in Listing 3-2. Notice that the addresses of the instructions are represented as two 4-digit hex numbers. The X's to the left of the colon represent the current contents of the $\overline{CS}$ register. The 4 digits to the right of the colon represent the offset of the first byte of a given instruction in the code segment. The parts of the program that are produced by the assembler program are shown in color. All others are entered by the programmer. The comments are shown to clarify the operation of the program. The assembler would ignore them; that is, they would actually be part of the source code that is written using an editor. In this chapter, it is assumed that the editor is not required, and that the assembler translates each mnemonic and its operand as they are entered. Let us also assume that the assembler interprets all numbers as being in hexadecimal form.

Listing 3-2

Address	Mnemonics	Comments
A 0100		
XXXX:0100	MOV AL,00	;CLEAR AL (00 IS TEST NO)
XXXX:0102	MOV CX,00FF	;SET COUNT
XXXX:0105	MOV DI,0200	;SET MEMORY POINTER
XXXX:0108	MOV [DI],AL	;WRITE AL TO MEM (START LOOP)
XXXX:010A	INC DI	;INCREMENT MEMORY POINTER
XXXX:010B	LOOP 0108	;REPEAT LOOP TILL CX + 0000
XXXX:010D	HLT	;END
XXXX:010E		

If the program just written was disassembled, the display presented in Listing 3-3 would result (of course, without the headings). U is an instruction to a debugger that tells it where to begin and end disassembly of the program. This, and other debugging options, will be presented later in this chapter.

Listing 3-3

Address	Opcodes	Mnemonics
U 0100,010D		
XXXX:0100	B000	MOV AL,00
XXXX:0102	B9FF00	MOV CX,00FF
XXXX:0105	BB0002	MOV BX,0200
XXXX:0108	8807	MOV [BX],AL
XXXX:010A	43	INC BX
XXXX:010B	E2FB	LOOP 0108
XXXX:010D	84	HLT

This program is shown in the form that many debugging programs would produce when disassembly is invoked. The only things that would be different in an actual disassembly are the code segment designations in the far left column. In actual use, the disassembly process would print the hex contents of the $\overline{CS}$ register in place of the X's in this area. Examine the mnemonics section of the listing. Notice that the destination operand for the MOV is presented before the source operand and that they are separated by a comma. This format has been used in all previous mnemonic forms presented in this chapter and in Chap. 2. Although it has not been stated explicitly until now, this is the standard format for all 8088 assemblers. For example, MOV AL,00 means "load AL with the immediate operand 0." Brackets are used to signify that an operand is located in memory and is pointed to by the register/offset that is being bracketed. In the program above, MOV [DI],AL means "move the contents of AL into the address pointed to by the DI." Notice that no decimal numbers appear in the program listing. Again, we shall assume that the assembler works only with hex representations of instructions and data.

One final point in regard to the sample program. Notice that the mnemonic representation for the LOOP instruction has its destination specified in what appears to be absolute terms. As mentioned in the section on the jump and loop instructions in Chap. 2, these instructions actually require relative addresses in their operand fields. The assembler will automatically convert the absolute address (0108_{16}) into a relative address (in this case, FB_{16}) location in the current code segment. This makes the program much easier to follow when compared to using the two's complement opcode version; however, the actual machine language program still uses the relative addressing mode.

Example 3-1

Write the mnemonics for the instructions that perform the following tasks. Addresses are not required, only the mnemonics as would appear if written using the assembler.

1. Move the contents of a word, whose location is pointed to by the sum of the contents of the BX and DI registers, into the AX register.
2. Add the contents of the AX register to the contents of a memory location whose offset is specified by the sum of BX and the constant 50_{16}.
3. Rotate right the contents of a memory location (1 byte) that is pointed to by the BP register.

Solution

```
1. MOV AX,[BX + DI]
2. ADD [BX +50],AX
3. ROR BYTE PTR [BP],1
```

The first two instructions are assumed by the assembler to use only word-length operands because a 16-bit register is used as a destination [in (1)] and as source [in (2)]. Because of this, in both cases, the memory-based operands are considered to be 16 bits long by default. If 8-bit registers had been used, the assembler would have defaulted to 8-bit memory-based operands also. The third part of the example, however, requires that the operand size be given explicitly by the programmer. The reason is that ROR (and many other instructions) may operate on memory-based operands that are either 8 or 16 bits wide. In such cases, the operand pointer that is enclosed in brackets must be designated as either a BYTE

PTR (byte pointer) or a WORD PTR (word pointer). You will recall that the WORD and BYTE PTRs were mentioned in the section on the logic instructions in Chap. 2.

The digit 1 separated from the pointer by a comma in [BX],1 indicates that this is to be a single rotate. You will recall that the rotate and shift instructions can also perform their respective operations more than one time per execution, depending on the setting of the v field. If $v = 1$, the number of operations is contained in the CL register. If multiple shifts or rotates are desired, the ending 1 is replaced with CL. Another example should help clarify these concepts.

Example 3-2

Write the mnemonics for the instructions that perform the following tasks.

1. Invert the contents of a byte whose location is specified by the sum of BP, SI and the constant offset $A0B5_{16}$.
2. Increment the contents of a word whose location is specified by the constant offset AA_{16}.
3. Rotate left, CX times, the contents of DX.

Solution

```
1. NOT BYTE PTR [BP + SI + A0B5]
2. INC WORD PTR [AA],1
3. ROL DX,CL
```

You have just seen how word and byte pointers are used with some of the logic instructions. The string manipulation instructions also must have operand size stated explicitly. The size of string element(s) to be operated upon is designated by appending B (for byte) or W (for word) onto the mnemonic. For example, the MOVS instruction, when using byte-length operands, is written MOVSB. A word-length operand is designated with MOVSW. The remaining string instructions are handled in a similar manner.

The instruction prefixes may also be used by the assembler. Since a prefix has no operand other than the instruction to which it applies, it is entered on a line by itself, followed by a colon. The four different segment override prefixes are designated as $\overline{\text{CS}}$:, DS:, SS:, and ES: by the assembler. A prefix is entered immediately before the instruction to which it applies.

Example 3-3

Write the mnemonics for a program that will read through the contents of offset locations $A000_{16}$ through $B000_{16}$ in the current extra segment. The program is to count the number of times that 00_{16} is found in the specified range of memory. The program is to begin at offset address 0100_{16} in the current code segment.

Solution

The program shown in Listing 3-4 will perform the required task. An arbitrary segment address ($\overline{CS}$ = 08A0) has been added.

Listing 3-4

```
08A0:0100        MOV  AL,00        ;Load AL with test byte
08A0:0102        MOV  BX,A000      ;Load pointer BX with first offset
08A0:0105        MOV  CX,0000      ;Clear match counter
08A0:0108        ES:               ;Segment override prefix
08A0:0109        CMP  AL,[BX]      ;Compare memory with AL test byte
08A0:010B        JNE  0110         ;If not equal don't increment counter
08A0:010E        INC  CX,1         ;If equal increment counter
08A0:0110        CMP  BX,B000      ;Compare BX to last address to test
08A0:0113        JE   011B         ;If equal then jump to The End
08A0:0116        INC  BX,1         ;Increment address pointer
08A0:0118        JMP  0108         ;Go back and test next location
08A0:011B        HLT               ;The End
```

3-2.2 Pseudo-Ops

Two pseudo-ops that are included in most assemblers will now be briefly discussed. You will recall that a pseudo-op is an instruction to the assembler and not a valid CPU opcode. The pseudo-ops that will be covered here will be called define byte (DB) and define word (DW).

The DB pseudo-op informs the assembler that all characters that follow it in quotes are to be stored sequentially in memory in ASCII code format. Each character will occupy 1 byte of memory. For example, the statement

```
XXXX:0100 DB 'Don't leave home without it.'
```

will cause the binary ASCII code for each character (including spaces and punctuation, except for the quotation marks) located within the quotes to be placed in memory, beginning at XXXX:0100. Numbers may also be stored in memory in ASCII code form if they are enclosed in quotes, as in DB '12345'. If you wanted these same numbers to be stored in normal binary form, the format would be DB 1,2,3,4,5. Each number is now entered into a memory location in 8-3-2-1 binary form. Any number being stored must not exceed the capacity of a single byte (FF_{16}). The DW pseudo-op works in a similar manner, except that characters and numbers are assigned to two memory locations (a word) each.

Since DB and DW are not true opcodes, they will not be shown when the program is disassembled. Instead, the data that was specified by either DB or DW will be shown.

3-2.3 Further Programming Examples

Some computer displays use a technique called bit mapping to produce graphics displays. Basically, bit mapping means that each of the dots that make up a picture on the screen can be turned on or off by writing a 1 or 0 in a specific bit location in memory. The details of this technique will be presented in Chap. 8, but for now, this is all that we need to know. Let us assume that the section of RAM in which these bits are located begins at address B800:0000 and ends at B800:3E80. Assuming that for testing purposes, this section of RAM is to be sequentially loaded with all 0s and then all 1s (screen blank, screen fully lit). This process is to repeat 5 times. The program that will perform this task is shown in Listing 3-5.

Listing 3-5

```
XXXX:0100        MOV AX,B800        ;LOAD AX WITH SEGMENT OF VIDEO RAM
XXXX:0103        MOV ES,AX          ;TRANSFER VIDEO SEGMENT INTO ES
XXXX:0105        MOV BX,0005        ;NO. OF TIMES TO PERFORM LOOP
XXXX:0108        MOV AL,00          ;SET FIRST TEST BYTE
XXXX:010A        MOV CX,3E00        ;INITIALIZE LOOP COUNTER
XXXX:010D        MOV DI,0000        ;RESET MEMORY POINTER
XXXX:0110        ES:                ;SEGMENT OVERRIDE PREFIX
XXXX:0111        MOV [DI],AL        ;WRITE TEST BYTE TO VIDEO RAM
XXXX:0113        INC DI             ;INCREMENT MEMORY POINTER
XXXX:0114        LOOPNZ 0110        ;LOOP TO 0110 UNTIL CX + 0000
XXXX:0116        CMP BX,0001        ;LAST TEST DONE?
XXXX:0119        JZ 011F            ;IF YES THEN JUMP TO END
XXXX:011B        DEC BX             ;DECREMENT TEST COUNT
XXXX:011C        NOT AL             ;INVERT AL FOR NEXT TEST
XXXX:011D        JMP 010A           ;PERFORM NEXT TEST
XXXX:011F        HLT                ;THE END
```

In the program of Listing 3-5, the CX register is used by the LOOPNZ (loop if CX $\neq$ 0000) instruction to delineate the sequence of instructions that write the test bytes to the proper section of RAM. Since the test byte alternates from 00_{16} to FF_{16}, the NOT instruction is used to modify it on each pass through the test. The BX register is used as a counter to keep track of how many times the RAM is filled with the test byte. Each pass decrements BX by 1, until BX is equal to 0001_{16}. When BX contains 0001_{16}, the CMP conditions set the ZF (flag), and the conditional jump is executed, terminating the program. If BX is not equal to 1, the JZ conditions are not met, BX is decremented, and the unconditional jump (JMP) causes execution to continue from offset address 010A. The segment override prefix ES: and the destination index (DI) register are used to send the test byte to the locations that are designated as the video RAM area. The contents of the ES register are modified by transferring into AX the desired segment address and then transferring the contents of AX into ES. Since no string movement instructions are used in this program, the ES register can be used for this purpose. You will recall that string moves reference the current extra segment.

For a final example of assembly language programming, let us assume that a certain application requires a program to control an analog to digital converter that is connected to ports $FFFF_{16}$ and $FFFE_{16}$. The output of the A/D converter is an 8-bit digital representation of an analog voltage, and this byte is sent to port FFFF. Port FFFE is used by the converter circuitry to inform the computer that it has made a conversion and is ready to be read (the conversions are not instantaneous). The converter signals that it is ready to be read by driving bit 0 (D_0) of port FFFE low. The remaining bits are indeterminate, and should be ignored. Once a conversion is completed and the byte is read from port FFFF, the converter must be reset by sending a dummy byte to port FFFE. A dummy byte can have any value, just as long as it is sent to the correct place (port FFFE). The program is to read 10_{10} consecutive samples from the converter and store them in 10 consecutive memory locations beginning at offset 0200_{16} in the current data segment. A detailed list of the steps that must be performed to implement this sequence of events is presented below.

1. Initialize the various pointers.
2. Initialize the A/D converter (send dummy byte to port FFFF).
3. Poll the converter (read port FFFE).
4. Read the LSB of the status byte.
5. If $D_0 = 0$, then conversion is complete. Go on to Step 6. If conversion is not complete ($D_0 = 1$), then go back to Step 3.
6. Read the output of the converter (port FFFF).
7. Store the byte.
8. Has the last byte been stored? If yes, then jump to Step 9; otherwise increment the memory storage pointer and go back to Step 2.
9. Terminate the program.

The steps just listed are presented in flowchart form in Fig. 3-2. This gives a more understandable idea of how the program could be constructed.

One possible implementation of this program is presented in Listing 3-6.

Listing 3-6

```
XXXX:0100     MOV DI ,0200     ;SET INDEX POINTER TO START OF STG AREA
XXXX:0103     MOV DX ,FFFF     ;SET I/O PTR TO LOCATION OF A/D CONV
XXXX:0106     OUT DX ,AL       ;RESET A/D WITH DUMMY BYTE
XXXX:0107     MOV DX ,FFFE     ;SET I/O PTR TO
XXXX:010A     IN AL ,DX        ;READ A/D STATUS
XXXX:010B     AND AL ,01       ;MASK OFF BITS 1-7 OF THE STATUS BYTE
XXXX:010D     CMP AL ,00       ;IS THE STATUS BIT CLEARED?
XXXX:010F     JNZ 010A         ;IF STATUS NOT CLEARED, CHECK IT AGAIN
XXXX:0111     MOV DX ,FFFF     ;CONV DONE, SET I/O PTR TO FFFF
XXXX:0114     IN AL ,DX        ;READ A/D CONVERTER OUTPUT BYTE
XXXX:0115     MOV [DI] ,AL     ;STORE A/D OUTPUT
XXXX:0117     CMP DI ,0209     ;LAST BYTE STORED YET?
XXXX:011B     JZ 0120          ;IF SO,JUMP TO PROGRAM TERMINATE
XXXX:011D     INC DI           ;INCREMENT MEMORY POINTER
XXXX:011E     JMP 0103         ;REINITIALIZE A/D AND READ OUTPUT AGAIN
XXXX:0120     INT 20           ;END, RETURN CONTROL TO OPERATING SYSTEM
```

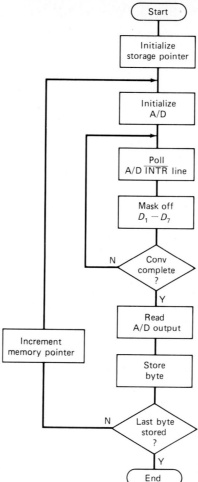

Fig. 3-2 Flowchart for polled operation of A/D converter.

In the program of Listing 3-6, the DI register is used to point to the locations in which the A/D converter output bytes are to be stored. It is also used to control the number of bytes that are read and saved; that is, when the DI = 0209, 10 samples have been read and saved, and the program is finished. The LOOP instruction could have been used just as easily, but either method will work. The AND instruction is used to mask off the 7 most significant bits of the converter's status byte. Since the state of only bit 0 is of interest, it is left unaffected (it is ANDed with 1) by this operation, while the remainder of the bits are cleared (ANDed with 0). This technique is used quite often to clear irrelevant bits. The program is terminated with software interrupt 20_{16}. This is a practical alternative to using the HLT instruction. In this case, it is assumed that interrupt 20_{16} returns control of the system to the operating system. Hex 20 was used as an example. In a given system there may be other interrupt types that will perform this function, and other functions as well. The actual interrupt types that cause certain functions to be performed depend on the operating system being used.

Review Questions for Section 3-2

1. How are operand pointers designated in assembly language?
2. In general, which instructions require the use of the BYTE PTR and WORD PTR designations?
3. How are control transfer destinations expressed in the assembly language program of Listing 3-6?
4. What 8088 instruction could be used in a masking operation such that unnecessary bits are set to binary 1?
5. Which 8088 register is used to point to locations in which operands are to be moved?
6. Which 8088 instruction will cause a jump to occur if a CMP operation results in the setting of the ZF (flag)?

3-3 PROGRAM DEBUGGING

For most of us, there is a good chance that an assembly language program will not run correctly on the first try. This is especially true when programs are long and contain numerous conditional transfer instructions. To aid in the task of correcting the problems that can occur when writing assembly language programs, debuggers are used. A debugger is a program that allows the disassembly and modification of machine language programs. You will recall that machine language is the object code that is produced by an assembler. Debuggers allow the assembled object code to be executed, analyzed, and modified with ease.

3-3.1 Common Debugger Characteristics

Most debuggers have a large assortment of commands that are used to facilitate the debugging process. The commands to be discussed in this section are representative of those that are available on most debuggers. There will be various differences in the actual structure of the commands that are used with debuggers designed to operate on different computers, and there will be differences between debuggers that are designed to work with a specific machine but are written by different people. The commands that are presented in this section are based on those that are available on the DEBUG assembler, supplied with the disk operating system of the IBM PC. This program has been used as a model, because it is a surprisingly powerful, yet relatively easy to use development tool, and many other assemblers have very similar characteristics.

3-3.2 Typical Debugger Commands

If you have been performing the activities in the accompanying *Laboratory Manual*, you are no doubt aware of some of the assembler features that will be presented. For the sake of completeness, those features that were introduced in the activities manual will be described here also.

The Assemble Command The process of writing an assembly language program for the 8088 CPU begins when the programmer instructs the assembler to begin accepting instructions. Entering the following command will initiate assembly.

A [[seg addr:]offset]

A means *assemble*, and the offset field contains the 3-digit hex representation of the starting location of the program to be assembled, relative to the 4-digit hex segment address code field [seg addr]. The braces [ ] are not used when the command is written. They are used here only to separate the command from the various fields that are optional. Fields that must be specified are not enclosed in braces.

If the segment address field [seg addr] is omitted, the offset specified in the offset field [offset] is relative to the current code segment by default. If both the segment and offset address fields are omitted, assembly begins at offset 0100_{16} in the current code segment, again, by default.

Example 3-4

Write the commands that would be required to begin assembly of programs at the following locations:

1. Absolute address $500FC_{16}$
2. 2A40:0000
3. Offset 0350 of the current code segment

Solution

1. This address could be specified in many different ways. In order to leave maximum room for coding, the segment address will be specified such that 64K byte of memory is available in the offset portion of the address field.

A 50FC:0000

2. This address is entered in the form presented in the problem statement.

A 2A40:0000

3. Since the current code segment is the default location of assembled programs, no segment address is required. An offset address must be supplied, however, because the default offset is 0100_{16}.

A 0350

The Unassemble Command   In order to view the mnemonics and opcodes that constitute an assembly language program, the unassemble command (U) is used. Unassembly is the same thing as disassembly, and the terms are used interchangeably. The unassemble command is structured as shown on the following page.

U [seg addr:][start offset,][end offset]

The [start offset] field is the 4-digit hex offset of the point at which disassembly is to begin in the segment specified by [seg addr], and [end offset] is the hex offset of the last instruction to be disassembled. The disassembly will produce a listing of the program which includes the segment address, offset addresses, hex equivalents of instructions and operands, and instruction mnemonics.

If the [seg addr] field is not specified, disassembly will be performed on the code within the limits given in the offset fields, in the current code segment. If the [end offset] field is omitted, a minimum of 32 bytes of code will be disassembled, starting at the [start offset] address. If, on the encounter of the 32nd byte, it is the first byte or an intermediate byte of an instruction, that whole instruction will be displayed, including the immediate operand, if applicable. The actual number of bytes shown will depend on the length of the last instruction encountered.

If no segment address is included, disassembly begins in the current code segment. If the offset address fields are also left out, disassembly automatically begins at offset 0100_{16} in the current code segment.

Example 3-5

Construct the commands that will disassemble the assembly language programs that occupy the following memory locations.

1. 0A00:0000 through 0A00:0AA2
2. 0100 through 0600 in the current code segment

Solution

1. U 0A00:0000,0AA2

2. U 0100,0600

The Go Command   The debugger is instructed to begin execution of a program by entering the command G. Program execution will begin in the current code segment, at the location given in the [= seg addr:offset] field.

G [= seg addr:offset] [bkpt bkpt . . .]

If the [= seg addr:offset] field is omitted, execution begins at the location pointed to by the current values of the $\overline{CS}$ and IP registers. The optional address parameters [bkpt] represent the hex offset addresses of the instructions at which breakpoints are to be inserted. A breakpoint is a 1-byte type 3 software interrupt that is automatically executed when the offset address(es) specified by the [bkpt] field are reached. This interrupt causes program execution to halt, and the contents of all of the registers to be displayed. Breakpoints can be placed in programs to temporarily suspend operation at points where problems are suspected of occurring. Entering G following a breakpoint will result in normal execution starting at the location at which the breakpoint was placed. For proper operation, the breakpoint must be placed at the location of the first byte of an instruction opcode.

Example 3-6

Construct the commands that will perform the following functions.

1. Start execution of a program beginning at 0355:0010.
2. Start execution of a program beginning at the current CS:IP location, with break points inserted at offsets 0230, 0240, and 0250.

Solution

1. G 0355:0010

2. G 0230,0240,0250

The Dump Command   Often, it is desirable not to disassemble a program, but to look at the hexadecimal or ASCII code contents of a section of memory. The dump (D) command allows the assembler to display the contents of a contiguous block of memory, displaced from the beginning of any current segment address by a 4-digit hex offset. The format of the dump command is shown below.

D [seg reg]:start offset,[end offset]

The contents of this contiguous block of memory will be displayed in hex and ASCII forms. If the [seg reg] field is omitted, the offsets will be relative to the current value of the DS register. If the [end offset] field is omitted, 128 bytes will be dumped, starting at the offset supplied in the [start offset] field.

Example 3-7

Write the commands that will perform the following tasks.

1. Dump the contents of a 50_{10} byte block of memory that begins at address 0300:0000.
2. Dump the contents of 256_{10} consecutive memory locations, beginning at offset 0200 in the current code segment.

Solution

1. D 0300:0000,0032

2. D CS:0200,02FF

The Fill Command   A command that is complementary to dump is the fill (F) command. This command allows each byte within a contiguous block of memory to be written to and filled with a specific number, list of numbers, or ASCII code character equivalents. The structure of this command is as follows.

F [seg addr:]start offset,[LN],end offset,operand(s)

The current data segment is the destination of the operands listed in this command by default if no value is entered for the [seg addr] field. The [LN] field is used if a list of byte-long numbers or a list of characters is to be written sequentially, beginning at the start offset. When L is used, the end offset is not used and only the values or characters specified in the operand field are written, beginning at the specified location. N is the number of bytes to be stored.

Example 3-8

Write the commands that will perform the following tasks.

1. Clear the memory locations from 0200:0000 through 0200:0500.
2. Enter the hex numbers 1, 2, 3 and 4 into four consecutive locations, starting at offset 0100 in the current data segment.

Solution

1. F 0200:0000,0500,00

2. F 0100 L 4 1,2,3,4

A sequence of ASCII codes can be written into successive bytes of memory using the F command. Characters must be enclosed in quotes. The following example uses this technique.

Example 3-9

Write the command that will load the ASCII code representation for the characters A, a, B, b, C, and c into the current data segment, starting at offset 100.

Solution

F 0100 L 6 "AaBbCc"

The characters that are enclosed in quotes are not separated by spaces, commas or any other symbols. This is because the ASCII code for the space, or other character would be written into RAM in between each of the desired ASCII codes.

The Enter Command   The enter command (E) allows a sequence of bytes to be written into RAM manually, 1 byte at a time. The format for this command is as follows.

E [seg addr:]offset byte byte byte . . .

If the segment address is not specified, then the offset is assumed to be in the current data segment. The bytes are entered sequentially by pressing the space bar after each is typed. After the last byte is entered, pressing the return key ends the E procedure. As bytes are entered, the current contents are displayed, followed by a period (.). If it is desired not to change the contents that are displayed, the space bar is struck without prior entry of a new byte. A typical display using the E command to enter the sequence 0B, AA, 22, 67, EE, starting at offset 0100 in the current data segment, is shown below. The colored parts are those that are entered by the programmer.

E 0100

0627:0100 14.0B 00.AA 00.22 9F.67 01.EE

The Register Dump Command   Register contents may be displayed using the register dump (R) command. Entering R causes the contents of all of the 8088's registers to be displayed on the CRT. The contents of a given register may be altered by specifying the register when entering the R command. For example, entering

RIP

will cause the contents of the IP register to be displayed, followed by a colon as shown below.

RIP   (This was entered by the programmer)
IP ????   (???? are the current hex contents of IP)
:-   (The new hex contents are entered here)

The programmer may now enter any 4-digit hex number into the IP register. Any register (8- or 16-bit) may be altered in this manner, except for the flag register. The codes shown in Fig. 3-3 are used to decode and set the states of the flag registers. In order to set a given flag to a particular state, the code representing that state is entered at the prompt. The contents of all of the registers may be displayed simultaneously by entering R with no register specification added.

Flag	Name	Set	Clear
OF	Overflow	OV	NV
DF	Direction	DN	UP
IF	Interrupt	EI	DI
SF	Sign	NG	PL
ZF	Zero	ZR	NZ
AF	Auxiliary carry	AC	NA
PF	Parity	PE	PO
CF	Carry	CY	NC

Fig. 3-3 Interpretation of flag status codes.

The Trace Command The trace command (T) is used to single step through a program one instruction at a time. Single-stepping is closely related to break point insertion. Effectively, break points are automatically inserted after each instruction when single stepping is used. To activate the trace function, instead of entering G at the start of the program, T is entered. Each time T is entered, the instruction pointed to by the IP register will be executed. After execution of the instruction, the contents of all of the registers, and the next instruction in line to be executed, are printed automatically. This provides a very useful program debugging tool. When trace is used and a LOOP instruction is encountered, the loop is executed at normal speeds. The registers are displayed after the loop is exited.

The Load and Name Commands The load command (L) is used to load a file from disk into memory or to load the data from a series of sectors. The sector by sector load from disk format is constructed as follows.

L seg addr:offset,drive, sector,n

In this option, *seg addr* and *offset* specify the memory location for storage of the data contained in consecutive disk sectors, beginning with the disk sector number (in hex) specified in the sector field. The drive field specifies disk drive A: (0) or B: (1). For example, the entry of

L 092C:0100 0 02 A0

causes the contents of $A0_{16}$ (160_{10}) consecutive sectors, beginning at sector 02_{16}, to be written into RAM, beginning at address 092C:0100.

The second option is used to load files from disk. The format for this option consists of two separately entered parts.

N [drive] name.ext
L [[seg addr:]offset]

The name command (N) precedes the name of the file, and *ext* is the file extension. The file extension is normally used to identify the format of the file, such as COM, EXE, or BAS. If a file has no extension, the period and ext field are omitted. If the file is on drive A:, the drive field is omitted. If the file is on a disk in drive B:, then B: is entered in the drive field. The beginning of the memory block in which the file is to be loaded is specified following L. If no load address is specified, the file is loaded into memory starting at offset 0100_{16} in the current code segment. The following command will load a file named GAME.COM from drive B: into the current code segment, beginning at offset 0100_{16}.

```
N B:GAME.COM
L
```

Example 3-10

Write the command that will load the program SCAN.COM from drive A: into memory.

Solution

```
N SCAN.COM
L
```

The Write Command   This command (W) is used to save data that is currently in memory by writing it to a disk. There are two options available that are similar to those used with the load command. The first option is configured as follows.

W [seg addr:]offset,drive,sector,n

The *seg addr:offset* field represents the beginning of the block of memory from which data is to be transferred to disk. If the seg addr portion of this field is omitted, the offset is referred to the current code segment by default. The drive field is used to select drive A: (drive = 0) or drive B: (drive = 1) as the destination. The sector field specifies the first sector at which data is to be transferred. The *n* field specifies the number of consecutive sectors that are to be written to. The contents of the memory are sequentially transferred to disk until all of the sectors specified have been filled.

The second option is used to write a file to disk, with a file name and the extension EXE. The name (N) function is used to assign the name to the file. The format for this option is as follows.

N [drive]name.EXE
W

The W command causes the block of data, beginning at offset 0100_{16} in the current code segment, to be written either to drive A:, if the drive field is omitted, or to the second disk drive, if B: is entered in the drive field. Before the file can be written to the disk, however, the number of bytes to be written to the file must be loaded into the BX and CX registers. BX contains the four high-order hex digits of the byte count, and CX contains the four low-order hex digits of the byte count. The following example should clarify the use of these commands.

Example 3-11

Write the sequence of commands that would be required to save an assembly language program, in which the first instruction begins at offset 0100_{16} in the current code segment and the last instruction ends at offset $010A_{16}$. The program is to be stored under the name THING.COM.

Solution

First, the length of the program is determined as being $0A_{16}$ bytes long. The BX register must contain 0000_{16}, and CX must contain $000A_{16}$ in order to specify the correct number of bytes to be saved. The register dump command is used to examine and change, if necessary, the contents of BX and CX as follows.

```
RBX         (This is entered by the programmer)
BX ????     (The current contents of BX are displayed)
:0000       (Enter the desired contents after the : prompt)
RCX         (This is entered by the programmer)
CX ????     (The current contents of CX are displayed)
:000A       (Enter the desired contents after the : prompt)
```

Now the program name is entered, followed by the write command.

```
N THING.COM
W
```

After the file has been saved, the message "Saving 000A bytes" will be produced, indicating that no problems have occured.

SUMMARY

This chapter has provided an introduction to some of the main features and characteristics of assemblers, assembly language programming, and debugging programs. The function of an assembler is to accept a program in mnemonic form and convert it into executable machine code. The mnemonic form is the source code, and the machine language form is the object code. Most assemblers allow the use of symbolic names for program segments, variables, and instruction sequences. Macro assemblers allow the user to create instruction sequences that may be executed as if they were native CPU instructions. These are called *macros*. Instructions that tell the assembler program how and where to assemble the machine language object code are called pseudo-ops, or assembler directives.

The testing of programs and the correction of program errors (the latter called *bugs*) are facilitated with the use of a debugging program. Debuggers allow machine code instructions to be disassembled, examined, and modified. Most debuggers allow the contents of memory and various registers to be manipulated with ease. Some debuggers even allow the creation of assembly language programs. These features make the debugger one of the most useful tools that can be used for programming and troubleshooting purposes.

CHAPTER QUESTIONS

3-1. In which segment will the opcodes for an assembly language program be located?

3-2. Using 8088 instructions, it is not possible to load an immediate operand into a segment register. It is possible to load a given segment register with an operand that is pointed to by another register. State another way in which the contents of a segment register may be altered. More than one instruction may be necessary.

3-3. From the information presented in this chapter, explain what a file is.

3-4. How is the length of a program that is to be saved on a disk specified when the name (N) and write (W) commands are used?

3-5. What is the term given to a label that represents a sequence of instructions that is executed as if it were a normal opcode?

3-6. What is the term given to an instruction to an assembler that does not always result in the generation of machine code, but rather informs the assembler to take some specific action?

3-7. In the mnemonic representations of the instructions presented in this chapter, how are pointers designated?

3-8. What is wrong with the following instruction mnemonic, and how could it be corrected?

    ROR [DI]

3-9. In the instruction mnemonic MOV AL,[SI] what is the purpose of the brackets around the operand field?

3-10. In what segment are indirect operands located?

CHAPTER PROBLEMS

3-11. Write the assembler mnemonic for the instruction that will exchange the contents of the DI register with AX.

3-12. Write the assembler mnemonic for an instruction that causes the BP register contents to be swapped with the contents of AX.

3-13. Write the mnemonic for the instruction that will add the contents of AL to the contents of CH.

3-14. Write the assembler mnemonic for the instruction that will compare the immediate byte-length operand F0 with the contents of the AL register.

3-15. If the instruction CMP AX,BX is performed, and the operand in AX is greater than the operand in BX, how will the SF (flag) be affected?

3-16. Write the assembler mnemonic for the rotate through carry left (RCL) instruction such that the contents of the BX register will be rotated the number of times as defined by the contents of CL.

3-17. Assuming that $CL = 05_{16}$, $BX = 01EA_{16}$, and $CF = 0$, what will be the hex contents of BX immediately following the execution of the RCL instruction specified in Problem 3-16?

3-18. Write the mnemonics for the instruction sequence that will load a byte from port $1C_{16}$ into AL. If AL contains FF_{16} after the port is read, the program should repeat the port read/test sequence. Otherwise, the contents of AL are to be moved to port $1D_{16}$, and the program should terminate. Assume that assembly begins at offset 0100_{16} in the current code segment (CS = XXXX).

3-19. Write the mnemonics for a program that will assign the following values to the segment registers: $DS = 0000_{16}$, $SS = AB00_{16}$, $ES = C000_{16}$. Assume that the program begins at offset address 0100_{16} in the current code segment. The operands that are to be written into the DS, ES and SS registers are to be transferred from AX.

3-20. Write the mnemonics for a short program that will move 100_{10} contiguous bytes of data beginning at offset address 0000_{16} from the current data segment into the current extra segment beginning at offset address $10F0_{16}$. The string should be moved, beginning with the element at the lowest address. The program should begin at offset address 0100_{16} in the current code segment.

3-21. Write a program in mnemonic form that will implement the flowchart in Fig. 3-4. The program begins at offset address 0100_{16} in the current code segment.

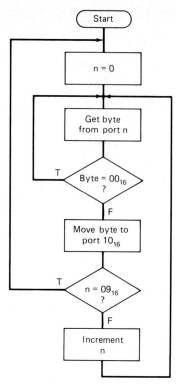

Fig. 3-4 Program flowchart.

3-22. Write the mnemonics for a program that will read the value of a word present at port $A0_{16}$ and determine whether the word is even or odd. If it is even, the program should initiate interrupt 25_{16}. If the word is odd, interrupt 26_{16} should be initiated. This sequence of operations is to repeat indefinitely. Assume that the program begins at offset address 0100_{16} in the current code segment.

3-23. Refer to the program fragment shown below. What will the hex contents of the AX register be after the DIV instruction is executed?

```
08F1:0100   B8321F   MOV AX,1F32
08F1:0103   B1B3     MOV CL,B3
08F1:0105   F6F1     DIV CL
```

THE 8088 CPU— OPERATION AND SYSTEM ORGANIZATION

Chapter 2 provided an introduction to the 8088 CPU, largely from a software point of view. This chapter will present the 8088 from a hardware perspective. A review of some of the basic principles behind the digital logic circuits that are used in 8088-based systems and 8088 power, timing, and bus interfacing requirements will be presented. The basic functional structure of the 8088 and techniques employed to create a practical system featuring separate address and data buses will be examined. In addition, introductory explanations and observations of the characteristics of a few of the available 8088 support devices and their uses will also be presented.

4-1 8088 OPERATIONAL CHARACTERISTICS

The 8088 is an N-channel, depletion load silicon gate HMOS (high-density MOS) microprocessor. The term *depletion load* refers to the use of depletion-mode MOSFETs (metal-oxide semiconductor field-effect transistors) as active loads on the drains of the transistors (also MOSFETs) used to form the switching elements in the IC. A single $+5$ V voltage source is required for proper operation of the CPU. The 8088 dissipates a maximum of 2.5 W when in operation. The pin diagram of the 8088 is presented in Fig. 4-1. All pins that carry data, address, and status information constitute what is referred to as the local bus. The 8088 local bus is 20 bits wide.

Referring to Fig. 4-1, you will notice that certain pins (24 through 31 and pin 34) may be defined either of two different ways. The function that is performed by any of these dual-purpose terminals is determined by strapping the MN/$\overline{\text{MX}}$ (minimum mode/maximum mode) pin either low (to ground) or high (to V_{CC}). Do not confuse these redefinable pins with those that are multiplexed (the address/data and address/status lines) onto the local bus. The pins that are multiplexed serve different purposes at various

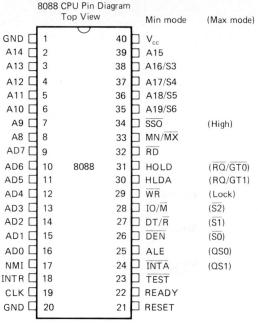

Fig. 4-1 8088 CPU pin designations.
(Courtesy of Intel Corporation.)

times, but their functions are not defined by the user. The 8088 itself defines the function of a given multiplexed pin, as required for addressing, data transfer, or control purposes during instruction fetch and execution cycles. The MN/$\overline{\text{MX}}$ pin strapping is determined by the designer at the outset, before any further system design is done, based on the various design requirements. The differences between the minimum and maximum modes of operation will be discussed later in the chapter.

4-1.1 System Timing

Microprocessors are largely synchronous devices, and as such, they require a timebase from which to coordinate their activities. Basic CPU timing is derived from a master clock. Some CPUs, such as the Motorola 6805, contain built-in clock generation circuitry. The clock signal required by the 8088 must be supplied by an external device (a clock generator). The recommended clock signal for the 8088 is a 5 MHz 33 percent duty cycle rectangular waveform. This translates to a clock period of 200 ns, with t_{on} = 66.7 ns and t_{off} = 133.3 ns. Such a waveform is illustrated in Fig. 4-2.

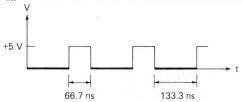

Fig. 4-2 8088 33 percent duty cycle clock waveform.

A higher-speed version of the 8088 (the 8088-2) is available which will operate at a clock frequency of 8 MHz, with the same 33 percent duty cycle requirement as the 5 MHz version.

The minimum recommended clock frequency for the 8088 is 2 MHz. This limit has been imposed because internally, the 8088 retains data in dynamic storage cells. Dynamic cells require periodic refreshing (rewriting of current stored data) in order to maintain their integrity. When the 8088 is operated at clock frequencies below 2 MHz, the cells may not be refreshed frequently enough, resulting in lost data and unreliable operation.

The basic time interval in which the microprocessor performs a given operation is called a bus cycle T_{cy}. The basic system timing diagram illustrated in Fig. 4-3 shows the relationships between the clock and the

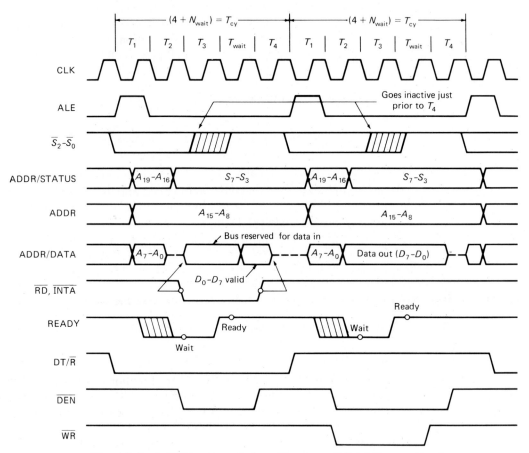

Fig. 4-3 Basic 8088 system timing. (Courtesy of Intel Corporation.)

various 8088 address, data, and control lines. During any operation in which the 8088 accesses the local bus (reading or writing to memory or I/O ports), a bus cycle will be produced. When not executing a bus cycle, as in the case of prefetched instructions being operated on from within the queue, the 8088 BIU generates idle cycles T_i. During idle cycles the 8088 continues to output updated status information on the most significant address lines. If the previous active bus cycle was a write operation, the 8088 continues to output data on the local bus until the next bus cycle is started. If the previous active bus cycle was a read operation, the 16 least significant address lines are tristated until the beginning of the next bus cycle.

Any given bus cycle may be a minimum of four clock periods long. This produces a minimum bus cycle time of 800 ns, when a 5 MHz clock is used. The 8088 may lengthen the period of a given bus cycle by inserting one or more wait states T_{wait} as required by a given operation. For example, if the CPU is to send or receive data from a peripheral device and the peripheral is not ready for data transfer, additional wait states must be inserted in the bus cycle. The peripheral (or its control circuitry) causes this to happen by pulling the 8088 READY line low. Each wait state added to the bus cycle is one clock period in duration. When the external device is ready for data transfer, it must then pull the READY line high.

Review Questions for Section 4-1

1. When will the 8088 insert wait states in a bus cycle?
2. Assuming a certain 8088 operates at a clock frequency of 4.614 MHz, what is the minimum length of a bus cycle?
3. Referring to Question 2, for what length of time would the clock line be high (logic 1) if the clock generator has a 33 percent duty cycle?
4. What is the term given to the time interval during which the 8088 performs an instruction?
5. What is the minimum number of clock cycles in a bus cycle?
6. A certain 8088-based microcomputer has been functioning erratically. A technician looks at the clock signal on an oscilloscope and measures the following parameters: clock period $(T) = 455$ ns, $t_{on} = 273$ ns. Could the clock signal possibly be responsible for the computer's erratic behavior? Explain your reasoning.

4-2 8088 PIN DEFINITIONS

As stated in the preceding section, the functions of several of the 8088 pins are dependent on the state of the MN/$\overline{\text{MX}}$ pin. When this input is tied high ($+5$ V), the 8088 operates in what is called the minimum mode. In the minimum mode, the 8088 alone generates all necessary bus control signals on pins 24 through 31, and on pin 34. When the MN/$\overline{\text{MX}}$ input is tied to ground, the above-mentioned pins are redefined, and some of the bus control signals must be generated by a second IC called a bus controller. The bus controller produces the command and control signals required to synchronize devices that are connected to the local bus with the CPU. The Intel 8288 is a bus controller that is designed to be used with a maximum mode 8088. Further details of the operation of the 8288 bus controller will be presented later in this chapter.

4-2.1 Mode Independent Pin Functions

The functions of most of the pins on the 8088 are not affected by the state of the $MN/\overline{MX}$ pin. These pins are described below. The relationship between a given pin or set of pins and the timing diagram of Fig. 4-3 is also given in the pin descriptions. The letter(s) enclosed in parentheses before the pin descriptions indicate whether a given pin serves as an input, an output, or both.

CLK	(I) Clock line.
V_{CC}	Supply voltage, $+5$ V 5 percent.
GND	Ground (both pins 1 and 20).
$MN/\overline{MX}$	(I) Minimum or maximum mode selection.
$AD_0 - AD_7$	(I/O) Bidirectional, tristate lines that form the 8-bit data bus and the 8 least significant address lines. Addresses and data are time multiplexed onto these lines. Valid memory or I/O addresses are present on these lines during the T_1 portion of the bus cycle. Valid data is present on these lines during T_2, T_3, T_w, and T_4. Float high-Z (tristate) during local bus hold acknowledge.
$A_8 - A_{15}$	(O) Tristate address lines. Output valid memory or I/O addresses for entire bus cycle. Addresses change during T_1. These lines float high-Z during local bus hold acknowledge.
$A_{16}/S_3 - A_{19}/S_6$	(O) Address/status lines. Output a valid memory address during T_1 of bus cycle. Lines are driven low during I/O operations. During both memory and I/O operations, processor status data is output during T_2 through T_4 of the bus cycle. Float to high-Z (tristate) during local bus hold acknowledge. See Fig. 4-4 for decoding of status lines.

$S_3 S_4$ Decoding

S_4	S_3	Characteristics
0 (low)	0	Alternative data (extra segment)
0	1	Stack
1 (high)	0	Code or none
1	1	Data

$S_6 = 0$

$S_5 = $ status of IF flag

Fig. 4-4 S_3, S_4 decoding table.
(Courtesy of Intel Corporation.)

$\overline{RD}$	(O) Read line. Goes low indicating CPU read operation that is CPU reading memory or I/O data from local bus. Active during T_2, T_3, and T_w. Floats to tri-state during local bus hold acknowledge.

READY	(I) Active high, indicates memory or I/O device ready to transfer data to or from CPU. If READY is held low by memory or I/O device, 8088 inserts wait states until READY is brought high. Must be synchronized external to CPU.
INTR	(I) Interrupt request, level triggered (high). Internally synchronized.
NMI	(I) Nonmaskable interrupt, rising (low to high) edge triggered. Internally synchronized.
$\overline{\text{TEST}}$	(I) The $\overline{\text{TEST}}$ pin is automatically examined by the CPU during the execution of the wait for test (WAIT) instruction. If $\overline{\text{TEST}}$ = low, then 8088 resumes normal execution. If $\overline{\text{TEST}}$ = high, then wait state extended.
RESET	(I) Active high (minimum of 4 clock cycles). Causes termination of present operation. Clears flags, IP, instruction queue, DS, ES, and SP registers. Sets CS = $FFFF_{16}$. This causes execution to begin at address $FFFF0_{16}$. At this address is a jump which sends the CPU to a system reset routine. The RESET input is internally synchronized by the 8088.

4-2.2 Minimum Mode Pin Functions

The following pin designations are valid when $MN/\overline{MX} = V_{CC}$. In such a case, the 8088 is defined as operating in the minimum mode. Use of the minimum mode produces the simplest, lowest chip count 8088-based system.

$IO/\overline{M}$	(O) Differentiates between memory and I/O accesses. Active (valid) during T_4 preceding bus cycle until T_4 of current bus cycle. Floats to high-Z (tristate) during local bus hold acknowledge.
$\overline{\text{WR}}$	(O) Write line, active low. Indicates to external devices that CPU is performing a memory or I/O write operation. Active during T_2, T_3, and T_w. Floats tristate during local bus hold acknowledge.
$\overline{\text{INTA}}$	(O) Interrupt acknowledge, active low during T_2, T_3, and T_w of each interrupt acknowledge cycle.
ALE	(O) Address latch enable, active high during clock low portion of T_1.
$DT/\overline{R}$	(O) Data transmit/receive. Used in conjunction with a data bus transceiver. Indicates direction of data transmission to or from CPU. Floats tristate during local bus hold acknowledge.
$\overline{\text{DEN}}$	(O) Data enable, active low. Indicates presence of valid data on local bus. For a read cycle, $\overline{\text{DEN}}$ is low from the middle of T_2 to the middle of T_4. For write cycles, $\overline{\text{DEN}}$ is low from the beginning of T_2 to the middle of T_4. Floats tristate during local bus hold acknowledge.

HOLD (I) Hold, active high. HOLD is driven high by some other device, such as another processor, that requires use of the local bus. Return of the local bus to the 8088 is achieved by driving HOLD low. HOLD operates in conjunction with HLDA.

HLDA (O) Hold acknowledge. HLDA is driven high by the CPU when it is relinquishing control of the local bus. Activation of HLDA indicates that the output lines of the 8088 have been tristated. HLDA is issued during either T_1 or T_4.

$\overline{\text{SSO}}$ (O) Status line. Used with IO/$\overline{\text{M}}$ and DT/$\overline{\text{R}}$ to decode current bus cycle status. See Fig. 4-5 for decoding of $\overline{\text{SSO}}$, IO/$\overline{\text{M}}$ and DT/$\overline{\text{R}}$.

Status Decoding

I/O/$\overline{\text{M}}$	DT/$\overline{\text{R}}$	$\overline{\text{SSO}}$	Characteristics
0	0	0	Code access
0	0	1	Read memory
0	1	0	Write to memory
0	1	1	Passive
1	0	0	Interrupt acknowledge
1	0	1	Read I/O port
1	1	0	Write to I/O port
1	1	1	Halt

Fig. 4-5 Status line decoding table. (Courtesy of Intel Corporation.)

4-2.3 Maximum Mode Pin Functions

The following pin definitions are implemented when the 8088 is operated in the maximum mode (MN/$\overline{\text{MX}}$ = GND). In the maximum mode, the 8088 no longer generates all of the required system timing signals. A bus controller must be used to develop bus control signals based on the states of the 8088 status lines $\overline{S}_0$, $\overline{S}_1$ and $\overline{S}_2$.

$\overline{S}_2$, $\overline{S}_1$, $\overline{S}_0$ (O) Status lines, active during clock high of T_4, T_1, and T_2. Passive or inactive (all status lines high) during T_3 or T_w. These lines are used by the bus controller to generate memory and I/O control signals. Changes in any of these lines during a T_4 cycle indicate the beginning of a new bus cycle. Changes in any of these lines during a T_3 or T_w cycle indicate the end of the current bus cycle. These status lines are decoded as shown in Fig. 4-6. $\overline{S}_0$, $\overline{S}_1$ and $\overline{S}_2$ are floated tristate (high-Z) during local bus hold acknowledge.

$\overline{\text{RQ}}/\overline{\text{GT0}}$, $\overline{\text{RQ}}/\overline{\text{GT1}}$ (I/O) Request/grant pins, bidirectional, active low. Force the CPU to relinquish control of the local bus to another device at the end of the current bus cycle.

Status Decoding
(Maximum Mode Only)

$\overline{S_2}$	$\overline{S_1}$	$\overline{S_0}$	Characteristics
0	0	0	Interrupt acknowledge
0	0	1	Read I/O port
0	1	0	Write to I/O port
0	1	1	Halt
1	0	0	Code access
1	0	1	Read memory
1	1	0	Write to memory
1	1	1	Passive

Fig. 4-6 Maximum mode 8088 decoding. (Courtesy of Intel Corporation.)

$\overline{\text{LOCK}}$ (O) Active low, activated by $\overline{\text{LOCK}}$ prefix, this pin stays low until the prefixed instruction is completed. Prevents other devices (coprocessors and the like) from using local bus. Floats tristate during local bus hold acknowledge.

QS0, QS1 (O) Queue status lines. Allow external monitoring of instruction queue. Figure 4-7 shows queue status decoding.

Pin 34 Always high in maximum mode.

Queue Status Decoding
(Maximum Mode Only)

QS1	QSØ	Indication
0	0	No operation
0	1	First byte of opcode from queue
1	0	Empty the queue
1	1	Subsequent byte from queue

Fig. 4-7 Maximum mode 8088 queue status decoding (Intel). (Courtesy of Intel Corporation.)

Review Questions for Section 4-2

1. When is a bus controller required in an 8088-based system?
2. What are some advantages of using the 8088 in the minimum mode?
3. How does the 8088 acknowledge a local bus hold request?
4. Which 8088 output lines are used by a bus controller to determine the state of the CPU?
5. At what address should the 8088 reset routine reside?
6. Which 8088 output pin indicates the presence of valid data on the local bus in the minimum mode?

Nearly all modern CPUs are configured such that control signals, data, and addresses are sent and/or received over one or more buses. A bus is a group of conductors that are used to carry signals to and from the CPU and external devices. As stated before, the 8088 uses a 20-bit multiplexed local bus structure. The multiplexing of several bus lines was done to allow a very large, directly addressable memory to be implemented without the added cost of increasing the IC pin count. One disadvantage of bus multiplexing is increased support circuit complexity and system chip count (multiplexed buses usually must be demultiplexed). Most of the older CPUs—such as the Intel 8080, the Motorola 6800, and the MOS 6502—did not use a multiplexed bus architecture. The reason for this is simple enough: A 40-pin DIP was large enough to accommodate an 8-bit data bus, 16-bit address bus, and the necessary power and control lines without having to resort to bus multiplexing. The block diagram in Fig. 4-8 shows a microprocessor system that is typical of those based on the 8080 or similar 8-bit CPUs.

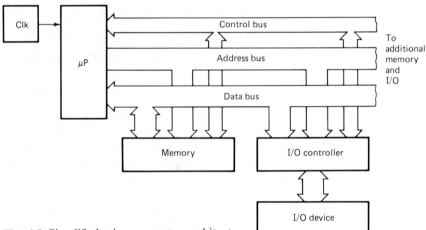

Fig. 4-8 Simplified microcomputer architecture.

4-3.1 Tristate Logic

Almost without exception, all modern microprocessors send and receive data over buses that are shared among many different devices. The ability to share a given line among several different devices is made possible through the use of tristate logic. The logic symbols for two different types of tristate inverters and their truth tables are shown in Fig. 4-9a and b. A control signal (G or $\overline{\text{G}}$) is used to force the output of the inverter into a high impedance (floating) state. When the gate is in the high-Z state, the input logic level has no effect, and for all practical purposes, the output of the gate is disconnected from the rest of the circuit. When the output of a gate is in the high impedance state, that output is sometimes said to be tristated.

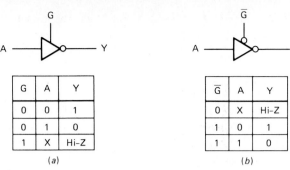

G	A	Y
0	0	1
0	1	0
1	X	Hi-Z

(a)

$\overline{G}$	A	Y
0	X	Hi-Z
1	0	1
1	1	0

(b)

Fig. 4-9 Tristate inverters with function tables.

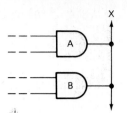

Fig. 4-10 Direct connection of TTL outputs (to be avoided).

The need for such tristate gates is demonstrated in Fig. 4-10. Suppose that gates A and B were each to alternately drive line X. Suppose, also, that device C is synchronized such that it expects to receive its input from a given gate at some particular times. Obviously, there is a good chance that the two gates will be driving line X (and device C) with conflicting data at any given time. For example, suppose the inputs to the two gates are such that gate A would output logic 1 and gate B would output logic 0. What logic level would exist on line X? Well, if they are standard TTL gates, the gate whose output is at logic 0 will override the other (TTL can sink 16 mA and source only 400 μA). The consequences of this state of affairs are the loss of data and possible excessive heating of the gates. You should recall that the outputs of TTL gates are never connected together directly (with the exception of open collector TTL).

By using tristate logic to buffer the gates that share a common output line, such conflicts can be resolved. Figure 4-11 illustrates one way in

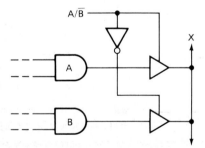

Fig. 4-11 Use of tristate logic to allow use of common lines for several gate outputs.

which two gates may share the same output line. The line labeled A/$\overline{B}$ is connected such that when it is low, the output of gate A is directed to line X and gate B is disconnected. When line A/$\overline{B}$ is high, gate A is disconnected and gate B drives line X. As you can see, many more outputs could be connected to line X using tri-state buffers or inverters.

So far, only unidirectional signal transmission has been considered. Many devices that are connected to the data bus must be able to send or receive data at different times. In these cases, a tristate bus transceiver is used. The internal logic diagram for the 74LS243 quad bus transceiver is shown in Fig. 4-12a. This tristate buffer could be used to connect four I/O lines to a bidirectional bus. If lines GAB and GBA are used to control the direction of data flow (from side A to side B, or from B to A). The function table for the 74LS243 is shown in Fig. 4-12b. Notice that it is possible to enable data transmission in both directions simultaneously (GAB = 0, GBA = 0). This is to be avoided, as oscillation may occur, possibly resulting in the destruction of the IC. A circuit that is connected to a bus via the 74LS243 may be totally isolated from the bus (neither sending nor receiving) when GAB = 1 and GBA = 0.

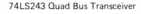

74LS243 Quad Bus Transceiver

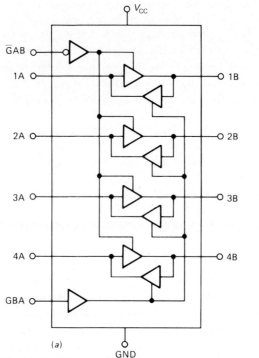

(a)

Function Table

Control inputs		Data port status	
$\overline{GAB}$	GBA	A	B
0	0	Input	Output
0	1	?	?
1	0	Isolated	Isolated
1	1	Output	Input

? = undefined

(b)

Fig. 4-12 Internal circuitry of 74LS243 transceiver (a) and function table (b).

Example 4-1

Draw the logic diagram for a quad bus transceiver circuit that is described by the function table in Fig. 4-13.

Control input G	Data port status	
	Side A	Side B
0	Input	Output
1	Output	Input

Fig. 4-13 Function table for Example 4-1.

Solution

The circuit shown in Fig. 4-14 will meet the design requirements.

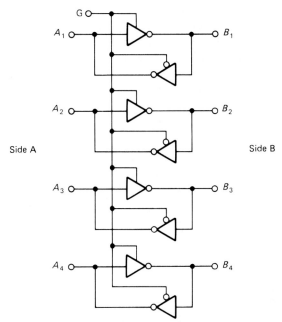

Fig. 4-14 Solution to Example 4-1.

4-3.2 Bus Multiplexing

In general, most devices that are used in microcomputer systems are designed to operate from separate control, data, and address buses. If these devices are to be used in an 8088-based system, the local bus must be demultiplexed. Before the actual details of demultiplexing the 8088 local bus are discussed, let us review some of the basics of multiplexers and demultiplexers that are commonly studied in digital electronics courses. Figure 4-15a shows the logic diagram for a 2 to 1 multiplexer that is representative of the internal circuitry of the 8088 at pin 38 (A_{16}/S_3). The select line (Y) would be controlled by circuitry inside the 8088, and is used to output either bit 16 of the address or the S_3 status bit, depending on which portion of the bus cycle is in effect at a given time. The output of the multiplexer is sent through a tristate buffer so that the output line may be floated to allow other devices to use this bus line. The truth table for the output line multiplexer is shown in Fig. 4-15b. Any of the 8088's multiplexed, tristate output lines could be modeled by this circuit.

The multiplexed lines that are bidirectional may be represented by the logic diagram in Fig. 4-16a. In this example, the multiplexer drives a tristate buffer just as in the previous case. Additional gating has been

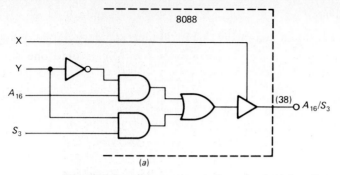

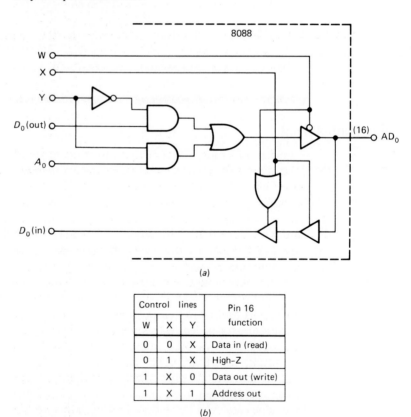

Fig. 4-15 Possible representation of a dual-function output line on 8088 (*a*) and function table (*b*).

Control lines		Pin 38 output function
X	Y	
0	0	A16
0	1	S3
1	X	High–Z

added to prevent the possibility of occurrences such as reading and writing data simultaneously. The function table in Fig. 4-16*b* describes the operation of this circuit. Keep in mind that the circuits of Fig. 4-15*a* and Fig. 4-16*a* represent the 8088 internal circuitry from a functional standpoint, and are presented only to help demonstrate how bus multiplexing and tristate functions could be implemented. The actual internal circuitry of the 8088 may be quite different.

Control lines			Pin 16 function
W	X	Y	
0	0	X	Data in (read)
0	1	X	High–Z
1	X	0	Data out (write)
1	X	1	Address out

Fig. 4-16 Possible circuitry for a bidirectional, dual function pin of the 8088 (*a*) and function table (*b*).

4-3.3 Bus Demultiplexing

Whereas multiplexing (in the microprocessor context) is the combining of information carried on several different lines onto one single line in a timeshared manner, demultiplexing is the routing of data from a single line to several different lines. Figure 4-17 presents the logic diagram for a 1 to

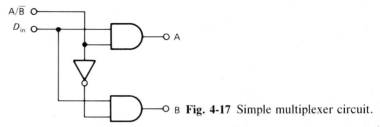

Fig. 4-17 Simple multiplexer circuit.

2 demultiplexer, or data distributor as it is also called. This is the classical form of demultiplexer that is usually studied in digital electronics courses. The operation of this circuit is straightforward, but it is not quite what is needed to demultiplex the 8088 local bus. The problem that prevents the use of this circuit is that demultiplexed data must be held for future use. A multiplexer like that in Fig. 4-17 outputs data on a given line only as long as it is present on the input, and that output line is selected.

In order to separate or demultiplex the data and addresses (and the status bits and addresses) from one another, we need to know when and for how long such information is present on the local bus. The exact details of this information are presented in the bus timing diagrams of the 8088 data sheets. Rather than get too bogged down in the timing diagrams, let us take a more intuitive approach to the creation of separate address and data buses.

Demultiplexing the Address Bus Let us begin by concentrating on isolating and holding the address information sent from the 8088 to the local bus. From what has been covered so far, it is known that lines A_8 through A_{15} are not multiplexed, so we need not worry about them; that is, valid address information is present on these lines for the entire bus cycle. It will be shown shortly, however, that it is a good idea to buffer these address lines anyway. Lines A_{16}/S_3 through A_{19}/S_6 and lines AD_7 through AD_0 present valid addresses during the clock high portion of T_1. The presence of a valid address is signaled by the occurrence of an ALE pulse. This can be seen in the timing diagram of Fig. 4-3. Now, since the complete address code is presented during one time interval (the interval of the ALE high pulse), all that needs to be done to hold the address for the entire bus cycle is the controlled storage of the address in a group of latches. Address latch control is the whole purpose of the ALE signal; that is, ALE is used to trigger the storage of the address in some sort of latching circuit. The latches hold the address for the remainder of the current bus cycle, allowing access to the proper memory location or I/O device. The address latching circuitry could be designed using devices such as the Intel 8282 or the 74LS373 tristate octal latches. The logic diagrams for these two latches are shown in Fig. 4-18*a* and *b*.

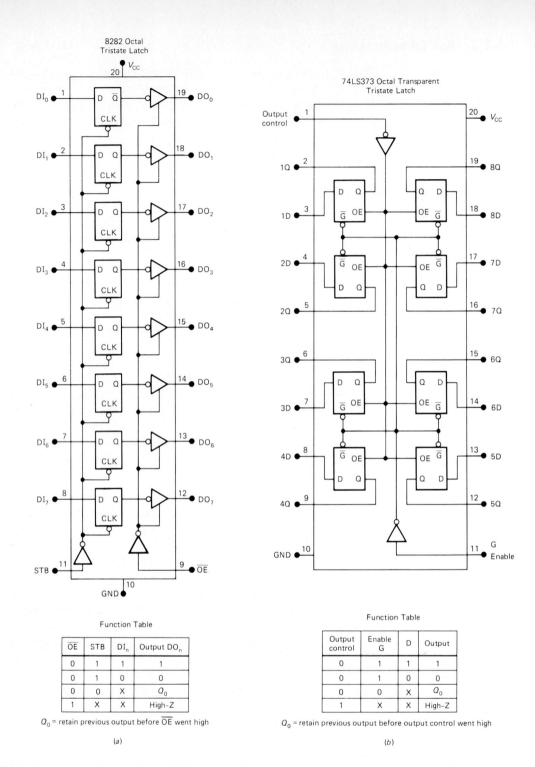

Function Table

$\overline{OE}$	STB	DI_n	Output DO_n
0	1	1	1
0	1	0	0
0	0	X	Q_0
1	X	X	High–Z

Q_0 = retain previous output before $\overline{OE}$ went high

(a)

Function Table

Output control	Enable G	D	Output
0	1	1	1
0	1	0	0
0	0	X	Q_0
1	X	X	High–Z

Q_0 = retain previous output before output control went high

(b)

Fig. 4-18 8282 octal tristate latch with function table (Courtesy of Intel Corporation) (a), and 74LS373 octal tristate latch with function table (b).

Tristate latches must be used to allow other devices to gain control of the address bus. This would be necessary if another CPU was sharing the same memory, or if direct memory access (DMA) was required by a device such as a disk drive.

The address demultiplexer circuit is shown in Fig. 4-19. It has been designed using 8282 octal latches, although a 74LS373-based design would

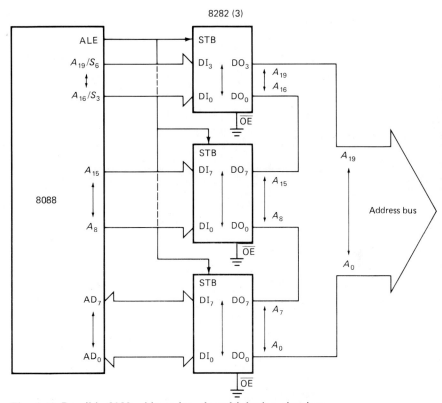

Fig. 4-19 Possible 8088 address bus demultiplexing circuitry.

work just as well. The output of the address latch effectively creates a separate (demultiplexed) full-time address bus that is updated on successive bus cycles. As an added benefit, the use of the address latches produces an address bus with a higher fan-out than the 8088 alone could provide. Any given 8088 output line can source 400 μA and sink 2 mA, whereas an 8282 latch can source 5 mA and sink 32 mA. The use of the 8282 increases the address bus drive capability tremendously. This is the reason that the dedicated address outputs of the 8088 would generally be buffered along with the multiplexed output lines. It should also be mentioned that when the 8088 is operated in the maximum mode, the ALE signal is produced by the bus controller and not by the 8088. The maximum mode equivalent of Fig. 4-19 is shown in block diagram form in Fig. 4-20. This circuit uses the 8288 bus controller to derive the ALE and several other signals based on the condition of the 8088 status lines $\overline{S}_0$, $\overline{S}_1$ and $\overline{S}_2$. The details of the bus controller will be presented later in this chapter.

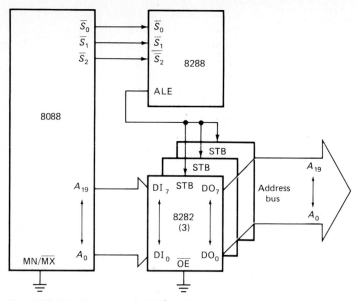

Fig. 4-20 Maximum mode 8088 address bus demultiplexing circuit.

Isolating the Data Bus Now that a basic approach to demultiplexing the address bus has been presented, the creation of a full-time data bus will be considered. The presence of valid data on the local bus is indicated when the 8088 (in the minimum mode) or the bus controller (in the maximum mode) drives the $\overline{\text{DEN}}$ line low. The direction of data transfer is indicated by the state of the DT/$\overline{\text{R}}$ line. If DT/$\overline{\text{R}}$ = 0, then data is read from the local bus by the CPU. If DT/$\overline{\text{R}}$ = 1, then the CPU is writing data to the local bus. Just as with the ALE signal, in the maximum mode, the $\overline{\text{DEN}}$ and DT/$\overline{\text{R}}$ signals are produced by the bus controller and not by the 8088.

The data bus is bidirectional; therefore a bus transceiver, such as the Intel 8286 or a 74LS245, should be used to interface the data bus with the local bus. The logic diagrams for these two ICs are shown in Fig. 4-21*a* and *b*. Both ICs have tristate outputs, which will allow other devices aside from the 8088 to use the demultiplexed data bus as necessary. A possible data bus demultiplexing circuit based on the 74LS245 has been added to the previous address bus demultiplexer and is shown in Fig. 4-22. Here's how the circuit works. Assume that an instruction opcode has been fetched and decoded, a valid address has been latched in, and this is a memory read operation. The selected memory location will have placed its contents on the data bus. DT/$\overline{\text{R}}$ will go low, causing the bus transceiver to pass data from side B (the data bus) to side A (the local bus). While DT/$\overline{\text{R}}$ is low, $\overline{\text{DEN}}$ goes low, bringing the transceiver buffers fed from the data bus out of their high-Z states and enabling data transfer from the data bus to the 8088. The sequence of events is very similar for a write operation also, with the main difference being that the transceiver is enabled while DT/$\overline{\text{R}}$ is high, reversing the direction of data flow.

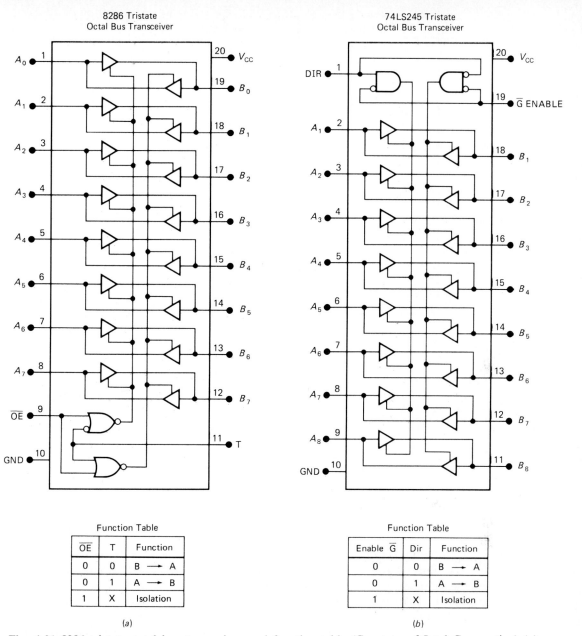

Fig. 4-21 8286 tristate octal bus transceiver and function table (Courtesy of Intel Corporation) (*a*), and 74LS245 tristate octal bus transceiver (*b*).

The circuit shown in Fig. 4-22 was designed based on the operation of the 8088 in the minimum mode. If the maximum mode was used, the line going to the *G* pin of the 74LS245 would require the addition of an inverter, possibly inserted where the *X* is drawn. This would be necessary because the 8288 bus controller drives the $\overline{\text{DEN}}$ line high upon the occurrence of valid data on the local bus. This is just the opposite of the $\overline{\text{DEN}}$ signal

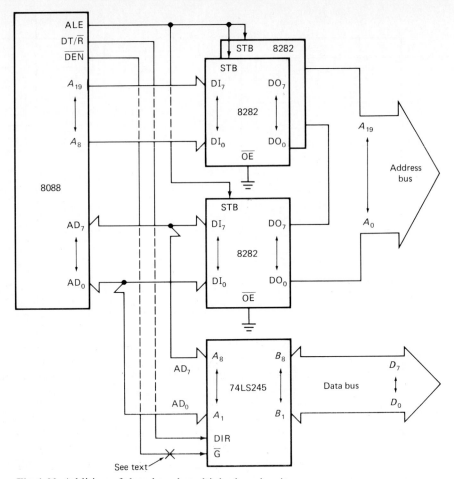

Fig 4-22 Addition of data bus demultiplexing circuitry.

developed by the 8088 in the minimum mode. Other changes required in the maximum mode include the routing of the 8282 STB lines and the DIR line of the 74LS245 to the appropriate bus controller outputs. These changes are shown in Fig. 4-23.

The circuits just described provide a good starting point for the development of a complete microcomputer system; that is, with the address and data latching circuits presented, the 8088 can now be used just like any of its earlier 8-bit predecessors that have separate address and data buses.

The IBM PC is an example of a microcomputer that uses the 8088 in the maximum mode, with address and data latching performed in essentially the same manner as has been presented here. The main difference is that IBM used 74LS373 latches in the design of the PC address bus demultiplexing circuit, while 8282 latches were used in the text. From a functional standpoint, both approaches are identical.

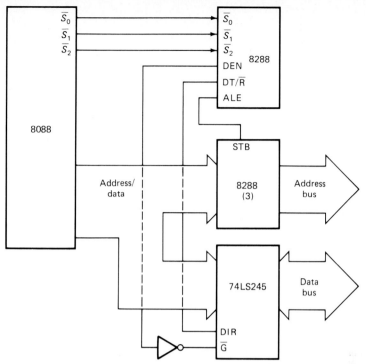

Fig. 4-23 Simplified maximum mode 8088 system bus demultiplexing.

Data and Address Bus Timing Demultiplexing the 8088 local bus has produced two separate buses: a 20-bit address bus and an 8-bit data bus. It is to these two demultiplexed buses that other devices, such as memory and interfacing adapters, will be interfaced. The signals that are produced on the address bus, data bus, and various control lines are shown in Fig. 4-24. The waveforms shown in a broken line are those that are produced in the minimum mode only. The waveforms labeled $\overline{\text{AMRDC}}$ or $\overline{\text{AIORC}}$, $\overline{\text{MRDC}}$ or $\overline{\text{IORC}}$, $\overline{\text{AMWC}}$ or $\overline{\text{AIOWC}}$, and $\overline{\text{MWTC}}$ or $\overline{\text{IOWC}}$ are generated by the 8288 bus controller in place of $\overline{\text{RD}}$ and $\overline{\text{WR}}$. These signals are used to control memory and I/O devices.

Review Questions for Section 4-3

1. What are the advantages and disadvantages of using multiplexed lines in a CPU design?
2. Why must the address and data latches have tristate outputs?
3. What is the advantage in buffering lines A_8 through A_{15} of the 8088 local bus?
4. How are address latches signaled that a valid address is being output onto the local bus?
5. How does the operation of the $\overline{\text{DEN}}$ signal generated by the 8088 differ from that generated by the bus controller?
6. Which 8088 control output is used to indicate the presence of a valid address on the local bus?

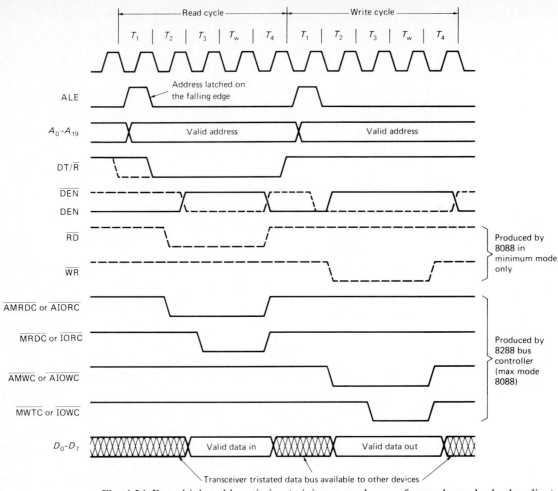

Fig. 4-24 Demultiplexed bus timing (minimum mode waveforms shown by broken line).

4-4   8088 SUPPORT CHIPS: THE 8284A AND THE 8288

Two of the most important of the 8088 support chips that have been mentioned so far have been the 8284A clock generator and the 8288 bus controller. The 8284A is required for the generation of a clock signal with the characteristics needed by the 8088. This IC also provides several other functions that would otherwise require additional design time and board area. The 8288 bus controller provides a means of increasing the performance of the 8088, by acting as an extension of the CPU. This, in effect, is equivalent to having a CPU that has a greater number of pins, without having to resort to a larger, more exotic package. The operational details of the clock generator and the bus controller will be presented in this section.

4-4.1 The 8284A Clock Generator

The 8284A has been designed to do more than just produce the 33 percent duty cycle clock signal as required by the 8088 CPU. Two other important functions that are performed by the 8284A are the synchronization of the READY and RESET signals that are applied to the 8088. You will recall that these two lines are not internally synchronized by the 8088, and so synchronization must be performed externally. Using the 8284A for this purpose saves some extra design work and also some circuit board real estate. The pin diagram and internal logic diagram for the 8284A are shown in Fig. 4-25a and b. The pin functions of the 8284 are described on the following page.

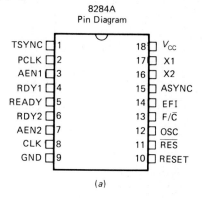

8284A
Pin Diagram

(a)

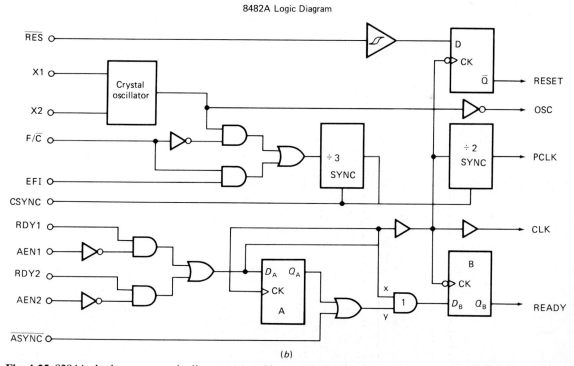

(b)

Fig. 4-25 8284A clock generator pin diagram (a) and internal logic diagram (b). (Courtesy of Intel Corporation.)

*X*1, *X*2	(I) Crystal inputs. Provide stable timing reference for internal series-resonant oscillator. Crystal should be chosen for oscillation at three times the desired clock frequency.
OSC	(O) Buffered output of internal crystal oscillator.
CLK	(O) Clock output. Provides 33 percent duty cycle clock at ⅓ of crystal oscillator frequency.
PCLK	(O) Peripheral clock line. TTL compatible 50 percent duty cycle waveform. Operates at ½ of CLK frequency.
EFI	(I) External frequency input. Driven by external TTL square wave source. Used as alternative to crystal-controlled internal oscillator.
F/$\overline{\text{C}}$	(I) Frequency/crystal. Determines operating mode. F/$\overline{\text{C}}$ = 0: crystal = control mode, F/$\overline{\text{C}}$ = 1: EFI = driven mode.
$\overline{\text{RES}}$	(I) Active low reset signal input. Controls generation of system reset pulse.
RESET	(O) Provides clock synchronized reset pulse to 8088 system.
CSYNC	(I) Clock synchronization, active high. CSYNC = 0: internal counters operational, CSYNC = 1: internal counters reset. Used to synchronize multiple 8284A clocks. Tied low for normal (crystal controlled) operation.
AEN1,AEN2	(I) Address enable, active low. Qualify (validate) associated RDY input line. AEN1 qualifies RDY1, AEN2 qualifies RDY2. One or both may be used. Unused lines are pulled high.
RDY1,RDY2	(I) Bus ready, active high. Driven by devices on bus to signal that data has been received or is ready to be sent to bus. One or both may be used. Unused line tied low.
READY	(O) Synchronized output of either RDY1 or RDY2, whichever has been qualified. Automatically cleared after minimum guaranteed hold time of 8088 READY input has been achieved. Drives READY input of 8088.
$\overline{\text{ASYNC}}$	(I) Ready synchronization select. Used in conjunction with READY output. $\overline{\text{ASYNC}}$ = 0: READY output is synchronized to both the rising and falling edges of CLK. Asynchronous devices that signal ready (to an RDY input) on a rising or positive-going edge are synchronized to the rising edge of CLK. Asynchronous devices that signal ready on a falling edge are synchronized with the falling edge of CLK. This mode is used with devices that might not meet the required setup time for the 8284A RDY inputs. $\overline{\text{ASYNC}}$ = 1: RDY inputs are synchronized to falling edge of CLK. Used with synchronous devices that are guaranteed to meet RDY setup time requirements.

From the pin descriptions given above, it is found that the 8284A may be operated in either of two basic configurations: (1) a crystal oscillator referenced mode or (2) a TTL square wave-driven mode. The crystal oscillator-based configuration is shown in Fig. 4-26. A crystal Y_1 is chosen

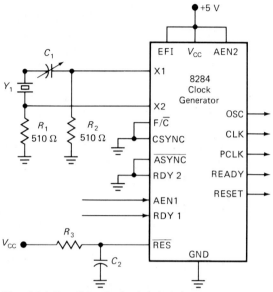

Fig. 4-26 Possible clock circuit using the 8284A.

for a resonant frequency of three times the desired clock frequency. Resistors R_1 and R_2 are used to stabilize the crystal oscillator. Capacitor C_1 serves two purposes. First, it may be used to trim the frequency of oscillation to the desired value. A range of from about 5 to 30 pF would be typical for this application. Second, C_1 isolates the crystal from the dc bias voltage produced by the 8284. This isolation protects the crystal from undue stress that may occur because of the dc bias. In this discussion, the 8284 is used in the crystal-controlled mode; therefore, the F/$\overline{C}$ pin must be tied low. CSYNC is also tied low to enable the internal dividers to operate properly. Notice that although EFI has been tied high in this particular configuration, it could be tied either high or low, because F/$\overline{C}$ is grounded. Line AEN2 has been tied high, and RDY2 has been tied low. This eliminates one of the bus ready inputs, leaving AEN1 and RDY1 available for peripheral device control of the READY line.

The $\overline{\text{ASYNC}}$ line has been tied low. This connection provides two stages of synchronization with the clock. Refer to the internal logic diagram in Fig. 4-25 for the following description of the action of the 8284A in terms of the $\overline{\text{ASYNC}}$ line. Since $\overline{\text{ASYNC}}$ is low, the output of flip-flop A will be passed through the OR gate to input Y of AND gate 1. The occurrence of a qualified RDY signal will be passed to the D input (D_A) of flip-flop A, and input X of AND gate 1. The next rising edge of the CLK signal will latch the RDY signal onto the output of flip-flop A, and hence input Y of the AND gate. The output of the AND gate is directed to the D input (D_B) of flip-flop B. The next falling edge of CLK will cause flip-flop B to latch the READY line high. As was presented in the previous $\overline{\text{ASYNC}}$ line description, this mode of operation is used when asynchronous devices that might not meet RDY input setup time requirements are used in the system.

Components R_3 and C_2, connected to V_{CC} and RES, are used to initiate a *power-on reset* command. In order to understand the operation of the RC circuit, you will recall that when $\overline{\text{RES}}$ is pulled low, the 8284 latches its RESET line high on the falling edge of CLK. This output is applied to the 8088 CPU RESET line, and causes the system to be initialized. The actual details of the power-on reset are as follows. When power is first applied, the system is for the most part in total chaos. Capacitor C_2 begins to charge through R_3. Until the capacitor is charged to a value of about 1.5 V, the $\overline{\text{RES}}$ pin is held at logic 0, causing the 8284A RESET output to be latched high. This means that when the CPU becomes active, rather than possibly attempting to execute the random garbage that may be present in memory, it will begin executing a system reset service routine, because its RESET input will be held high by the RESET output of the 8284A. This sequence of events is called *booting-up*, and the start-up routine(s) used in this operation are usually located in read-only memory (ROM) operating systems. An operating system is a master program that handles the interface between the computer, operator, and peripheral equipment. The power-on reset routines are responsible for all system initialization, self-test, and any other housekeeping chores that are required for proper system operation.

Now that the system is in the process of initialization, let us return to the 8284A's $\overline{\text{RES}}$ pin. As capacitor C_2 charges, it will eventually reach the trip point of the 8284A's internal Schmitt trigger. The Schmitt trigger converts the slowly rising edge of the capacitor charging voltage into a rapidly rising voltage that is compatible with the digital components in the IC. The values of R_3 and C_2 are chosen such that during charging to the trip point, the 8284 $\overline{\text{RES}}$ input is held low for about 100 μus after all devices are up and running. The actual delay time required depends on the exact Schmitt trigger trip voltage. As the trip voltage increases, so does the required delay time. For example, an 8284A with trip voltage of 1.05 V requires a time delay of at least 50 μ, while a trip voltage of 2.6 V requires a time delay of at least 162 μ. Both of the previous time delay requirements were based on a minimum power supply voltage of 4.5 V.

In the most general of terms, the reason for holding the reset on power-up signal active is this: The extended time during which the RESET command is present gives the system time to settle down after the rude awakening it receives when power is first applied.

4-4.2 The 8288 Bus Controller

As stated earlier, when the 8088 is operated in the maximum mode, some of the required bus control signals must be generated by an external device.

This situation has arisen because a 40-pin DIP is not large enough to handle all of the signals that must be produced. The 8288 bus controller has been designed to simplify large system design, by relieving the 8088 of these control signal generating duties. The pin diagram and internal block diagram for the 8288 are presented in Fig. 4-27a and b.

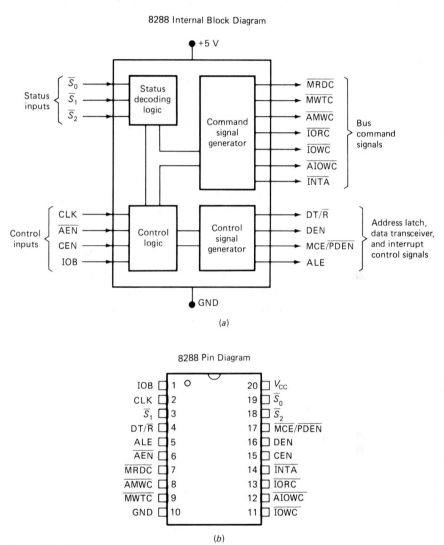

Fig. 4-27 8288 bus controller logic diagram (a) and pin designations (b). (Courtesy of Intel Corporation.)

A review of Fig. 4-23 shows that when operating in the maximum mode, the 8088 produces three signals ($\overline{S}_0$, $\overline{S}_1$ and $\overline{S}_2$) that are used by the bus controller to derive its outputs. The only 8288 outputs shown in Fig. 4-23 were the ones necessary for control of the bus latches. Descriptions of all of the 8288 pins are given on the following page.

$\overline{S}_0, \overline{S}_1, \overline{S}_2$ (I) Status inputs. Tied to associated 8088 status outputs. The 8288 decodes these inputs as presented in Fig. 4-28.

8288 Status Input Decoding

$\overline{S}_2$	$\overline{S}_1$	$\overline{S}_0$	Processor status	8288 command
0	0	0	Interrupt acknowledge	$\overline{INTA}$ (low)
0	0	1	Read I/O port	$\overline{IORC}$ (low)
0	1	0	Write to I/O port	$\overline{IOWC}$, $\overline{AZOWC}$ (low)
0	1	1	Halt	None
1	0	0	Code access	$\overline{MRDC}$ (low)
1	0	1	Read memory	$\overline{MRDC}$ (low)
1	1	0	Write to memory	$\overline{MWTC}$, $\overline{AMWC}$ (low)
1	1	1	Passive	None

Fig. 4-28 8288 bus controller status decoding. (Courtesy of Intel Corporation.)

IOB   (I) Input/output bus mode. Allows two different modes of bus control. IOB = 0: system bus mode. The 8288 assumes that external bus arbitration circuitry is in use. The bus arbiter informs the 8288 that the bus is free for use via the $\overline{AEN}$ line. If the bus is not free ($\overline{AEN}$ = 1), the 8288 command output lines are tristated. IOB = 1: I/O bus mode. All 8288 output lines are active at all times. No external bus arbitration.

CLK   (I) Clock input. Connected to CLK output of the 8284A clock generator. Provides basic timing reference.

ALE   (O) Address latch enable. Provides address latch enable pulse (for latching on trailing edge of pulse). Active when a valid address is present on the local bus.

$\overline{DEN}$ (O) Data enable. Used to enable transceivers driving the demultiplexed data bus. Active when valid data is present on the local bus.

DT/$\overline{R}$ (O) Data transmit/receive. Determines data direction through data bus transceivers.

$\overline{AEN}$ (I) Address enable. Enables 8288 command output lines in system bus mode (IOB = 0). Command outputs respond a minimum of 115 ns after $\overline{AEN}$ goes low. If $\overline{AEN}$ goes high, command outputs are tristated. $\overline{AEN}$ has no effect when IOB = 1. When active, it allows command lines to be taken over by other controllers.

CEN   (I) Command enable. CEN = 0: the 8288 command outputs and control outputs $\overline{DEN}$ and $\overline{PDEN}$ go to their respective inactive states. CEN = 1: command outputs, $\overline{DEN}$, and $\overline{PDEN}$ are enabled.

$\overline{IOWC}$ (O) I/O write command. Instructs I/O device to read data bus. Issued during T_3 of bus cycle.

$\overline{\text{AIOWC}}$	(O) Advanced I/O write command. Issues I/O write command early in bus cycle. Issued during T_2 of bus cycle. This signal (and all advanced commands) helps prevent the 8088 from adding unnecessary wait states by allowing slow devices to get ready to access the data bus.
$\overline{\text{IORC}}$	(O) I/O read command. Instructs I/O device to write to the data bus.
$\overline{\text{MWTC}}$	(O) Memory write command. Instructs addressed memory location to read and store data on data bus. Issued during T_3 of bus cycle.
$\overline{\text{AMWC}}$	(O) Advanced memory write command. Issues memory write command during T_2 of bus cycle.
$\overline{\text{MRDC}}$	(O) Memory read command. Instructs memory to place data onto data bus.
$\overline{\text{INTA}}$	(O) Interrupt acknowledge. Informs the device that is requesting interrupt service to place the desired interrupt number onto the data bus.
MCE/$\overline{\text{PDEN}}$	(O) Function determined by IOB logic level. IOB = 0: defined as master cascade enable (MCE), active high. Goes high during interrupt. Used to initiate reading of address from a programmable interrupt controller. IOB = 1: defined as peripheral data enable ($\overline{\text{PDEN}}$), active low. Enables data bus transceiver for I/O operations.

It is apparent that the bus controller relieves the 8088 of most of the necessary control duties. In order to obtain maximum 8088 system performance, the 8288 bus controller is required. The 8288 is also directly compatible with the 8086 CPU.

Review Questions for Section 4-4

1. At what logic level should the 8284A $\overline{\text{ASYNC}}$ line be tied if the RDY input(s) are driven by asynchronous devices?
2. How may the 8284A internal dividers be reset?
3. Why is power-on reset necessary?
4. What is the function of a Schmitt trigger?
5. What is the purpose of having advanced command outputs on the 8288?
6. Which 8288 command lines would be used to control memory devices?

4-5 MEMORY AND I/O ADDRESSING

Up to this point, very little has been said about the actual ways in which memory and I/O devices are connected to and used by the CPU. This section will provide some basic preparation for upcoming treatments of these topics.

4-5.1 Memory and I/O Operations

The information supplied in Chap. 2 on the instruction set and assembly language programming provided some insight into the ways in which the 8088 can handle memory and I/O transfers. Since there are separate memory- and I/O-referenced instructions, it may be deduced that memory and I/O devices are interfaced to the system in somewhat different ways. For example, the assembly language instruction MOV AL,[0FC2] transfers, into the AL register, the contents of the memory location whose absolute address would be given by $(16_{10} \times DS) + 0FC2$, where DS represents the 16-bit contents of the data segment register. Referring to the timing diagrams presented earlier in this chapter, it may be seen that moving data from memory to the CPU is accomplished during a memory read cycle. A memory device is informed of this fact when the 8088 pulls the IO/$\overline{M}$ and $\overline{RD}$ lines low (or the bus controller just pulls $\overline{MRDC}$ low). Conversely, an instruction such as MOV [0FC2],AL is accomplished during a write cycle. The memory is instructed to output the contents of this location when the 8088 pulls the IO/$\overline{M}$ and $\overline{WR}$ lines low (or the bus controller pulls $\overline{MWTC}$ and $\overline{AMWC}$ low). In either case, a memory-referenced operation is indicated by the activation of the memory command lines. Memory read and write control signal timing diagrams based on the demultiplexed bus structure are shown in Fig. 4-29. The colored waveforms are those produced by the 8088 in the minimum mode.

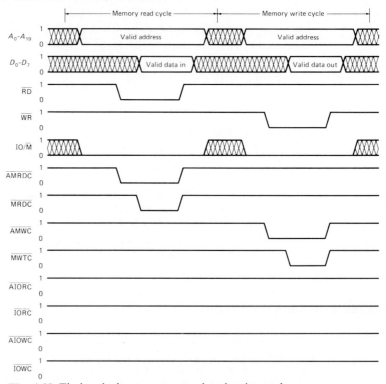

Fig. 4-29 Timing during memory read and write cycles.

The 8088 can perform similar read and write operations to and from I/O ports, via the IN and OUT instructions. These two instructions are accumulator-specific; that is, they can transfer data only to and from the accumulator (either AL or AX) and a given port. As far as instruction timing is concerned, the only difference between reading a memory location and reading a port (IN) is that in the minimum mode, IO/$\overline{M}$ remains high while $\overline{RD}$ goes low; while in the maximum mode, $\overline{IORC}$ goes low and $\overline{MRDC}$ remains high. A port is selected or activated using the address lines, just as in the case of addressing a memory location. The address that specifies a given port is called the port number. The 8088 can directly address up to a maximum of 64K (65,536) different ports.

You will recall that there are two types of I/O transfer instructions: fixed port and variable port. Fixed port I/O transfers can reference only the first 256 ports, while variable port I/O transfers can access any of the 64K possible ports. Now, the question arises that since the address bus is 20 bits wide and it takes only 16 bits to specify one port in 64K, how does the address bus respond during I/O transfers? The answer is simple. During any I/O transfer (IN or OUT), the four most significant address lines A_{16} through A_{19} are driven low. This means that segment addresses are not required in port locations. In other words, any ports, if used, will reside alongside the first 64K of memory. The control lines are used to select either a memory location or a port.

The bus timing for the IN and OUT instructions is shown in Fig. 4-30.

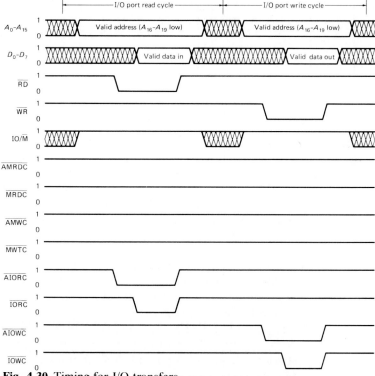

Fig. 4-30 Timing for I/O transfers.

This diagram is very similar to that of the memory transfers because, in fact, they are both basically read and write cycles. The only difference is in the behavior of the command lines and the four most significant address lines.

A simplified block diagram of a system containing memory and I/O ports is shown in Fig. 4-31. This figure illustrates the control structure that is used in 8088-based systems.

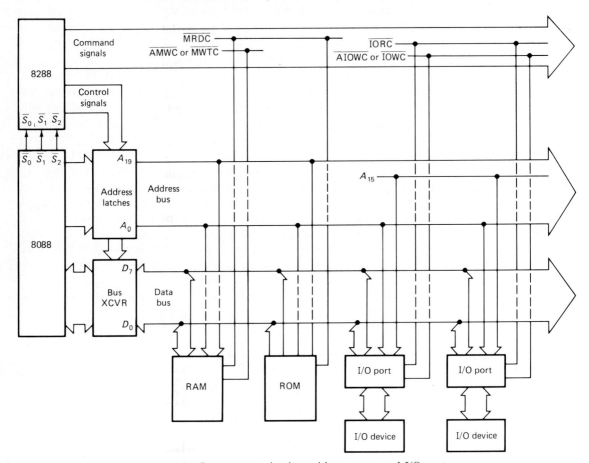

Fig. 4-31 System organization with memory and I/O ports.

4-5.2   I/O Control

There are several different ways in which I/O operations can be handled by the 8088. This section will introduce some of the basic ideas behind I/O operations and control techniques. Additional information regarding I/O interfacing will be presented in Chap. 6. One method of handling I/O operations is called polling. Polled I/O relies on software to repeatedly or occasionally poll a port or series of ports in order to determine whether service is required. A possible flowchart for a program that performs polled I/O is shown in Fig. 4-32. The problem with this approach is that if a port

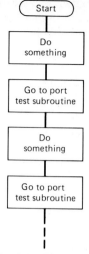

Fig. 4-32 Flowchart for polled I/O operations.

must be polled frequently, the CPU will have to spend a large portion of its time performing the polling operation. This reduces processor throughput drastically. Also, should a port require immediate service, it still has to wait for the CPU to get around to polling it first. This time delay may be unacceptable in some applications.

In order to alleviate some of the problems associated with polled I/O, another technique, interrupt-driven I/O, may be used. In this method, an external device may inform the CPU that it requires service by initiating an interrupt sequence. In other words, the peripheral receives service only when service is requested. You will recall that the 8088 has two hardware interrupt inputs: Nonmaskable interrupt (NMI) and interrupt request (INTR). The NMI is usually reserved for response to the most critical of occurrences, and cannot be ignored by the 8088. The INTR input may be used for general purpose interrupt control and is maskable. Using either of these inputs, an external device may get the attention of the CPU whenever service is required. Since polling is not required, throughput is increased.

Normally, a microcomputer system will require several ports for devices such as a keyboard, disk drive, monitor, printer, and so on. A device that provides easier control over several I/O ports is the interrupt controller. The Intel 8259A priority interrupt controller (PIC) is an example of such a device. The logic symbol for the 8259A is shown in Fig. 4-33. The 8259A

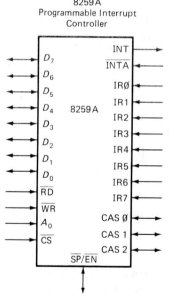

Fig. 4-33 Logic symbol for 8259A PIC. (Courtesy of Intel Corporation.)

is designed to accept service requests from up to eight different devices. A given device signals the 8259A that it requires service by pulling one of the interrupt request (IR) lines high. When the 8088 is ready to service the interrupt, it will pull the interrupt acknowledge line ($\overline{\text{INTA}}$) low. In general, the transfer of control signals between various peripheral devices and the CPU is called handshaking. Interrupt request and acknowledgment are forms of handshaking.

The circuit in Fig. 4-34 shows how the 8259A may control several ports that are connected to the 8088-based system. The 8259A may be assigned any address in the I/O address space. The address decoder detects the presence of this address and activates the PIC (if it is an I/O operation). Input line A_0 may also be used to address the 8259A. The PIC may be programmed for several different modes of operation via the data bus lines while it is being addressed. Again, further details regarding the use of the 8259A and I/O operations in general will be presented in Chap. 6.

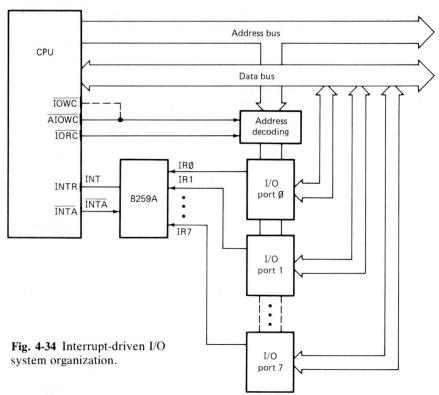

Fig. 4-34 Interrupt-driven I/O system organization.

4-5.3 Direct Memory Access

It is apparent from the preceding discussions that very often a peripheral device will transfer data to or accept data directly from the CPU. For example, if it is necessary to transfer a byte from memory to a peripheral, that memory location must first be read and its contents loaded into the accumulator. The contents of the accumulator must then be transferred to the port to which the peripheral device is connected. Transfer of data from the peripheral to memory would be handled in a similar manner. However, such data transfer methods are relatively slow. A second method of data transfer called direct memory access (DMA) provides a much faster means of I/O data transfer.

The idea behind DMA is to allow a peripheral device to bypass the CPU and communicate directly with memory. During such times, the CPU should remain inactive; that is, the CPU must relinquish control of the data, control, and address buses to DMA control circuitry. In the minimum mode, this is done by driving the 8088's HOLD input high. The requests for I/O service that require direct memory access must be sent to DMA control circuitry, which in turn requests the CPU and any other devices that may have control of the buses to allow the DMA operation to occur. Upon receipt of the DMA request, the CPU finishes executing its current instruction, sends out a HOLD acknowledgment, and then tristates its address, data, and command lines. At this time, the DMA controller is responsible for generating the command signals (such as $\overline{MRDC}$, $\overline{IORC}$, and so on) that coordinate the transfer of data over the bus. When the DMA operation is finished, the DMA controller signals this to the CPU by returning the HOLD line low, which in turn causes the 8088 to resume normal operation. In the maximum mode the bus controller would be the destination and source of HOLD and HLDA signals, respectively.

A widely used DMA controller is the Intel 8237A-5. A very simplified logic symbol for the 8237A-5 is shown in Fig. 4-35. Peripheral devices

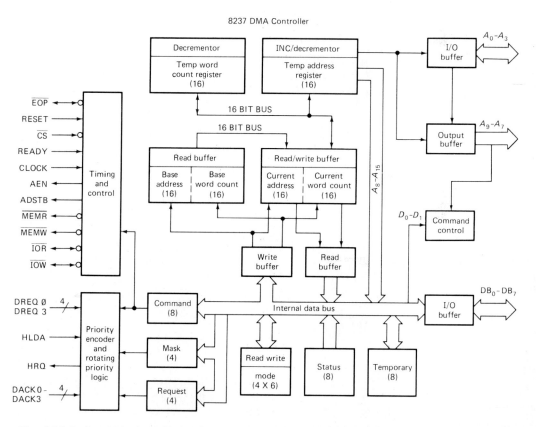

Fig. 4-35 Internal block diagram for the 8237 DMA controller. (Courtesy of Intel Corporation.)

make requests for DMA by driving one of the DMA request lines (DREQ0 through DREQ3, whichever it is connected to) high. The 8237A responds by driving its Hold Request (HRQ) output high, which in turn drives the CPU (or bus controller) HOLD input high. The CPU will then tristate its control, address, and data lines, giving control to the DMA controller. The DMA controller then drives the appropriate DMA Acknowledge (DACK) line high, indicating that a DMA cycle has been granted.

The DREQ input lines are prioritized such that DREQ0 has the highest priority and DREQ3 has the lowest priority. This means that if a channel of higher priority requests DMA while a channel of lower priority is in a DMA cycle, the lower priority cycle will be suspended.

This prioritizing of DMA channels is very important in some microcomputer systems. For example, a DMA channel can be dedicated for the purpose of refreshing the memory in the system. To do this, a programmable timer (an Intel 8253 timer, for example) could be configured such that a pulse is applied to the 8237A-5 DREQ0 line at predetermined intervals. This pulse would initiate a memory refresh operation each time it occurs. The highest-priority input would be used for refresh operations, because loss of data could occur if refresh is not performed within certain periods of time. Essentially, during the refresh operation, the data contained in the RAM is read and then written back into the same locations. DMA is used to speed up the entire process. Further details concerning dynamic RAM operation will be presented in Chap. 5. In the IBM PC system, DREQ2 is used for disk-memory transfers (DREQ1 and DREQ3 are not dedicated to any specific devices or operations). A given device may terminate the DMA operation by driving the 8237A-5's $\overline{\text{EOP}}$ input low.

Review Questions for Section 4-5

1. Which method of I/O control requires scanning of the ports?
2. To which interrupt input of the 8088 is the INT output of the 8259A usually connected?
3. How may the number of ports that are controlled by the interrupt controller be increased beyond 8?
4. Which 8237A DREQ input has the lowest priority?
5. Which input line is used to enable the 8259A?
6. What is the advantage of DMA I/O versus CPU-controlled I/O?
7. Assume that it takes 16 clock cycles to read a port and 16 clock cycles to write to a memory location using IN and OUT instructions, and the 8088 is operating at a clock frequency of 4.77 MHz. How long will it take to read and store 1000 bytes of data from a given port?

SUMMARY

The 8088 provides the microcomputer designer with many different design options. In most cases, though, a design will require the demultiplexing of the 8088 local bus. Such demultiplexing may be accomplished with the addition of a few tristate latches and data bus transceivers. Latch and transceiver control may be provided by the 8088 alone when operated in the minimum mode, or by a bus controller if the 8088 is operated in the maximum mode.

The 8284A clock generator is used to provide the 8088 with its required 33 percent duty cycle clock (CLK) signal. The 8284A provides synchronization of reset and ready signals as well as a 50 percent duty cycle TTL-compatible output that runs at one-half the rate of the CLK output.

Maximum mode 8088 systems require the use of the 8288 bus controller. This device produces the necessary bus timing signals based on the 8088 status outputs. The 8288 also allows the use of multiple processors and coprocessors to share the same local bus with the 8088.

The 8088 has been designed to handle I/O transfers through the use of specific I/O instructions. Polled I/O and interrupt-driven I/O are two possible methods of I/O servicing. Control of interrupt-driven I/O configurations is simplified by the use of an interrupt controller.

High-speed data transfer between memory and peripheral devices may be accomplished using direct memory access (DMA). DMA requires that the CPU turn over control of the address and data bus to a DMA controller. The DMA controller is responsible for the generation of bus control and command signals while a peripheral device is reading from or writing to memory.

Further details of the operation of the 8088 family of devices mentioned may be found in the *Intel Microsystem Components Handbook*.

CHAPTER QUESTIONS

4-1. Which 8088 output pin controls the address latches?

4-2. On which portion of the ALE pulse will an 8282 octal latch strobe (STB) input cause latching to occur?

4-3. How long must the 8088 RESET line be held high to ensure that it will be honored?

4-4. Which 8088 output line controls the direction of data flow through the data bus transceivers?

4-5. At what address does the 8088 begin executing instructions following a RESET signal?

4-6. Why must some inputs to the 8088 be externally synchronized?

4-7. Which I/O technique allows the highest data transfer rate?

4-8. Which CPU-controlled I/O service technique is generally the fastest to respond when an I/O device requires service?

4-9. Which 8288 output lines control the direction of I/O transfers?

4-10. During I/O transfers, how are the four most significant address lines driven by the 8088?

4-11. What is the term given to the request and acknowledgment signals that are transferred between the CPU and an external device?

4-12. What is the maximum number of 8-bit ports that the 8088 can address using the IN and OUT instructions?

CHAPTER PROBLEMS

4-13. An 8088 CPU is to be operated with a 4.77 MHz clock. What should the values of t_h and t_l be if the clock has a 33 percent duty cycle?

4-14. Based on the clock frequency of Problem 4-13, what is the minimum length of a bus cycle?

Refer to Fig. 4-36 to answer Questions 4-15, -16, and -17.

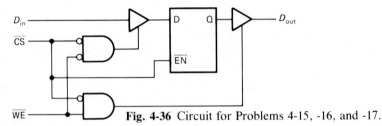

Fig. 4-36 Circuit for Problems 4-15, -16, and -17.

4-15. What logic levels must be present on lines $\overline{CS}$ and $\overline{WE}$ in order to activate the D_{in} line?

4-16. Which combinations of $\overline{CS}$ and $\overline{WE}$ will cause D_{out} to be tristated?

4-17. What combination (if any) of $\overline{CS}$ and $\overline{WE}$ will cause both tristate buffers to go to the high-Z state?

4-18. Draw the logic diagram for a 1 of 4 data selector that will output logic 0 on the selected line.

4-19. An 8284A clock generator is to be used to produce a 4.77 MHz clock signal. What is the internal crystal oscillator's operating frequency?

4-20. In Fig. 4-22, how can the demultiplexed address bus be controlled so that an external device can take control of it in some situations?

4-21. Refer to Fig. 4-26. Assuming that the 8284A has a trip level of 1.5 V, V_{CC} = 5.0 V, R_3 = 1kμ, and C_2 = 0.022 μF, how long will the RESET output be held high?

4-22. A certain 8088-based system operates with a clock frequency of 5.2 MHz. If it takes 16 clock cycles to move a byte from memory to CPU or from CPU to a port, how long will it take to transfer the contents of a 16K byte block of memory to a peripheral device?

MEMORY DEVICES AND MEMORY INTERFACING

5

Almost all of the information presented in previous chapters is predicated upon the concept of memory, that is, the storage of information, data, and instructions for future use. This chapter will present a review of the characteristics and classifications of the various memory devices available. The advantages and disadvantages associated with several of the different types of semiconductor memory devices will be presented. The concepts behind the design of memories using ICs and memory decoding will also be covered.

5-1 MEMORY FUNDAMENTALS

The fundamental storage elements that make up the heart of some widely used memory devices are what are referred to as bistable multivibrators. A bistable multivibrator has two stable output states, and may assume either state when driven properly. Once the bistable device is forced into a given state, it will remain there until it is forced into its complementary state. This, in effect, is equivalent to having a device with the ability to remember a past event, which is, of course, the whole idea behind memory devices in general.

5-1.1 Flip-Flops

One of the first bistable devices introduced in most digital electronics courses is the set-reset (SR) flip-flop or latch. Figure 5-1 shows the logic diagram and function table for a simple SR flip-flop designed with NOR gates. Flip-flops rely on the use of positive feedback to maintain a stable output state. The function table for this flip-flop indicates that it has active-high inputs, and is in a quiescent or storage mode when both inputs are tied low. What this means is that when the inputs are in the quiescent state, the flip-flop remembers whichever input was active last.

You will recall that if the inputs to a TTL gate are left open, they will float high. This would cause the outputs of the flip-flop in Fig. 5-1 to assume invalid states. To prevent this from happening, pull-down resistors could be connected from the input lines to ground. This places the latch in the memory state when the inputs are removed. An equivalent latch could also be constructed using NAND gates, with the main operational difference being that this flip-flop would have active-low inputs.

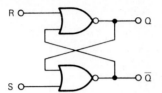

S	R	Q	$\overline{Q}$	State
0	0	Q_0	$\overline{Q}_0$	Memory
0	1	0	1	Reset
1	0	1	0	Set
1	1	0	0	Illegal

Fig. 5-1 NOR latch and function table.

A large memory could be constructed by arranging many flip-flops in an array. This approach to memory design is used quite frequently. The flip-flops located within the matrix are frequently referred to as *cells*. Although flip-flops are relatively simple, they are usually composed of five or six transistors. This imposes a limit on the density (the number of cells per unit chip area) of a given memory device that is constructed in this manner. There are other cell design alternatives that require fewer transistors to store a bit, and hence can be integrated more densely. The various types of memory devices and their major features will be discussed next.

5-1.2 Memory Classifications

Currently, the most widely used memory devices are fabricated using bipolar and metal-oxide semiconductor MOS IC technology. In the MOS category, the two major types used are N-channel MOS (NMOS) and complementary MOS (CMOS) devices. Memories constructed using any of these devices can be divided into three main categories: random access memory, (RAM), read-only memory (ROM) and serial memory. The term *random access* is actually applicable to ROM also, because both ROM and RAM are random access devices. Random access means that it is possible to access any given storage location without having to sequentially progress through any other locations. What is actually being referred to when the term RAM is used is random access read-write memory. The various IC memory devices available may be broken down as shown in Fig. 5-2.

Random access memory is the type of memory that most microcomputer users and advertisers are particularly concerned with. RAM makes up the memory in which user-written or externally loaded programs and data are stored. In other words, the RAM is the program work space.

ROM is used to permanently store instructions and data that are vital to the operation of the computer. Such things as interrupt service routines and vectors, high-level language facilities, operating system instructions, and initialization routines are often programmed into ROM.

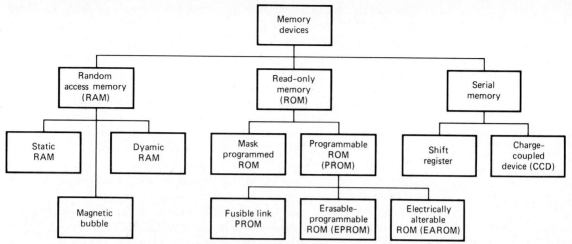

Fig. 5-2 Classification of memory devices.

Serial or sequential memory devices are not as popular as the random access memories for several reasons, although they can be used in the same applications as RAMs and ROMs. One of the main reasons for the relative unpopularity of serial memories is their slow average access speed. Consider the steps required to read a given cell within a RAM as compared to a serial memory with equivalent storage capacity. To read the RAM, first the desired address is placed on the address bus, and hence to the memory device's internal decoding circuitry. Next, the chip is informed that a read operation is to be performed. Finally, the chip is enabled, and it outputs the contents of the selected cell(s) to the data bus. Regardless of which location is being read, the read operation takes the same length of time. In order to read the contents of a given cell in a serial memory, however, all of the data that precedes the data of interest must first be shifted out. In other words, the data that is to be read must itself be shifted out, possibly through a large number of storage cells. The data that is shifted out during the read operation must also not be lost, and therefore it must be recycled into the memory. It is obvious that this could be a rather complex and time-consuming process. This has limited the use of serial memory in many applications.

Review Questions for Section 5-1

1. If NAND latches are used to build a latch, what combination of input levels is illegal?
2. How are cells usually arranged in a random access memory?
3. How would the arrangement of cells in a serial memory differ from that of a random access memory?
4. A certain serial memory device operates in a system with a clock frequency of 4 MHz. The memory device has 4096 memory cells. How long would it take to read all of the locations in the device?

5. What type of feedback is responsible for a latch's ability to store information?

6. What type of memory usually constitutes the program work space?

5-2 RANDOM ACCESS MEMORY

Both bipolar- and MOS-type devices can be used to form flip-flop-based memory cells. All memory devices that use flip-flops as the basic storage elements are classified as static RAMs. Because static RAM devices store information in active flip-flops, as long as power is supplied to the chip, the data is retained. Reading a given storage cell in the static RAM also has no effect on the stored information. This is called nondestructive read out (NDRO).

Speed and timing are usually very important factors when one is considering interfacing memory to a microprocessor. The time required for a given device to present the contents of a cell or a group of cells at its output line(s) once the address and enable signals have been applied is called the device access time t_a or t_{ac}. Access time is often used as a general guide as to how fast a memory can respond to a request for data.

In general, RAMs constructed using bipolar technology are faster (they have lower access and cycle times) than equivalent MOS devices. This is about the only advantage of bipolar over MOS, and even this is being eliminated as faster MOS devices are developed. The advantages of MOS-technology RAMs over bipolar RAMs are summarized below.

1. Low power dissipation. In general, MOS static RAMs dissipate about ⅓ as much power per cell as bipolar RAMS. RAMs constructed using CMOS devices have even lower power dissipation per cell than NMOS devices.

2. Higher density. Because of their low power dissipation, MOS devices can be packed into a smaller area. This means more bits can be stored on a given size chip.

3. Low cost. Bipolar RAMs are about 10 to 20 times as expensive per bit as MOS RAMs.

Bipolar RAMs are usually used in the design of smaller memories, such as those that store around 256 bytes or so. Such small memories are often called scratch-pad memories. They are useful for storage of intermediate results of calculations and other frequently modified information that must be accessed quickly.

5-2.1 Static RAM

There are literally hundreds of different static RAM devices on the market. One typical example of a commonly used static RAM is the Motorola MCM6810. The pin diagram and internal functional block diagram for the MCM6810 are shown in Fig. 5-3*a* and *b*. The MCM6810 is a 128 × 8 NMOS static RAM. As noted in the block diagram, the MCM6810 stores data in 128 separate 8-bit blocks that are arranged in a matrix. A more

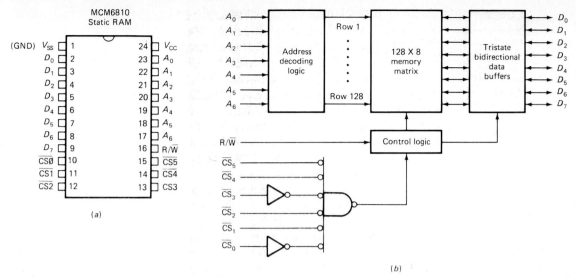

Fig. 5-3 Pin diagram for Motorola MCM6810 static RAM (*a*) and internal block diagram (*b*). (Courtesy of Motorola, Inc.)

detailed representation of the storage matrix is shown in Fig. 5-4. Each storage cell within the matrix is a flip-flop made up of NMOS transistors. A given byte (row of cells) is selected for reading or writing by the address

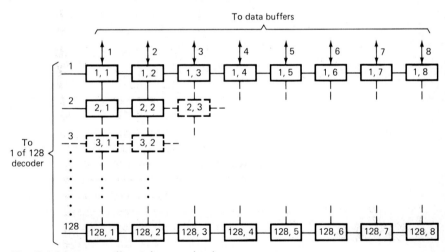

Fig. 5-4 Memory cell matrix organization.

decoder. A more detailed representation of the address decoder is shown in Fig. 5-5. The 6810 is configured for a read or write operation via the R/$\overline{\text{W}}$ input. This particular IC provides 6 chip select $\overline{\text{CS}}$ lines ($\overline{\text{CS0}}$ through $\overline{\text{CS5}}$) for easier decoding. Not all applications will require the use of all 6 $\overline{\text{CS}}$ lines. Those chip select lines that are unneeded may be connected to ground or V_{CC}, whichever is appropriate.

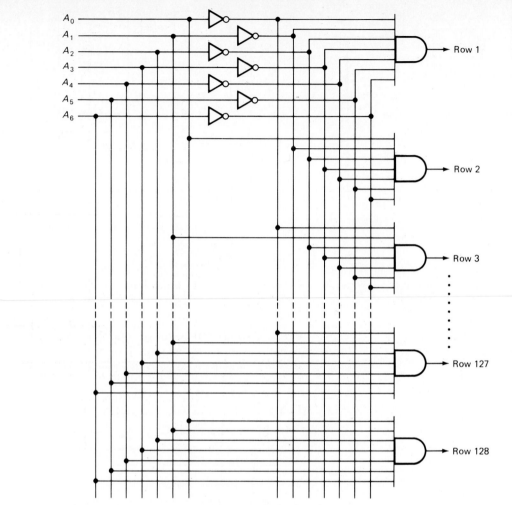

Fig. 5-5 Partial logic diagram for a 1 of 128 decoder.

Another commonly used static RAM is the 2112. The 2112 static RAM pin diagram and internal block diagrams are shown in Fig. 5-6a and b. This device stores data in 256 separate 4-bit blocks. Inputs A_0 through A_4 are used to select one of 32 different rows. Each column in the memory matrix is 4 cells wide, hence the column decoder is a 1 of 8 selector. Lines A_5 through A_7 are used to select a given 4-bit wide column. In terms of the number of bits stored per chip, the 2112 and the 6810 are the same; that is, both ICs store a total of 1024 bits. The main difference between the two ICs, aside from different packages (which in itself is relatively important), is in their storage formats. The 6810 is a byte-oriented device, while the 2112 is a 4-bit-oriented (sometimes called a *nibble*) device. Two 2112s are needed to store byte-length data.

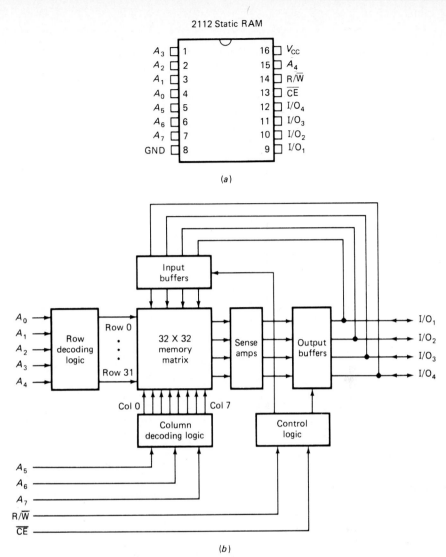

Fig. 5-6 2112 static RAM pin diagram (*a*) and internal block diagram (*b*).

Example 5-1

Draw the logic diagram that shows how 2112 RAMs would be connected to a data bus to produce a memory that will store 256 bytes.

Solution

Two 2112s would be required, since each 2112 holds 256 separate 4-bit long blocks. You should be aware that the CPU will address both ICs as if they were one device; that is, both 2112s will be enabled and either read

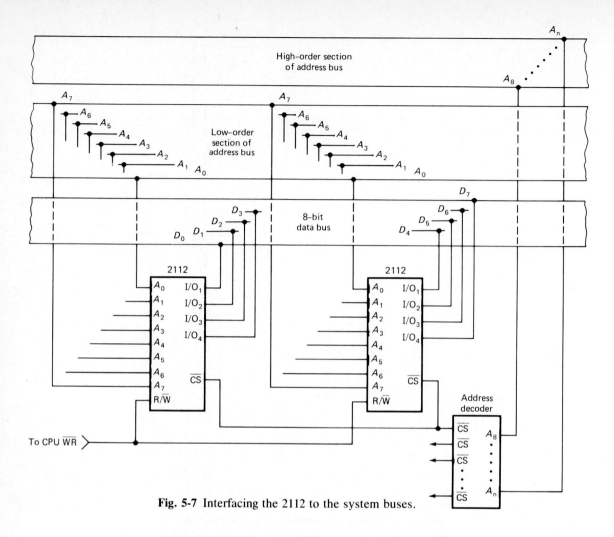

Fig. 5-7 Interfacing the 2112 to the system buses.

from, or written to simultaneously. Additional blocks have been added to complete this diagram. These sections will be explained later in this chapter.

Bit-oriented RAMs are also available, and are actually used more often today than nibble- and byte-oriented RAMs. When accessed, a bit-oriented RAM will enable only one cell for reading or writing. Eight separate chips are required for the storage of byte-length data. Figure 5-8 illustrates how bit-oriented RAM could be connected to an 8-bit microprocessor data bus. Although address bus connections are shown, they will not be discussed yet. Also note that all eight chip select lines are driven simultaneously. This allows the CPU (via the address decoder) to treat the memory chips as if they were one large device.

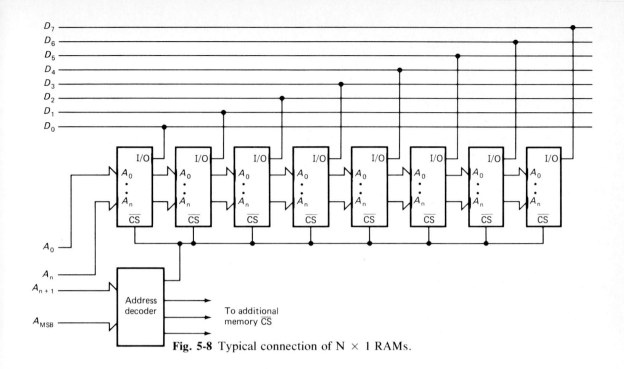

Fig. 5-8 Typical connection of N × 1 RAMs.

5-2.2 Dynamic RAM

Dynamic RAM differs from static RAM in several respects. One difference between these two types of RAM is the construction of the basic storage cells that are the heart of the memory chip. Where static RAM uses flip-flop cells to store data, dynamic RAM utilizes small capacitors as the basic storage cells. Also, dynamic RAM is fabricated using MOS technology exclusively. Figure 5-9 shows a simplified dynamic RAM circuit that is representative of widely used high-density memory designs. A single E-MOSFET (enhancement-MOSFET) is used to control access to a low-value capacitor (typically about 0.05 pF in value). It is this capacitor C_c that is used to store a bit of information in the form of an electrical charge, or lack thereof. The storage capacitors are made low in value to conserve chip real estate, which is of prime importance to high-density integration. The single-transistor dynamic RAM cell is much simpler and takes up much less space than a flip-flop-type static RAM cell.

The dynamic RAM depicted in Fig. 5-9 is typical of many devices currently on the market. It is a bit-oriented RAM in which a given cell is accessed by selecting its row and column coordinates. Let us assume that conceptually this circuit represents a 65,536 × 1 dynamic RAM, such as the 4164. Let us also assume that the memory cells are arranged in a 256 × 256 matrix (although often such memories are divided internally into four 128 × 128 matrices; either way, both methods are functionally the same). This requires that the row and column decoders each have 8 select inputs. It is standard design practice for such RAMs to have their row and

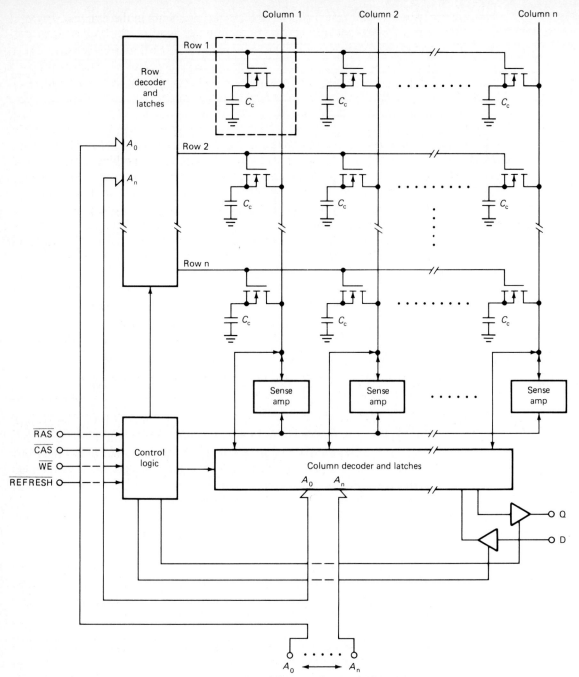

Fig. 5-9 Representative circuitry of a dynamic RAM.

column select inputs multiplexed onto a single group of pins. In this case, the 16 row and column address pins would be reduced from 16 to 8. This multiplexing scheme allows the smaller and more inexpensive 16-pin DIP to be used to house the chip.

Since small capacitors are the storage elements in the dynamic RAM, it stands to reason that charge leakage could lead to the loss of data after some time. As it turns out, most dynamic RAM cells will lose their charge within 2 to 5 ms after the charging voltage is removed. Such rapid data loss is unacceptable, and is prevented by periodically *refreshing* each cell. Basically, a cell is refreshed by reading its contents, and then rewriting those contents back into it.

As may be suspected, reading and writing to dynamic RAM are more complex procedures than reading and writing to static RAM. In this case, as in most others, one doesn't get something for nothing. The trade-off for the high density of dynamic RAM is added design complexity. In fact, the design of the dynamic RAM interfacing circuitry is quite often one of the most difficult tasks encountered in the design of a computer.

Descriptions of typical dynamic RAM write and read cycles are presented below. Refer to the read and write timing diagrams shown in Fig. 5-10a and b and the circuit in Fig. 5-9 while following these explanations.

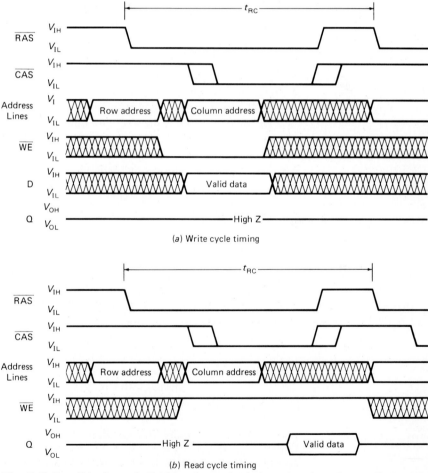

(a) Write cycle timing

(b) Read cycle timing

Fig. 5-10 Possible dynamic RAM write cycle timing (a) and read cycle timing (b).

The Write Operation

1. The desired row address is presented to the RAM address lines.

2a. $\overline{RAS}$ is driven low. The row address is latched in on this falling edge. This causes the selected row line to go high, forcing the MOSFETs on that row to go into conduction. This connects the storage capacitors to their associated column lines.

  b. The sense amps detect the charge or lack of charge on the capacitors, and in turn, each sense amp recharges its associated capacitor to either V_{DD} or 0 V, depending on whether is was charged or discharged when activated.

3. $\overline{WE}$ is driven low.

4. The desired column address is presented to the RAM address lines.

5. $\overline{CAS}$ is driven low. This activates the column decoder, which in turn routes the logic level from the D input to the cell at the intersection of the activated row and column. If a logic 1 is being stored, the capacitor is charged to V_{DD}. If a logic 0 is being stored, the capacitor is discharged to 0 V.

6. $\overline{RAS}$ and $\overline{CAS}$ are driven high.

The Read Operation

1. The desired row address is applied to the address pins.

2. $\overline{WE}$ is driven high.

3a. $\overline{RAS}$ is driven low. The row address is latched in on this falling edge. The selected row is driven high, connecting the capacitors on that row to their associated column lines and sense amps.

  b. Each sense amp will detect the charge or lack of charge on its associated capacitor, and will in turn drive the column line to the correct voltage. This will recharge the capacitor to V_{DD} if a logic 1 was stored, or discharge the capacitor to 0 V if a logic 0 was stored.

4. The output of the sense amp is buffered and sent out to the Q pin of the RAM.

5. $\overline{CAS}$ and $\overline{RAS}$ are driven high.

Several important points should now be mentioned concerning the operation of dynamic RAM. It was stated previously that the capacitors used to store logic levels will tend to discharge in a short period of time. In order to retain the integrity of the data stored in dynamic RAM, the cells must be refreshed periodically. Typically, most dynamic RAMs require each cell to be refreshed at least once every 2 ms. This means that contents of the RAM must be read and then rewritten at frequent intervals. This need for refreshing is the major drawback of dynamic RAM. The discussion of the read and write operations above, however, indicates that all of the cells in a given row are refreshed any time that the row is addressed. This means that all that need be done to refresh the memory is the sequential activation of the various rows, possibly with the column decoder disabled. This is known as row address select-only ($\overline{RAS}$-only) refresh. The time required to refresh any given row is the same as t_{rc} (read-write cycle time), as shown on Fig. 5-10a and b. There are actually many different ways in which a dynamic RAM may be refreshed. Some dynamic RAMs have a $\overline{REFRESH}$ input that allows easier refreshing of the chip. Several possible refresh methods will now be presented.

RAS-Only Refresh   There are two ways that the $\overline{RAS}$-only method of refresh can be implemented; the burst mode and the distributed mode (sometimes called transparent or hidden refresh). In both cases, the $\overline{CAS}$ input is held high (inactive), and $\overline{WE}$ and D are in don't care states while refresh is occurring. An external counter applies row addresses to the RAM address pins. You will recall that any time a given row is selected, all of the cells in that row are refreshed. If the RAM has 128 rows, a 7-bit counter would be used. A RAM with 256 rows would require an 8-bit counter, and so on.

The burst refresh operation would proceed as follows. Assume that this is a 65,536 × 1 RAM, whose cells are in a 256 × 256 matrix, and the external refresh counter begins at 0000 0000. First, $\overline{RAS}$ is pulsed low. This causes all 256 cells in row 1 to be refreshed. The counter is incremented, and $\overline{RAS}$ is again pulsed low. This process repeats until all 256 rows have been refreshed (most 65,536 × 1 RAMS are actually refreshed two rows at a time, cutting refresh time in half). All of the rows are refreshed in one long burst. This is an effective refresh method; however, during the time that refresh is occurring, the RAM cannot be accessed by external devices. On the time scale of the CPU, a burst refresh is a very long time interval.

The distributed refresh method operates in a manner similar to the burst method, except that the refresh operations are distributed in between read and write cycles, throughout each 2-ms period; hence the term distributed refresh. Distributed refresh may be preferable to burst refresh because it allows refresh cycles to occur at times when the CPU is doing other things that don't require memory access. This is where the term hidden refresh comes from.

Example 5-2

The 4116 is a 16K × 1 dynamic RAM. The storage cells in this device are arranged in a 128 × 128 matrix, and each cell must be refreshed once every 2 ms.

1. If the row and column inputs are multiplexed, how many address pins should this IC have?
2. Assuming $\overline{RAS}$-only refresh is used and each refresh cycle takes 300 ns, on the average, what percentage of time is the RAM available for use by the CPU or some other device?

Solution

1. Rows and columns are selected with 1 of 128 decoders. Each decoder will have 7 input lines. Since the decoders are multiplexed, the 4116 will have only 7 input lines.

2. Since each refresh cycle takes 300 ns, and a total of 128 cycles are performed, the total time required in each 2-ms period is 128×300 ns $= 38.4 \mu$s. The percentage of time that the RAM is available is found to be about 98 percent; that is, about 2 percent of the time the memory cannot be accessed due to the refresh operation. The percentage of time required for distributed refresh would be the same as above, however, there is a high probability that the CPU would not be prevented from accessing the memory when required, because the refresh cycles are spread evenly throughout each 2-ms period.

Automatic Refresh Some dynamic RAMs have provisions for automatic refresh operation. An example of such a device is the Motorola MCM6664 65,536 × 1 dynamic RAM. The pin diagram for the MCM6664 is shown in Fig. 5-11. This RAM has a $\overline{\text{REFRESH}}$ input that is used to control its

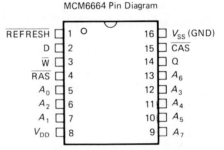

MCM6664 Pin Diagram

Fig. 5-11 Pin diagram for the MCM6664 dynamic RAM (Motorola). (Courtesy of Motorola, Inc.)

mode of operation. The MCM6664 also has a built-in row counter and a timer that may be used to refresh the chip. There are three different ways that automatic refresh can be accomplished using the MCM6664: single-pulse automatic refresh, multiple-pulse automatic refresh, and self-refresh. The first two methods are similar to burst and periodic refresh, respectively, except that the RAM chip takes care of the counting itself.

In order to enter the single-pulse mode of refresh, the $\overline{\text{RAS}}$ line is held high and $\overline{\text{REFRESH}}$ is pulsed low. This refreshes the first row. After the first row is refreshed, a normal read or write cycle is allowed to occur, after which, $\overline{\text{RAS}}$ is pulsed again. This sequence of events occurs repeatedly, with the internal refresh counter incrementing each time $\overline{\text{REFRESH}}$ is pulled low. This is similar to distributed refresh.

In the multiple-pulse mode, $\overline{\text{RAS}}$ is pulled high and $\overline{\text{REFRESH}}$ is pulsed 128 consecutive times (the MCM6664 refreshes two rows at a time). Each falling edge of the $\overline{\text{REFRESH}}$ pulse increments the internal counter, causing it to point to the next higher row. The pulses applied to $\overline{\text{REFRESH}}$ must begin on 2-ms intervals. Timing diagrams that illustrate these two modes of operation are shown in Fig. 5-12*a* and *b*.

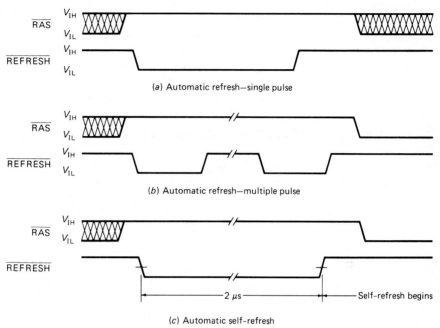

(a) Automatic refresh—single pulse

(b) Automatic refresh—multiple pulse

(c) Automatic self-refresh

Fig. 5-12 Automatic refresh timing diagrams for the MCM6664 RAM. (Courtesy of Motorola, Inc.)

The self-refresh mode of operation is entered by pulling $\overline{\text{RAS}}$ high and holding $\overline{\text{REFRESH}}$ low for at least 2 µs. The occurrence of these conditions causes the 6664's internal timer to activate. The timer automatically increments the row counter, causing bursts of refresh cycles to occur at 2-ms intervals. This mode of operation can be used to hold data without outside intervention while the RAM is not being used, such as when battery backup of the system is in use. Timing for automatic self-refresh is shown in Fig. 5-12*c*.

Since the interfacing of dynamic RAM is such a complex design task, IC manufacturers have produced devices specifically designed to make dynamic RAM easier to use. These devices are called dynamic RAM controllers. Two such devices are the Intel 8202A and 8203. The 8202A is designed to provide all required control signals for 2117- and 2118-type 16,384 × 1 dynamic RAMs. The 8203 is designed to control both 16,384 × 1 and 65,536 × 1 dynamic RAMS. In addition, these devices also arbitrate access to the RAM. In other words, they will prevent external devices from accessing the memory during a refresh cycle and vice versa.

Review Questions for Section 5-2

1. What is the main advantage of dynamic RAM over static RAM?
2. What devices are used to produce memories with very low power dissipation?
3. A certain static RAM is listed as being 1K × 8 in size. How many cells are in this device? How many address pins will it have?
4. Why is address multiplexing used with dynamic RAMs?
5. What are the signals that are used to multiplex the address into the row and column decoders of a dynamic RAM?
6. What are the two main refresh techniques?
7. A certain 4K × 1 dynamic RAM has t_{rc} = 600 ns. How long would it take to refresh this device using the burst method?

5-3 READ-ONLY MEMORY

Read-only memories (ROMs) are devices that contain previously written information. They are not reprogrammable during normal device operation. In use, an address is supplied to the ROM, the device is enabled (selected), and the contents of the location that is addressed are driven onto the ROM data pins.

ROMs are most often used to store programs and data that must be present in a system at all times. Such programs are often called *firmware*. Firmware is software that is contained in hardware (the ROM chip).

5-3.1 Diode Matrix ROMs

Perhaps the simplest ROM that can be made is the diode matrix ROM. One possible design for such a ROM is shown in Fig. 5-13a. In this circuit, the ROM is programmed by placing diodes at various intersections of the row and column lines. To understand exactly how this circuit works, we must first examine the operation of the 74154. The 74154 is a 4 to 16 decoder. A given output (row) line is selected by applying its address to the select inputs. The line that is selected is driven low. All other lines (the deselected lines) are driven high. The two $\overline{\text{ENABLE}}$ inputs may be used to place all of the outputs in the logic high state.

Let us now look at the operation of the diode matrix ROM of Fig. 5-13a from a functional standpoint. Beginning with all address inputs at logic 0, row 0 will be driven low (approximately 0 V), and the rest of the rows will remain high (approximately +5 V). Because row 0 is low, all of the diodes connected to it are forward biased. This causes the column lines that these diodes are connected to to drop to about 0.7 V. This is the barrier potential of silicon diodes. So, when row 0 is active (low), outputs D_0 through D_3 are pulled to logic 0. Now, let us assume that the address lines are driven by 0110 (6_{10}). This activates row 6, pulling output lines D_3 and D_1 low. The two remaining output lines D_0 and D_2 will remain high because the diodes that are connected to them also have their anodes connected to high (+5 V) rows. Those diodes are not forward biased. Stepping through the 16 possible input combinations results in the outputs

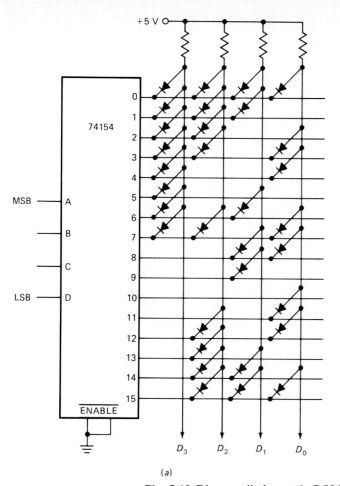

Address inputs				Outputs			
A	B	C	D	D_3	D_2	D_1	D_0
0	0	0	0	0	0	0	0
0	0	0	1	0	0	0	1
0	0	1	0	0	0	1	1
0	0	1	1	0	0	1	0
0	1	0	0	0	1	1	0
0	1	0	1	0	1	1	1
0	1	1	0	0	1	0	1
0	1	1	1	0	1	0	0
1	0	0	0	1	1	0	0
1	0	0	1	1	1	0	1
1	0	1	0	1	1	1	1
1	0	1	1	1	1	1	0
1	1	0	0	1	0	1	0
1	1	0	1	1	0	1	1
1	1	1	0	1	0	0	1
1	1	1	1	1	0	0	0

(a)   (b)

Fig. 5-13 Discrete diode matrix ROM (a) and output listing (b).

presented in Fig. 5-13b. Examining this truth table, we see that the ROM is an 8-4-2-1 binary to Gray code converter. Gray code is a code in which only 1 bit changes from one sequential pattern to the next. It is often used in digital positional sensing applications.

It should now be clear that it is a relatively simple task to program a diode matrix ROM, such as the one just presented. One simply connects diodes at the intersections where logic 0s are required when a given decoder output is active (low). This ROM could be expanded to longer words by adding more columns as required. It should be mentioned that the output of this ROM is not TTL-compatible, although it does make a good demonstration device.

5-3.2 Mask-Programmed ROM

The general internal structure of a mask-programmed ROM (and most other ROMs for that matter) is shown in Fig. 5-14. It is readily apparent that ROMs are organized in much the same manner as RAMs.

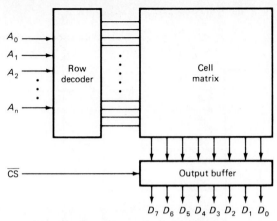

Fig. 5-14 Block diagram of a typical ROM.

Mask-programmed ROMs are programmed during the chip manufacturing process. In this process, an etch-resistant mask is formed over certain parts of the chip. This mask is used to prevent the etching of the conductive paths that are deposited on the chip. Fig. 5-15 shows part of a MOS mask-

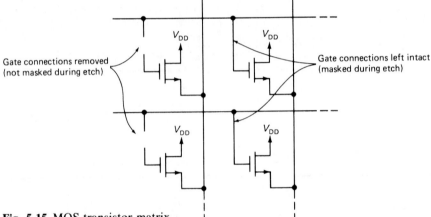

Fig. 5-15 MOS transistor matrix.

programmed ROM matrix. The transistors whose gate connections have been etched away will remain in a nonconducting state when their row (gate) lines are driven high. These cells are programmed to represent logic 0. The cells whose transistors still have gate connections pull their associated column lines high when their row lines are activated. Simplified symbols for N-channel enhancement MOSFETs have been used in Fig. 5-15. Many times, even the drain arrow is left off of the symbol.

Mask-programmed ROMs are generally used when a large number of ROMs are to be produced. The initial cost of producing a mask-programmed ROM is high (several thousand dollars), because the mask must be custom made based on the customer's requirements. However, once the mask is made, many ROMs with the same contents can be produced quickly and inexpensively. Most microcomputer manufacturers use mask-programmed ROMs to hold their operating systems and BASIC interpreters.

5-3.3 Fusible Link Programmable ROM

Fusible link PROMs are user-programmable. A cell of a bipolar fusible link PROM is shown in Fig. 5-16. This cell operates in much the same

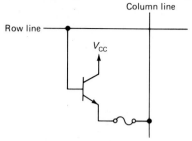

Fig. 5-16 Fusible link PROM cell.

manner as the mask-programmed MOS ROM just discussed; that is, transistors that have their emitter fuses blown will have no effect on their associated column lines when base drive is applied. Transistors that still have their fuses intact will pull their associated column lines high when base drive is applied. The user programs the fusible link PROM by causing specific fuses to blow. The fuse is an extremely thin trace of nichrome or polysilicon. Polysilicon fuses are used more often, because they are more reliable than nichrome. Nichrome fuses have a tendency to relink occasionally after being blown.

Figure 5-17 shows a circuit that may be used to program Intel 3601 bipolar PROMs. The programming process works as follows. The address

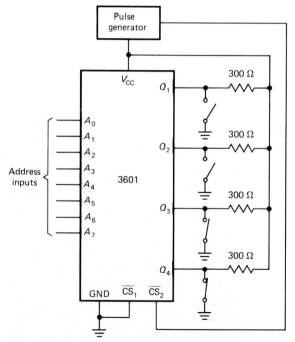

Fig. 5-17 Programming setup for 3601 PROM.

of the first row of cells is applied to the address pins of the PROM. The transistors connected to that row are all supplied with base drive. The collectors are connected (via the V_{CC} pin) to a pulsed voltage source. The output (column) lines that go to the transistors whose emitter fuses are to be blown are grounded. The output lines of the transistors whose fuses are to remain intact are connected to the pulsed V_{CC} line. A series of well-defined pulses is then applied to the V_{CC} pin. This causes high emitter current pulses to occur, which melt and open those fuses that are connected to the grounded output lines. The address is incremented, the switches are set for the next row, and the V_{CC} source again applies pulses to the circuit. This process is repeated for each row of cells in the PROM.

Once programmed, a fusible link PROM cannot be reprogrammed. Therefore, if a mistake is made, or the program requirements change, a new PROM must be programmed and the old one replaced. These types of PROM are usually employed in applications where relatively few ROMs are required, and program changes are made very infrequently.

5-3.4 Erasable PROM

Erasable PROM (EPROM) is a very popular form of memory because it is programmable and erasable by the user. It has the advantages of being nonvolatile and reprogrammable. A memory is said to be nonvolatile if it retains its data without power being applied. It is reprogrammability that largely accounts for the popularity of EPROM.

An EPROM is illustrated in Fig. 5-18. A quartz window is bonded into the ceramic DIP which allows the chip to be viewed. The window is there

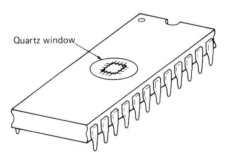

Quartz window

Fig. 5-18 Typical EPROM packaging.

for erasure purposes. As with most other memory devices, the block diagram presented in Fig. 5-14 is a reasonable representation of the internal structure of an EPROM. In the case of the EPROM, special E-MOSFETs, each built with an extra floating gate are used to form the cells. A cross-sectional view of an EPROM storage cell is shown in Fig. 5-19a. The schematic symbol for the transistor is shown in Fig. 5-19b.

A cell may be programmed by applying about 15 to 20 V from drain to source, while at the same time applying about $+25$ V to the gate. Because of the high V_{ds}, electrons are injected into the channel between the drain and source. However, since the gate is at an even higher potential than

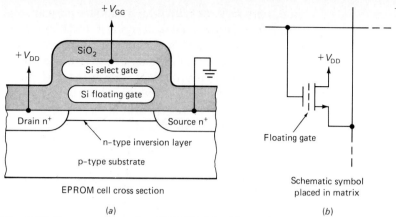

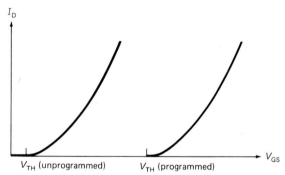

Fig. 5-19 Cross section of an EPROM EMOStransistor (*a*) and schematic symbol (*b*).

the drain, a strong electric field is produced which pulls electrons through the SiO_2 barrier and into the floating gate. Once in the floating gate, the electrons become trapped. The cell is now programmed. What this trapping of electrons in the floating gate does is effectively increase the threshold voltage (V_{th}) of the FET. The transconductance curves in Fig. 5-20 illustrate the shift. Studies have shown that once programmed, an EPROM will remain programmed for more than 10 years.

Fig. 5-20 Effect of stored gate charge on EPROM MOSFET transconductance curve.

When reading the EPROM, if the cell has remained unprogrammed, its associated row line will easily exceed V_{th}, causing the formation of a conductive inversion layer between the drain and source. This in turn causes the column line to be pulled to V_{DD}. If a programmed cell is addressed, the applied gate voltage does not exceed V_{th}, and the FET remains nonconducting. What happens is that the accumulated negative charge on the floating gate cancels out the applied gate field, and no inversion layer is created.

From the preceding discussion, it may be deduced that a programmed cell represents logic 1 and an unprogrammed cell represents logic 0. In order to erase the cells, a source of ultraviolet (UV) radiation is shined into the window of the device. Unlike normal glass, quartz is transparent to UV radiation; that is why it is used in the window. When the UV radiation penetrates the floating gate, the trapped electrons are driven into high energy states. These excited electrons have enough energy to penetrate the SiO_2 insulation, and are absorbed into the substrate. The erasing process usually takes about 30 min or so.

5-3.5 Electrically Alterable ROM (EAROM)

EAROMs (sometimes called electrically erasable ROM or EEROM) are very similar to the EPROM just discussed. The main difference between them is that the EAROM may be erased electrically rather than with UV radiation. Programming and erasing the EAROM require special circuitry that must be designed into the system in which it is used. The programming cycle takes about 1 ms. Erasing takes about 100 ms. However, access time is around 400 ms.

EAROMs are relatively expensive, and they are also low in storage density when compared to other MOS-type memory devices. Some other problems associated with EAROM are that they have shorter program storage times than EPROM and they are not as reliable as other ROMs when erased and reprogrammed several times.

5-3.6 General Comparisons of ROMs

Of the read only memories discussed, the highest density devices are the mask-programmed ROM and the EPROM. These ROMs are typically available with up to $32K \times 8$ storage capacity. Typically, these two types of devices are interchangeable; that is, most manufacturers produce mask programmed ROMs and EPROMs with the same pin designations and voltage requirements. Fusible link PROMS have lower density than EPROMs (typically up to $2K \times 8$), but are much less expensive.

Access time is another parameter that is important when considering which ROM to use in a system. Maximum access times and storage capacities are listed below for several examples of ROMs that are readily available.

ROM Type	Example Device	Size	Maximum Access Time
Mask prog.	MCM6830	$1K \times 8$	350 ns
	IM7364	$8K \times 8$	350 ns
EPROM	2708	$1K \times 8$	450 ns
	27256	$32K \times 8$	250 ns
Fused link	74S474	512×8	250 ns
	82S191	$2K \times 8$	250 ns

Review Questions for Section 5-3

1. What term is given to software that is stored in ROM?
2. What type of ROM is used most often when a large number of identical units are required?

3. What logic level is represented by a programmed PROM cell?
4. Some bipolar PROMs are available with either tristate or open collector outputs. Which do you think would be compatible with an 8088 microprocessor? Why?
5. What effect does the storage of a negative charge on the floating gate have on an enhancement mode MOSFET storage cell?
6. Which type of ROM is likely to be used when prototype systems are being developed?

5-4   SERIAL MEMORY

Serial memories are classified as read-write memories. The structure of serial memory is typified by the serial-in serial-out (SISO) shift register. A SISO shift register is shown in Fig. 5-21. Notice that this is also a first-in first-out (FIFO) type of structure. Data to be stored must be clocked in, 1 bit at a time. In order to read such a memory, all bits that were entered prior to the data to be read must be clocked out first. This is a time consuming process, and is the main reason why such memories are not used often in microcomputer systems. There are two major types of serial memory currently available: charge coupled devices and magnetic bubble memories. Each will be discussed briefly in this section.

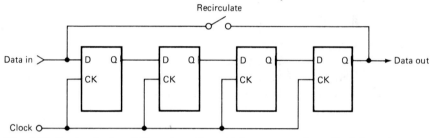

Fig. 5-21 Recirculating shift register for serial storage and recall of data.

5-4.1   Magnetic Bubble Memory

Magnetic bubble memories (MBMs) are not fabricated from silicon as were the memories discussed previously. Instead, a special garnet substrate is used as the foundation for the device. A thin film of magnetic material is deposited on the surface of the garnet, and extremely small chevron shaped guide elements are then deposited on the film. This structure is then wrapped in orthogonally (perpendicular) oriented coils of fine wire. Finally, small permanent magnets are placed above and below the chip. This structure is shown in Fig. 5-22. The magnets above and below the chip force most of the magnetic domains in the film to become aligned. However, some domains will not align, and these domains form the "bubbles." The bubbles line up below the chevron-shaped elements, and may be moved from one place to another by applying current through the orthoganal coils. The movement of a bubble past a Hall effect detector signifies logic 1. The lack of a bubble moving by a detector when pulses are applied to

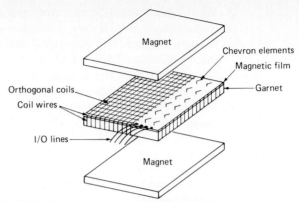

Fig. 5-22 Construction of a magnetic bubble memory device.

the coils signifies logic 0. The actual details of operation of the magnetic bubble memory are quite complex and will not be presented here.

The strong point of MBMs is their storage density. More than 1 million bits can be stored on a single chip about 1 cm square. Such extreme density is very attractive in miniaturized systems. Also, MBMs are nonvolatile; that is, they retain their stored data when power is removed.

The biggest weakness of the MBM is the time it takes to read data that is located deep within the device. The average delay created by this condition is called latency time. For most MBM devices, the latency time is around 1 ms.

5-4.2 Charge Coupled Devices

Charge coupled devices (CCDs) are fabricated using MOS technology, and are currently used much less often in computers than even MBMs. CCD storage density is relatively high, with 65,536 bits/device readily available. Charge coupled devices are members of the dynamic memory group; that is, they must be periodically refreshed in order to retain their contents. Refresh may be accomplished by recirculating the contents of the register. The colored lines in Fig. 5-21 would be used for this purpose. Refresh logic would be used to control the operation of the switch.

As with MBMs, the latency time of CCDs is a major drawback. The added refresh time delay and refresh circuitry also have prevented widespread application of CCDs in computer systems. However, CCDs may be used to form analog shift registers. These devices are used to form time delay lines in some analog and digital circuits.

Review Questions for Section 5-4

1. What is the term given to the time interval that occurs in between a serial memory read request and presentation of data at the memory's output?
2. What part of an MBM causes bubble movement to occur?
3. What sequential logic circuit closely resembles MBMs and CCDs from a functional standpoint?

4. How is bubble movement detected in an MBM?
5. A certain MBM is used in a microcomputer, and has a maximum data output rate of 500K bits/s. If this device contains 262,144 storage locations, how long would it take to read the entire contents of the device?
6. How is an EPROM erased?

5-5 MEMORY INTERFACING AND DESIGN CONSIDERATIONS

After all of this talk about memories, it is time to see how they are connected to the computer system. Much of the information required has already been presented. This section will cover the basic aspects of address decoding. Specifically, interfacing memory to the 8088 based system will be discussed.

Let us begin by defining how much total memory is to be used, how much will be RAM, how much will be ROM, and where (from an addressing point of view) these devices will be located.

5-5.1 The Memory Map

The first thing that will be done is the development of a memory map. This map will be used as a guide to memory device selection and organization. In order to create a memory map for the computer, certain details of the operation of the 8088 must be recalled. Upon power-up, the 8088 is reset and vectored to absolute address $FFFF0_{16}$. The 8088 expects to find a valid instruction opcode at this location, and will begin normal program execution at this point. If the computer is to be self-starting, the beginning of an initialization routine should be placed here. The distance from $FFFF0_{16}$ to $FFFFF_{16}$ is probably not long enough to hold much of an initialization routine, so a jump to an initialization instruction will probably be located here. Such an instruction could be a maximum of 5 bytes in length. In any case, it is for this reason that an 8088-based design practically requires the highest memory locations to be ROM. The process by which a computer initializes itself is called booting-up, or just booting. This term comes from the fact that the computer essentially "pulls itself up by its own bootstraps."

An important fact that should be recalled is that the 8088 always fetches interrupt vectors from absolute addresses 00000_{16} through $003FF_{16}$. These vectors must be contained in memory when the computer is operating. There are two practical ways that the storage of the interrupt vectors can be handled: A ROM containing the vectors could be located at the beginning of memory, or the reset initialization routine could load the vectors into RAM at the beginning of memory. There are some advantages and disadvantages associated with both methods. For instance, programming the interrupt vectors into ROM ensures that they will always be present and cannot be erased or altered accidentally by the user. However, if the vectors are loaded into RAM, the user can create interrupt service routines, and write the vectors for them over the default vectors. The RAM located vector approach is used by IBM in the PC. It is standard practice to design a microcomputer such that the ROM occupies either the very highest or the very lowest address locations (rarely both). Also, since the 8088 vectors to location FFFF0 automatically on power-up, the design that is presented in this section will locate the ROM at the top (highest addresses) of memory. Any RAM that is to be added to the system will begin at the bottom of memory and will be expanded toward higher addresses as the need arises.

Now that the interrupt vector storage method and general ROM address locations have been taken care of, a memory map may now be started. Let us assume that an 8K × 8 ROM will be located at the top (highest addresses) of memory, and that the rest of the address space is available for other uses such as RAM. The memory map of Fig. 5-23 shows the

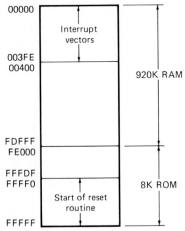

Fig. 5-23 Memory map showing vector locations for the 8088.

memory configuration up to this point. Notice that the addresses increase from top to bottom. This is the format used by IBM in its personal computer literature. In contrast, Intel literature, for example, reverses the address ordering in its memory maps; that is, the lowest addresses are located at the bottom of the map. Both methods are acceptable.

Many decisions must be made before the details of the memory map can be filled in. For example, will more ROM be required? Will dynamic or static RAM be used? Are peripheral interfacing devices going to be assigned addresses? These are questions that must be answered by the engineers designing the system, based on the intended purpose of the machine and possible future applications and modifications.

5-5.2 Address Decoding

An address decoder is a circuit that enables devices that are connected to the address bus when the address of that particular device is present on the bus. In terms of memory devices, the address decoder enables the chip when access to any location within that device is desired.

There are two major methods of decoding the address space: fully decoded addressing and partially decoded addressing. The design of either type of decoder may be little more than a relatively simple combinational logic circuit. Figure 5-24 shows a maximum mode 8088 with address and data bus demultiplexing circuitry. This will be the model to which the memory will be added.

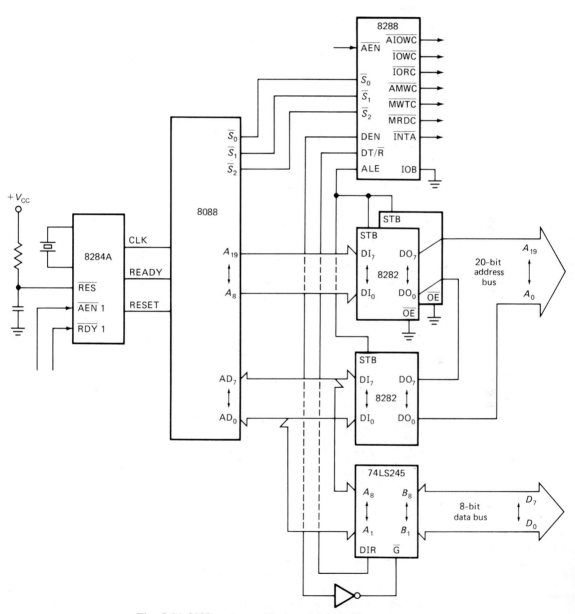

Fig. 5-24 8088 system with demultiplexed bus structure.

Interfacing the ROM   Let us begin this phase of design by choosing a particular 8K × 8 ROM chip and designing a circuit that will enable it when and only when a location within the range of $FE000_{16}$ through $FFFFF_{16}$ (the space that will be occupied by the ROM) is addressed. Arbitrarily, let us assume that the ROM to be used is an Intersil IM7364 mask-programmed HMOS device. The logic symbol for the IM7364 is shown in Fig. 5-25.

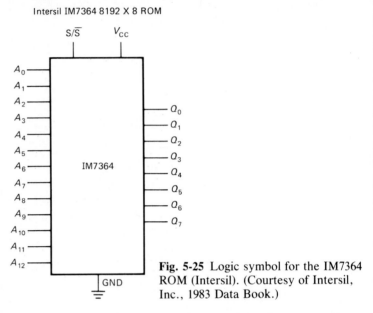

Intersil IM7364 8192 X 8 ROM

Fig. 5-25 Logic symbol for the IM7364 ROM (Intersil). (Courtesy of Intersil, Inc., 1983 Data Book.)

Pins Q_0 through Q_7 are the data outputs, pins A_0 through A_{12} are the address inputs and $S/\overline{S}$ is a programmable chip select input. The chip select input is programmed as either active high or active low during the masking process per the customer's specifications. Since most memory devices have active-low chip selects, let us assume that this ROM has been programmed as such. The IM7364 operates from a single +5 V supply and is TTL compatible, as are the latches and buffers used in the circuit of Fig. 5-24.

The starting and ending addresses of the area that will be occupied by the ROM are presented in Fig. 5-26. Comparing these two addresses and the logic diagram of the ROM, it is obvious that the seven most significant

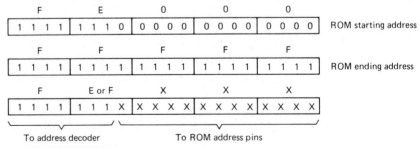

Fig. 5-26 ROM address decoding charts.

address lines must be used to decode (select) the ROM. The lines that are used to select a given location within the ROM are marked with an X, signifying "don't care" states in the third box in Fig. 5-26. Examining the third box, it is found that when the seven most significant address bits are high, the ROM is being addressed. Any other bit pattern that might occur on these lines would indicate that an address somewhere below that of the ROM is being accessed. It is these seven bits which will be used to select (enable) the ROM.

Using some basic digital electronics theory, it is easily determined that if the seven most significant address lines are NANDed, the NAND gate will output logic 0 when the ROM is accessed. This is just what is needed to select the ROM . . . almost. It must also be remembered that the ROM should be only activated when a correct address is present and a read operation is being performed. A read operation is signaled when $\overline{RD}$ is driven low by a minimum mode 8088, or when $\overline{MRDC}$ is driven low by the bus controller (maximum mode 8088). No matter which line is used, it must be used in the control of the ROM select input. Inverting the given read signal and then applying it to the NAND gate with the address lines will produce the desired results. The decoded ROM circuit is shown in Fig. 5-27. Since each location within the ROM has its own unique address, by definition, the ROM is said to be fully decoded.

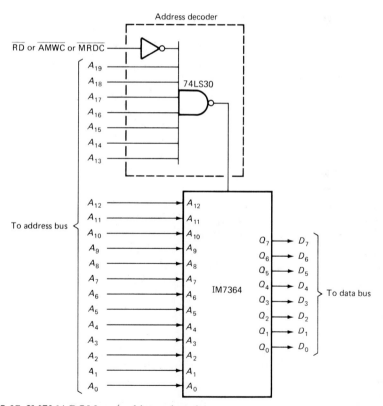

Fig. 5-27 IM7364 ROM and address decoder.

Interfacing the RAM Once the ROM has been mapped and decoded, the RAM may be added. There are a large number of different RAM chips available, so the next step is to determine which one to use. In order to keep the circuits relatively simple, let us use static devices. Arbitrarily, let us choose the Intel 2167 16K × 1 static RAM in this design. The logic symbol and the control function table for the 2167 are shown in Fig. 5-28a and b. Notice that this RAM has separate data input and output lines. None of the static RAMs presented so far have had such a data input/ output arrangement, but it shall soon be seen that this presents no problem.

It is now time to decide how much RAM will be included in the system. According to the memory map of Fig. 5-23, there is enough free space for 920K (actually 1,040,384) byte of RAM. That's an awful lot of RAM! Let's be a little conservative and add only 64K byte of RAM to this particular system. Until recently, 64K byte of RAM was considered a fairly large memory for a microcomputer. With the question of how much RAM to add settled, the general arrangement of the RAM chips must be considered. Since the 2167s are bit-oriented devices, they will be connected to the data bus in the same general manner as the devices that were shown in Fig. 5-8. Using this information as a starting point, we find that a group of eight 2167 RAMs is required to produce a 16K × 8 (16K byte) section of memory. In order to create a 64K byte section of memory, four groups of eight 2167 RAM chips are required. Let us refer to each group of eight 2167s as a block. The boundaries of the blocks are illustrated in Fig. 5-29.

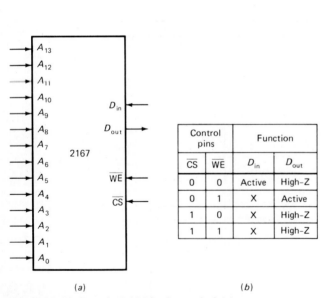

Control pins		Function	
$\overline{CS}$	$\overline{WE}$	D_{in}	D_{out}
0	0	Active	High-Z
0	1	X	Active
1	0	X	High-Z
1	1	X	High-Z

Fig. 5-28 2167 static RAM logic symbol (a) and function table (b).

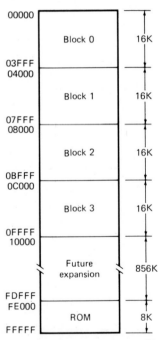

Fig. 5-29 System memory map with ROM and RAM addresses listed.

The eight 2167 RAMs that constitute each block must be treated as if they were one single device; that is, all RAM chips in a block should receive the same control signals at the same time. The logic diagram of Fig. 5-30 shows how the blocks of RAM are connected to the data bus, address bus, and CPU write enable line. Again, refer to Fig. 5-8 for the details of how the individual RAMs within the blocks are connected. The write enable ($\overline{\text{WE}}$) pin of each block is connected to whichever write control pin is applicable in the system, depending on whether the minimum or maximum mode is being used.

The D_{in} and D_{out} lines of each individual 2167 RAM are connected as shown in the colored inset in Fig. 5-30. The $\overline{\text{CS}}$ and $\overline{\text{WE}}$ signals will control the data I/O lines such that after a valid address is present ($\overline{\text{CS}}$ is low on a given block), if $\overline{\text{WE}}$ is high, the D_{in} pins of the selected block are in don't care states, and the D_{out} pins are active. This is a memory read

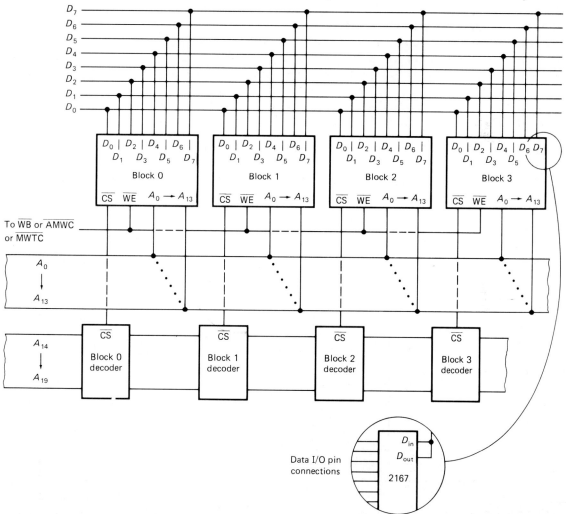

Fig. 5-30 Interfacing the RAM chips to the buses.

operation. If $\overline{WE}$ is low when a valid address is present ($\overline{CS}$ is low), the D_{in} pins are active, and the D_{out} pins of that block are tri-stated. This is a memory write operation. Any other combinations of $\overline{CS}$ and $\overline{WE}$ disable D_{in} and tristate D_{out}.

Developing the RAM Decoders   The RAM decoding circuits may be developed in the same general way as the ROM decoding circuit. Beginning with block 0, and using the memory map of Fig. 5-29 as a guide, the decoding chart in Fig. 5-31 may be produced. From the decoding chart we find that

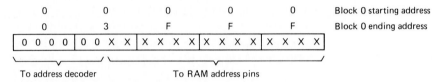

Fig. 5-31 Block 0 RAM decoding chart.

the six most significant bits of the address bus will be 0 whenever block 0 is being addressed. A circuit that produces logic 0 only when all inputs are 0 is shown in Fig. 5-32. Low-power Schottky logic gates were used in this design because they present a lighter load on the bus than standard TTL gates, and yet they have a slightly lower propagation delay. Propagation delay is the time required for a device to produce a valid output response to a valid input level.

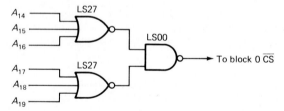

Fig. 5-32 Partially complete block 0 address decoding circuit.

There are still a few more points that must be considered before this circuit is fully completed. You will recall from Chap. 4, that I/O devices may also have their addresses placed on the address bus. The difference between I/O addressing and memory addressing is that different command lines are used for each operation; that is, during I/O read and write cycles, $\overline{IOWC}$, $\overline{AIOWC}$, and $\overline{IORC}$ control a given I/O device, while $\overline{MWTC}$, $\overline{AMWC}$, and $\overline{MRDC}$ control a given memory device. What this all means is that it is possible for a memory device that has only a single $\overline{WE}$ (or equivalent) control input to have the same address as an I/O device. Unless precautions are taken, there is a chance that both an I/O port and a memory location could be read at the same time. This clearly would produce a bus conflict. Examination of Fig. 5-30 reveals that if an I/O device with the same address as the RAM is written to, the RAM will not be overwritten because it is controlled by the $\overline{WR}$, $\overline{AMWC}$, or $\overline{MWTC}$ lines. Any of these lines will be active only during a memory write operation. However, when reading an I/O port, it is possible that the memory will also attempt to drive the data bus whenever $\overline{\text{WR}}$, $\overline{\text{AMWC}}$, or $\overline{\text{MWTC}}$ (whichever is applicable) is inactive (high), and $\overline{\text{CS}}$ is low. The only way that the memory could know that it is not to be read (that is, it shouldn't drive the data bus) is by monitoring the $\overline{\text{MRDC}}$ line or, in the minimum mode, the $\text{IO}/\overline{\text{M}}$ line.

The address decoder of Fig. 5-32 may be modified as shown in Fig. 5-33 to prevent I/O-memory conflicts. Basically, the circuit works by disabling

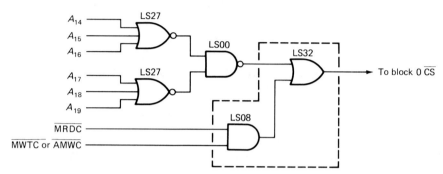

Fig. 5-33 Complete block 0 address decoder.

(deselecting) the memory block whenever both $\overline{\text{MRDC}}$ (or $\overline{\text{RD}}$) and $\overline{\text{WR}}$ are high. The truth table used to develop this modification is shown in Fig. 5-34. This circuit will be used to control the $\overline{\text{CS}}$ outputs of each decoding circuit. Some memory devices have separate read and write, or output disable, command lines. For an example of how a memory device such as this could be connected to an 8088-based system, consult the *Intel Microsystem Components Handbook*.

Truth Table for $\overline{\text{CS}}$ Control

Memory read line A	Memory write line B	Address decoder output C	Output to $\overline{\text{CS}}$ f	Operation
0	0	0	d	Impossible
0	0	1	d	Impossible
0	1	0	0	Memory read
0	1	1	1	Memory read of different block
1	0	0	0	Memory write
1	0	1	1	Memory write to different block
1	1	0	1	I/O operation
1	1	1	1	Nonmemory operation

Fig. 5-34 Truth table for block 0 address decoder.

The decoder for block 1 of the RAM is developed based on the decoding chart shown in Fig. 5-35. The only difference between this decoding chart and the one in Fig. 5-31 is that the LSB of the decoder input address lines is always logic 1 when block 1 is being addressed. Using this information,

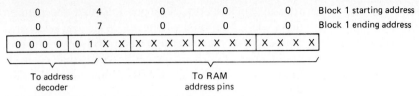

| 0 | | | | 4 | | 0 | | 0 | | 0 | Block 1 starting address |
| 0 | | | | 7 | | 0 | | 0 | | 0 | Block 1 ending address |

To address decoder

To RAM address pins

Fig. 5-35 Block 1 RAM decoding chart.

the decoder circuit shown in Fig. 5-36 may be developed. Again, the decoder has been modified to prevent memory-I/O conflicts. It should be mentioned that the ROM, or any other memory beyond the first 64K, does not need this extra control because the I/O space is only 64K bytes long. During I/O transfers, the four most significant address lines are always 0. The first two blocks (32K) of memory have now been fully decoded.

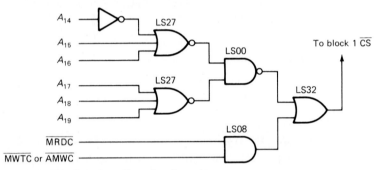

Fig. 5-36 Block 1 decoding circuit.

The remaining two decoders will not be presented here, but the general ideas behind their design should now be apparent. Adding even more blocks of memory up to the ROM limit could be accomplished in this manner, although the decoding circuitry would begin to take up a lot of board space. Should this present a problem, there are other decoding circuits that may be more space efficient. Another approach to memory decoding will be presented next.

5-5.3 Other Decoding Alternatives

The problem with the decoding approach taken with the RAM has already been pointed out: It would take up too much space on the circuit board to decode a larger portion of the available memory space. One decoding circuit design approach that might result in some design time and board space savings is to use a 1 of N decoder. In this approach, the memory is broken down into N different sections or blocks. The 1 of N decoder is used to select a given block of memory. For example, using the four blocks of RAM just discussed in the previous section, the design of the decoder using this technique would progress as follows.

The decoding charts of Fig. 5-37 show that address lines A_{14} and A_{15} may be used to select a given block of RAM. Our choice of memory chips seems to have worked out rather nicely from a decoding standpoint. It is

RAM Decoding Charts

	A_{19}																			A_0
Block 0	0	0	0	0	0	0	X	X	X	X	X	X	X	X	X	X	X	X	X	X
Block 1	0	0	0	0	0	1	X	X	X	X	X	X	X	X	X	X	X	X	X	X
Block 2	0	0	0	0	1	0	X	X	X	X	X	X	X	X	X	X	X	X	X	X
Block 3	0	0	0	0	1	1	X	X	X	X	X	X	X	X	X	X	X	X	X	X

Fig. 5-37 Decoding charts for all four blocks of RAM.

also seen that address lines A_{16} through A_{19} are always logic 0 when any location within the first 64K of memory is addressed.

All of the information presented in the preceding paragraph points to the choice of the 74LS139 dual 1 of 4 decoder as the heart of the decoding circuit. The logic symbol and function table for the 74LS139 are shown in Fig. 5-38. When a given half of the decoder is disabled ($\overline{G1}$ or $\overline{G2}$ = 1),

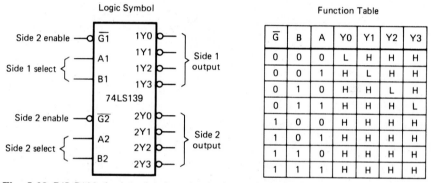

Fig. 5-38 74LS139 dual 1 of 4 decoder logic symbol and function table.

all of that half's outputs are driven high. When either or both halves of the decoder are enabled, the selected outputs will go low, while the deselected outputs will remain high. Since our application requires only a 1 of 4 selection, only side 1 of the decoder will be used. A small circuit must be designed to disable the decoder when memory outside of the first 64K locations is being addressed (to decode the decoder, so to speak). The finished circuit is shown in Fig. 5-39. Each output of the decoder is

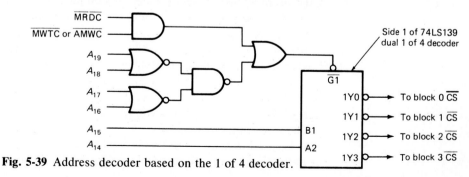

Fig. 5-39 Address decoder based on the 1 of 4 decoder.

Memory Devices and Memory Interfacing section

connected to chip select inputs of its associated block. The 74LS139 is enabled whenever the four most significant bits of the bus are at the logic zero level, and the transfer is not to or from I/O device. This occurs when the first 64K of memory is being addressed and the proper read or write command line is low. A given block of RAM is enabled by lines A_{14} and A_{15} in accordance with the function table in Fig. 5-38. Notice that using the 1 of 4 decoder reduced the number of gates required to decode the first 64K of memory significantly.

If, at some future date, another 64K of RAM was to be added, the additional RAM and the second half of the 74LS139 could be wired into the system. This will be left as an exercise at the end of the chapter. Another alternative would be to replace the 74LS139 with a 74LS138 1 of 8 decoder. This would be a simpler approach than using the 74LS139 (at least if a contiguous 128K byte section of RAM was required). Another way to decrease the amount of circuit board space taken up by the memory circuits is to use higher density memory chips. For example, if 64K $\times$ 1 static RAM chips were available, they might be used in place of the 2167 16K $\times$ 1 devices in the design just presented. Each block would be 64K byte in size, and would consist of eight of the larger memory devices. This would allow more memory to be decoded with a given 1 of N decoder. Of course, the decoding circuitry would have to be redesigned, because such memory chips would have more address pins (unless multiplexed address inputs were used, which is another design task in itself). The problem here is that static RAMs are not available with such high storage density; therefore, dynamic RAM would have to be used. This would make the design much more complex.

Partial Decoding Partial decoding is another memory control method that saves circuit board space. Smaller systems that do not require the use of the full address space can benefit the most from partial decoding. The best way to understand partial decoding is to look at an example.

Let us design a decoder that will place a 256-byte block of RAM in the circuit of Fig. 5-24, beginning at absolute address 10000_{16}. This block will be constructed with two 2112 256 $\times$ 4 RAMs. The 2112s would be connected to the data and address bus as shown in Fig. 5-7. The section of the decoder that selects this block of RAM could be designed just like the previously discussed decoders. In order to demonstrate the savings that may be achieved using partial decoding, let us first fully decode this block of RAM using the same approach as was done for blocks 0 and 1 originally.

The decoding chart for the new RAM is shown in Fig. 5-40. Based on the bit pattern of lines A_{19} through A_8, the decoder shown in Fig. 5-41 may

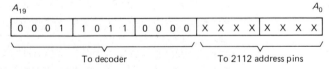

Fig. 5-40 Decoding chart for the 2112 RAM.

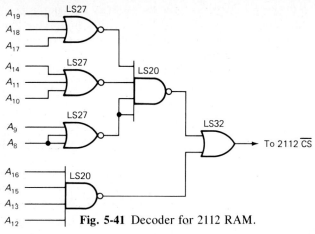

Fig. 5-41 Decoder for 2112 RAM.

be constructed. There are many other possible designs for this circuit; however, all of the gates shown are readily available members of the low-power Schottky family. In any event, this circuit or an equivalent is required to fully decode the 2112 RAM chips as specified in the memory map.

Let us now reduce the number of gates in the decoder circuit by using the technique of partial decoding. From an examination of the decoding chart in Fig. 5-40, it is found that if the inputs of a three input NOR gate are connected to address lines A_{14}, A_{11}, and A_{10}, that gate may be used to select the new block of RAM. The decoding chart and actual circuit for such a decoder are shown in Fig. 5-42a and b.

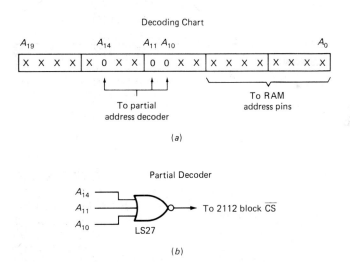

Fig. 5-42 Partial decoding chart (*a*) and circuit (*b*) for 2112.

It is obvious that this circuit is much simpler than that of Fig. 5-41. However, there is a price that is paid for this simplification; that is, a partially decoded section of memory (or anything else that is partially decoded in the system) will actually occupy more than the intended addressing space. To fully understand the implications of this statement, it must be realized that only 13 of the 20 possible address lines have been used to decode this block of RAM. Those address lines marked with colored X's in Fig. 5-42a have no effect at all on the selection of the new RAM. What this means is that any address that produces 0 on lines A_{14}, A_{11}, and A_{10} will access a location somewhere within the 256-byte block of RAM just added. To determine how many 256-byte sections of the address space will be taken up by the partially decoded RAM, just count the number of unused address lines (n), and raise 2 to that power. This is demonstrated in the example below.

Example 5-3

Determine how many 256-byte long sections of memory are effectively occupied by the RAM that is decoded by the circuit in Fig. 5-42b.

Solution

There are a total of 20 address lines available. Lines A_0 through A_7 are used to address locations within the RAM chips. Address lines A_{14}, A_{11} and A_{10} are used as inputs to the address decoder. This leaves nine unused address lines. Therefore, there are 2^9 or 512 different places in the total address space where the RAM that is decoded by the circuit in Fig. 5-42b may be accessed; that is, each of the 256 bytes of this RAM may be read from or written to from any of 512 different addresses. This is a waste of 130,816 memory locations.

Obviously, partial decoding is an inefficient memory management technique. This is why it is used only in smaller systems. For example, if the partially decoded RAM just discussed was actually added to the existing circuit, and it was desired to add even more RAM, it would be necessary to ensure that the additional RAM was not located at one of the areas where the partially decoded RAM exists. The replication of the partially decoded memory at several different addresses is sometimes called foldback; that is, foldback addresses are those address locations which the partially decoded devices inadvertently occupy.

5-5.4   Memory Error Checking

With the trend toward greater and greater amounts of RAM being used in microcomputer systems, the reliability of the memory becomes a major concern. The loss of 1 bit from an instruction or an operand that is stored in memory can make the difference between successful operation and total failure of a program. The loss of data from memory can indicate that a memory device is failing, or possibly that some other malfunction has occurred.

Parity checking is a commonly used memory error-checking method. Parity checking capability may be implemented by adding a parity generator/checker, such as the 74AS280 (AS means advanced Schottky), and 1 extra bit of RAM for each byte of normal RAM. In effect, when such modifications are made, each memory location becomes 9 bits wide. The 9th bit of each location is used to store a parity bit.

Here's the basic idea behind this type of parity checking. Whenever a byte is written into a location in RAM, that byte is also applied to the input of a parity generator. Let us assume that the parity generator used here operates such that if the applied byte contains an even number of logic 1s, the generator will output a logic 0. Conversely, if the applied byte contains an odd number of 1s, then the parity generator will output logic 1. The output of the parity generator is then stored in the extra bit of RAM, resulting in an even number of 1s in the overall 9-bit word. Using this technique, each memory location in the entire RAM will contain an even number of bits set to logic 1.

Now, when a given byte of RAM is read, the 8 normal bits plus the 9th parity bit are sent to the parity checker. If there is not an even number of logic 1 bits present at the input of the parity checker, its output will assume whatever state that is used to indicate a parity error. This signal could be used to initiate an interrupt that informs the user of the problem. Such an interrupt could possibly even track down the faulty RAM location and report that device to the user. One possible design for such a circuit is shown in Fig. 5-43. The operation of this circuit is outlined below.

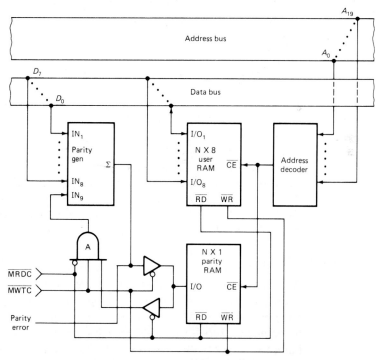

Fig. 5-43 Memory interface with addition of parity bit generation, storage, and checking functions.

Memory Write Cycle Operation

1. The memory address is driven onto the address bus. At this time, $\overline{MRDC}$ and $\overline{MWTC}$ are both high, resulting in the output of gate A being driven low.
2. The $\overline{MWTC}$ line is driven low, indicating that data is to be written to RAM. The output of gate A is still low. This level is applied to the 9th input of the parity generator. In this way the parity of the byte that will be driven onto the data bus can be determined properly.
3. A byte is placed on the data bus. This byte is stored in RAM as usual, and is also applied to the eight remaining inputs to the parity generator. The output of the parity generator is written into the $N \times 1$ RAM location corresponding to that of the user RAM.
4. $\overline{MWTC}$ returns high, ending the memory write cycle. The 9-bit word stored in RAM now has even parity.

Memory Read Cycle Operation

1. The address is driven onto the address bus. Again, both $\overline{MWTC}$ and $\overline{MRDC}$ are high.
2. The $\overline{MRDC}$ line is driven low, indicating that a memory read cycle is in progress.
3. The selected address is activated, and that byte is driven onto the data bus and also to eight of the parity generator inputs. Since $\overline{MRDC}$ is low and $\overline{MWTC}$ is high, gate A will pass the output of the bit in the $N \times 1$ parity RAM on to the 9th input of the parity generator. The 9-bit input to the parity generator should have even parity, producing logic 0 at the parity generator output. If the 9-bit input has odd parity, the output will be driven high, which indicates a parity error.
4. $\overline{MRDC}$ returns to logic 1, terminating the memory read cycle.

Parity checking is a relatively simple but effective method of verifying the integrity of data stored in memory. Parity checking is done automatically any time a location is read. There is one major weakness of simple parity checking that should be mentioned: The parity checker will indicate an error only if an odd number of bits are "lost." A lost bit is one that has somehow changed states undesirably. For example, suppose that the following byte and extra parity bit were written into memory.

Data Byte   **Parity Bit**
0111 0101   1

If, when this pattern of bits was read out, an odd number of bits (1, 3, or 5) had been lost, the parity of the word would be odd, indicating an error. However, if an even number of bits (0,2,4,6,8) had been lost, the parity of the word would still be even, indicating no parity error. That is to be expected; after all, parity is being checked, not the actual composition of the byte. If all of the bits in the least significant nibble of the byte were to be cleared, as shown below, the parity bit that was stored would still be valid, although the loss of these 2 bits could be disastrous.

Data Byte	Parity Bit
0111 0000	1

Other more sophisticated error-checking methods are available. In fact, some methods will locate exactly which bit was lost and correct it. These methods are usually employed in data communication applications. In general, modern memory devices are quite reliable, except when operated at extremes in temperature. Many microcomputers run through various sophisticated memory-testing routines when power-on initialization is performed. If these tests are passed, parity checking is normally all that is required to monitor the performance of the memory during actual computer operation.

Review Questions for Section 5-5

1. Which command lines could be used to enable a ROM in an 8088-based system?
2. What is the advantage of using partially decoded addressing as opposed to fully decoded addressing?
3. What is the advantage to programming the 8088 interrupt vectors in RAM?
4. A certain ROM chip is to be activated (selected) when and only when address bus lines A_{12} through A_{19} and $\overline{\text{MRDC}}$ are low (logic 0). Draw the logic diagram for a decoder circuit that will meet these requirements.
5. When using bit-oriented memory devices in the design for an 8088-based microcomputer, how many chips will be selected during a given read or write cycle?
6. Why are low-power Schottky devices often used in the design of address decoding circuits?
7. Under what conditions will a parity check detect memory errors?

SUMMARY

This chapter has presented some of the basic principles behind the operation and interfacing of memories and memory circuits. Several of the available memory decoding circuits and methods of designing them have also been presented. With this information, the reader should now be able to understand how memory devices work, why certain types of memory are preferred in certain situations, and the advantages and disadvantages of using one type of memory versus another.

Most current memory devices are random access devices, which are available in static and dynamic forms. Static RAM is relatively easy to interface to a system, but has low storage density (fewer bits for a given chip area). Dynamic RAM can be produced with extremely high storage density, but is difficult to design into a system. The various types of ROM available include mask programmed ROM, fusible link PROM, erasable

PROM (EPROM), and electrically alterable PROM (EAPROM). The transistors used to make up the storage cells in EPROMS and EAROMS are enhancement-mode FETs. Mask-programmed and fusible link read-only memories may be constructed using either MOS or bipolar technology.

Serial or sequential memory devices are also available for computer applications. These devices are accessed in such a way that information is shifted out 1 bit at a time. The average time delay produced by this serial access is called latency time. Magnetic bubble memories and charge coupled devices are the main types of serial memories being produced.

Memory maps are used as a guide to memory placement in microcomputer design and in interfacing applications. Once a memory map is completed, the various memory decoding circuits are designed. Most often, a given device or group of devices will be fully decoded, which gives each byte of memory its own unique address. Standard LS TTL gates may be used in the design of the decoder, and often medium-scale integration (MSI) decoders are used to select a given block of memory locations.

The technique of partial decoding simplifies hardware design, but creates foldback addresses, those addresses at which a given device may be accessed but which were not necessarily intended in the original design.

CHAPTER QUESTIONS

5-1. What are the basic storage cells that are used to produce static RAM?

5-2. If very low power dissipation was a major concern in the design of a microcomputer, what type of static RAM devices would be used?

5-3. What class of semiconductor memory devices is not considered to be random access?

5-4. What is the purpose of the $\overline{CAS}$ input on a dynamic RAM?

5-5. Which dynamic RAM refresh method will probably delay the CPU access to memory most frequently?

5-6. What is the term given to the average time required for a given bit to be shifted out of a serial memory device?

5-7. Why are bipolar static RAMs not produced with storage densities as high as MOS static RAMs?

5-8. Refer to Fig. 5-41. Why is it not necessary to make the output of this address decoder dependent upon the memory read or write command lines as well as the given address lines?

5-9. How often must a typical dynamic RAM cell be refreshed?

5-10. Quite often, NAND gates are the primary gates used in the design of address decoding circuits. Why do you think this is so? (*Hint:* Check a logic data reference book.)

CHAPTER PROBLEMS

5-11. A certain dynamic RAM's storage cells arranged in a 256×256 matrix. Assume that each cell must be refreshed once every 4 ms, $t_{cy} = 350$ ns, and rows are refreshed one at a time. Using $\overline{RAS}$-only burst-mode refresh, how long does it take to refresh the device?

5-12. How many address pins would the dynamic RAM of Problem 5-11 require if the row and column decoders are multiplexed?

5-13. In reference to the RAM of Problem 5-11, on the average, what percentage of the memory's time is taken up by the refresh operation?

5-14. Redraw the diode matrix section of Fig. 5-13a such that the ASCII code representations for the letters A through P are produced when binary inputs are 0000 through 1111, respectively.

5-15. Are static RAMs considered to be volatile devices? Why?

5-16. Redesign the decoder of Fig. 5-27 such that the starting address of the ROM is at absolute address $FA000_{16}$.

5-17. Design a decoder based on the 74LS139 that will select one of four $8K \times 8$ ROMs, beginning at absolute address $F0000_{16}$.

5-18. Design the decoding circuits for blocks 2 and 3 of Fig. 5-30, based on the memory map of Fig. 5-29.

5-19. Obtain the logic diagram for the 74LS138 1 of 8 decoder, and redesign the circuit in Fig. 5-39 based on this substitution.

5-20. A certain $64K \times 8$ block of RAM is partially decoded by the circuit in Fig. 5-44. How many address locations are actually occupied by the RAM, and what are the starting and ending addresses of each "image" of the RAM? (The images of the RAM are those address spaces where the RAM appears to be located.)

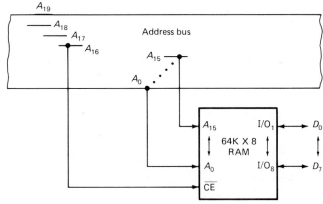

Fig. 5-44 Circuit for Problem 5-20.

I/O INTERFACING FUNDAMENTALS

A microprocessor would be of little practical use if there was no way of enabling it to communicate with the outside world. The computer is given access to the outside world through input and output channels called ports. Most often, some type of peripheral device provides the interface between the user and the computer. A few obvious examples of practically indispensable peripheral devices are keyboards and video displays. Since the first step required that allows the computer access to the outside world is a port, this chapter will start by presenting the details of several different port options.

The addition of ports permits the computer to control and respond to events that occur outside of itself. It is in the area of interfacing where some of the most interesting of computer circuits are encountered. Interfacing may often involve a wide range of both linear (analog) and digital circuitry. For example, in order for a computer to read a certain type of joystick (a potentiometric joystick), two resistance values that represent the position of the joystick must be converted into digital format. Such applications rely on both linear and digital circuit design techniques.

A few of the concepts behind I/O interfacing were presented in Chap. 4. This chapter will expand on those basic 8088 interfacing techniques that were previously introduced, and also present some others. The I/O port designs presented in this chapter will be based upon the operation of the 8088 in the maximum mode, with demultiplexed address and data buses implemented.

6-1 I/O FUNDAMENTALS

There are as many different port designs as there are persons designing them. As such, a very generalized approach to I/O concepts will be presented in this section.

6-1.1   Programmed I/O

Perhaps the simplest way of interfacing a computer with the outside world is through the use of a technique called programmed I/O. In this method of strict programmed I/O, a given port is entirely under control of the program currently in progress. For example, let us assume that a certain device is connected to an output port that is controlled strictly by software. Depending on the nature of the device being controlled by the computer, it may be possible that data or control signals can be sent to it at any time without regard to the status of that device. In such a case, it must be assumed that the external device will operate or respond properly regardless of how frequently or infrequently control signals and/or data is sent to it. This is programmed I/O in its simplest form, and is roughly analogous to the accessing of a location in RAM (for a bidirectional port) or ROM (in the case of an input-only port).

6-1.2   Polled I/O

A more flexible method of I/O control that is a variation of strict programmed I/O is called polled I/O. In polled I/O, the software must take into account consideration of whether or not the external device is ready to accept or transmit further data or control signals to or from the port. Many different peripheral devices such as printers, power control circuits, and various pieces of electronic test equipment are good candidates for polled I/O control.

When the device that is connected to the I/O port cannot be accessed at unspecified, arbitrary points in time, polling may be used to detect a state of readiness. This is accomplished by having the CPU read 1 or more status bits that are generated by the peripheral device. The signals used to indicate whether the device (or even the CPU) is ready or not for a given operation are called handshaking signals. In many applications, strict programmed I/O cannot be used. In such cases, polled I/O may be just the right technique. In general, polled I/O has the advantage of being relatively simple from both hardware and software standpoints, although not as simple as strict programmed I/O. On the debit side, however, polled I/O has the disadvantage of possibly wasting much of the CPU's time on repetitive polling operations when the external device does not require service. For example, if a certain device occasionally requires service at 500-μs intervals, the software that runs in conjunction with this device must be written such that the device is polled at this rate. However, if the majority of the time the device requires service, say, once every 10, the program must still be written such that polling occurs at the highest rate required (once every 500 μs, in this case), just in case the need arises. These possible problems limit the usefulness of polled I/O techniques in some applications.

6-1.3   Interrupt-Driven I/O

It is apparent that an external device that is connected to a programmed or polled I/O port may not have the ability to directly or immediately notify the CPU that it requires service. When such a port is given service (the port is written to or read from), it may occur arbitrarily under program control, or it may be polled. You will recall that polled I/O has the disadvantage of wasting a lot of CPU time that could be used to perform useful tasks, and programmed I/O can really be used only with devices that can be accessed at arbitrary intervals. These problems aside, programmed and polled I/O techniques are relatively simple, and that fact is enough to make them viable I/O control methods.

A more efficient way to handle peripheral devices that require service at various unpredictable times is through the use of interrupts. Basically, interrupt-driven I/O control provides the peripheral device with the ability to interrupt the execution of the program currently in progress and initiate a service routine. In this way, the peripheral device takes the computer away from its other tasks only when service is absolutely required. The net effect is an increase in processor throughput, especially when several ports are being used. As with practically all other aspects of computer operation and design, there are disadvantages that come along with the advantages. In this case, the main disadvantage is increased hardware and programming complexity in comparison with programmed and polled I/O techniques.

6-1.4   Dedicated I/O

The term dedicated I/O refers to ports (programmed, polled, or interrupt driven) that occupy locations within the I/O address space of the computer. Devices that are connected to such ports are often referred to as being I/O-mapped. The I/O address space is used for control of and communication with peripheral devices only. The 8088's IN and OUT instructions are designed to access dedicated I/O ports (as are the BASIC statements INP and OUT, which are constructed from the 8088 IN and OUT instructions). Execution of an IN or an OUT instruction will cause the bus controller to send command signals to the ports via the $\overline{\text{IORC}}$, $\overline{\text{IOWC}}$, and $\overline{\text{AIOWC}}$ lines, while a specific port address is driven onto address lines A_0 through A_{15}. This allows the 8088 to control up to 65,536 different 8-bit wide ports. All things considered, this is an astoundingly large number of ports, and in practice, it is likely that only a small fraction of this number would be used. It is important to realize though, that the potential for direct control of an extremely large number of ports does exist.

6-1.5   Memory-Mapped I/O

Although the 8088 has a separate address space and instructions that are designed specifically for I/O port access, there are still other alternatives. I/O ports may also be memory-mapped. A memory-mapped port is assigned a location within the system's memory address space, and is accessed just like a normal memory location. The Motorola 6800 CPU is an example of a microprocessor that is designed to use memory-mapped I/O exclusively, for it has no I/O instructions or I/O command lines.

The advantage to using memory-mapped I/O is that fewer command output pins are required of the CPU, and any operation that may be performed on a memory location may also be performed on a port. In an 8088-based system, memory mapped I/O ports would be controlled by the memory command lines $\overline{\text{MWTC}}$ (or $\overline{\text{AMWC}}$) and $\overline{\text{MRDC}}$. The disadvantage of memory mapped I/O is that the ports will occupy addresses in the memory space, hence reducing the available memory to some degree.

Memory-mapped I/O is normally used in smaller systems where the possibility of needing the entire memory address space for actual memory devices is not very likely. An example of such a system could be a small microprocessor-based process control device. This type of device might not require large amounts of memory, leaving much memory space available for I/O port implementation. Of course, if such a device is designed around a CPU that has no dedicated I/O instructions (such as the Motorola 6800), then memory-mapped I/O is the only alternative available.

6-1.6   Direct Memory Access

Up to this point, all of the I/O port techniques presented have had one thing in common; that is, whether a given port is to send information to the computer or receive information from the computer, that information must pass through the CPU. For example, if a series of data elements that are to be stored in RAM is to be sent to the RAM by a peripheral device, any given piece of data must be loaded into the accumulator (AL if it is byte-wide data) using the IN instruction, and then sent to the proper memory location using another instruction (probably MOV). When the previous sequence of events is presented in a little more detail, the possible speed limitations of this type of data transfer become more apparent. Consider that the transfer of each byte of data requires an instruction fetch (IN), an instruction decode, loading of data into the accumulator and then writing the contents of the accumulator into a memory location (MOV). If many bytes are to be INputed from the port, this process must be repeated over and over again. An I/O device that requires data that is stored in RAM to be supplied to it must go through a similar sequence of operations. Some applications require that many thousands of bytes of data be transferred rapidly between the peripheral and the memory in a short period of time. The time spent fetching and decoding the same instructions (most likely MOV, IN and OUT) will slow down the effective data transfer rate significantly. If there was some way of bypassing the CPU and transferring data to and from the memory and the peripheral device(s) directly, speed could be increased greatly. Direct memory access (DMA) is an I/O technique that provides a way around the CPU bottleneck, by allowing the peripheral device to do just that: read or write directly to the system's memory. A graphical representation of the paths of data flow in CPU-mediated I/O and DMA-type I/O operations is shown in Fig. 6-1a and b.

Direct memory access is relatively complex from a hardware perspective; however, implementation has been facilitated by the availability of VLSI

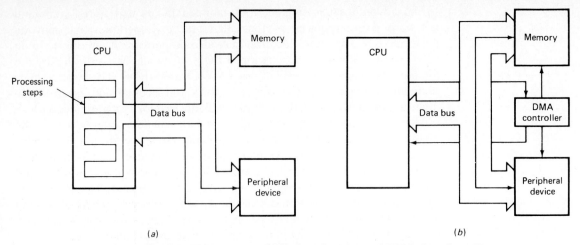

Fig. 6-1 CPU processed I/O data flow (*a*) and DMA data flow (*b*).

DMA controllers, such as the Intel 8237A. The operation of the 8237A was described in Chap. 5. Basically, a DMA transfer requires that the CPU tristate its address, data, and control lines so that the DMA controller can take over the generation of address and command signals that are required to control memory and I/O devices. You will recall that a device may take control of the various system buses by driving the 8088's HOLD input high. The 8088 acknowledges the hold request by driving HLDA high. Two examples of operations that benefit tremendously from high-speed DMA transfer are those of writing to and reading from magnetic disks. Since disk transfers are serial in nature, and data is transferred 1 bit at a time, reading and writing data would require many instructions to be fetched and decoded repetitively for each byte transferred. The DMA controller allows the direct movement of data between the memory and the disk drive without the intermediate steps of CPU generated IN and OUT operations. In fact, quite often, the maximum rate of data transfer is limited only by the speed of the memory devices in the system. If data is transferred in a parallel manner, 8 bits at a time, at a rate of 1 byte every 1000 ns (within the speed limits of most RAMs), an effective transfer rate of 8 million bits/s can be achieved.

Review Questions for Section 6-1

1. Which port control technique will generally provide a given peripheral device with the quickest service when required?
2. State two advantages associated with using memory-mapped I/O in relation to dedicated I/O.
3. What is the main disadvantage of memory-mapped I/O?
4. A certain 8-bit microprocessor has 12 dedicated I/O address lines. How many ports could be controlled directly using this CPU?
5. A certain peripheral device that uses DMA transfers data to RAM at a rate of 10,000 bits/s. How much time would be required for the device to fill a 64K byte block of memory?

6. How does a DMA controller signal the 8088 that it requires control of the address, data, and control buses? How does the 8088 acknowledge that it has transferred control to the DMA controller?

6-2 BASIC PORT DESIGN AND OPERATION

As stated previously, ports may often be treated by programs just as though they were memory locations. In many cases, the design of port circuitry is also very similar to that which is used for control and access of memory devices. This is especially true in the case of a port that is to be used for programmed I/O. The control circuitry required to implement ports that are to be driven using polled I/O techniques is also very similar to that used in memory addressing designs. Interrupt-driven ports, however, while retaining many major similarities to programmed and polled I/O ports, are more complex and require additional control circuitry. This section will cover the fundamental aspects of the implementation and applications of the various types of ports that have been introduced.

6-2.1 Dedicated Output Port Operation

The block diagram for a simple dedicated output port is presented in Fig. 6-2. This particular port is designed to occupy one location within the I/O

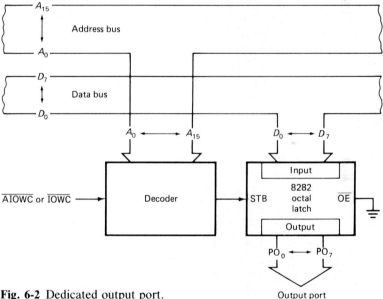

Fig. 6-2 Dedicated output port.

addressing space of an 8088-based system. Since this is an output-only port, either of the $\overline{AIOWC}$ or $\overline{IOWC}$ command lines may be used to enable the decoder. The choice of which command line is used depends on the propagation delay characteristics of the decoder and the port output circuit. In most cases, if high speed devices such as LS TTL are used, the $\overline{IOWC}$ and $\overline{AIOWC}$ command lines may be used interchangeably. The 8088's advanced command lines, $\overline{\text{AIOWC}}$ and $\overline{\text{AMWC}}$, provide extra time for slower devices (many EPROMs, for example, are relatively slow in comparison to the 8088) to respond to the CPU. The I/O address decoder itself may be designed in the same manner as the memory decoders discussed in Chap. 5. Notice, however, that only address lines A_0 through A_{15} are required to fully decode a port address, whereas fully decoding a memory location requires the use of all 20 address lines. This reduction in the number of address lines will generally allow for a reduction in the number of gates required in the port decoding circuitry, in comparison with the decoding of a single memory-mapped location.

A latch has been used to form the actual output port. This is necessary because a given byte that is being sent to the port will be present on the data bus for only a short time (less than one bus cycle). The latch holds the output for use by the peripheral after the computer has gone on to some other operation. Let us assume that the actual latch used in the port circuit of Fig. 6-2 is an Intel 8282. The pin and internal logic diagrams for the 8282 are shown in Fig. 6-3a and b. Keep in mind that another device, such as a 74LS373 octal tristate latch, could be used in place of the 8282 just as easily.

The decoder must be designed such that the occurrence of the correct port address and a low $\overline{\text{IOWC}}$ (or $\overline{\text{AIOWC}}$) signal will produce a high logic level on the 8282 STB (strobe) input. When STB is high, the inputs to the

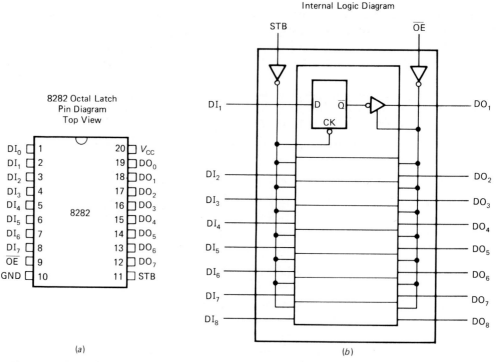

Fig. 6-3 Pin designation for the 8282 octal latch (*a*) and internal block diagram (*b*). (Courtesy of Intel Corporation.)

latch are enabled and a byte is accepted from the data bus. When the command signal ($\overline{\text{IOWC}}$ or $\overline{\text{AIOWC}}$) goes high indicating the end of the I/O write operation, STB will be driven low. This will cause the 8282 to latch the byte accepted from the data bus into the port output lines. The output of the latch (the port) will now retain this data until it is overwritten in another port output operation.

An output port such as that just described is useful for supplying a predefined sequence of control or data bytes to some external device in an asynchronous manner. In reference to this application, asynchronous means that there is no fixed time reference upon which a series of data output intervals is related. Notice, also, that no polling has to occur to allow a byte to be sent to the port. The port driver program has total control over the port.

Example 6-1

Design an address decoder for the circuit in Fig. 6-2 such that the port is located at address $AAAA_{16}$ in the I/O address space. Assume that the 8282 octal latch is to be controlled by the decoder. Standard LS TTL gates are to be used in the decoder design.

Solution

The circuit shown in Fig. 6-4 will meet the stated design requirements. The reader should notice that the port circuits presented in Figs. 6-2 and 6-4 would be used in programmed I/O applications, as no provisions have been made to allow for the input of status information (handshaking).

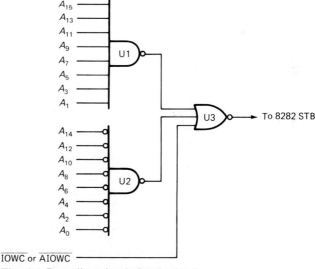

Fig. 6-4 Decoding circuit for the latch.

Example 6-2

Write the assembly language mnemonics for a program that will sequentially output the contents of absolute memory locations 00000_{16} through $003FF_{16}$ to a device that is connected to the port that was decoded in Example 6-1. Assume that the program being written will begin at address $0806:0100_{16}$.

Solution

The following program represents one solution to the assignment.

```
0806:0100        MOV DX,AAAA        ;LOAD PORT ADDRESS IN DX
0806:0103        MOV SI,0000        ;CLEAR THE SOURCE INDEX
0806:0106        MOV DS,SI          ;SET THE DATA SEGMENT POINTER TO 0000
0806:0108        MOV AL,[SI]        ;LOAD BYTE INTO AL (START OF LOOP)
0806:010A        OUT DX,AL          ;WRITE AL BYTE TO PORT (DX + AAAA)
0806:010B        CMP SI,03FF        ;LAST BYTE TRANSFERRED?
0806:010F        JE 0114            ;IF SO, PROGRAM FINISHED
0806:0111        INC SI             ;INCREMENT SOURCE INDEX
0806:0112        JMP 0108           ;REPEAT LOOP
0806:0114        INT 20             ;TERMINATE PROGRAM (DOS FUNCTION)
```

6-2.2 Dedicated Input Port Operation

The design of a dedicated input port is not quite as simple as that of the previously presented output port. An additional factor that must be considered is that since the port is to drive the data bus, provisions must be made to disable the output side of the port when the CPU is not reading it. Failure to allow for isolation of the input port will result in severe bus conflicts. In other words, when not in use (not being read), the input port should be electrically disconnected or isolated from the data bus. This may be easily accomplished by using tristate buffers in between the latch and the data bus. The block diagram for such a circuit is shown in Fig. 6-5. As noted in the block diagram, the separate octal tristate buffer and octal latch may be integrated into a single device such as an 8282 or a 74LS373. Again, let us assume that the 8282 latch is to be used in this application, since it is an octal latch with tristate outputs.

Let us now step through the sequence of events that would occur during the operation of the circuit shown in Fig. 6-5 when it is used by an IN instruction. Assuming that an IN instruction is being executed, the port address will first be driven onto the address bus. This causes the output of the address decoder to drive the 8282 STB input low. The transition from high to low on the STB pin causes data to be latched into the 8282. After the address has stabilized, $\overline{IORC}$ will go low. The $\overline{IORC}$ line is ORed with the output of the address decoder (which is still low) and applied to the $\overline{OE}$ pin of the tristate buffer section, causing the data that was previously latched (when STB went low) to be driven onto the data bus.

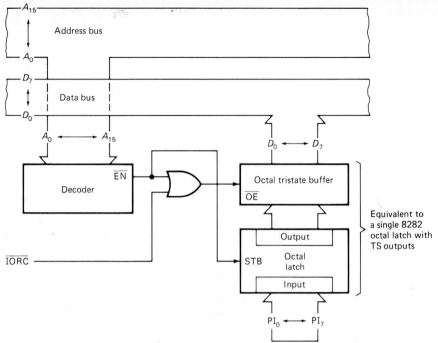

Fig. 6-5 Possible design for a latched input port.   Input port

Once the port read cycle is complete, $\overline{\text{IORC}}$ will go high, disabling the tristate buffer and isolating the port from the data bus. At the beginning of the next instruction fetch, the address will change, bringing the output of the decoder high and allowing new data to be sent into the latch.

It may be helpful to reread the preceding paragraph while turning back to the I/O read and write timing diagram in Fig. 4-30 if you are still not certain as to how the input port operates.

6-2.3   Bidirectional Ports

A bidirectional port is a port that occupies one address (memory or I/O), and may be used as either an input or an output. It is a fairly simple matter to configure the two previously discussed input and output ports such that they form a bidirectional port. Figure 6-6 illustrates one possible bidirectional port configuration.

The address decoder is comprised of gates U3, U4, and U5. The presence of the correct port address is indicated when the output of U5 is low. If an I/O write to this port is being performed, the $\overline{\text{AIOWC}}$ (or the $\overline{\text{IOWC}}$) command line will go low, causing the output of U7 to go high, strobing data from the data bus into U1. When $\overline{\text{AIOWC}}$ (or $\overline{\text{IOWC}}$) returns high, U7's output goes low, latching the data into the output of U1. All of this time, the $\overline{\text{IORC}}$ line remains high, which in turn holds $\overline{\text{OE}}$ of U2 high, tristating the output of U2. Notice that the input to U2 will be enabled whenever the correct I/O address is *not* present on the bus. This should

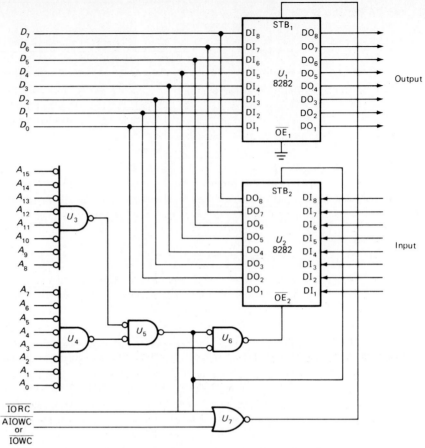

Fig. 6-6 A latched, bidirectional I/O port with address decoder.

pose no problems since the output of U2 is disabled during these times. However, at the times when U5's output does go low and a port input operation is not being performed (possibly frequently, as many different memory addresses could activate the output of U5), random garbage may be strobed into U2, overwriting previous data that was strobed in. This should not be a matter of concern, because the input port latch is not intended to be used for long-term storage. The input latch is really to be used only to hold data stable until the CPU has time to read it. If the past data applied to the input port that was overwritten was important, it would have been stored in memory at some earlier time, such as immediately after it was read.

During a read operation, the output of U5 is again driven low, latching input data into U2. This time however, both $\overline{\text{AIOWC}}$ and $\overline{\text{IOWC}}$ will remain high while $\overline{\text{IORC}}$ is driven low. When $\overline{\text{IORC}}$ is driven low, the $\overline{\text{OE}}$ pin of U2 will go low, causing transfer of data onto the data bus. $\overline{\text{IORC}}$ will then go high, tristating the output of U2 and allowing new data to be written into the input side of U2.

6-2.4 Additional Dedicated I/O Port Concerns

The three previously presented I/O mapped (dedicated) port designs (Figs. 6-2, 6-5, and 6-6) may require some modification in order to function properly in a microcomputer that uses dynamic RAM. You will recall that dynamic RAM requires periodic refreshing in order to retain the integrity of its contents. The refresh operation is usually a DMA-type operation; that is, the contents of a memory location are read and then rewritten into the original location by a refresh controller. During the times when the memory is being refreshed (or any other DMA operation is being performed), the $\overline{IORC}$, $\overline{IOWC}$ and $\overline{AIOWC}$ command lines may assume active states that would not occur under normal CPU-controlled conditions. This, in conjunction with the activity that will occur on the address bus, may result in dedicated I/O ports being activated inadvertently, possibly resulting in bus conflicts and false inputs to, and outputs from, the ports. This is obviously a situation to be avoided. In most 8088-based systems, a DMA controller (possibly an 8237A) will be used in the design of the refresh circuitry, and the CPU is not involved in the refresh operation. Circuitry that generates an address enable signal (AEN) that indicates when a DMA operation is being performed will also be included in such a system. The 8237A generates an AEN signal for just this purpose. The AEN control signal is used to disable the I/O ports (except possibly a port that is used in the DMA process) when DMA operation occurs. Figure 6-7 illustrates the addition of an active-high AEN control line to the decoding circuit of Fig. 6-4. With this modification, the port will be activated only when AEN is low. AEN is driven low by the DMA controller during normal CPU operations and it is driven high during DMA operations.

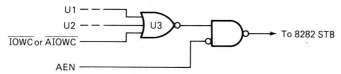

Fig. 6-7 Use of the AEN control line in an I/O address decoder is required in systems with DMA.

6-2.5 Memory-Mapped I/O Ports

The design of a memory-mapped port may be approached in a manner almost identical to that used in the design of the dedicated I/O ports discussed in the previous section. In fact, there are only two major differences between a dedicated I/O port and a memory-mapped I/O port: (1) The memory-mapped ports are controlled by the $\overline{MRDC}$ command line and either of the $\overline{MWTC}$ or $\overline{AMWC}$ command lines instead of $\overline{IORC}$, $\overline{IOWC}$, and $\overline{AIOWC}$, respectively; and (2) the address decoder output will be dependent upon the states of all 20 of the address bus lines A_0 through A_{19}, if the port address is to be fully decoded. The same basic latching and decoding circuits that were used in the dedicated I/O port may also be used in the design of a memory-mapped port. The block diagram for a memory-mapped output port is shown in Fig. 6-8.

The logic diagrams for the input and bidirectional memory-mapped ports will not be presented because they are so similar in design to the dedicated I/O ports. For example, in order to modify the diagram of Fig. 6-5 for operation as a memory-mapped port, the decoder would be expanded to the entire width of the address bus (again, if full decoding is required) and either $\overline{\text{AIOWC}}$ would be replaced by $\overline{\text{AMWC}}$, or $\overline{\text{IOWC}}$ would be replaced by $\overline{\text{MWTC}}$. Also, AEN control would not be required, if the address lines are fully decoded.

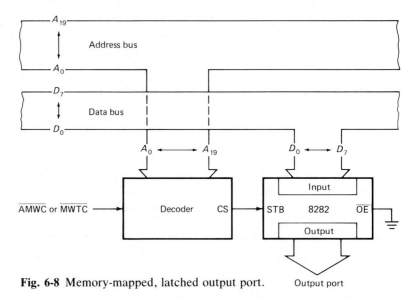

Fig. 6-8 Memory-mapped, latched output port.

Example 6-3

Draw the logic diagram for the decoder circuit that will place a memory-mapped input port at absolute address $0F000_{16}$. An 8282 octal latch is to be used in the design.

Solution

The circuit shown in Fig. 6-9 meets the stated requirements.

With slight modifications, any of the decoders presented in Chap. 4 can be used in either dedicated or memory-mapped I/O addressing designs. For example, if eight different dedicated or memory-mapped output ports are to be interfaced to a system, a 74LS138 1 of 8 decoder could be used to form the port select function. The logic symbol and function table for the 74LS138 are shown in Fig. 6-10a and b. The following example demonstrates the use of this IC in a dedicated I/O port decoding application.

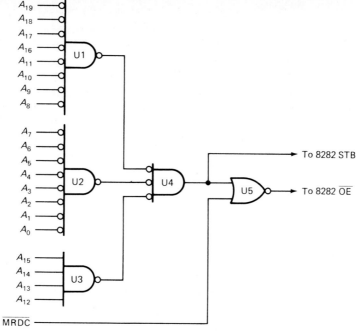

Fig. 6-9 Memory-mapped output port address decoder.

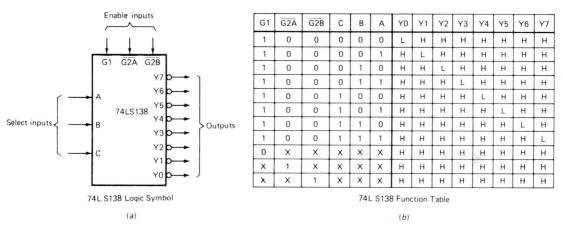

G1	$\overline{G2A}$	$\overline{G2B}$	C	B	A	Y0	Y1	Y2	Y3	Y4	Y5	Y6	Y7
1	0	0	0	0	0	L	H	H	H	H	H	H	H
1	0	0	0	0	1	H	L	H	H	H	H	H	H
1	0	0	0	1	0	H	H	L	H	H	H	H	H
1	0	0	0	1	1	H	H	H	L	H	H	H	H
1	0	0	1	0	0	H	H	H	H	L	H	H	H
1	0	0	1	0	1	H	H	H	H	H	L	H	H
1	0	0	1	1	0	H	H	H	H	H	H	L	H
1	0	0	1	1	1	H	H	H	H	H	H	H	L
0	X	X	X	X	X	H	H	H	H	H	H	H	H
X	1	X	X	X	X	H	H	H	H	H	H	H	H
X	X	1	X	X	X	H	H	H	H	H	H	H	H

74L S138 Logic Symbol

(a)

74L S138 Function Table

(b)

Fig. 6-10 74LS138 1 of 8 decoder and function table.

Example 6-4

Design the interfacing circuitry required to implement eight 8-bit dedicated output ports in a demultiplexed maximum-mode 8088-based system. The ports are to occupy I/O address locations $FF00_{16}$ through $FF07_{16}$. The 74LS138 is to be used in the port selection circuitry. Assume that AEN control is not required.

Solution

The circuit shown in Fig. 6-11 illustrates one possible solution. The occurrence of an address within the correct range will cause the output of U1 to go low, while the output of U4 will go high. When either $\overline{\text{IOWC}}$ or $\overline{\text{AIOWC}}$ goes low, indicating a read operation, U5 will be enabled. During the time interval that the output command line is low, the selected latch will be strobed to accept data (STB = 1). This occurs because the active-low outputs of U5 have been inverted. When the write command line returns high, U5 will be disabled, latching data into the selected 8282.

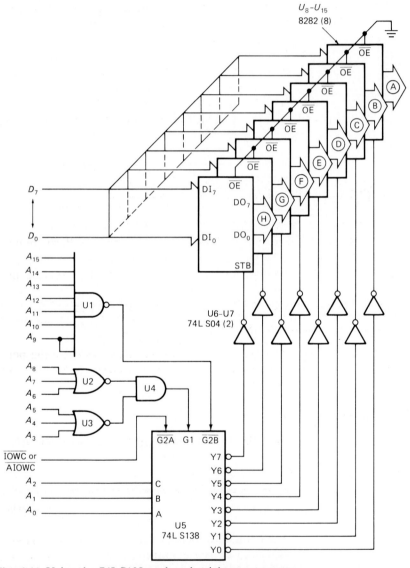

Fig. 6-11 Using the 74LS138 to decode eight output ports.

At this point, the reader should be able to adapt the circuit presented in Example 6-5 to the memory-mapped I/O approach with little difficulty. This will be left as an exercise at the end of the chapter.

Review Questions for Section 6-2

1. Refer to Fig. 6-5. If, during a memory read operation, the correct address of this port was present on the address bus, what logic levels would be present on the STB and $\overline{OE}$ inputs of the latching circuit?
2. Why is tristate buffering necessary on an input port?
3. What logic function is performed by U2 in Fig. 6-4?
4. How is an output port "informed" that there is valid data present on the data bus?
5. What logic function is performed by U4 in Fig. 6-9?
6. Refer to Fig. 6-11. Assuming the 74LS138 is enabled, which output port will be active if $A_0 = 1$, $A_1 = 0$, and $A_2 = 1$?
7. Refer to Fig. 6-11. Assuming that any given latch is active (reading data from the data bus), will any of the other seven remaining latches respond to the data on the bus? If so, how?
8. On the basis of the block diagram presented in Fig. 6-8, in general, how long will a given latch output data that was previously sent to it?

6-3 INTERRUPT-DRIVEN I/O

The problems associated with the I/O port circuits introduced in Secs. 6-1 and 6-2 should be apparent: (1) Ports requiring periodic service at relatively unpredictable intervals require large amounts of CPU time for polling; and (2) a port that requires service might not receive service quickly enough for some applications unless the CPU spends a great amount of time polling it. Both of these problems can be overcome by using interrupt-driven I/O techniques. A peripheral device that can initiate an interrupt does not have to be polled, because it can signal the CPU whenever it requires service. Also, since the peripheral can interrupt the operation of the CPU, it will generally receive service more quickly than a device that is polled.

6-3.1 8088 Interrupt Operation

The 8088 has two interrupt inputs: the interrupt request (INTR) and the (nonmaskable interrupt) (NMI). Almost all interrupt-generating I/O devices are connected to the 8088's INTR input line. You will recall that the NMI input is generally reserved for devices that signal situations of extreme emergency. The NMI pin is a positive edge triggered input that always generates a type 2 interrupt, while the INTR input is level triggered, and may be used to initiate an interrupt of any type. The significance of edge triggering versus level triggering on the interrupt inputs may be better understood when the requirements of each type of input are restated: Although the NMI input is edge triggered, the only requirement of this input is that it be held high for a minimum of two clock cycles. The NMI command will be responded to only one time, regardless of how long the NMI input is held high. Conversely, since the INTR input is level triggered, if an interrupt request remains present (INTR held high) for extended periods of time, it is possible to have repeated responses to the request. This situation may or may not present a problem, but it is easily resolved. The details of the interrupt request response will now be discussed.

The 8088 tests the INTR input during T_4 of each bus cycle. An interrupt request is initiated when an external device drives the 8088's INTR input high. Since the INTR input is level triggered, it must be held high by the external device until the 8088 senses its presence. The external device must then be informed that the interrupt request has been detected, and is ready to be acted upon. Such a response is a sequence of events called an interrupt acknowledge cycle. The interrupt acknowledge timing diagram is shown in Fig. 6-12. Notice that the interrupt acknowledge cycle consists of two parts, each 4 clock cycles long.

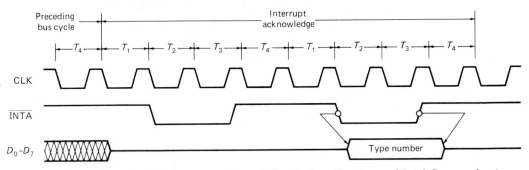

Fig. 6-12 8088 interrupt acknowledge timing. (Courtesy of Intel Corporation.)

Referring to Fig. 6-12, it is assumed that an interrupt request has occurred (the device has driven INTR high) sometime prior to T_4 of what is labeled the "preceding bus cycle." The detection of an interrupt request by the 8088 will cause the interrupt acknowledge cycle to begin. Interrupt acknowledgment is signified when the bus controller drives its $\overline{\text{INTA}}$ output low. This provides a convenient control signal that can be used to cause the interrupting device to remove the interrupt request; that is, the device that is requesting service should return the INTR line low in response to the acknowledgment. The bus controller next drives its $\overline{\text{INTA}}$ line back to logic high during T_3 of the first part of the interrupt acknowledge cycle. The bus controller will drive the $\overline{\text{INTA}}$ line low a second time during T_2 of the second half of the interrupt acknowledge bus cycle. $\overline{\text{INTA}}$ will then be driven high during T_3. The interrupting device must supply an interrupt type number to the 8088 (via the data bus) during the time that $\overline{\text{INTA}}$ is low within the second bus cycle. The first half of the interrupt acknowledgment cycle is also used by the 8088 to generate a bus $\overline{\text{LOCK}}$ signal. This prevents other processors (or possibly a DMA controller) that may be sharing the same bus in a multiprocessor system from interfering with the interrupt housekeeping chores.

The interrupt type number that is supplied to the 8088 by the interrupting device is automatically multiplied by four within the CPU. This is done to allow any of the 256 available interrupt vectors to be addressed by a 2-digit (1 byte) hex number. You will recall that the interrupt vectors occupy absolute addresses 00000_{16} through $003FF_{16}$ in memory, and each vector occupies 4 consecutive bytes. Since the data bus is only 8 bits wide, and a 3-digit (12-bit) hex value is required to specify the vector, the internal multiplication by four allows the vector type to be specified by 1 byte in a single read operation. A conceptual diagram showing how the absolute address of the first byte of an interrupt vector is generated is shown in Fig. 6-13. This address is used to access the vector corresponding to a given interrupt number (Int.# $B1_{16}$, in this case). A given vector is written into the CS and IP registers, and is used to specify the beginning of an interrupt service routine.

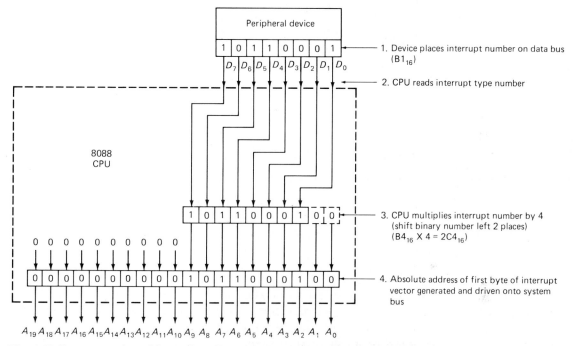

Fig. 6-13 Representation of formation of the absolute address from an interrupt type number.

Before the interrupt vector is loaded into the CS and IP registers, the contents of both of those registers and the flags are automatically pushed into the stack. Any other registers that contain critical data that may be altered by the service routine must be saved (most likely pushed into the stack) by the service routine itself in order to prevent their contents from possibly being overwritten or altered in some way. Also, after the flags are pushed, the IF (flag) is cleared. This prevents other INTR inputs from being honored while the 8088 is performing the internal housekeeping required to begin execution of the current interrupt request. Once the service routine has begun, the IF will remain cleared. If it is necessary to have the IF set, this must be done by the service routine itself. Such setting of the IF by the service routine allows for the possibility of nested interrupts. Nested interrupts are interrupts that occur within interrupts; that is, if during the course of execution of an interrupt routine another interrupt request should occur, the current service routine would be suspended and the device requesting service would be honored. Of course, if the IF is not set after the service routine has begun, no further interrupt requests will be honored until the current service has been completed (if IF = 1 when the flags are popped at the end of the service routine), with the exception of a nonmaskable interrupt.

Example 6-5

A certain I/O device initiates an interrupt request. The interrupt type number supplied to the 8088 is 0018_{16}. What absolute hex addresses are occupied by the vector that is being pointed to?

Solution

The address of the first byte of the interrupt vector is found by multiplying the interrupt number times 4.

$$18_{16} \, 4 = 60_{16}$$

The vector occupies the following absolute addresses expressed as 8-bit hex numbers.

00060_{16} [IP LOW]
00061_{16} [IP HIGH]
00062_{16} [CS LOW]
00063_{16} [CS HIGH]

Note that a hexadecimal number may be multiplied by 4 rather easily by converting it into binary form and shifting left two places. The shifted binary number may then be converted back into a hexadecimal number that is 4 times the original value.

6-3.2 An Interrupt-Driven Input Port

On the basis of the somewhat complex sequence of actions of the 8088 during an interrupt request-acknowledge operation, we find that an I/O port can use the INTR line to request service. However, the timing constraints imposed in such a case require more sophisticated port circuitry than that discussed earlier. The circuit shown in Fig. 6-14 is one possible interrupt-driven port design. This particular circuit is designed specifically to control a 1-byte-wide input port. The operation of this circuit is described

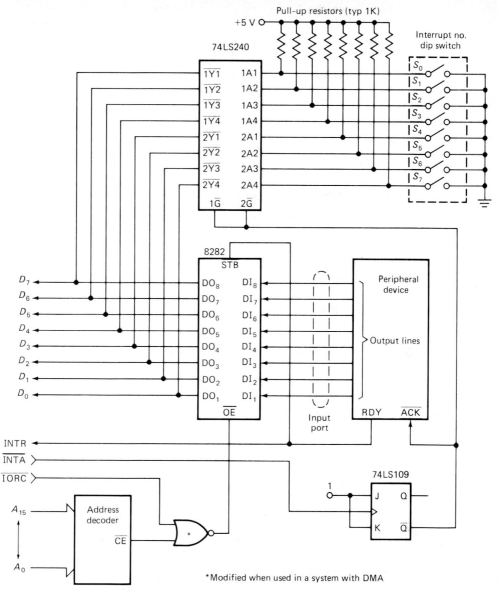

Fig. 6-14 Circuit for an interrupt-driven input port.

by the following steps and the timing diagram of Fig. 6-15. At the outset, let us assume that the 74LS109 JK flip-flop is cleared ($\overline{Q} = 1$). This would be the case under normal circumstances.

1. The peripheral device signals the 8088 that it is ready to supply a byte of data to the data bus by driving its RDY output high. This drives the 8088's INTR input high, and also enables the 8282 latch to accept the input byte. It is assumed that the input device continues to assert the interrupt request until its $\overline{ACK}$ input is driven low.

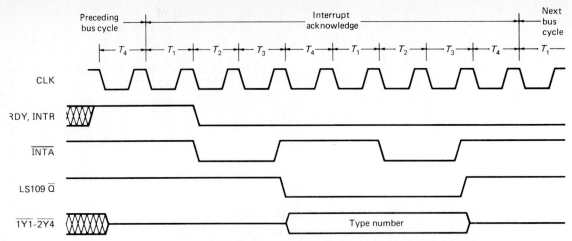

Fig. 6-15 Timing diagram for the interrupt-driven input port during interrupt acknowledge.

2. The 8088 detects the interrupt request, and if the IF = 1, it initiates the first interrupt acknowledge cycle, during which $\overline{\text{INTA}}$ is driven low. Note that the 74LS109 will remain in the cleared state because it is a positive (rising) edge triggered device.

3. The 8088 then drives $\overline{\text{INTA}}$ high, which toggles the 74LS109 positive edge triggered flip-flop. This causes $\overline{Q}$ to go low, signaling to the peripheral device that the interrupt has been acknowledged. $\overline{Q}$ also enables the 74LS240 tristate octal bus driver, which places the interrupt type number onto the data bus.

4. The input device now responds by driving its RDY output low, which removes the interrupt request and latches the data into the 8282.

5. In the second interrupt acknowledge cycle, the 8088 fetches the interrupt number from the data bus while $\overline{\text{INTA}}$ goes low a second time.

6. The 8088 drives $\overline{\text{INTA}}$ high, which toggles the flip-flop, and tri-states the output of the 74LS240. This removes the interrupt type number from the data bus.

7. The data stored in the 8282 may now be accessed by the interrupt service routine via the IN instruction. The address of the port would be determined by the circuitry within the address decoder.

Observe that in Fig. 6-14, the interrupt number is user-programmable via a DIP switch. It is common practice to allow the system user to make some operational feature and hardware changes with DIP switches. For example, many printers use such a method to allow the user to enable or disable certain features, such as slashed 0s, italics, special graphics symbols, and so on. In the port design just presented, the interrupt number is programmed prior to operation based on the following considerations.

1. When a given switch is open, its associated 74LS240 input is pulled to logic 1 by a pull-up resistor. That level is inverted by the 74LS240, and may then be applied to the data bus as a logic 0 when the output is enabled.

2. When a given switch is closed, that input of the 74LS240 is pulled to ground (logic 0). When the output of the 74LS240 is enabled, a logic 1 will be presented to that line of the data bus.

In this particular design, S_0 represents the most significant bit of the interrupt type number and S_7 represents the least significant bit.

In reference to Fig. 6-14, it should also be mentioned that if this port is to be used in a system that has DMA capability, the AEN control line should be taken into account in the port design, since bus conflicts could arise if the port is inadvertently activated during a DMA operation. The modification of Fig. 6-14 that would be required for an active-high AEN control is shown in Fig. 6-16. A three input OR gate is all that is needed to combine the three control lines that drive the $\overline{OE}$ pin of the tristate latch, because all three lines ($\overline{INTA}$, AEN, and $\overline{IOWC}$ or $\overline{AIOWC}$) must be low in order to enable the output of the latch.

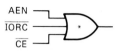

Fig. 6-16 Required modification to the circuit in Fig. 6-14 if used in a system with DMA.

Most often, the I/O port circuitry required by a given peripheral will be built into that particular device, that is, designed to work with a particular system (an IBM PC, Apple IIe, Commodore 64, and so on). In this way, the user need not be concerned (hopefully) about the compatibility of the device and the port circuitry. Many peripheral devices are also supplied with software that allows them to be used more easily. Such software could possibly be written such that the interrupt vectors and service routines that the device requires for proper operation are written into RAM upon start-up. It is also common for various I/O devices to use the various interrupt service routines that reside in the system ROM.

6-3.3   An Interrupt-Driven Output Port

An interrupt-driven output port can be designed that is very similar in many respects to the input port of Fig. 6-14. Using the design of Fig. 6-14 as a starting point, one might ask what different requirements an output port would need as opposed to the input port? Let us begin by outlining the basic characteristics for a hypothetical application. These requirements are listed below.

1. When the peripheral device that is connected to the port requires data from the computer, it will request service via the INTR input of the 8088. This particular peripheral is requesting a byte of data to be sent to it via the data bus.
2. If the CPU honors (acknowledges) the request, it will require the interrupt type number to be placed on the data bus. At this time, the device requesting service should remove the interrupt request (pull the 8088 INTR line low).
3. The CPU begins execution of the service routine.
4. The service routine addresses the port and sends data to the output latch to which the interrupting device is connected.

Now that some general guidelines have been presented, the actual circuit design process may begin. Rather than duplicating previous efforts, let us adapt as many features of the input port in Fig. 6-14 as practical in the design of the output port. A review of the description of the operation of the port in Fig. 6-14 reveals that the same interrupt number generating circuitry (the 74LS240, DIP switch, and pull-up resistors) and the interrupt acknowledge flip-flop may be employed, as is, in the output port design. This is so because the actions of these sections of the circuit are independent of whether a port read or write operation is being requested. Such details are determined by the service routine whose vector is supplied by the circuit. It may also be concluded that the 8282 tristate octal latch may also be used, except that now the input side will be connected to the data bus, while the output side will be connected to the external device. In this case, however, since data is being taken from the data bus, the CPU (actually the bus controller) will be used in conjunction with the address decoder to strobe data into the output latch. The address decoder section of the output port could be designed using any of the techniques presented earlier in this chapter. With all of this information taken into consideration, the circuit shown in Fig. 6-17 is one possible result. This circuit is very similar

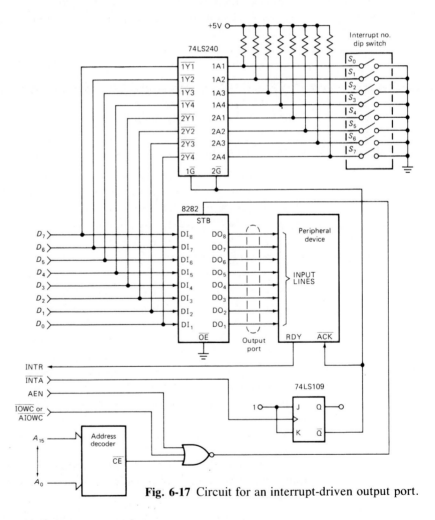

Fig. 6-17 Circuit for an interrupt-driven output port.

to the interrupt-driven input port from which it was derived. For the sake of clarity, those parts of Fig. 6-17 that differ from those of Fig. 6-14 are shown in color. Also notice that the design has been modified to allow the AEN control line to be implemented.

A step-by-step description of the operation of the interrupt-driven output port will now be presented. The DIP switches $\overline{S}_0$ through $\overline{S}_7$ operate as described earlier, and are used to program in the desired interrupt number. The timing diagram in Fig. 6-15 is valid for this circuit also.

1. The peripheral device needing service drives its RDY output high, starting the interrupt request sequence.
2. The CPU responds by pulsing $\overline{\text{INTA}}$ low two consecutive times. On the rising edge of the first pulse, $\overline{Q}$ of the flip-flop toggles low, enabling the tristate bus driver (74LS240) to drive the interrupt type number onto the data bus. (See Fig. 6-15.) This also signals the peripheral device that the interrupt request has been received and is being acted upon. The peripheral device should now drive its RDY output low.
3. On the rising edge of the second $\overline{\text{INTA}}$ pulse, $\overline{Q}$ of the flip-flop toggles back to the logic high state, tristating the 74LS240, which removes the vector type number from the data bus.
4. When the service routine has a byte available for the port, it will address the port, causing $\overline{\text{CE}}$ and $\overline{\text{IOWC}}$ or $\overline{\text{AIOWC}}$ to go low. These two signals are NORed with the AEN line (AEN is normally low) to produce a logic 1, which in turn strobes the byte present on the data bus into the 8282 latch. When $\overline{\text{IOWC}}$ or $\overline{\text{AIOWC}}$ returns high, the input side of the latch will be disabled. Data is now available to the peripheral device that is connected to the output of the latch.

For the most part, the operation of this circuit is very much like that of the input port of Fig. 6-14. The differences between the two circuits are few. Notice in Fig. 6-17 that the output enable ($\overline{\text{OE}}$) pin of the 8282 is connected to ground. This connection causes the latch to hold the byte that was strobed into it until new data is strobed in again at some later time. If it was necessary to tristate the output of the 8282, the peripheral device itself would probably be given this task, as the CPU would have no way of knowing exactly when the peripheral required such a condition to exist, without the addition of more circuitry and therefore greater complexity.

A few other points regarding the operation of the circuits of Figs. 6-14 and 6-17 are now in order. As with any other dedicated I/O port design, DMA transfers (such as those that occur during memory refresh operations) could activate the port, causing bus conflicts. This problem was discussed earlier in this chapter, and would be handled in the same way as before; that is, the I/O address decoder must be designed such that the AEN control line (or its equivalent) is used to enable the interrupt type number generating and port latching circuitry.

A second problem that must be overcome will occur when more than one interrupt-driven device or port is connected to the system. As an example, let us consider a situation in which the RAM refresh operation is initiated by control circuitry that generates an interrupt request. Most microcomputers use a timer that generates refresh interrupts at periodic intervals as required by the RAM. This is the case with the IBM PC. The bus controller responds to the refresh request in the same manner that it would for an interrupt request generated by the circuits in Figs. 6-14 and 6-17 (see Fig. 6-15). It is apparent that when the bus controller drives $\overline{\text{INTA}}$ high, in response to the refresh interrupt request, we wish to activate only the refresh circuitry. However, in the designs that have been presented (Figs. 6-14 and 6-17), any given interrupt response that occurs (the two $\overline{\text{INTA}}$ pulses) would cause the 74LS109 to respond to the bus-controller-generated $\overline{\text{INTA}}$ signal and force the 74LS240 to drive an interrupt number onto the data bus. Here again, bus conflicts will arise, as the port can be activated while DMA is taking place.

All of the aforementioned information, plus the fact that the 8088 has only one interrupt request input, means that some sort of interrupt control circuitry must be devised to handle several different interrupt-driven devices (including refresh circuitry). Such a circuit would be responsible for the coordination of all devices that request service through the generation of interrupt signals, and possibly for the prioritization of the various interrupt-generating devices.

Interrupt prioritization is often required in many applications. For example, refreshing the contents of the system's dynamic RAM is most likely going to be more critical to system operation than sending data to a printer that also generates an interrupt when it requires service. After all, it would be foolish to sacrifice the contents of the RAM just so that higher printer speeds can be achieved. Also, it could be useful to have the interrupt control circuitry allow its interrupt request inputs to be selectively ignored or masked off. The design of this type of interrupt controlling device could be quite complex, especially if options such as program control of masking and priority reassignments are desired. Fortunately, the 8088 family provides a solution to this problem, which is presented in the next section.

Review Questions for Section 6-3

1. How long and at what logic level must the 8088's NMI input be held in order to guarantee response?
2. What device generates the $\overline{\text{INTA}}$ signal in a maximum mode 8088-based system? To which device are interrupt request signals applied?
3. Where are the contents of the status flag, CS, and IP registers saved when an interrupt is serviced?
4. When should a peripheral device remove an interrupt request signal?
5. Which 8088 interrupt input has the highest priority?
6. What is the term given to the assignment of various levels of importance to multiple interrupt inputs?

In the most general terms, the act of connecting any device to the CPU (memory devices included) could be considered interfacing, although not necessarily to the outside world. Interfacing various devices (dynamic RAM and disk drives, for example) to a computer can prove to be among the most difficult of tasks. To help ease the burden on designers and programmers, various single-device building blocks are available. Two such devices that will be covered in this section are the Intel 8259A programmable interrupt controller and the 8255A programmable peripheral interface. Both of these devices are very flexible and allow the programmer and designer many different options. Because of their flexibility, it is rather difficult to fully understand and appreciate the various modes and applications in which these two devices can be used. To this end, only introductory explanations of these chips will be presented. The interested reader is referred to the *Intel Microsystem Components Handbook* for full operational and programming details of these two devices.

6-4.1 The 8259A Programmable Interrupt Controller

The Intel 8259A programmable interrupt controller (PIC) is a very flexible interrupt-driven I/O controller that is compatible with both the 8088 CPU and the older 8080 and 8085 CPUs. This discussion will be limited to 8088-based operation. The internal block diagram for the 8259A is shown in Fig. 6-18.

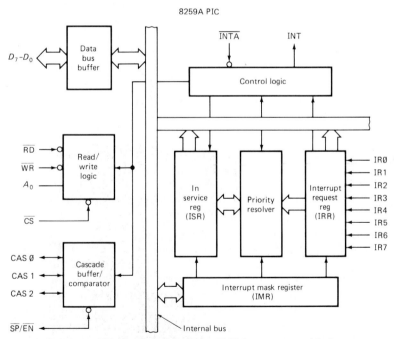

Fig. 6-18 Internal block diagram of the 8259A programmable interrupt controller. (Courtesy of Intel Corporation.)

The 8259A is designed to handle up to eight prioritized vectored interrupts for the CPU, via its interrupt request lines IR0 through IR7. These interrupt request inputs are prioritized, and unless programmed otherwise, the IR0 input is assigned the highest priority. The remaining interrupt request inputs are assigned descending values of priority down to IR7, which is the lowest. Any combination of the various IR inputs may also be masked under program control. A block diagram representation of how the 8259A PIC may be set up to control eight I/O devices is shown in Fig. 6-19. Using

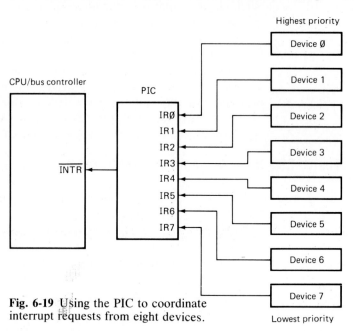

Fig. 6-19 Using the PIC to coordinate interrupt requests from eight devices.

prioritized interrupts allows devices whose operation is more critical to be serviced more quickly and efficiently. For example, if two devices request service at the same time, say the devices connected to lines IR0 and IR4, the one with the highest priority (IR0) will be serviced first. However, since the 8259A is programmable, the priority assignments can be changed as required in a given situation.

For greater flexibility, the PIC can be programmed to ignore any or all of the IR inputs, depending on the state of the interrupt mask register (IMR). The IMR is an 8-bit register. Each bit in the IMR is associated with a specific interrupt request (IR) input line. Writing logic 0 into a given mask bit will enable the corresponding IR input line, while setting the mask bit to logic 1 will disable the IR line. All IR inputs that are not masked (their mask register bits are low) retain their normal priorities. A specific instruction or command word is supplied to the PIC to program the mask register contents. Whenever an interrupt request is sent to the CPU, by the PIC, the bit that represents the interrupt line within the interrupt service register (ISR) that was activated is set. The PIC will not respond to further interrupt requests until the ISR bit is reset to 0 with a special programming word called an end of interrupt (EOI) instruction, or EOI command word. Command word instructions will be discussed in more detail later in this section.

The PIC can be written to or read from for programming and control purposes. The $\overline{CS}$ input is active low, and is used in conjunction with $\overline{RD}$, $\overline{WR}$, and A_0 to enable the chip. Normally, the PIC will be assigned a location within the I/O address space of the system in which it is used. The PIC is programmed by writing command words to it through normal CPU OUT operations. The status of the 8259A's internal registers can be ascertained by reading them with the IN instruction. As usual, an I/O address decoder could be designed to provide the necessary chip select control signal.

Command words that are issued to the PIC fall into two categories: initialization command words (ICWs) and operation command words (OCWs). As the name implies, ICWs are used to determine the initial operating mode of the PIC. Default ICWs would be written to the PIC upon power-up or during a system reset. If so desired, the PIC may be reinitialized at any time. The first ICW is issued to the PIC through a port write operation where $A_0 = 0$ and $D_4 = 1$ (the A_0 input is used by the PIC to decode command words and is usually connected to A_1 of the address bus). This instruction is called initialization command word 1 (ICW1), and its structure is shown in Fig. 6-20. The bits shown in color are used only in 8080/8085-based systems and may be ignored when the PIC is used with the 8088. Writing ICW1 automatically clears the PIC interrupt mask, which enables all of the IR inputs. Bit D_0 (IC4) must always be set when the PIC

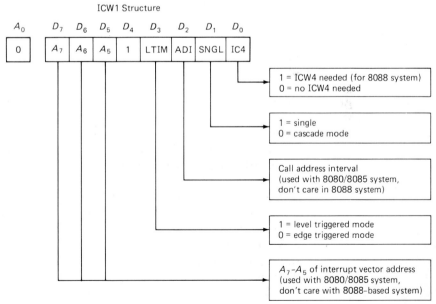

Fig. 6-20 Format for initialization control word 1 of the PIC. (Courtesy of Intel Corporation.)

is used with the 8088, because a later instruction (ICW4) is required to set the PIC up for operation with the 8088. D_1 (SNGL) is used to select single or cascade operation. Cascading is required when the PIC is used to control other PICs. Bit D_3 (LTIM) configures the interrupt request register such that the IR inputs are either rising edge or level triggered. Bit D_4 must be set for proper decoding of the control word. The remaining bits that are written to the PIC are ignored when the PIC is used in 8088-based systems.

Interrupt command word 2 (ICW2) is written to the PIC following ICW1 and is used to define the address of the first byte of eight successive interrupt vectors. This group of vectors is used by the devices that are coordinated by the PIC. You will recall that an 8088-based system reserves the first 400_{16} bytes (00000_{16} through $003FF_{16}$) of memory for interrupt vectors. The 8259 uses ICW2 to determine which group of eight vectors it is to use when it is requesting service for a given device. The device connected to the IR0 input of the PIC will be serviced by the routine pointed to by the first vector of the group. Successively lower priority inputs are assigned to the vectors such that IR7 is serviced by the routine that is pointed to by the last vector of the group. The format for the ICW2 byte is shown in Fig. 6-21a. Once again, the colored sections of the

ICW2 Structure

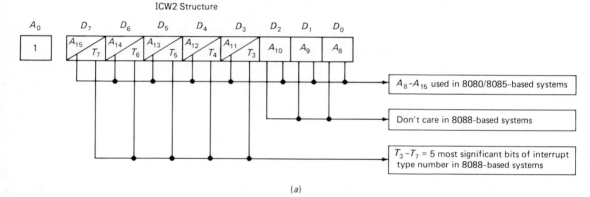

(a)

Interrupt Vector Byte Content
(8088-based system)

	D_7	D_6	D_5	D_4	D_3	D_2	D_1	D_0
IR7	T_7	T_6	T_5	T_4	T_3	1	1	1
IR6	T_7	T_6	T_5	T_4	T_3	1	1	0
IR5	T_7	T_6	T_5	T_4	T_3	1	0	1
IR4	T_7	T_6	T_5	T_4	T_3	1	0	0
IR3	T_7	T_6	T_5	T_4	T_3	0	1	1
IR2	T_7	T_6	T_5	T_4	T_3	0	1	0
IR1	T_7	T_6	T_5	T_4	T_3	0	0	1
IRØ	T_7	T_6	T_5	T_4	T_3	0	0	0

(b)

Fig. 6-21 Structure of ICW2 (a) and interrupt vector byte composition table (b). (Courtesy of Intel Corporation.)

illustration represent those functions that are used with the 8080 and 8085 CPUs. ICW2 controls operation in the following manner. After an interrupt has been requested by an external device, and the 8088 has acknowledged the interrupt, the PIC will issue an interrupt type number to the CPU that is derived from ICW2 and the particular IR pin that was activated. A table that defines the interrupt type response of the PIC is shown in Fig. 6-21b. The 5 most significant bits of the type number T_3 through T_7 will be those that were entered in ICW2 bits D_3 through D_7. The 3 least significant bits of the type number are derived according to which IR input was activated (see Fig. 6-21b). An example should help clarify the purpose of ICW2.

Example 6-6

During initialization, an 8259A was programmed such that ICW2 = 10_{16}. If at some time after initialization, a device requests service on IR3 of the 8259, which interrupt number will be produced by the PIC? At what absolute address will the interrupt vector begin?

Solution

When the interrupt request is honored, the 8259A will set the three least significant bits of the interrupt type number such that $D_2 = 0$, $D_1 = 1$, and $D_0 = 1$, as shown in the IR3 row of Fig. 6-20b. The five most significant bits of the interrupt type number will be set equal to the values of the five most significant bits of ICW2. The three least significant bits of ICW2 are ignored. Using this information, the interrupt type number is produced as shown below.

$$\text{Output from ICW2} = 0001\ 0XXX_2 \text{ (X is effectively 0)}$$
$$\text{Output from IR3} = XXXX\ X011_2$$

Adding the two quantities above produces

$$\text{Int. type no.} = 0001\ 0011_2 \ (13_{16})$$

The absolute address of the first byte of the interrupt vector may now be computed by shifting the binary representation of the type number two places to the left and setting the remaining higher order bits that compose the 20-bit address to zero. This yields

$$0000\ 0000\ 0000\ 0100\ 1100_2 \qquad (0004C_{16})$$

A third ICW is used if several 8259As are cascaded. In cascaded operation, several PICs are controlled by a master PIC. Sixty-four prioritized interrupts

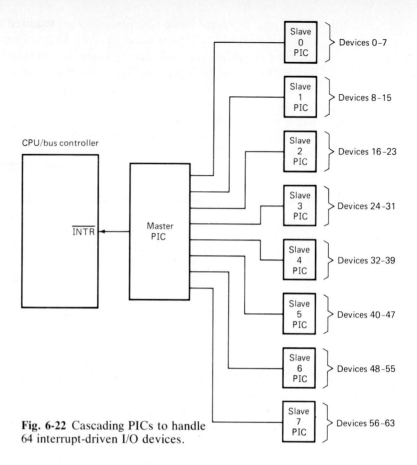

Fig. 6-22 Cascading PICs to handle 64 interrupt-driven I/O devices.

may be handled in the cascade mode, as shown in Fig. 6-22. The cascade (CAS_0, CAS_1, and CAS_2) inputs and the ICWs are used to configure the PIC for use in such systems. When a single PIC or several independent PICs are used, they will be programmed as operating in the single mode by ICW1, and ICW3 will be skipped automatically during the initialization process. The cascade mode of operation will not be covered in this text, although for the sake of completeness, the structure of ICW3 is shown in Fig. 6-23.

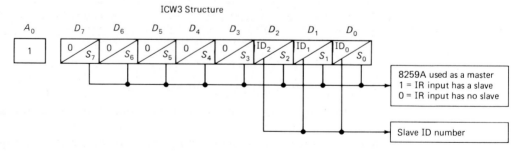

Fig. 6-23 ICW3 control word structure. (Courtesy of Intel Corporation.)

The fourth control word (ICW4) is always required when the 8259A is used with the 8088. This is because if ICW4 is skipped, the 8259A will assume the 8080/8085 mode of operation by default. The ICW4 byte is structured as shown in Fig. 6-24. Bit D_0 microprocessor mode (μPM) is

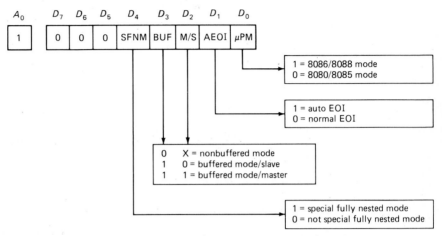

Fig. 6-24 ICW4 control word structure. (Courtesy of Intel Corporation.)

used to select between 8080- and 8088-type operation. In an 8088-based system this bit must always be set. The automatic end of interrupt (AEOI) bit D_1, is used to select the end of interrupt mode. In the automatic mode (AEOI = 1), the PIC will issue an interrupt request, wait for acknowledgment, supply a type number, and then automatically clear the in-service register (ISR). As soon as the ISR bit is cleared, higher-level interrupt requests may be sent to the CPU by the PIC, possibly allowing multiple-level interrupts. If AEOI is left cleared (no AEOI), the service routine being executed is responsible for informing the PIC that other interrupts may be processed, by supplying an end of interrupt (EOI) command. Bit D_2 (M/S) sets up the PIC as either a master or a slave device. When the PIC is used singly (noncascaded mode), D_2 is set. If D_3 is set, then the PIC is in the buffered mode. The 8088 system that has been developed all along in this text is buffered; that is, the data bus was buffered by latches when it was demultiplexed off of the system bus. This requires that the PIC be initialized to operate in the buffered mode. When the buffered mode is enabled, the $\overline{SP/EN}$ line acts as an output that enables and disables the bus data latches. If the PIC is not in the buffered mode, $\overline{SP/EN}$ is an input that is used to select between master and slave operation. In the nonbuffered mode, the PIC is a master if $\overline{SP/EN}$ is tied high, and if $\overline{SP/EN}$ is low, the PIC is a slave device. If ICW4 is not used, then $\overline{SP/EN}$ is used to select between master and slave operation by default. Bit D_4 is used to select operation in the special fully nested mode (SFNM is active if $D_4 = 1$). SFNM must be enabled in the master PIC of a group of cascaded devices.

After the PIC has been initialized, further instructions may be supplied to it at any time. These instructions are called operational command words (OCWs). Although the OCWs are numbered, they may be written to the PIC in any order, at any time, as required by a given application. OCW1 controls the PIC's interrupt mask register (IMR). The structure of OCW1 is shown in Fig. 6-25. Bits M_0 through M_7 are written into the IMR such

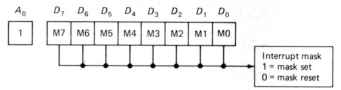

Fig. 6-25 Operation control word 1 (OCW1) structure. (Courtesy of Intel Corporation.)

that if a given bit is set to 1, its associated interrupt request input is disabled. This allows any given IR input to be masked off, or ignored.

OCW2 is constructed as shown in Fig. 6-26. This control word is used to cause rotation or to indicate the end of a given interrupt service routine.

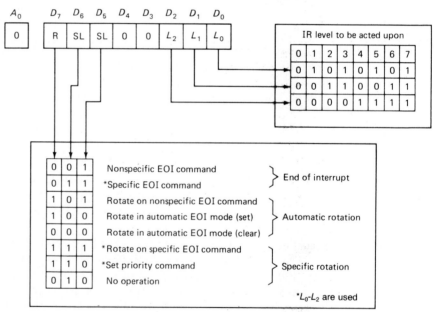

Fig. 6-26 Operation control word 2 (OCW2) structure. (Courtesy of Intel Corporation.)

Rotation refers to the changing of the priorities of the various IR inputs. There are two types of rotation: automatic rotation and rotation on nonspecific EOI. Briefly, here is what this means: In automatic rotation, the device that was serviced most recently is automatically assigned the lowest priority. This kind of operation would be used when all of the interrupt inputs are of about equal priority. Another priority modifying command that is available is the specific rotation command. Specific rotation allows the interrupt inputs to be assigned arbitrary priorities by either a service routine or a main program. There are also several other priority rotation commands available. Those commands will not be discussed in this text.

The final operational command word is OCW3. The structure of this command is shown in Fig. 6-27. Bits D_1 and D_0 of OCW3 are used to allow

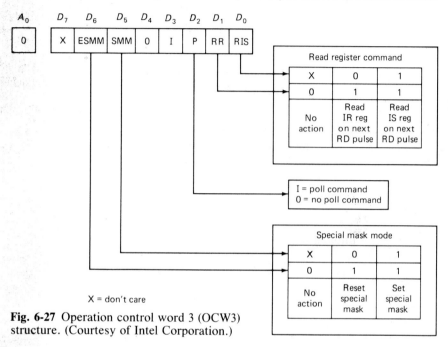

X = don't care

Fig. 6-27 Operation control word 3 (OCW3) structure. (Courtesy of Intel Corporation.)

the CPU to read the status of the various registers within the 8259A. That is, RR enables register read when set, and RIS is used to select between the IR and IS registers. D_2 is used to select either polled operation ($P = 1$) or unpolled (interrupt-driven) operation ($P = 0$). When in the polled mode, the interrupt output (INT) is not used. In this mode, the 8259A treats the next read operation (generated by polling software) as an interrupt acknowledge. The 8259A will then drive the number of the highest priority interrupt request input that was active onto the data bus in the form shown in Fig. 6-28. The polling software must then decode this information and

D_7 D_6 D_5 D_4 D_3 D_2 D_1 D_0

| I | – | – | – | – | W2 | W1 | W0 |

W0–W2: Binary code of the highest priority level requesting service

I: equal to a "1" if there is an interrupt

–: determined in ICW2

Fig. 6-28 Format of the interrupt type number sent by the PIC to the CPU. (Courtesy of Intel Corporation.)

take the appropriate action. D_5 (SMM) and D_6 (ESMM) are used to activate and select options in what is called the special mask mode. If ESMM is set, the special mask mode is enabled. In the special mask mode, the contents of OCW1 are interpreted differently than is normal; that is, normally (when the special mask mode is not active), when an interrupt is being serviced, all lower-priority IR inputs are disabled automatically. In the special mask mode, any interrupt request input (IR) whose mask bit was set by OCW1 will be enabled, whether it is of higher or lower priority than the interrupt currently being serviced. This allows lower-priority interrupt requests to be honored while a given interrupt request is being serviced.

Generally speaking, the 8259A is a fairly complex device. A complete examination of this chip and its uses could not be presented here, but a few programming examples should help clarify some of the major aspects involved in its use.

Example 6-7

Determine the initialization command words (ICWs) required to configure an 8259A for operation under the following conditions: it is an 8088-based system; a single PIC is used in the buffered mode, with auto EOI; the PIC is to use interrupt numbers $F0_{16}$ through $F7_{16}$; the IR inputs are to be in the edge triggered mode.

Solution

The ICWs are constructed and written to the PIC as presented below. Starting with ICW1:

Bit	Name	Value	Comment
D_0	IC4	1	8088 requires use of ICW4.
D_1	SGL	1	Single 8259A mode (non-cascaded).
D_2	ADI	X	Don't care (used in 8080/8085 systems).
D_3	LTIM	0	Sets IR inputs to edge triggered mode.
D_4	–	1	Always set in ICW1.
$D_5 - D_7$	$A_5 - A_7$	X	Don't care (used in 8088/8085 systems).

Arbitrarily setting all don't cares to 0:

$$\text{ICW1} = 0001\ 0011_2\ (13_{16})$$

ICW2:

Bit	Name	Value	Comment
$D_0 - D_2$	$A_8 - A_{10}$	X	Don't care (used in 8080/8085 systems).
$D_3 - D_7$	$T_3 - T_7$	01111	5 MSBs of INT TYPE number (note reversed order here).

Again, setting don't cares to 0:

$$ICW2 = 1111\ 0000_2\ (F0_{16})$$

ICW3:

Skipped automatically by 8259A when single mode selected in ICW1.

ICW4:

Bit	Name	Value	Comment
D_0	μPM	1	Selects 8088 mode.
D_1	AEOI	1	Enables automatic end of interrupt.
D_2	M/S	1	In single mode, PIC is always a master.
D_3	BUF	1	Buffered operation
D_4	SFNM	0	SFNM only used with master in a multiple PIC system.
$D_5 - D_7$	—	000	Always 0.

$$ICW4 = 0000\ 1111_2\ (0F_{16})$$

The reader must also keep in mind that the A_0 input of the 8259A must have the correct logic levels applied to it when the ICWs are written. Intel suggests that A_0 be connected to address line A_1 in 8088-based systems. As a natural consequence of this requirement, the PIC occupies at least two I/O address locations. An address decoder could be designed to decode the remaining 15 address lines, or partial decoding could be used. Again, the necessity of the AEN (or equivalent) control line would also have to be accounted for in the design of the decoder.

One possible way of connecting a single 8259A to an 8088-based system is presented in Fig. 6-29. In this example, address line A_0 and AEN alone are being used to select (enable) the PIC. This is a very simple way of decoding the 8259A, but the number of possible I/O devices that can be connected to the system is decreased dramatically (because of address foldback). However, if more than eight I/O devices are required, additional 8259As can be cascaded as necessary. Notice that as shown, the 8259A is in the buffered mode; that is, the $\overline{SP}/EN$ pin must be defined as a data latch enable line ($\overline{EN}$). This output is combined with the bus-controller-produced data enable ($\overline{DEN}$) output to demultiplex the system bus. Refer to Figs. 5-22 and 5-23 for a review of the bus demultiplexing circuitry. The reader should also notice that each peripheral device still requires its own decoding circuitry. The service routine that is initiated by the specific interrupt request is responsible for actually providing communication between the peripheral and the computer.

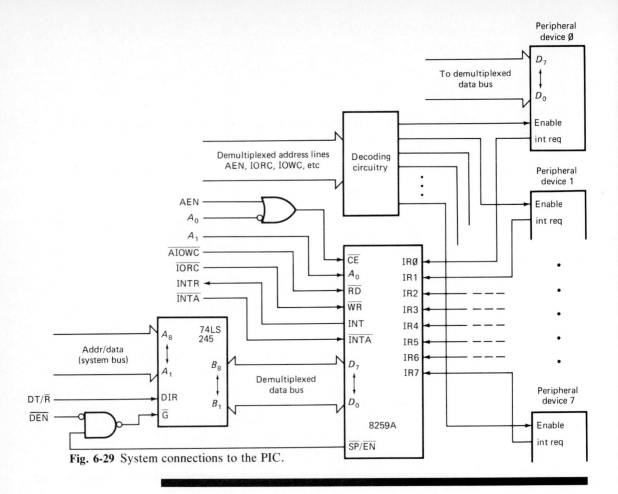

Fig. 6-29 System connections to the PIC.

Example 6-8

Assume that an 8259A, initialized as in Example 6-5, is decoded such that it occupies I/O addresses 0000_{16} and 0002_{16}, and input A_0 of the PIC is connected to address bus line A_1. Determine the construction of the OCWs that will allow the CPU to read the contents of the IR register and mask off the four most significant IR inputs. Then write the mnemonics for an assembly language program that will implement the OCWs such that the four least significant IR inputs are masked off only if they all were initially enabled (clear) when the IR register contents were read. The program is to skip the masking step if the IR inputs were already disabled (masked). The four least significant IR inputs are to be enabled if the masking step is executed.

Solution

(1) OCW construction

OCW3 and OCW1 must be used in this example. These control words are constructed as shown below.

OCW3:

Bit	Name	Value	Comment
D_0	RIS	0	Set to read ISR (not needed here).
D_1	RR	1	Read IMR on next $\overline{RD}$ pulse if set.
D_2	P	0	Polling not wanted, so write 0 here.
D_3	–	1	Always set.
D_4	–	0	Always clear.
D_5	SMM	X	Special mask mode not required here.
D_6	ESMM	0	No action (as above in D_5).
D_7	–	X	Don't care.

Arbitrarily setting all don't cares to 0:

$$OCW3 = 0000\ 1010_2\ (0A_{16})$$

OCW1:

Bit	Name	Value	Comment
$D_0 - D_3$	$M_0 - M_3$	1111	Mask off the most significant IR inputs.
$D_4 - D_7$	$M_4 - M_7$	0000	Enable the least significant IR inputs.

$$OCW1 = 0000\ 1111_2\ (0F_{16})$$

(2) Assembly Language Implementation

Since the 8259A resides at I/O locations 0000_{16} and 0001_{16}, and A_1 of the address bus is connected to the PIC's A_0 input, the addresses of the PIC must be determined accordingly.

Assuming a starting address of 0100_{16}:

```
XXXX:0100      MOV AL,0A        ;LOAD AL WITH OCW3
XXXX:0102      OUT 00           ;WRITE OCW3 TO THE 8259A
XXXX:0104      IN 00            ;READ THE CONTENTS OF THE ISR
XXXX:0106      OR AL,F0         ;SET (MASK) THE 4 MSBs OF AL
XXXX:0108      CMP AL,F         ;ARE THE 4 LSBs ALL CLEAR (IRs ACTIVE)?
XXXX:010A      JE 0110          ;IF YES THEN SKIP IMR SET OPERATION
XXXX:010C      MOV AL,OF        ;LOAD ICW1 INTO AL
XXXX:010E      OUT 02           ;WRITE OCW1 TO THE PIC (MASK IR0   R3)
XXXX:0110      ??? ??           ;THE REST OF THE PROGRAM BEGINS HERE
```

6-4.2   The 8255 Programmable Interface Controller

Up to this point, as long as interrupt-driven I/O is not required, the port designs that may be used are relatively simple. Data transfers of a byte at a time either to or from the CPU have also been the only I/O operations presented thus far. In some applications, however, it may be necessary to configure several port lines as inputs and, at the same time, configure some or all of the remaining port lines for use as outputs and/or for handshaking purposes. It may also be desirable to allow the possibility of having a program redefine the operation of a given I/O line. Designing port circuits with this kind of flexibility could be quite a complex task using standard SSI and MSI devices alone. As such, these types of circuits are generally best designed around VLSI programmable peripheral interface or control devices. Two examples of such devices are the Motorola MC6821 Peripheral interface adapter (PIA) and the Intel 8255A programmable peripheral interface (PPI). These two devices provide the designer and the user of the computer with many port options. This section will present a brief description of the 8255A PPI.

8255A Functional Description The internal block diagram for the 8255A is shown in Fig. 6-30. The I/O ports of the 8255A PPI are divided into two

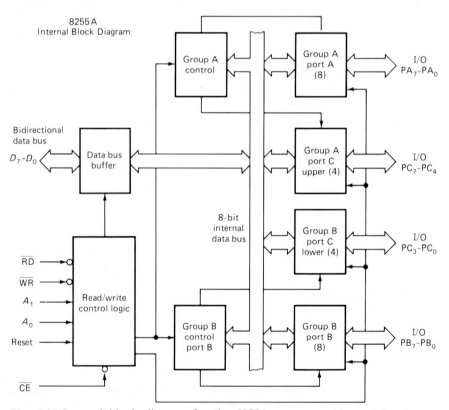

Fig. 6-30 Internal block diagram for the 8255A programmable peripheral interface. (Courtesy of Intel Corporation.)

sections: group A, which includes all 8 bits of port A and the upper 4 bits of port C, and group B, which includes all 8 bits of port B and the lower 4 bits of port C. Ports A, B, and C, and their control circuits, can be set up to operate in three different ways, called mode 0, mode 1, and mode 2. A functional block representation of the 8255A in its three operating modes is shown in Fig. 6-31.

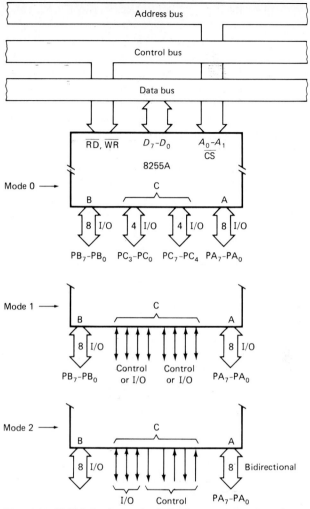

Fig. 6-31 8255A basic mode definitions and bus interface. (Courtesy of Intel Corporation.)

The operating mode for a given port is defined according to the codes presented in Fig. 6-32. Notice that in the mode definition control word format, there are no provisions for defining the operation of port C. The definitions of the port C I/O lines are not independently programmable. Instead, port C's I/O lines are automatically configured, based on the modes of operation that are selected for port A and port B. More will be said about this relationship later in this section.

As shown in Fig. 6-33, pins A_0 and A_1 are used to select a given port within the 8255A, and are normally connected to system bus address lines A_0 and A_1, respectively. The $\overline{RD}$ and $\overline{WR}$ inputs determine the direction of data transfer, and would be connected to the bus controller's $\overline{IORC}$ and $\overline{IOWC}$ (or $\overline{AIOWC}$) pins, respectively. If $\overline{WR} = 0$, then the 8255A will

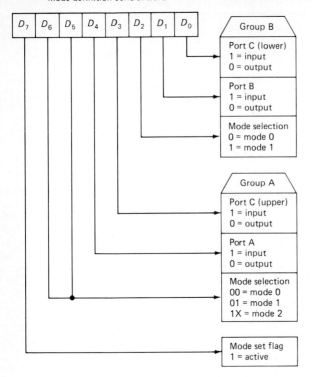

Group B

Port C (lower)
1 = input
0 = output

Port B
1 = input
0 = output

Mode selection
0 = mode 0
1 = mode 1

Group A

Port C (upper)
1 = input
0 = output

Port A
1 = input
0 = output

Mode selection
00 = mode 0
01 = mode 1
1X = mode 2

Mode set flag
1 = active

Fig. 6-32 8255A mode definition control word structure. (Courtesy of Intel Corporation.)

8255A Basic Operation

	A_1	A_0	$\overline{RD}$	$\overline{WR}$	$\overline{CS}$	Input operation (read)
1	0	0	0	1	0	Port A → data bus
2	0	1	0	1	0	Port B → data bus
3	1	0	0	1	0	Port C → data bus
						Output operation (write)
4	0	0	1	0	0	Data bus → port A
5	0	1	1	0	0	Data bus → port B
6	1	0	1	0	0	Data bus → port C
7	1	1	1	0	0	Data bus → control
						Disable function
8	X	X	X	X	1	Data bus → tristate
9	1	1	0	1	0	Illegal condition
10	X	X	1	1	0	Data bus → tristate

Fig. 6-33 8255A basic operation function table. (Courtesy of Intel Corporation.)

accept data from the bus (the CPU performs a write operation); while if $\overline{RD}$ = 0, then the 8255A will transfer data to the bus (a CPU read operation). The $\overline{CS}$ input is used to enable or select the 8255A. This pin would be connected to the output of an I/O address decoder, whose inputs are driven by system address bus lines A_3 through A_{15} (for dedicated I/O addressing) and the AEN control line, if applicable. Any time the $\overline{CS}$ input is high (the 8255A is deselected), the data bus buffer (see Fig. 6-29) is tristated and the 8255A is effectively disconnected from the data bus. The RESET input is normally connected to the master system reset line. In an 8088-based system, this signal is produced by the clock generator (see Fig. 5-2). When the reset input is driven high, all of the 8255A's internal registers are cleared and the I/O lines and the data bus buffer are tristated.

Initialization and Programming   The 8255A is programmed by writing a control byte into its control logic section using the 8088's OUT instruction. The format of such a control byte is shown in row 7 of Fig. 6-34.

As mentioned before, the ports of the 8255 may be programmed to operate in any of three modes: mode 0, mode 1, or mode 2. In mode 0 operation, the 12 I/O lines are programmed in four groups, given as PA_0 through PA_7, PB_0 through PB_7, PC_0 through PC_3, and PC_4 through PC_7. Intel refers to this as the basic input/output configuration. The basic I/O mode makes no provisions for handshaking between the peripheral side of the PPI and the CPU. Data is latched only onto the I/O lines that are

A		B		Group A		Group B		
D_4	D_3	D_1	D_0	Port A	Port C (upper)	#	Port B	Port C (lower)
0	0	0	0	Output	Output	0	Output	Output
0	0	0	1	Output	Output	1	Output	Input
0	0	1	0	Output	Output	2	Input	Output
0	0	1	1	Output	Output	3	Input	Input
0	1	0	0	Output	Input	4	Output	Output
0	1	0	1	Output	Input	5	Output	Input
0	1	1	0	Output	Input	6	Input	Output
0	1	1	1	Output	Input	7	Input	Input
1	0	0	0	Input	Output	8	Output	Output
1	0	0	1	Input	Output	9	Output	Input
1	0	1	0	Input	Output	10	Input	Output
1	0	1	1	Input	Output	11	Input	Input
1	1	0	0	Input	Input	12	Output	Output
1	1	0	1	Input	Input	13	Output	Input
1	1	1	0	Input	Input	14	Input	Output
1	1	1	1	Input	Input	15	Input	Input

Fig. 6-34 Mode 0 port definitions. (Courtesy of Intel Corporation.)

programmed as outputs. Lines that are programmed as inputs are not latched. A given port, when programmed to act as an input or output, can be redefined only by writing the appropriate command to the PPI. In Fig. 6-31, it is seen that port C is divided into two 4-bit sections. Lines PC_4 through PC_7 will automatically be set up for the same function as the I/O lines of port A, while lines PC_0 through PC_3 will assume the same function as the I/O lines of port B. A complete summary of the mode 0 port definitions is presented in Fig. 6-34. Mode 0 provides the simplest I/O configurations that are available with the 8255A.

In mode 1, called the strobed I/O mode, the 8255A's port C lines can be used for transfer of either control (handshaking) signals or data, via 4-bit I/O operations (see Fig. 6-31). Again, port C is not an independently programmable port. It is divided into two sections that are associated with the programming of ports A and B, as was the case in mode 0 operation. In mode 1, the I/O lines are latched in both input and output configurations. As with mode 0, a given port must be programmed with a control word to act as either an input or an output. Mode 2 operation allows port A to be used as a bidirectional port. Handshaking signals are sent and received over lines PC_7 through PC_3. Port B can be programmed for either input or output operation in either mode 0 or mode 1. Notice that the programmed modes of the ports can be mixed. In this case, Port A is programmed to operate in mode 2, and lines PC_3 through PC_7 are defined as being handshaking lines for port A. The three remaining port C I/O lines are defined as operating in the same mode as port B.

Ports A and B can also be programmed to operate in different mode combinations. For example, port A could be programmed to operate in mode 2, while port B is operating in mode 0 or mode 1. Port C would automatically be defined in relation to the modes chosen for ports A and B. In order to provide more insight into the 8255A, a programming example will now be presented.

Example 6-9

An 8255A PPI is used in a simple programmed I/O 8088-based system. The PPI is decoded such that it occupies I/O addresses 0000_{16} through 0003_{16}. Write the mnemonics for an assembly language program that will configure port A as an input, and port B as an output. Port C upper is to be programmed as an input, and port C lower is to be programmed as an output. Mode 0 is to be used in this application.

Solution

Using the 8255A basic operation decoding shown in Fig. 6-33, we find that address lines A_0 and A_1 must be high when a byte is to be written to the control register. This corresponds to I/O address 0003_{16}. Therefore, the control word will be written to this address when the 8255A is configured. The mode definition word that must be written to the PPI is determined using Fig. 6-32. Starting with the MSB:

Mode set flag: $D_7 = 1$

This allows the PPI to be programmed for various operating modes; that is, if the mode flag is set, the control word is interpreted by the 8255A as being a mode definition control word.

Group A mode selection Bits: $D_6 = 0$, $D_5 = 0$

Selects mode 0 operation for port A and port C upper.

Port A function selection: $D_4 = 1$

Configures port A as an input port.

Port C upper function selection: $D_3 = 1$

Configures port C upper as an input port.

Group B mode selection Bit: $D_2 = 0$

Selects mode 0 operation for port B and port C lower.

Port B function selection: $D_1 = 0$

Configures port B as an output port.

Port C lower function selection: $D_0 = 0$

Configures port C lower as an output port.

The entire control word may now be written.

$$\text{Control word} = 1001\ 1000_2\ (98_{16})$$

The assembly language mnemonics required to initialize the PPI could be written as follows.

```
XXXX:0100      MOV  AL,98      ;LOAD THE CONTROL WORD INTO AL
XXXX:0102      OUT  AL,03      ;SEND THE CONTROL WORD TO THE PPI
```

Notice that the fixed port version of the OUT instruction has been used in this example. This is possible when the port that is being read from or written to is within the first 256_{10} I/O address locations.

Because of the wide range of operating configurations available with the 8255A PPI, complete coverage of all of the functional options cannot be presented in this text. Further details of the operation of the 8255A may be found in the *Intel Microsystem Components Handbook*.

Review Questions for Section 6-4

1. Which of the 8259A's interrupt request inputs normally has the highest priority?
2. What is the function of the $\overline{\text{SP}/\text{EN}}$ pin when the 8259A is used in a demultiplexed 8088-based system?
3. Which 8259A initialization control word determines the base interrupt vector location?
4. What is the term given to the act of disabling an interrupt request input?
5. Which 8255A operating mode provides a means for handshaking between the peripheral device and the PPI?
6. If bits D_4 through D_0, respectively, are set to 1000_2 in the mode definition control word for the 8255A, and mode 0 operation is selected, which ports will be programmed as inputs and which will be programmed as outputs?

6-5 TYPICAL I/O APPLICATIONS

A few simple I/O applications will now be presented. The circuits to be discussed are typical of many that are encountered in industrial environments. In many applications, simple programmed or polled I/O is all that is required. An example would be an interface that turns certain pieces of equipment on and off at predetermined times. This would require only a simple output port and some circuitry that will isolate the computer circuitry from the devices that are being controlled. In other cases, various types of switches may be used as inputs to the computer. These switches could be used to signal the movement of parts on an assembly line, doors that are left open or closed, and many other occurrences. It is these types of applications that will be examined briefly in this section.

6-5.1 An Output Port Control Application

The circuit for a latched output port is shown in Fig. 6-35. The details of the port address decoder have been omitted for clarity. In general, this circuit is very similar to the output ports that were presented earlier in this chapter. As the usual practice for 8088-based port designs, I/O mapping has been used.

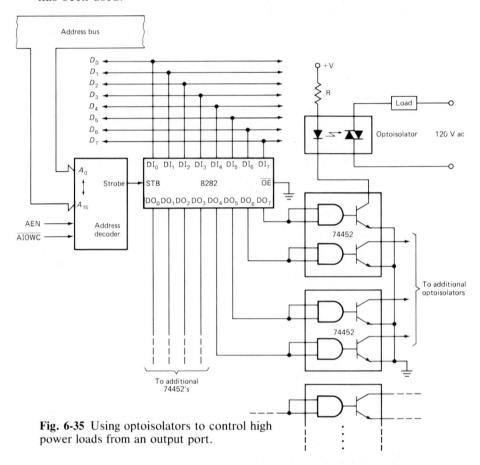

Fig. 6-35 Using optoisolators to control high power loads from an output port.

The main feature to be noted about this circuit is that the computer circuitry (the buses, address decoder, and latch) has been isolated from the devices that are being controlled. The devices used for isolation purposes are called optoisolators or optocouplers. The optoisolators used in this example contain a LED and a light-activated triac. These two devices are typically mounted inside a plastic or ceramic DIP, which allows the light emitted by the LED to illuminate the junction area of the triac. There is no electrical contact between the triac and the LED.

Triacs are members of the thyristor family of devices, with other examples being SCRs and 4-layer diodes. Triacs are bidirectional or bilateral devices, while SCRs are unidirectional. This means that a triac can be gated on during either half cycle of the ac line. Once a thyristor is gated on, it will remain on until the current flow through the device is reduced below a certain level called the holding current. This feature makes thyristors very useful for controlling the average power dissipation of a load that will operate from the ac line. Each time the line voltage crosses 0, the thyristor will turn off. In reference to Fig. 3-35, a given load will receive 100 percent power as long as the LED in the optoisolator is turned on. The LED is controlled by an integrated AND gate/NPN transistor switch (the 74452) This device is required, because most LEDs need from 20 to 100 mA for specified brightness. Writing a logic 1 to a given bit of the port will cause the transistor in the associated 74452 to be driven into saturation. This forward biases the optoisolator LED, which in turn gates on the triac. Since the port output is latched, the load will receive power for 360 degrees of the ac line cycle. Writing logic 0 to a given bit of the port will allow the appropriate triac to unlatch on the next line 0 crossing.

Circuits such as that in Fig. 6-35 are typically used to provide automatic control of motors, lights, heaters, and solenoids, just to name a few. Optoisolators can be obtained that will handle up to 5 or 10 A, with isolation ratings from a few hundred volts to over 5 kV. If even higher voltages and currents must be handled, the optoisolator can be used to drive larger SCRs, triacs, or relays.

6-5.2 An Input Port Application

The circuit in Fig. 6-36 shows how an input port may be used to monitor external events with the use of simple switches. Once again, optoisolators

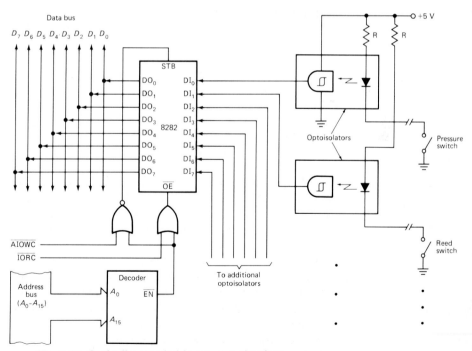

Fig. 6-36 Optically coupled input port circuitry.

are used to isolate the port circuitry from the outside world. It is always a good idea to provide such isolation. If the unexpected should occur, such as the switch line accidentaly being shorted to the 120-V ac line, only the optoisolator will be destroyed, and the computer will most likely escape serious harm. Notice that the AND gates within the optoisolators are light activated, and they also exhibit hysteresis. These are Schmitt trigger devices, which will snap on and off rapidly even if the brightness of the LED should vary at a slow rate when being turned on or off. Hysteresis also produces a deadband, which must be transited before the AND gate will change states. This provides noise immunity that may be necessary in an industrial environment.

Let us now analyze the way that this port is controlled by the computer. This circuit requires a two-step process in order for the switch status to be made available to the computer. First, in order to strobe the current status of the switches into the latches, the port must be written to. It does not matter what is sent to the port, as long as the correct address is presented, along with the $\overline{\text{AIOWC}}$ command (and AEN if required). The byte sent to the port is called a dummy byte. The occurrence of these events will pulse the 8282's STB input high, transferring the outputs of the optoisolators into the latches. Now that the switches have been read, the latched switch states are input to the computer by reading the port using the IN instruction. At this point, the computer can evaluate the conditions indicated by the switch positions and take the appropriate actions.

Although it is relatively simple, an interfacing design like that of Fig. 6-36 can be very useful in many applications. The switches shown in this circuit are representative of many different types that may be used. The pressure switch, for example, could be used to monitor the steam pressure in a boiler. A sectional view of a pressure switch is shown in Fig. 6-37a. When pressure exceeds a certain level, the diaphragm is forced down (colored in Fig. 6-37a), a switch is closed, which turns on the optoisolator. The second switch shown in Fig. 6-34 is a magnetic reed switch. This kind

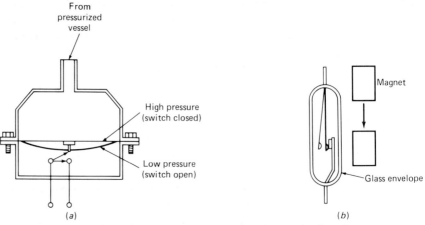

Fig. 6-37 Construction of a pressure switch (*a*) and a reed relay (*b*).

of switch is closed (or possibly opened) when brought in proximity to a strong magnet. An enlarged illustration of a reed switch is shown in Fig. 6-37b. The colored parts of the drawing represent the closing of the contacts when a magnet is brought near. There are many other switching possibilities, such as Hall effect devices, centrifugal switches, and so on. They all may be interfaced to the computer using relatively simple port circuits. Of course, there are a multitude of other ways in which the computer can sense and control its environment, and some are quite sophisticated. Chapter 7 will deal with some of the more advanced interfacing applications.

6-5.3   Low-Level I/O Programming Techniques

When interfacing the computer to the outside world, one must also consider the application from the software side. Generally, throughout this text, programming of the computer has been approached via low-level languages, such as machine or assembly language. In many applications this would be the approach that would be the most practical. In a system designed for dedicated I/O operation, such as the 8088, the IN and OUT instructions provide direct access to the ports. In systems that use memory-mapped I/O, the usual memory-referenced instructions provide equivalent capabilities. A simple I/O programming application is presented in the following example.

Example 6-10

A certain 8088-based microcomputer has programmed I/O input ports located at I/O addresses $A000_{16}$ and $A001_{16}$. The ports used here could be part of a hypothetical computerized system that automatically monitors temperature, for example. Write the mnemonics for a program that will continuously monitor port A000 for the presence of 00_{16}. When 00_{16} is detected, the program is to input and store the byte that is present at port A001. This process is to repeat until 100_{16} bytes have been stored, with each byte in consecutive memory locations, beginning at offset 0200_{16} in the current data segment. The actual program is to begin at offset 0100_{16} in the current code segment.

Solution

One of several possible solutions to this programming problem is presented below. This program is rather straightforward, and is quite similar to many others that were presented earlier. Notice that in line XXXX:010C the DX register is incremented in order to point to port A001 after detection of hex 00. This was done to save a few bytes of program length. An equally effective, and perhaps more easily recognizable, method would be to load DX with $A001_{16}$ instead.

```
XXXX:0100        MOV DI,0200        ;LOAD DI WITH START ADDR OF STORAGE AREA
XXXX:0104        MOV DX,A000        ;SET DX TO POINT TO PORT A000
XXXX:0107        IN AL,DX           ;READ PORT A000
XXXX:0108        CMP AL,00          ;DID PORT CONTAIN 00?
XXXX:010A        JNE 0107           ;IF NOT, GO BACK AND POLL AGAIN
XXXX:010C        INC DX             ;INCREMENT DX TO POINT TO PORT A001
XXXX:010D        IN AL,DX           ;READ THE PORT
XXXX:010E        MOV [DI],AL        ;STORE THE BYTE IN MEMORY
XXXX:0110        CMP DI,02FF        ;LAST BYTE STORED?
XXXX:0113        JE 0118            ;IF YES, JUMP TO XXXX:0118
XXXX:0115        INC DI             ;IF NO, INCREMENT STORAGE POINTER
XXXX:0116        JMP 0104           ;GO BACK AND POLL A000 AGAIN
XXXX:0118        ???                ;MORE INSTRUCTIONS COULD START HERE
```

There are several advantages in using machine or assembly language programming techniques for I/O control. Probably the primary advantage is that of speed. About the only way to transfer data to memory from the outside world, as done by the program in Example 6-10, would be through the use of DMA techniques. However, DMA is generally a much more complex operation, and it is not always the best-suited method for a given I/O application. Likewise, machine language programming is not always necessary in all I/O applications.

6-5.4 High-Level Language I/O

Many versions of BASIC that are available for microcomputers have statements that allow direct control of I/O ports. For example, BASIC for an 8088-based microcomputer could have two statements that allow input from and output to a port, just as are available in the 8088 instruction set. INP and OUT are analogous to IN and OUT for the 8088. Actually, INP would be considered a function, because its execution would cause a value to be returned to the program.

The availability of I/O instructions from BASIC simplifies many programming tasks. Using interpreted BASIC as an example, the interpreter would be responsible for loading the DX register with the appropriate port number, and all other register and memory manipulations required to perform a given I/O task. The syntax for the BASIC I/O statements is as follows:

OUT x,y

where x is the port number (0 to 65,535) and y is the value of the byte to be output (0 to 255).

INP(x)

where x is the port number as defined previously.

The port numbers x and the byte to be output y may be in explicit numeric form, as in the statement on the following page.

$$10 \; I \; = \; INP \; (10)$$

They may be variables as shown in the following program fragment.

```
10 PORT = 10
20 I = INP (PORT)
30 OUT PORT,I 1
```

The following example will aid in understanding the use of the INP instruction in a programming application.

Example 6-11

Repeat the programming assignment presented in Example 6-10 using BASIC. Rather than storing inputed values in specific memory locations, however, store them in a one-dimensional array.

Solution

The program below is one possible solution to the problem. Before discussing the operation of the program, an explanation of the symbol &H is in order. &H is a prefix that is used to indicate to the interpreter that the number being referenced is in hexadecimal form. This means that &H100, for example, is 100_{16}. This allows the programmer to use hex numbers directly in a program. If you prefer, you could use the decimal equivalents, but this would require manual conversion from the hex values used in Example 6-10. Also notice that all variables used in this program are defined as integers. This was used because it is good programming practice, as integers take up less memory than real numbers.

Line 10 dimensions the integer variable A% to 100_{16} (256). A FOR-NEXT loop is used to control the number of times that bytes are read from PORT2 (port $A001_{16}$). Prior to reading PORT2, PORT1 (port $A000_{16}$) is polled and tested for the occurrence of 0. This determines whether or not PORT1 should be read. Upon the detection of 0 at PORT1, PORT2 is read and its value assigned to A%(I%). The index I% is incremented on each pass through the loop until 100_{16} bytes have been input.

```
10 DIM A%(&H100)
20 FOR I% = 1 TO &H100
30 PORT1% = &HA000
40 PORT2% = &HA001
50 X% = INP (PORT1%)
60 IF X% =0 THEN 70 ELSE 50
70 A%(I%) = INP(PORT2%)
80 NEXT I%
```

Example 6-12

Assuming that 100_{16} bytes of data were stored in the array in Example 6-11, continue the program such that it will output the contents of the array to an output port located at I/O address 50_{16}.

Solution

The program lines presented below will perform the requested operation. This section of the program is basically very similar to that in Example 6-11, except that it uses the OUT instruction.

```
90 OUTPORT =&H50
100 FOR I% = 1 TO &H100
110 OUT OUTPORT,A%(I%)
120 NEXT I%
```

The advantage of performing I/O operations with higher level languages lies in the ease with which the data that is input or output can be processed. The main disadvantage is that speed of operation is severely compromised. For example, the assembly language program presented in Example 6-10 will run hundreds of times faster than the program in Example 6-11. This, however, is the classic trade-off between programming in high- and low-level languages.

The reader should recall that not all microprocessors use dedicated I/O. A system that uses memory-mapped I/O would not have the use of the IN and OUT instructions available in its higher-level language implementation. This is because the CPU does not have IN and OUT instructions in its instruction set. In such a case, where BASIC is used, memory locations are accessed through use of the POKE statement and the PEEK function. As the terms imply, PEEK allows the program to return the value of a byte at some particular address, while POKE allows the programmer to write a byte to a particular memory location. These two instructions are also available in most versions of BASIC that are used in systems with dedicated I/O to allow manipulation and examination of memory locations. We shall not devote time to these two instructions here, but they will be used later in the text and in the lab manual.

Review Questions for Section 6-5

1. What is the main difference between a standard logic gate, such as a NAND gate, and an equivalent Schmitt trigger device?
2. Refer to Fig. 6-35. What value must R have if $+V = 12$ V and $I_{LED} = 50$ mA, when the optoisolator transistor is in saturation?
3. From a functional standpoint, how do triacs and SCRs differ?

4. In general, how is a thyristor turned off?

5. Refer to Fig. 6-36. How is the status of the switches strobed into the 8282 latch?

6. What could be used as an electronic equivalent of a reed switch?

SUMMARY

There are many different methods of port design used in microcomputer systems. Many microprocessors, such as the 8088, are designed primarily to use dedicated I/O ports, which means that the instruction set of the CPU contains special instructions that are port-specific. The advantages of dedicated I/O in 8088-based systems are that fewer address lines need to be decoded, in comparison to memory decoding, and shorter instructions are used, because all I/O instructions are accumulator-specific.

Memory-mapped I/O is another alternative, in which the port(s) occupy addresses in the memory space of the CPU. This method is also popular. Ports may also be polled, interrupt-driven, or strictly under program control. To help ease the design burden, special programmable interfacing adapters are available. These devices may be programmed for a number of different modes of operation, such as polled or interrupt-driven.

The transducers used to supply data to an input port may be nothing more than simple switches. These switches are usually electrically isolated from the computer by optoisolators. Output ports can also be used to control high power loads, when optoisolators are included in their design. There are many industrial applications in which the computer can be used for equipment monitoring and control purposes. The I/O port provides the pathway between the computer and the outside world.

Many implementations of BASIC provide for peripheral device control via the I/O ports. The INP function and the OUT statement are examples of these instructions. High level language control of I/O operations can simplify the programming process in many cases, but speed is lost.

CHAPTER QUESTIONS

6-1. In a certain application, 1 bit of a computer's output port is to be used to drive an LED such that it blinks at fixed intervals. Which I/O control technique would be suited to this application?

6-2. An analog to digital converter is to sample a voltage level, convert it into an equivalent 8-bit binary number, and then send the byte to the input port of a computer. The time required for the circuit to make a conversion is not constant, but, once a conversion is complete, the A/D circuit will present the byte to the port for only 1 ms. A new conversion will then be started, and the previous byte will be lost. Which I/O control technique would be the most appropriate for this application if it is important that no samples be lost or skipped?

6-3. Which I/O control technique requires the use of handshaking?

6-4. In reference to an 8088-based system, what disadvantage(s) are there in using memory-mapped I/O?

6-5. In terms of I/O interfacing, what is the function of the AEN control line in an 8088-based system?

6-6. Why are output ports usually latched?

6-7. How many dedicated I/O ports can the 8088 address?

6-8. Briefly describe how an 8088 acknowledges an interrupt request.

6-9. Name two commonly used peripheral devices that would require bidirectional ports.

6-10. During what type of operation can an I/O-mapped port be inadvertently activated?

6-11. What type of I/O control would be used when it is important that a peripheral device receive service quickly upon request?

6-12. What interrupt type is generated when the 8088's NMI input is activated?

6-13. What action must be performed by an interrupt service routine that will allow multiple-level interrupts to occur?

6-14. What are the two types of commands that can be supplied to the 8259A programmable interrupt controller?

6-15. What effect does using the automatic end of interrupt (AEOI) mode have on the operation of the 8259A PIC?

6-16. How is the function of the 8259A's $\overline{SP/EN}$ pin determined? How is it defined in a buffered 8088-based system?

6-17. Which mode of operation provides facilities for handshaking with the 8255A programmable peripheral interface (PPI)?

6-18. What states are assumed by the registers and the data bus lines of the 8255A when a reset occurs?

CHAPTER PROBLEMS

6-19. Modify the circuit in Fig. 6-5 such that it could be used in a system that incorporates a DMA controller.

6-20. Design an 8-bit-wide programmed I/O input port and the required decoding circuitry such that the port occupies I/O address 8000_{16}. Use an 8282 latch in the design. The system to which the port is to be connected has DMA capability.

6-21. Refer to Fig. 6-14. Design the decoding circuitry such that the port is memory-mapped to address $FFF00_{16}$.

6-22. In the discussion concerning the circuit in Fig. 6-6, it was stated that U2 would accept, or strobe in, data when the port address was not on lines A_0 through A_{15}. Describe how the circuit could be modified so that data is strobed in from the peripheral device only when the correct port address is present on lines A_0 through A_{15}. It is an I/O read operation. A DMA operation is not in progress. (*Hint:* Additional gates are required. Also, consider the way that the 8282's strobe input is triggered; perhaps a substitution should be made for the 8282.)

6-23. Refer to Fig. 6-11. Modify the circuit such that it may be used in a system that has DMA capability.

6-24. At what absolute address will an 8088 fetch the first byte of an interrupt vector if interrupt type number $5A_{16}$ is requested?

6-25. Refer to Fig. 6-14. How must the switches be set to initiate interrupt type $2F_{16}$ when an interrupt request is acknowledged? Represent a closed switch by binary 1, an open switch by binary 0.

6-26. Write the ICWs required to set up an 8259A PIC for use in an 8088-based system based on the following requirements: interrupt request inputs must be level triggered, a single PIC is to be used, the data bus is buffered, automatic EOI is required, and interrupt vectors 10_{16} through 17_{16} are to be referenced. The PIC is fully decoded to occupy I/O addresses 0000_{16} through 0004_{16}. The A_0 input of the PIC is connected directly to line A_1 of the address bus, as Fig. 6-29 shows.

6-27. Referring to the 8259A as described in Problem 6-26, write the OCW that will allow the IS register to be read on the next occurrence of a read operation. No poll command is to be given, and no action is to be taken regarding the special mask mode.

6-28. In reference to Problem 6-27, what I/O address must the control word be written to? Remember that the PIC is selected (enabled) whenever address line A_0 is high (see Fig. 6-29).

6-29. Write the mode definition control word that will configure an 8255A PPI such that both port A and port B are operating in mode 0 as an output port, and port C (upper and lower) is an input port.

6-30. Write the mnemonics for an assembly language program that will continuously test D_0 of an input port at I/O address $A000_{16}$, for logic 1. If $D_0 = 1$, the program is to output FF_{16} to an I/O port at address $A001_{16}$, then go back and repeat the polling process. (*Note:* The remaining bits may assume random states.)

INTERFACING AND DATA CONVERSION

7

Once a computer has had one or more ports added to it, it is then ready to interact with the outside world. It is often the case that many devices that must be controlled and many signals that must be processed by the computer are continuous or analog in nature. For example, if a continuously variable analog quantity or device, such as a dc motor (its rotational velocity perhaps), is to be controlled by the computer, this requires that the digital output presented at the port be converted into an analog signal that is compatible with the analog device. Conversely, if an analog device, such as a positional transducer, is to supply data to the computer, the signal produced by that transducer must be converted from a continuous form into a digital logic format that is compatible with the computer system. This chapter will provide an overview of some commonly used digital to analog (D/A) and analog to digital (A/D) conversion circuits and their applications. Let us begin by examining some widely used D/A converters and their performance characteristics.

7-1 D/A CONVERSION

The main function of a D/A converter (DAC) is to accept a group of bits from a computer or some other digital device and convert that bit pattern into an equivalent analog voltage level. Normally, the bit pattern presented to the D/A converter is interpreted as being a binarily weighted number. The output of the D/A converter should be able to assume a different level for each unique digital input that is applied to it.

7-1.1 D/A Conversion Fundamentals

A commonly used block diagram representation for a D/A converter is shown in Fig. 7-1. The output produced by a given D/A converter may be

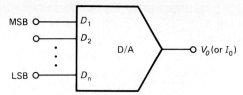

Fig. 7-1 Block diagram symbol for a digital to analog converter.

either a voltage or a current level. Whichever type of output is produced is determined by the circuitry used to construct the converter. The number of different voltage or current levels that can be produced at the output of the D/A converter is related to the number of bits that the converter has on its input by the equation

$$N = 2^n \qquad \text{(Eq. 7-1)}$$

where N is the number of different output levels that can be produced and n is the number of input bits that the converter has.

Example 7-1

A certain D/A converter has 10 binary inputs. How many different output levels can be produced?

Solution

$$N = 2^{10}$$
$$= 1024 \text{ levels}$$

The number of different levels that can be produced at the output of a D/A converter may be used to define what is termed the resolution of that device. Simply stated, the more input bits the D/A has, the higher its resolution. Using the 10-bit D/A converter presented in Example 7-1, it could be said that this converter has a resolution of 1 part in 1024. Resolution is one of the most important D/A converter specifications that must be considered in a given application. There are several ways in which resolution can be expressed. One method has just been presented; that is, resolution can be expressed in terms of 1 part in N ($N = 2^n$). Alternatively, resolution may be expressed as a percentage, as given by the equation

$$\text{Percent resolution} = (\tfrac{1}{2^n}) \times 100 \text{ percent} \qquad \text{(Eq. 7-2)}$$

Example 7-2

In reference to Example 7-1, what is the resolution of the D/A converter expressed as a percentage?

Solution

$$\text{Percent resolution} = (\tfrac{1}{2}^{10}) \times 100 \text{ percent}$$
$$= (1/1024) \times 100 \text{ percent}$$
$$= 0.098 \text{ percent}$$

The interpretation of Example 7-2 and resolution in general is that at the most, the output of the 10-bit D/A converter can be accurate to within 0.098 percent of the full-scale output. Full-scale output is the voltage or current level produced at the output of a hypothetical D/A converter that has infinite resolution with binary 1 applied to each input. Obviously, a real D/A converter can never quite reach the ideal full-scale output because of the finite number of input bits that will be present. For example, if we consider the D/A converter shown in Fig. 7-1 to have four input lines, a graph of V_O versus the binary input (the transfer function) for this 4-bit D/A converter can be produced. Such a graph is shown in Fig. 7-2. Notice that there are 16 distinct output voltage levels possible (counting 0 V) and 15

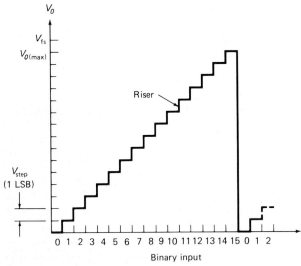

Fig. 7-2 Transfer characteristics for a 4-bit D/A converter.

risers. In order to achieve full-scale output, a 16th riser would be required. This means that at maximum V_O, the output will fall short of V_{fs} by one increment or step. The size of a single output increment is often called 1 LSB, as this is the smallest change that can be obtained and it occurs when the LSB of the digital input changes states. The increase of the output (voltage or current) for each of the steps is equal (ideally) and is determined by the number of steps (the resolution) and V_{fs} using the relationship

$$\text{Step size} = V_{fs}/2^n \qquad \text{(Eq. 7-3)}$$

where n is the number of binary inputs to the converter and V_{fs} is the full-scale voltage of an ideal equivalent D/A converter.

Using the information given above, it is possible to determine the D/A converter's output voltage for a given binary input. This will be demonstrated in the next example.

Example 7-3

Determine V_O for a 4-bit D/A converter that has a theoretical value of V_{fs} = 10 V, and the decimal equivalent of the binary input is 12.

Solution

The step size is calculated from Eq. 7-3.

$$\begin{aligned} \text{Step size} &= V_{fs}/2^n \\ &= 10\ \text{V}/16 \\ &= 0.625\ \text{V} \end{aligned}$$

The output voltage may be found by multiplying the step size by the value of the binary input.

$$\begin{aligned} V_O &= 0.625\ \text{V} \times 12 \\ &= 7.5\ \text{V} \end{aligned}$$

The resolution of a D/A converter may be used as a general indicator of its potential for accuracy, because resolution defines the limits of the accuracy of the converter (it is analogous to precision). It should be stressed, however, that accuracy and resolution (precision) are not the same thing. For example, a 16-bit D/A converter would generally be considered to have high resolution (1 part in 65,536), but it is not necessarily true that the value of V_O is an accurate representation of a given input. Under ideal conditions, the output of the D/A converter should be accurate to within $\pm \frac{1}{2} V_{step}$ (also referred to as $\pm \frac{1}{2}$ LSB because 1 step = 1 LSB). However, there are many possible sources for error in a typical D/A converter circuit. The actual error sources depend on the circuitry used to construct the D/A converter. Rather than list those specific error sources, the effects of the various error sources on the output of the converter will be summarized. Figure 7-3 illustrates the effects of the various errors on the graph of the transfer function of a perfect D/A converter. Note that the transfer function of a perfect D/A converter is exactly linear and is also continuous (it has infinite resolution). Of course, in practice such ideal characteristics cannot be realized.

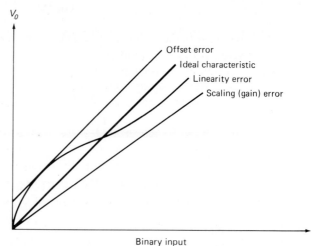

V_O

Offset error
Ideal characteristic
Linearity error
Scaling (gain) error

Binary input

Fig. 7-3 Graph of ideal (color) A/D converter transfer characteristics and the effects of various errors.

Offset Error An offset error results in the output of the D/A converter not being 0 when its binary input is 0. This results in a constant shift of V_O (or possibly I_O) over the entire range of binary inputs. If this is the only type of error present, the output will be in error by a constant amount regardless of the value of the input.

Gain Error This is sometimes called a scaling error. A gain error will produce step sizes that are either larger or smaller than what is desired (the LSB size is incorrect). Gain error causes V_O to deviate farther from the expected value as the value of the binary input is increased; that is, the output error increases (in either a positive or negative direction) as the value of the input increases.

Linearity Error This type of error is caused by nonlinearities inherent in the D/A converter circuitry. For example, if the gain of the D/A converter does not remain constant for all binary inputs, output steps of varying size will be produced. The net effect of nonlinearity on the converter is deviation of the transfer function from a straight line. Temperature variations and gradients often cause nonlinearity errors. This is often the most difficult type of error to correct.

Another D/A converter specification that is of importance is that specification which is related to the time that it takes a given circuit to perform a conversion. This characteristic is called settling time. Settling time is defined as the time it takes for the output of the D/A converter to reach and remain within some specified percent of the final output. A typical value that is used is ±½ LSB, where again, 1 LSB is the step size. Figure 7-4 illustrates the change of output level for a hypothetical D/A

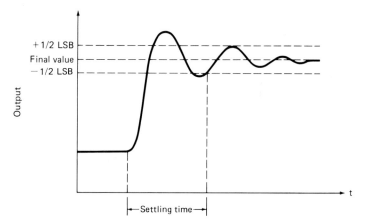

Fig. 7-4 Graph of D/A output response showing settling time.

converter and how settling time may be observed. In this particular illustration, the output exhibits a tendency to overshoot the desired final output level. This overshoot is common in many D/A conversion circuits, and is not a desirable occurence. Whenever the output has reached and stays within the desired range of values, the circuit is considered to have reached its final state. The worst case settling time will generally occur when the output of the D/A converter must change from one extreme to another, that is, from maximum output to minimum output or from minimum output to maximum output. To understand the limits imposed by this specification, consider a D/A converter that has a settling time of 10 ms. In order to obtain reliable output levels under all input conditions, the binary input must not change value faster than once every 10 ms. In practice, an even greater time interval would be used (possibly as much as 100 percent greater) to ensure that the circuit has time to respond properly to radically differing input values.

Review Questions for Section 7-1

1. Explain how an offset error at the output of a D/A converter could be detected.
2. What is the term given to the smallest step that a D/A converter can produce at its output?
3. How could the resolution of a D/A converter be increased?
4. What type of error would most likely be induced by temperature-related changes in D/A converter component parameters?
5. What D/A converter specification is a measure of the time required to perform a conversion to within specific limits?
6. How many bits would a D/A converter require for a resolution of 1 part in 10^3, or better?

D/A converters are generally designed using operational amplifier circuits, specialized monolithic (IC) D/A devices, or a combination of both. In this section, four different D/A converter circuits will be discussed. They are representative of those commonly used in many applications.

7-2.1 Weighted Resistor Summing Amplifier

One of the simplest types of D/A converters is the binary weighted summing amplifier. An example of such a circuit is shown in Fig. 7-5. In order to

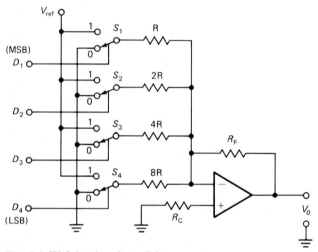

Fig. 7-5 Weighted resistor D/A converter.

keep the circuit simple, only four inputs have been used. The switches are controlled by the digital inputs D_1 through D_4 such that when a logic 1 is applied to a given input, that switch is connected to the V_{ref} (reference) voltage source. Using standard op amp circuit analysis techniques, the output voltage of this circuit can be determined using the equation

$$V_O = -V_{ref}(D_1 R_F/R + D_2 R_F/2R + D_3 R_F/4R + D_4 R_F/8R) \qquad \text{(Eq. 7-4)}$$

where $D_n = 1$ if the binary input is high (1) and $D_n = 0$ if the binary input is low (0).

The negative sign in Eq. 7-4 is present because the op amp is connected in the inverting mode. If V_{ref} is a positive voltage, V_O will be negative; and if V_{ref} is a negative voltage, V_O will be positive. The value of R_F used determines the D/A converter's overall gain or scaling constant. The larger R_F is, the higher the output voltage of the D/A converter for a given binary input. In most designs, S_1 through S_4 would not actually be mechanical switches; most likely they would be CMOS analog switches. An example of such a device is the LF11331 quad SPST JFET analog switch. A given switch within this IC may be opened or closed by applying a TTL-compatible logic level to the control line (as done with the D lines in Fig. 7-4) of that switch. The following example should clarify the operating details of the circuit.

Example 7-4

The component values for the circuit in Fig. 7-5 are as follows:

$$R_F = 10 \text{ k}\Omega, \ R = 10 \text{ k}\Omega, \ V_{\text{ref}} = 5 \text{ V}.$$

Determine the percent resolution for the circuit and V_O for the following input levels. Assume that a logic 1 connects a given input resistor to the reference voltage.

	D_1	D_2	D_3	D_4
(1)	0	0	0	1
(2)	0	0	1	0
(3)	1	0	0	0
(4)	1	1	1	1

Solution

$$
\begin{aligned}
\text{Percent resolution} &= (\tfrac{1}{2^n}) \times 100 \text{ percent} \\
&= (\tfrac{1}{2^4}) \times 100 \text{ percent} \\
&= (\tfrac{1}{16}) \times 100 \text{ percent} \\
&= 6.25 \text{ percent}
\end{aligned}
$$

Using Eq. 7-4, the output voltages are as follows.

Case 1

$$V_O = -5\text{V} \left(\frac{0 \times 10\text{k}}{10\text{k}} + \frac{0 \times 10\text{k}}{20\text{k}} + \frac{0 \times 10\text{k}}{40\text{k}} + \frac{1 \times 10\text{k}}{80\text{k}} \right)$$

$$V_O = -0.625 \text{ V}$$

Case 2

$$V_O = -5\text{V} \left(\frac{0 \times 10\text{k}}{10\text{k}} + \frac{0 \times 10\text{k}}{20\text{k}} + \frac{1 \times 10\text{k}}{40\text{k}} + \frac{0 \times 10\text{k}}{80\text{k}} \right)$$

$$V_O = -1.250 \text{ V}$$

Case 3

$$V_O = -5\text{V} \left(\frac{1 \times 10\text{k}}{10\text{k}} + \frac{0 \times 10\text{k}}{20\text{k}} + \frac{0 \times 10\text{k}}{40\text{k}} + \frac{0 \times 10\text{k}}{80\text{k}} \right)$$

$$V_O = -5.000 \text{ V}$$

Case 4

$$V_O = -5V \left(\frac{1 \times 10k}{10k} + \frac{1 \times 10k}{20k} + \frac{1 \times 10k}{40k} + \frac{1 \times 10k}{80k} \right)$$

$$V_O = -9.375 \text{ V}$$

The binary weighted relationship between V_O and the various inputs for the above example may be verified by noting that for case 1, the decimal equivalent of the input is 1 and $V_O = -0.625$ V. In case 2, the decimal equivalent of the input is 2 and $V_O = -1.250$ V. It is obvious that when the numerical value of the input doubles, the output voltage also doubles. Also, notice that the maximum output voltage produced (in case 4) is less than the full-scale output voltage (V_{fs}). This may be demonstrated by noting that for case 3, in which the MSB alone is at logic 1, V_O (-5 V) will be $\frac{1}{2} V_{fs}$. From this, it may be inferred that $V_{fs} = -10$ V. The addition of more and more inputs will result in a maximum output voltage that more closely approximates V_{fs}. Another way to look at it is that the maximum output of a given D/A converter will always be short by 1 LSB, assuming all other error sources (that is, gain, offset, and linearity errors) have been eliminated.

The conversion speed limit of the particular converter being used, as mentioned before, can be a very important consideration. Conversion speed is ultimately dependent upon all possible sources of delay in the entire circuit, with some finite, nonzero settling time as the end result. In op-amp-based circuits, such as in Fig. 7-5, the settling time will be primarily dependent on the slew rate and bandwidth characteristics of the op amp. Slew rate is a large signal specification that is a measure of the maximum rate of change of V_O that is possible at the output of the amp. Bandwidth is normally considered a small-signal frequency operating limit specification, and is related to slew rate. For the purposes of this discussion, slew rate is much more important than bandwidth, since we will be dealing with large, fast-rising output signals. If rapid conversions are required, a high-speed (high slew rate) op amp must be used. As most of us are well aware, digital circuits can change output states at remarkably high rates of speed. If the D/A converter cannot change its output voltage quickly enough in response to the changing input data, the circuit may be useless in certain applications. In the worst case, the output of the converter would have to change from maximum to 0, or vice versa in response to an input. It is this worst case delay that would be specified for a given D/A converter circuit. Settling times of 150 ns and lower are readily attainable with many commercially available D/A converter circuits. If a commercial grade 741 op amp were used in the converter of Fig. 7-5, the output could change at a maximum rate of 0.5 V/μs, which is the typical slew rate of the 741. This means that if the binary input was initially 0, and then 1111_2 was applied to the digital inputs, the output would take about 20 μs to slew from 0 to the desired output. This may seem like a rapid transition, but it is relatively slow when compared to the speeds attainable with most digital circuits.

Although the circuit in Fig. 7-5 is useful, there are some additional problems that prevent its use in practical D/A conversion applications. The main drawbacks associated with this circuit are related to the extreme range of resistor values that are required when high resolution is desired (a 256 to 1 maximum to minimum resistor ratio is required for 7-bit resolution). With such a large span of resistance values required, there is a definite possibility of the occurrence of temperature-related problems. Resistors that differ widely in value also tend to have different temperature coefficients (mainly because of differing composition). In order to overcome this problem, resistors with matched temperature coefficients must be used. Over a wide spread of values, such resistors are very expensive and quite possibly impossible to obtain. In other words, the more inputs that are used (to obtain higher resolution), the more impractical the weighted resistor summing amp D/A converter approach becomes, because an even greater range of input resistance values is required. These problems limit the usefulness of this circuit (Fig. 7-5), and in most practical circumstances, such a circuit would be used in noncritical low-resolution applications.

7-2.2   The R-2R Ladder D/A Converter

A practical alternative to the binary weighted D/A converter is a circuit called an R-2R ladder D/A converter. The schematic for such a circuit is shown in Fig. 7-6. In this particular example, the op amp is connected in the noninverting configuration. The similarity between the input voltage divider circuit and a ladder is easily seen. The "ladder" section of this circuit acts as a switch-selectable variable-voltage source. The voltage that

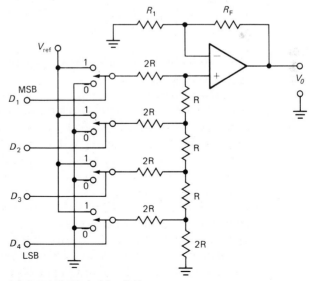

Fig. 7-6 R-2R ladder D/A converter.

is present at the noninverting input of the op amp is related to the switch settings according to the relationship

$$V_{in} = D_1 V_{ref}/2 + D_2 V_{ref}/4 + D_3 V_{ref}/8 + D_4 V_{ref}/16. \quad \text{(Eq. 7-5)}$$

Equation 7-5 may also be expressed as

$$V_{in} = V_{ref}(D_1/2 + D_2/4 + D_3/8 \ldots) \quad \text{(Eq. 7-5a)}$$

where $D_n = 1$ (switch connected to V_{ref}) or $D_n = 0$ (switch connected to ground).

The voltage gain of the noninverting op amp may be determined using the equation

$$A_V = 1 + R_F/R_1 \quad \text{(Eq. 7-6)}$$

Combining Eqs. 7-5a and 7-6, the general expression for V_O of the R-2R D/A converter is found to be

$$V_O = A_V V_{ref}(D_1/2 + D_2/4 + D_3/8 \ldots). \quad \text{(Eq. 7-7)}$$

The advantage of the R-2R ladder D/A converter over the weighted summing amp type is that only two different values of resistance need to be used at the input of the amplifier. The resistance range is only 2 to 1, regardless of the resolution desired; therefore temperature tracking problems can be more easily eliminated. The R-2R ladder converter is also more practical in that it is much easier to obtain precision resistors that are of two different values (2 to 1 ratio) than a larger number of binarily weighted ones. The analysis of the R-2R ladder D/A converter is also relatively simple, as is shown in the following example.

Example 7-5

The D/A converter of Fig. 7-6 has the following component values: $R_F = 10\ k\Omega$, $R_1 = 10\ k\Omega$, $R = 10\ k\Omega$, $V_{ref} = 5\ V$. Determine V_O for the following inputs. Assume that a logic 1 input connects a given switch to V_{ref}.

	D_1	D_2	D_3	D_4
(1)	0	0	0	1
(2)	0	0	1	0
(3)	1	0	0	0
(4)	1	1	1	1

Solution

V_O for each case is found using Eq. 7-7.

$$\text{Case 1: } V_O = 0.625 \text{ V}$$
$$\text{Case 2: } V_O = 1.250 \text{ V}$$
$$\text{Case 3: } V_O = 5.000 \text{ V}$$
$$\text{Case 4: } V_O = 9.375 \text{ V}$$

Notice the similarity between the outputs determined in Examples 7-4 and 7-5. For the resistance ratios given, both produce the same magnitude of V_O for a given input. Also note that the maximum values of V_O are the same (disregarding polarity) and are less than V_{fs} by 1 LSB.

7-2.3 Monolithic D/A Converters

The two D/A conversion circuits just presented are fairly popular in some simple designs. However, when high resolution is required, quite a few resistors must be used to implement the D/A circuitry. For example, a 7-bit R-2R converter requires 16 matched (in temperature coefficient and relative value) resistors just for the ladder circuit. These resistors are relatively expensive, take up excessive room on the circuit board, and add additional steps to the manufacturing process (they must be inserted into the circuit board). Monolithic (integrated circuit) D/A converters provide a convenient solution to these problems. Consider that components that are fabricated on an IC are inherently well matched in terms of relative value and temperature characteristics. This, plus the fact that the IC D/A converter will take up less circuit board real estate than an equivalent discrete circuit, makes them the overwhelming choice in most designs.

There are many different monolithic D/A converters available. A typical example of such a device is the National Semiconductor DAC0808. This is a 7-bit D/A converter with a current-source-type output; that is, the output current is proportional to the value of the binary input. The DAC0808 is supplied in a 16-pin DIP, and has a typical settling time of 150 ns. The pin diagram for this device is shown in Fig. 7-7.

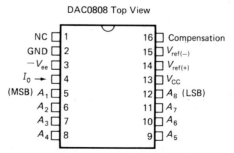

Fig. 7-7 Pin diagram for the DAC0808 monolithic D/A converter.

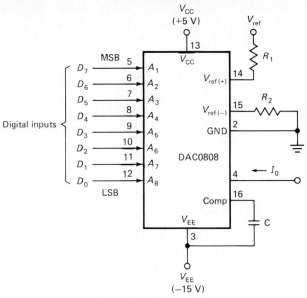

Fig. 7-8 A practical D/A converter circuit.

A D/A converter circuit based on the DAC0808 is presented in Fig. 7-8. The output current for this circuit may be found using the equation

$$I_O = -\frac{V_{\text{ref}}}{R_1}(D_7/2 + D_6/4 + D_5/8 + \ldots D_0/256) \qquad \text{(Eq. 7-8)}$$

where D_n is 1 or 0.

Notice the reversal of the subscript numbering for the D inputs. This was done to make the order of significance of the D/A inputs conform to that of an 8088 data bus. The negative reference pin $V_{\text{ref}(-)}$ is tied to ground through a resistor R_2 that is equal to R_1. The inclusion of this resistor helps null out offset errors. The compensation pin (pin 16) connects to $-V_{\text{EE}}$ via a low-value capacitor (typically around 0.001 µF). This capacitor helps to prevent ringing and overshoot at the output of the converter. Notice also that the output of the DAC0808 is a negative current level. As will be shown shortly, this presents no problem for most applications, and in fact is actually quite convenient in some cases.

The majority of the time, it is preferred that the output of a D/A converter be a voltage level rather than a current level. This requirement is easily met using an op-amp-based current to voltage (I/V) converter at the DAC0808's I_O pin. Figure 7-9 shows a simple I/V converter as would be used in this application. The output voltage of this circuit may be found using the equation

$$V_O = -I_O R_F \qquad \text{(Eq. 7-9)}$$

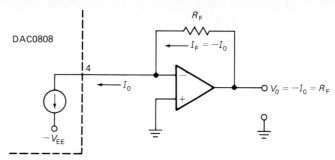

Fig. 7-9 Using an op amp as an I/V converter on the output of the 0808.

Notice that since I_O is negative to start with, V_O will be positive, and since I_O is proportional to the binary input, V_O will be proportional as well. The complete circuit using the DAC0808 and the I/V converter is shown in Fig. 7-10. The expression for V_O may be obtained by combining Eqs. 7-8 and 7-9 to form

$$V_O = \frac{V_{ref}R_F}{R_1} (D_7/2 + D_6/4 + D_5/8 + \ldots D_0/256) \quad \text{(Eq. 7-10)}$$

Example 7-6

The circuit in Fig. 7-10 has the following values: $V_{ref} = 5$ V, $R_1 = 5$ kΩ. Design a voltage to current (V/I) converter that will produce $V_O = 5$ V for the binary input 1000 0000 (128_{10}).

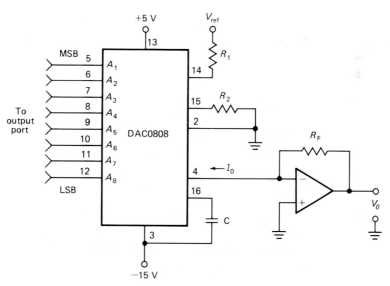

Fig. 7-10 Complete D/A converter circuit with voltage output.

Solution

The value of R_F is the only thing that must be determined for the V/I converter. This may be accomplished by calculating I_O for the DAC0808 under the specified input conditions. Using Eq. 7-10:

$$I_O = -\frac{V_{ref}}{R_1}(D_7/2) \quad \text{The remainder of the terms are 0.}$$
$$= -0.5 \text{ mA}$$

Since $V_O = -R_F I_O$

Then $R_F = V_O/I_O$
$$= 10 \text{ k}\Omega$$

An application in which the DAC0808 may be used is computer-controlled waveform generation. Figure 7-11 shows the block diagram repre-

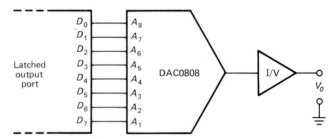

Fig. 7-11 Connection of the D/A converter to an output port.

sentation for a simple circuit that may be used in the waveform generation application. The D/A converter is driven by a latched output port. Most likely, an assembly language program would be written to output the necessary bit patterns that are used to produce a given waveform. For example, if a sawtooth waveform was required, the program would simply increment the accumulator (AL in the 8088) and successively output its contents to the port that drives the D/A converter. The output that would be produced is shown in Fig. 7-12a. Since there are 255 steps in each ramp, the waveform closely approximates that of an analog function generator. The frequency of the output signal would be limited by the rate at which the CPU could execute the increment and OUT operations, as it would require 255 loops to ramp from 0 to maximum output.

An increase in the frequency can be obtained at the expense of resolution. For example, if the contents of the accumulator are incremented by 15 on each step, only 17 loops will be required to ramp from 0 to maximum. The output waveform for this situation is shown in Fig. 7-12b. Notice that the steps are relatively large in comparison to the waveform in which all 255 steps are utilized.

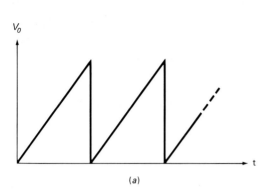

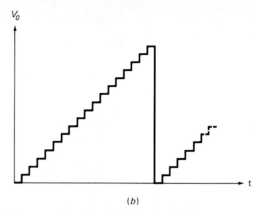

(a)   (b)

Fig. 7-12 Ideal sawtooth waveform (a) and digital approximation produced by D/A converter (b).

Because of the stair-step nature of the digitally produced waveform, the output signal will contain many high-frequency harmonics that may not be desired. These harmonics may be removed with a low-pass filter. Such a circuit is shown in Fig. 7-13. The high-frequency components contained in the signal will be shunted to ground by the capacitor, while the low-frequency components will appear at V_O relatively unaffected. If the waveform of Fig. 7-12b was applied to this circuit (Fig. 7-13), the output would appear as shown in Fig. 7-14. There are many other uses for the D/A converters presented. A few more examples would be process control, motor-speed control, and many robotics applications.

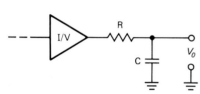

Fig. 7-13 Filtering the output of the D/A converter.

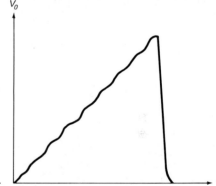

Fig. 7-14 The effect of filtering on the digitally generated sawtooth waveform.

A D/A converter could also be controlled very easily with a high-level programming language such as BASIC, using the techniques presented in Chap. 6. A few examples will demonstrate this application.

Example 7-7

Assume that an 8-bit D/A converter is located at I/O address 100_{16}. Write a BASIC program that will produce a sawtooth waveform as shown in Fig. 7-12a.

Solution

```
10 PORT = &H100
20 FOR I = 0 TO &HFF
30 OUT PORT,I
40 NEXT I
```

Examination of the program in Example 7-7 illustrates the ease with which the sawtooth waveform can be generated using the microcomputer. Of course, the trade-off for this simplicity is speed. The machine language version of this program would most likely run hundreds of times faster, producing a waveform that is also hundreds of times higher in frequency. The execution time of the BASIC program could be decreased significantly, however, if compiled BASIC is used.

It is interesting to note that when a waveform is generated using a microcomputer and D/A converter, the waveform is constructed in the time domain; that is, the instantaneous amplitude of the waveform is produced and outputted to the converter at specific times. When viewed from this standpoint, a waveform such as the sawtooth is relatively easy to produce using either high- or low-level programming languages. From the frequency domain perspective, however, the sawtooth waveform is rather complex, being composed of a summation of harmonically related sine functions. The point here is that it is relatively easy to produce nonsinusoidal waveforms using a computer, whereas it is somewhat more difficult to produce sinusoidal functions, because of the trigonometric functions that are involved. In general, the opposite is true of linear circuits.

To solidify the point of the preceding statement, let us consider how a sinusoidal waveform could be produced using the computer techniques presented thus far. In assembly language, there would basically be two different approaches that could be used. One method would be to write a subroutine that could compute the sine of an argument that is supplied to it. The argument of a function is the quantity that is operated on by that particular function, and in this case, the argument would be time or phase angle. A second alternative would be to create a lookup table that contained values of the sine of an angle between, say, 0 and 360 degrees. The rate at which the values in the table are read out would determine the period of the generated sine wave. This method would most likely provide a higher operating speed than the computational method, because it is quicker to grab a byte from memory than go through a long series of arithmetic operations, but it might also take up more space in memory. The lookup-table approach would be similar to that which was presented in Chap. 2 (see Fig. 2-30).

Using BASIC, the computational approach would be the easiest method to use because the sine function is already available. The lookup-table method could also be used, with the table itself stored in a one-dimensional array. The following example will help illustrate the concepts being presented.

Example 7-8

A certain microcomputer has an 8-bit D/A converter located at I/O address 30_{16}. Write a BASIC program that will produce a sinusoidal waveform at the output of the converter. The program is to use the full resolution of the converter.

Solution

The program listed below will produce the desired waveform. Line 10 defines the port number. Line 20 defines the value of 2π. This is done because nearly all versions of BASIC compute trigonometric functions for an argument supplied in radians. There are 2π radians in one complete cycle of a sine wave, and every cycle is identical to every other cycle. The value 2PI is used as the loop exit value. In order to use the full resolution of the converter, 256 different values of the argument (I) are required, hence I is incremented by the amount $2\pi/256$ on each pass through the FOR-NEXT loop.

```
10 PORT = &H30
20 2PI= 6.28318
30 INCREMENT =2PI/256
40 FOR I = 0 TO 2PI STEP INCREMENT
50 X = SIN(I)
60 OUT PORT,X
70 NEXT I
```

The preceding examples are just a few of the many interesting possibilities that could be presented in the use of the D/A converter. For example, rather than using the output of the D/A converter to produce just waveforms, the output could be used to position a cutting head on an automatic machine tool. The position of the head could be pulled from a lookup table, or possibly determined mathematically, say, as when a cam is being produced. For multiple axis control, several D/A converters could be used. The possibilities are nearly endless and are becoming more and more important as robotics and automated manufacturing become more prevalent. Some of the programming techniques that were presented in this section will be presented again in later chapters in a similar context.

Review Questions for Section 7-2

1. A certain D/A converter has 12 inputs. What is the percent resolution of this circuit?

2. A certain application requires a D/A converter with a resolution of at least 3 percent. What is the minimum number of input bits required of the D/A converter?
3. Refer to Fig. 7-5. If $R_F = 10$ kΩ and $R = 10$ kΩ, what value should R_C have in order to minimize offset voltage at V_O?
4. Refer to Fig. 7-10. What type of error would occur if the gain of the op amp varied as I_O changed levels?
5. Why do you think CMOS analog switches are used more often in D/A converter circuits than mechanical switches or relays?
6. A certain 5-bit D/A converter has $V_{fs} = 12$ V. What will be the value of V_O with all inputs at logic 1?

7-3 A/D CONVERSION

As stated before, there may be times when a computer must be used to process signals or data that are generated by analog devices. An example of such an application is the inertial guidance system of a missile. The computer in such a missile would have to accept signals from perhaps an infrared-sensitive transducer and various other transducers that indicate relative missile attitude, velocity, and so on, and control the direction of flight based on this information. Generally speaking, almost all transducers produce a continuous analog output. The job of the A/D converter (ADC) is to sample the analog signal and then produce a digital (numerical) representation of that quantity. Figure 7-15 shows a block diagram representation for an A/D converter. This circuit produces an n-bit binary output that is proportional to the input voltage. A graph of a 4-bit A/D converter transfer characteristic is shown in Fig. 7-16. Notice the similarity between this graph and that of Fig. 7-2. Some of the more important A/D converter parameters that affect this transfer characteristic will now be discussed.

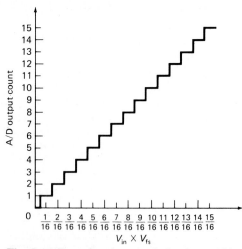

Fig. 7-16 Transfer characteristics for a 4-bit A/D converter.

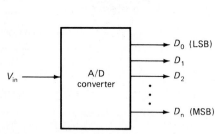

Fig. 7-15 Symbol for an A/D converter.

7-3.1 A/D Concepts

Several key observations relating to the characteristics of A/D conversion can be determined by examining Fig. 7-16. Just as in the case of D/A conversion, the number of bits used will determine the accuracy limitations (resolution) of the A/D converter. The stair-step representation of the A/D converter characteristics shown in Fig. 7-16 illustrates that for all but a few points (16 in this case), the output is an approximate digital representation of the input. A graphical representation of the error in the digital output at any point on the transfer characteristic is shown in Fig. 7-17.

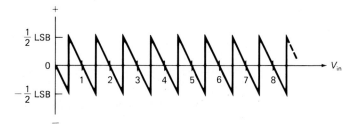

Fig. 7-17 Error plot for an A/D converter.

For a converter with higher resolution (more inputs), the peak amplitude of the error will decrease. A theoretically ideal A/D converter would have infinitely many outputs and, therefore, infinite resolution. This would result in an error graph that is a horizontal line with an amplitude of 0, which of course is unrealizable. The error that is inherent in all A/D converters due to the finite resolution is called quantization error. This error cannot be eliminated.

The output of an A/D converter is actually a digital representation of the input level that existed at some particular instant in time. This implies that A/D converters operate by sampling an analog quantity. As such, one must ensure that the input to the converter is held relatively constant while a conversion is in progress or being sampled. For inputs that are slowly varying, the output of the A/D converter may be considered to represent the instantaneous value of that particular signal. Sample and hold (S/H) circuits are often used to ensure that the input quantity does not vary while a conversion is being made. Conversion time and sample rate are important considerations in most, if not all, A/D converter applications. The speed-related parameter that is often used to determine the applicability of a given A/D converter in a given application is called conversion time. The conversion time t_c is a measure of the worst case time delay between the application of an input and the production of the equivalent binary output. The worst case occurs when the output must change from one limit (0 possibly) to the other extreme (max). Figure 7-18 illustrates this time delay. The input is presented to the converter at t_1, and the output responds at t_2. The difference between these times is the conversion time t_c. Conversion time defines the maximum rate at which a signal may be sampled.

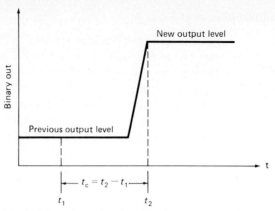

Fig. 7-18 Illustration of A/D conversion time response.

The interval of time in between samples is called the sample time. A more useful parameter is sample rate, which is just the reciprocal of sample time. In order to see the effects of finite sample rate on the conversion of an analog signal into a digital quantity, let us consider a sinusoidal input to an A/D converter. Figure 7-19 shows the possible response of an A/D

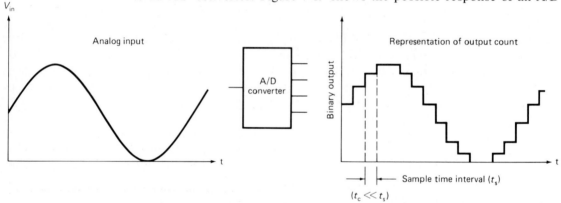

Fig. 7-19 Digitization of an analog signal with an A/D converter.

converter to a sinusoidal input. Let us assume that the conversion time of the A/D circuit is negligibly short, and that the sample time interval is about 1/10 of the period of the incoming signal. Keep in mind that the digitized waveform shown is just a graphical representation of the binary output of the A/D converter. The important thing to notice is that the digital output is a reasonably good representation of the analog input. Even more precise conversion is possible with a higher sampling rate, if the resolution of the A/D converter is also high.

A problem can occur, however, if the analog input signal is changing too rapidly, relative to the sample rate. In such a case, the A/D converter may not make enough conversions in a given period of time to accurately approximate the input signal, and a phenomenon known as aliasing will occur. It can be shown that in order for a time-sampled system, such as an A/D converter, to accurately represent at least the most fundamental characteristics of an input (the fundamental frequency and amplitude), the sampling frequency must be at least twice the frequency of the incoming signal. This requirement is known as the Nyquist sampling theorem. Figure 7-20 illustrates the effect of not meeting the Nyquist criterion, where the

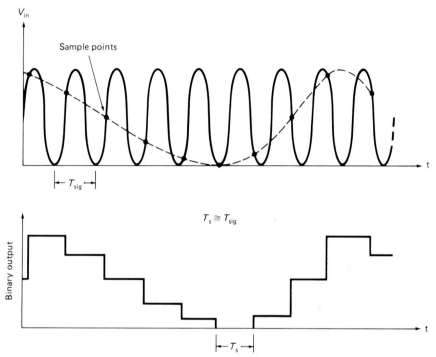

Fig. 7-20 Aliasing occurs when the sample rate is too low relative to the period of the analog signal.

time between samples is approximately the same as the period of the input signal. The output of the A/D converter is a false representation (an alias) of the input. Applications such as the digitization of speech and other rapidly varying signals rely on high sample rates for accurate conversion. Also, real-time control of systems (a guided missile, for example) requires very high sample rates for monitoring of rapidly varying conditions. The term real-time refers to the ability of a computer to operate so quickly that it simulates a continuous device or system rather than one that works in discrete intervals. The maximum sample rate that may be attained is limited by the conversion speed of the A/D converter. In other words, it would do no good to sample an input once every 10 ns if the A/D converter has a conversion time of, say, 500 ns. The result of such a situation would be meaningless garbage at the output of the converter. Fortunately, for many applications, the input level being converted will remain relatively constant.

It is also important to keep in mind that offset, gain, and nonlinearity errors can affect the accuracy of the A/D conversion just as occurs in

D/A conversion. The sources of these errors depend on the circuitry that constitutes a given A/D converter and will be discussed in the next section.

7-3.2 A/D Conversion Circuits

There are several different A/D conversion techniques in use today. The majority of A/D converters that are encountered will be one of the following types: the ramp A/D converter, the successive approximation A/D converter, and the dual-slope (integrating) A/D converter. Each has its own advantages and disadvantages, and the application in which the A/D converter is to be used will dictate which approach should be taken. Another less frequently used A/D circuit called a parallel converter will also be presented.

The Ramp A/D Converter Perhaps the simplest to understand is the ramp A/D converter as shown in Fig. 7-21. The heart of this circuit is a D/A

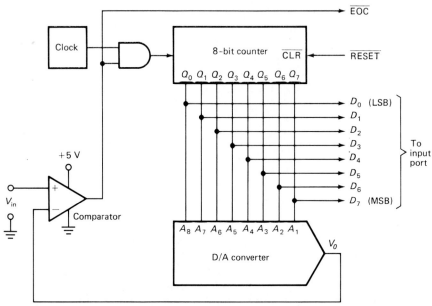

Fig. 7-21 A/D converter using a binary counter, comparator, and D/A building blocks.

converter. This is a common feature of several types of A/D converters. The operation of this circuit as it would be controlled by a computer will now be described. It is assumed that a positive dc voltage is present at the input of the comparator.

1. The computer sends a reset pulse to the counter. This places the inputs to the D/A converter at logic 0, forcing V_O of the D/A to 0 V. Since the noninverting input of the comparator is positive with respect to the inverting input, the output will be driven to saturation at about +5 V. This enables the AND gate to pass clock pulses to the up-counter.

2. As clock pulses are applied to the counter, the output of the D/A converter (V_O) ramps higher in voltage. Refer to Fig. 7-2 for an illustration of the D/A ramp output.

3. At some point, the count will have increased such that the output of the D/A converter exceeds that of V_{in}. When this occurs, the output of the comparator is driven to 0 V. This disables the clock, stopping the counter at the point where V_O just exceeded V_{in}. The end of conversion ($\overline{EOC}$) line is also pulled low, and is used to signal the computer that the digital output is ready to be read. The $\overline{EOC}$ line could be polled occasionally, or it could be used to initiate an interrupt, or it could be used to strobe the output of the converter into an input port latch.

4. After the computer has read the data, a reset pulse is sent to the A/D converter, starting the process over again.

A graphical representation of the operation of the ramp A/D converter is presented in Fig. 7-22. t_1 represents the time required for the counter

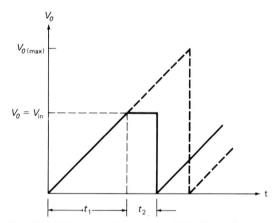

Fig. 7-22 Graph of the output of the D/A section of the A/D converter.

to ramp the output of the D/A converter just past V_{in}. t_2 represents the time interval during which the computer reads the data and then issues a reset pulse. Note that t_2 could vary depending on the details of the software that controls the reset line.

The time required to make a conversion t_1 is determined by the value of V_{in} and the frequency of the clock. The example below will illustrate this relationship.

Example 7-9

The A/D converter of Fig. 7-21 has f_{clock} = 50 kHz. The D/A converter section has V_{fs} = 10 V. If V_{in} = 6.00 V, how long will the circuit take to make the conversion?

Solution

Since this is a 7-bit converter and $V_{fs} = 10$ V, the step size is found using Eq. 7-3.

$$V_{step} = 10/2^8$$
$$= 0.03906 \text{ V}$$

The number of steps N required to cause the output of the D/A converter to reach 6.00 V is found by dividing V_{in} by V_{step}.

$$N = 6.00/0.03906$$
$$= 153.6$$

Since fractional steps cannot exist, N is rounded up to the next highest integer; therefore $N = 154$. The output of the D/A converter is increased by 1 step (LSB) for each clock period. The clock period is the reciprocal of the clock frequency; therefore

$$T_{clk} = 1/f_{clk}$$
$$= 1/50 \text{ kHz}$$
$$= 20 \text{ } \mu\text{s}$$

Now the length of time required by the conversion is found by multiplying the clock period by the number of steps required.

$$t = T_{clk N}$$
$$= 20 \text{ } \mu\text{s} \times 154$$
$$= 3.08 \text{ ms}$$

It is apparent from the preceding example that as V_{in} becomes larger, the conversion time will increase, because more clock periods must accumulate to cause V_O to reach or exceed V_{in}. The maximum length of time required for a conversion is given by the equation

$$t_c(\text{max}) = T_{clk}(2^n - 1) \tag{Eq. 7-11}$$

The absolute accuracy of the ramp A/D converter will be affected primarily by the characteristics of the D/A converter section (offset, nonlinearity, and gain) and the comparator. The comparator has got to be able to reliably control the AND gate in response to voltage differentials somewhat lower than 1 LSB on its input in order to take advantage of the resolution of the D/A converter. For example, if a 16-bit D/A converter is used to form the A/D with $V_{fs} = 10$ V, the LSB voltage value will be about 152.6 μV. This is a very small increment indeed, and would require a very sensitive (high-gain) comparator to resolve down to such a small voltage.

The Successive Approximation A/D Converter Successive approximation register (SAR) based A/D converters are close relatives to the ramp types. Figure 7-23 shows the block diagram for a SAR-type A/D converter. Both ramp

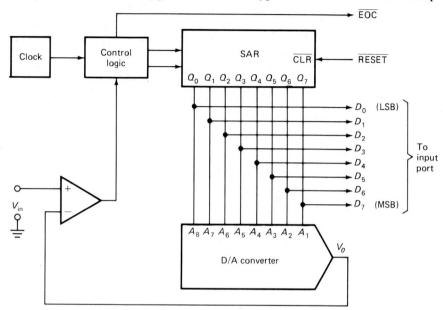

Fig. 7-23 A/D converter using the successive approximation register (SAR) technique.

and SAR converters use a D/A converter and comparator in their operation. The main difference between these two types of converters is in the digital counting section. The ramp converter usually works by counting up in the normal binary sequence until V_{in} is exceeded. The operation of the SAR converter proceeds is a manner that will be described in the following steps. Refer to Figs. 7-23 and 7-24 during the description.

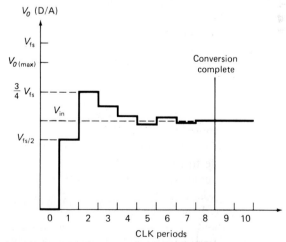

Fig. 7-24 Graph of D/A section response during a conversion using the SAR A/D converter.

1. At the beginning of the first clock period, the control logic applies a pulse to the SAR, which responds by setting its MSB and clearing the remaining outputs. This causes V_O to be equal to $V_{fs}/2$. In Fig. 7-24, this is less than V_{in}, and the output of the comparator will remain high. The control logic senses that the comparator has stayed high and sends a signal to the SAR that latches the MSB at logic 1.
2. On the occurrence of the next clock pulse, the next most significant bit of the SAR output Q_6 is set. In Fig. 7-24, the output of the D/A will exceed V_{in}, driving the comparator output low. The control logic senses this and does not latch Q_6 high.
3. On the next clock pulse, Q_6 is cleared and Q_5 is set. Again, the output of the comparator is high, so the control logic does not latch Q_5 high.

The sequence of steps outlined above will repeat eight times (until the LSB of the SAR is tested), because this is a 7-bit converter. Basically, the circuit tests a given output beginning with the MSB of the SAR, and if the output of the D/A converter exceeds V_{in}, that bit is discarded. If the setting of a given SAR output bit produces an output from the D/A converter that is less than that of V_{in}, then the bit is latched high. After all of the SAR bits have been tested, the binary output will be proportional to V_{in}. It is easy to see the advantage of this A/D converter over the ramp-type converter; that is, the conversion time is directly proportional to the number of bits in the SAR. Compare this with the conversion time of the ramp A/D converter, where the worst case conversion time is proportional to 2^n, where n is the number of bits in the counter. The SAR-type A/D converter is much more widely used than the ramp-type for this reason. The SAR A/D converter is susceptible to the same errors as the ramp converter; that is, offset, gain, and nonlinearity errors that are present in the D/A section will affect the accuracy of the digital output. Also, the comparator has to be able to reliably resolve a voltage differential less than 1 LSB.

Example 7-10

A 10-bit SAR A/D converter operates with a 25 kHz clock. How long will this circuit take to perform a conversion?

Solution

The converter will take 10 clock periods to perform the conversion. The period of the clock is found by taking the reciprocal of the clock frequency

$$T_{clk} = \frac{1}{25}\ kHz = 40\ \mu s.$$

The conversion time is found by multiplying T_{clk} by the number of bits n.

$$t_c = 40\ \mu s \times 10$$
$$= 400\ \mu s$$

Example 7-11

The D/A converter section of Fig. 7-23 has V_{fs} = 10 V. What is the smallest value of V_{in} that will produce a nonzero digital output? Assume the comparator is ideal.

Solution

The smallest input that could be detected would be equal to 1 LSB of the D/A section. Since this is an 8-bit converter and V_{fs} is 10 V, the LSB amplitude may be found using Eq. 7-3. This will also yield the smallest voltage that may be resolved.

$$1\,\text{LSB} = V_{\text{step}} = V_{fs}/2^8$$
$$= 0.0391\,\text{V}$$

The Dual-Slope A/D Converter Both of the previously discussed A/D converters were designed around D/A converters. Another alternative that is used quite often is the dual-slope A/D converter. Such an A/D converter is shown in Fig. 7-25. An integrator forms the heart of this circuit. Briefly, the circuit works in the following manner. Assume the counter is initially reset, and the integrator V_O is 0.

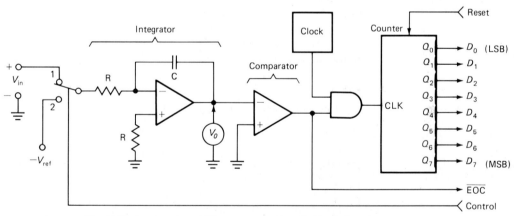

Fig. 7-25 Integrating A/D converter circuit (dual slope).

1. The switch is set to position 1, allowing V_{in} to be applied to the input of the integrator (V_{in} must be positive). The capacitor charges linearly as V_O slews negative at a constant rate. The negative-going output of the integrator forces the comparator output high, gating the clock to the up-counter.
2. As soon as the counter reaches a predetermined count (usually when the counter recycles to 0), the switch is set to position 2. Since the

clock frequency is constant, the sample time t_1 is also constant. This is illustrated in Fig. 7-26 for two different values of V_{in}. Note that the polarity of V_O has been inverted for clarity.

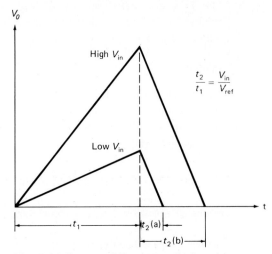

Fig. 7-26 Output of integrator during charge and discharge cycles of an A/D conversion for high and low input voltages.

3. The instant the switch is placed in position 2, the negative reference voltage is applied to the integrator. This causes V_O to slew back toward 0. Meanwhile, the counter is enabled and is accumulating a count. This action is also shown in Fig. 7-26.
4. When the reference voltage has driven the output of the integrator back to 0, the comparator output goes low, disabling the counter. The output of the comparator may be used to signal the end of the conversion ($\overline{EOC}$) as well as to degate the clock.
5. The count that was attained during the reference-driven time interval t_2 is directly proportional to V_{in}.

The relationship between the values of V_{in}, V_{ref}, t_1, and t_2 is given by the equation

$$t_2/t_1 = V_{in}/V_{ref} \qquad \text{(Eq. 7-12)}$$

Since t_1 and t_2 are both determined by the constant clock frequency, the ratios of the counts attained during t_1 and t_2 may be used in the ratio of Eq. 7-12. Applying this substitution and solving for V_{in}, the following equation is obtained.

$$V_{in} = (V_{ref} \times \text{count 2})/\text{count 1} \qquad \text{(Eq. 7-13)}$$

Example 7-12

A certain dual-slope A/D converter has an 8-bit counter, operates at a clock frequency of 10 kHz, and has $V_{ref} = -10$ V. The sample time t_1 is equal to the time that the counter takes to count up from 0 until it recycles to 0 again. If the decimal equivalent of the output count is 100 at the end of a conversion, what is the value of V_{in}?

Solution

It takes 256 (2^n, where n is the number of bits in the counter) clock pulses to recycle the counter from a starting count of 0. Therefore, 256 is substituted for $count_1$ in Eq. 7-13. V_{ref} and $count_2$ are given, and may also be substituted into Eq. 7-13, yielding

$$V_{in} = (V_{ref} \times count\ 2)/count\ 1$$
$$= 10 \times 100/256$$
$$= 3.91\ V$$

Dual-slope A/D converters can be made very accurate. This is the reason that they are frequently used in digital voltmeter circuits. The main disadvantage of dual-slope converters is their relatively slow conversion time in relation to the D/A-based converters. Also, the operation of the integrator circuitry is very critical to the overall accuracy of the conversion. Very low offset current op amps must be used, and the feedback capacitor must be very low in leakage and have a very low temperature coefficient. As is the case with the ramp converter, the dual-slope-type converters are not as popular in most computer applications as the successive-approximation-type converter, although they are used frequently in high-accuracy devices, such as digital voltmeters.

The dual-slope A/D converter is also sensitive to short-term variations in clock frequency, as well as variations in reference voltage and integrator component value. For example, if the clock frequency should vary during t_2, the output will be in error because the ramp time of the integrator will remain fixed, while the counter's rate of incrementation either increases or decreases. A constant short-term clock frequency is required to retain the validity of Eq. 7-13, because the count achieved in a given time interval is based on this assumption. However, the chances of the clock frequency changing appreciably in one sample/conversion cycle are quite small, especially if a stable source, such as a crystal oscillator, is used in the circuit.

Long-term variations in clock frequency will have virtually no effect on the accuracy of the dual-slope converter. For example, if $f_{clk} = 50.000$ kHz the moment that power is applied to the circuit, and 1 h later $f_{clk} = 50.100$ kHz (perhaps due to a temperature change), there would be no discernible effect on conversion accuracy. This would be true because the change in frequency over a given sample/conversion cycle would be very small. Considering that the maximum conversion time for a given circuit is most likely to be less than 1 s (typical conversion times are around 20 to 50 ms), let us very conservatively assume that the conversion time is actually 1 s. Assuming that the frequency drifted linearly over the 1-h period, a frequency drift rate of $+0.028$ Hz/s will have occurred. For a maximum conversion time of 1 s, the error introduced by this drift is about 0.0006 percent. This is an exceedingly small amount of error and may justifiably be ignored. In fact, such a small error would probably be swamped out by other factors, such as op amp offset error, component value variation, and so on.

Dual-slope A/D converters are often constructed using hybrid IC technology. A hybrid IC contains both monolithic devices, such as the counter and op amp sections, and thin- and thick-film components, such as resistors and capacitors. All of the components that make up the hybrid IC are mounted in close proximity to one another on the same substrate. This reduces temperature gradient related problems, as all of the components will be operating at about the same temperature. The values of the film resistors can be very accurately adjusted and matched using techniques such as laser trimming. Such close-tolerance (both relative and absolute) resistances are not possible using standard monolithic IC fabrication methods. As would be expected, the disadvantage associated with hybrid ICs is their high cost. But, in situations where conversion speed is not critical and accuracy is, such circuits can become quite attractive.

Monolithic A/D Converters More often than not, A/D conversion circuitry is designed around monolithic ICs. An example of one such device is the National Semiconductor ADC0804. Figure 7-27 shows a typical application

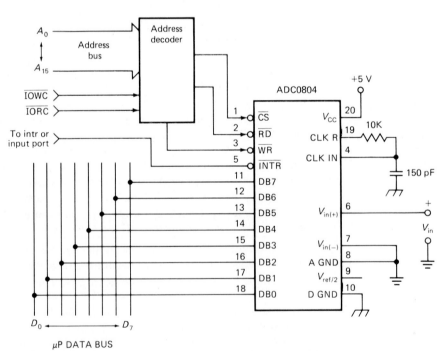

Fig. 7-27 Interfacing the ADC0804 A/D converter to the microcomputer.

using this IC. The ADC0804 was designed specifically to be used in computer and microprocessor-based systems, hence the chip select ($\overline{CS}$), read ($\overline{RD}$), write ($\overline{WR}$) and interrupt request ($\overline{INTR}$) pins. Internally, the ADC0804 uses an 8-bit SAR to perform the actual conversion. The clock is also internal and is programmed with an external RC circuit. Notice that in Fig. 7-27 the output lines of the ADC0804 are connected directly to the data bus. This is possible because the ADC0804 contains an internal tri-state latch. The output of the latch is enabled when the $\overline{CS}$ and $\overline{RD}$ pins are driven low (the CPU is reading the output of the converter). A conversion is initiated by pulling $\overline{CS}$ and $\overline{WR}$ low. The $\overline{INTR}$ output is driven low by the ADC0804 at the end of a conversion, and may be used to initiate an interrupt service request. It may also be connected to an input port line and polled under program control.

A potentiometric transducer may be used to supply the input voltage to the ADC0804 as shown in Fig. 7-28a. The maximum input voltage is 5 V. Potentiometers are often used as positional transducers in servomechanisms. If higher input voltages are to be digitized, a voltage divider such as that shown in Fig. 7-28b may be employed. Notice that the ADC0804 has two different ground pins. The A GND pin is the ground for the analog input, while the D GND pin is the digital circuit ground. This allows better isolation between the digital and analog section of the system.

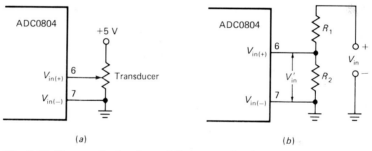

(a)   (b)

Fig. 7-28 Two methods of providing an analog input signal to the A/D converter.

The Parallel A/D Converter   When conversion speed is the primary concern in an application, the parallel A/D converter (sometimes called a flash converter) is an approach that could be considered. As the name implies, a parallel A/D converter does not sequentially step through a series of digital outputs or count the ramp time of an integrator until it has resolved the value of the input. Instead, the input voltage is applied simultaneously to the inputs of a group of parallel connected comparators, each operating from a different reference voltage. A 3-bit parallel A/D converter is shown in Fig. 7-29. A reference voltage is applied to a series of resistors that form a voltage divider. The inverting input of a given comparator is effectively driven by its own unique reference voltage as determined by the divider resistors.

Let us now step through the operation of the parallel A/D converter circuit. Assume that V_{in} is ramping positively from 0 V. At $V_{in} = 0$ V, the

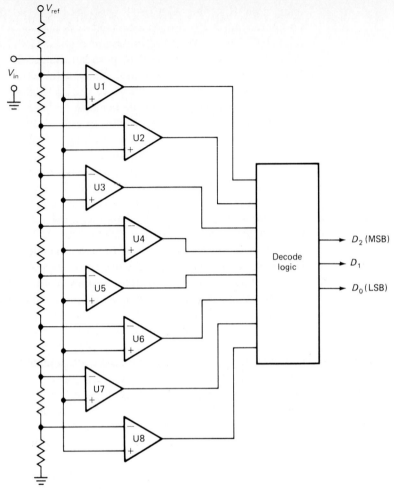

Fig. 7-29 Circuitry for a parallel or flash A/D converter.

outputs of all comparators will be driven to logic 0 and the decoder output is 000_2. As V_{in} increases, the first comparator to change states is $U7$, since it has the lowest applied reference voltage. This change of state is decoded and presented at the output of the decoder as 001_2. As V_{in} increases further, each comparator will consecutively drive its output high until finally $U1$ is triggered. It is important to note that whenever a given comparator is driven high by the input voltage, the outputs of all of the comparators below it will also remain high. The output logic levels respond to the increasing input voltage as shown in Fig. 7-30.

This circuit is called a flash converter because of its very high conversion speed. If very fast comparators and decode logic are used, the output will be able to track very rapidly varying input signals. This would be considered real-time digitization. Of course, if the digital output of the converter is to be stored and used at some later time, a very fast data storage system would be required to keep up with the data stream. Notice that no clock

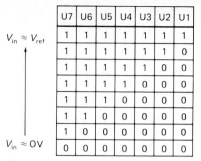

U7	U6	U5	U4	U3	U2	U1
1	1	1	1	1	1	1
1	1	1	1	1	1	0
1	1	1	1	1	0	0
1	1	1	1	0	0	0
1	1	1	0	0	0	0
1	1	0	0	0	0	0
1	0	0	0	0	0	0
0	0	0	0	0	0	0

$V_{in} \approx V_{ref}$

$V_{in} \approx 0V$

Fig. 7-30 Truth table describing the outputs of the comparators in the parallel A/D converter.

control is shown in Fig. 7-29. Clock control would be required to provide synchronization between the output of the A/D converter and the storage circuitry. The addition of a synchronizing clock circuit could provide almost any desired sample rate that is possible with the device that is driven by the A/D converter. The clock would control either latching circuitry at the output of the converter or sample and hold devices at the input of the converter, in order to prevent output changes from occurring during a port read operation.

The fundamental drawback in implementing parallel A/D converters is the necessity of the large numbers of comparators required to obtain relatively high resolution. The 3-bit converter of Fig. 7-29 has a resolution of ± 12.5 percent. This could not really be considered a high-resolution circuit. Generally, at least 7- or 8-bit resolution is desirable in most applications. The number of comparators required to construct an n-bit parallel converter is determined by the equation

$$N = 2^n - 1 \qquad \text{(Eq. 7-14)}$$

where N is the number of comparators necessary and n is the number of bits present at the output.

Using Eq. 7-14, it is found that the 7-bit parallel A/D converter requires 127 comparators, while the 8-bit converter will require 255. This is obviously going to be a costly conversion technique when high resolution is required.

Review Questions for Section 7-3

1. What type of error is inherent in all types of A/D converters?
2. Which type of A/D converter is capable of the highest conversion speed?
3. A certain 8-bit SAR A/D converter completes a given conversion in 80 ms. If the size of the SAR and D/A sections of this converter are replaced with 10-bit devices, what will be the resulting conversion time?
4. Which type(s) of A/D converters have a conversion speed that is independent of the value of V_{in}?

5. Refer to Fig. 7-25. What change(s) would be required to allow the conversion of negative values of V_{in}?

6. A certain A/D converter is to be used to digitize sinusoidal input signals of up to 1 kHz. What is the minimum conversion rate that will allow proper operation of the circuit?

SUMMARY

The addition of input and output ports is only the beginning of the computer/outside world interface. We live in a world that is to a large extent analog in nature. Digital to analog and analog to digital converters provide a means by which the computer can respond to and control analog signals and devices.

D/A converters are available or may be constructed in several different forms. The most commonly used D/A converters are the monolithic IC devices, which may employ weighted resistor summing amps, R-2R ladders, or any of a number of other circuits in their internal construction. The resolution of a D/A converter is related to the number of output bits available on that particular circuit. Resolution sets the lower limit on conversion accuracy. Errors that can adversely affect the accuracy of a D/A converter are gain errors, offset errors, and linearity errors. A graph of the transfer function or characteristic of a D/A converter can be used to determine the nature of any errors that may be present in the output of that circuit.

Analog to digital converters are somewhat more complex than D/A converters of similar resolution. In fact, many A/D converters are constructed around D/A converters. Two examples of these types of circuits are the ramp and SAR A/D converters. Of the two, the SAR converter is faster for a given resolution, at the cost of increased complexity. The resolution of the internal D/A circuitry limits the ultimate accuracy of these kinds of A/D converters.

Integrating dual-slope A/D converters are used in applications that require very high accuracy. These converters produce a digital output that is proportional to the time that an integrator ramps to 0 with an applied reference voltage relative to the length of time that an unknown input was present. Dual slope converters are generally slower than the counter and SAR converters. The fastest A/D converters available are the parallel converters. These converters use a group of comparators driven in parallel by the analog input. A voltage divider is used to develop the required reference inputs, based on a fixed reference voltage. High resolution parallel converters require large numbers of comparators and relatively complex decoding circuitry, which limits their usefulness under most circumstances.

CHAPTER QUESTIONS

7-1. If the sample rate of a given A/D converter does not meet the Nyquist criterion, what type of error will result?

7-2. In many A/D conversion applications where time-varying signals are to be digitized, the input signal is first processed through a low-pass filter. Give a possible explanation for this modification.

7-3. A certain D/A converter produces the transfer characteristic graphed in Fig. 7-31. What type(s) of error(s) are present? The ideal transfer characteristic is shown in color for comparison purposes.

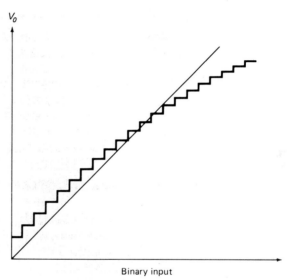

Fig. 7-31 Transfer characteristic plot for Question 7-3.

7-4. Which type of A/D converter would be most effective for the purpose of digitizing a rapidly varying analog signal?

7-5. State two different ways by which the EOC line of an A/D converter can be used to control the action of a CPU.

7-6. What D/A specification would be used to define the maximum rate at which various binary inputs may be applied?

7-7. Which type of D/A error results in output voltage increments that are either smaller or larger than desired?

7-8. Refer to Fig. 7-5. Suppose that the input switches were replaced with SPST-type switches such that the presence of logic 1 closed the switch (connected V_{ref}) and the presence of logic 0 opened the switch (the input or left side of the resistor would float open). What effect would this change have on the operation of the circuit? What problem(s) could be created?

7-9. State two major problems associated with the weighted resistor summing amp D/A converter.

7-10. What is the minimum quantization error that any A/D converter can exhibit (in terms of LSB size)?

7-11. Refer to Fig. 7-5. What is the function of R_C?

CHAPTER PROBLEMS

7-12. What is the maximum conversion time for the circuit shown in Fig. 7-21 if $f_{clk} = 1$ kHz?

7-13. Refer to Fig. 7-23. Assuming the D/A section has $V_{fs} = 5$ V and the comparator behaves ideally, what value of V_{in} will produce the binary output $0111\ 1111_2$?

7-14. A 10-bit SAR-type A/D converter has a 5-kHz test/discard test/retain rate. How long will it take this circuit to perform a conversion?

7-15. A 10-bit dual-slope A/D converter has $V_{ref} = -6$ V. If the sample time count t_1 is 1024_{10} and the reference time count t_2 is 768_{10}, what value of V_{in} is indicated?

7-16. A certain ramp-type A/D converter uses a 12-bit R-2R ladder-type D/A converter with $V_{ref} = 4.096$ V. If the clock frequency is 8 kHz, how long will the circuit take to perform a conversion if $V_{in} = 2.000$ V?

7-17. A certain assembly language program causes a D/A converter to produce the output waveform shown in Fig. 7-32. What simple modification of the D/A circuit could eliminate the large dc offset that is present in the output waveform?

7-18. Refer to Fig. 7-25. What would happen if V_{in} exceeded V_{ref}? How could such an occurrence be prevented (using additional components)?

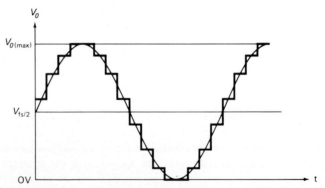

Fig. 7-32 D/A converter output waveform for Problem 7-18.

7-19. A certain ramp-type A/D converter requires a resolution of 0.20 percent or better. What is the minimum number of stages that the counter section (and also the D/A section) of this converter must have to achieve this resolution specification?

7-20. The circuit shown in Fig. 7-8 has the following component values and input conditions: $V_{ref} = +5$ V, $R_1 = R_2 = 12k$, and the binary input is $1001\ 1100_2$. What value will I_O have? What is the value of 1 LSB?

7-21. How many bits are required to form a D/A converter that will produce 32 different output levels?

7-22. Refer to Problem 7-20. An I/V converter is to be added to the circuit such that $V_{fs} = 10$ V. What value must R_F have?

7-23. How many comparators would be required to construct a 6-bit parallel A/D converter?

7-24. Refer to Fig. 7-21. A problem could be encountered in the counter section of this circuit if the flip-flops that constitute the counter toggle on the falling edge of the clock input signal (negative edge triggered devices are used). What effect would such a situation have on the output of the converter? Suppose that the counter was constructed with negative edge triggered devices. What modification(s) would be required to ensure proper operation of the converter?

7-25. A certain 4-bit D/A converter has $V_{O(max)} = 10$ V. What is V_{fs} for this circuit?

7-26. The outputs of the comparators in Fig. 7-33 are TTL-compatible. Design a decoding circuit that will produce the correct binary weighted output for the various states that will occur on the comparator outputs.

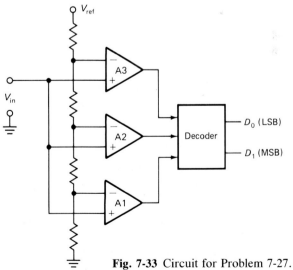

Fig. 7-33 Circuit for Problem 7-27.

VIDEO DISPLAYS AND GRAPHICS

8

The video display is the most widely used of all microcomputer output devices. This chapter will introduce the main ideas behind the operation of various types of character and graphics displays. The relationship between the bit patterns stored in memory and the image that appears on the screen of the display will be discussed from both character generator ROM and individually addressable bit-mapped video RAM standpoints. Some typical high-level language graphics statements will also be discussed, including their use in the plotting of various types of graphs and mathematical functions.

8-1   VIDEO DISPLAY FUNDAMENTALS

As mentioned before, there are several different types of video displays in use with computers today. This section shall focus on those that are designed around cathode-ray tubes (CRTs), as they are the most widely used.

8-1.1   Monochrome CRTs

The construction of a typical monochrome (one-color) CRT is shown in Fig. 8-1. Basically, here's how it works. Current flow through the heater causes the negatively charged cathode to become hot. This results in the formation of a cloud of electrons around the cathode. The electrons that are heated off of the cathode are attracted toward the positively charged accelerating anode. The focusing anode forces the electrons that are moving toward the face of the CRT to form a tight beam. The accelerating anode increases the velocity of the electron beam so that it takes a very short time for the beam to reach the face of the CRT. This is necessary because the electrons will repel each other rather quickly, causing the beam to spread and go out of focus.

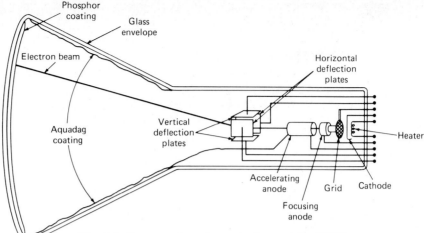

Fig. 8-1 Cross section of a cathode-ray tube (CRT).

As the electron beam is moving toward the CRT's face, it passes by charged deflection plates. There are two pairs of deflection plates. One pair deflects the electron beam back and forth horizontally across the CRT, and the other, up and down vertically across the CRT. The inside of the CRT face is coated with a phosphor that emits visible light when struck by the high-velocity electron beam. By applying time-varying voltages to the vertical and horizontal deflection plates, various images may be formed with the CRT.

The brightness of the images formed on the face of the CRT is dependent on the intensity of the electron beam when it passes over a given spot. The intensity of the beam is controlled by applying a negative voltage to the tube's grid. A high negative voltage present on the grid will prevent some electrons from leaving the cathode, hence reducing the intensity of the beam and the brightness of the display. A sufficiently high negative voltage applied to the grid will prevent any of the electrons emitted by the cathode from striking the phosphor coating. This is how the beam is turned off to produce a black portion of an image.

Many different types of phosphors may be used to form the coating on the inside of the CRT. One of the more important characteristics of a given phosphor is its persistence. Persistence is a measure of how long the phosphor glows after it has been excited by the electron beam. Low-persistence phosphors must be excited more frequently in order to maintain a relatively constant level of light, while high-persistence phosphors need to be excited less often for the same effective light level. The importance of persistence will become more apparent when scanning is discussed later in this chapter.

8-1.2 Magnetic Deflection

The CRT shown in Fig. 8-1 uses what is called electrostatic deflection; that is, electrostatic fields, produced by applying high voltages to the various control elements in the tube, are used to direct the electron beam to the desired position. This is the technique used in many computer monitors and in some oscilloscopes. However, electrons also have magnetic poles, and may therefore be deflected by magnetic fields. In such a case, the deflection plates are replaced by external coils of wire that form what is called a deflection yoke. The deflection yoke is mounted around the neck of the CRT, and it serves to move the electron beam to any desired point on the screen just as deflection plates do. Many computer monitors and all modern television sets use magnetic deflection to produce a display. A drawing of a CRT with a deflection yoke is shown in Fig. 8-2.

8-1.3 Color CRTs

In many respects, color CRTs are quite similar to monochrome ones, as the basic principles behind the operation of both are essentially the same. The main difference between them is that color CRTs use three different color phosphors on the CRT face, a part called a shadow mask, and, usually, three electron guns. A simplified cross section of a typical color CRT is shown in Fig. 8-3. Deflection of the electron beams may be either electrostatic or magnetic. A close-up view of the shadow mask and the phosphor coating is also shown in Fig. 8-3. The phosphor dots are arranged such that any given group of three (a triad) primary colors—red, blue, and green—forms a dot. By varying the relative intensity of the three phosphor spots in a group, different colors may be produced.

The three electron beams produced are not independently deflected; that is, all three electron beams are deflected simultaneously by an equal

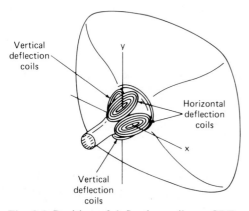

Fig. 8-2 Position of deflection coils on CRT.

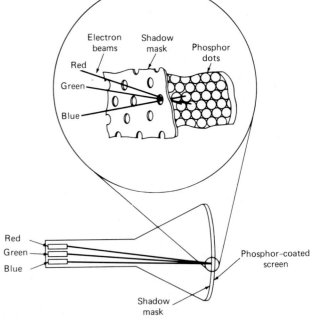

Fig. 8-3 Detail of phosphor coating and shadow mask of a three-gun color CRT.

amount. They must also be focused such that the electron beams converge on the holes in the shadow mask. Upon passing through a given hole in the shadow mask, the beams deconverge and strike their associated phosphor dot. This produces sharp, well-defined illumination of the three different color phosphors that make up a triad.

Some color CRTs use a single electron gun, from which the electron stream is split into three beams whose intensities are independently controllable just like the three-gun tube. A notable characteristic of the single-gun CRT is that the colored phosphors are rectangular in shape. The advantage of the single-gun CRT over conventional tubes is that convergence is more easily adjusted. These CRTs are usually found in high-quality monitors (and televisions).

8-1.4 Raster Scanning

Nearly all CRT-based video displays use raster scanning to generate characters and graphics. This is the same technique that is used to produce a picture on a standard television receiver. A raster-scanned display produces a picture that is formed by intensity modulated horizontal lines drawn one below another on the face of the CRT. These lines are called rasters, hence the term raster scanning. Raster scan action is illustrated in Fig. 8-4. Starting in the upper left-hand corner of the display, the

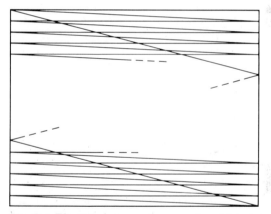

Fig. 8-4 Electron beam pattern produced by raster scanning.

electron beam is swept across and down to the right. When the right side of the screen is reached, the intensity of the electron beam is reduced to near 0, or blanked, and it is deflected rapidly back to the left. The colored lines in Fig. 8-4 represent the retrace portions of the scan. The rapid return to the left side of the display is called horizontal retrace. This process repeats until the last line is drawn, at the end of which the beam intensity is again reduced and driven to the upper left corner of the display, where the entire process is again repeated. The return to the beginning of the screen is called the vertical retrace, and again, during vertical retrace, the display is blanked. As the beam is swept across the screen on each raster, its intensity is modulated and the desired picture is produced, one line at a time.

With this type of raster scan (called noninterlaced scan), each complete scan of the screen (from left to right, top to bottom, and back to the beginning) is called a frame. The rate at which frames are produced is sometimes called the refresh rate; that is, when referring to video displays, the refresh rate is the frequency with which a complete picture or frame is updated.

8-1.5 Interlaced Raster Scanning

Quite often, a technique called interlaced raster scanning is used to produce the video display. Interlaced scanning is used in television sets and may also be implemented in video monitors. The idea behind interlaced scanning is that the information that is to be displayed on the screen is drawn every other line (even lines or odd lines) during each successive frame. Figure 8-5 illustrates this process. The black lines represent the path of the

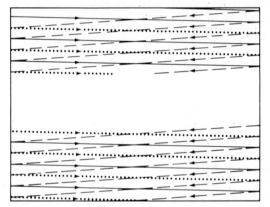

Fig. 8-5 Interlaced raster scanning pattern. Even field is shown by a dotted line.

electron beam in what is called the odd field, and the dotted lines represent the path of the beam in the even field. Dashed lines represent horizontal retrace. Assuming that scanning begins with the even field, the beam begins its journey at the center of the top line (line 0). During retrace, the beam is moved down to line 2, skipping line 1, where the process repeats until the final even line is drawn. At this time, vertical retrace occurs and the odd field is now drawn in the same manner, except that it begins in the upper left-hand corner (line 1) and ends in the center of the bottom of the display area, offset by one line from the even field. The end result is that half of the picture is filled in during each successive field, and two fields are required to complete a frame. This process is illustrated by the generation of the number 8 in Fig. 8-6a, b, and c.

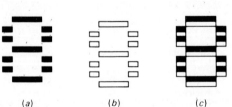

(a)   (b)   (c)

Fig. 8-6 Generation of a character with interlaced scanning. Even field (a) combined with odd field (b) produces solid character (c).

8-1.6 Further Details on Raster Scanning

The time it takes the beam to sweep across one horizontal line and return to start the next line is determined by a circuit called a horizontal oscillator. For North American television sets, the horizontal oscillator frequency is 15,750 Hz. This is also a common horizontal frequency used in computer monitors, although it is by no means the only one used. A typical horizontal oscillator waveform is shown in Fig. 8-7a.

The time that it takes the beam to move from the top of the screen to the bottom and back again is determined by the vertical oscillator of the monitor. A typical vertical oscillator is shown in Fig. 8-7b. The frequency of this signal will be much lower than that produced by the horizontal oscillator. In North America, the vertical oscillator frequency for television sets is 60 Hz, which is also commonly used in computer monitor applications.

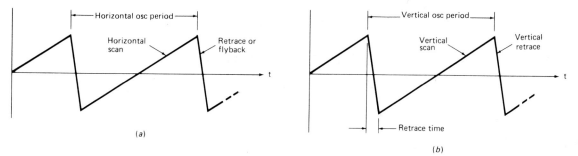

Fig. 8-7 Horizontal (a) and vertical (b) oscillator waveforms. *Note:* Time scales are not equal.

8-1.7 Overscan and Retrace

Most monitors actually begin scanning before the beginning of the display area, and continue scanning a short distance past the right side of the visible display area. This is called overscan. The time required for overscan plus the time needed for vertical retrace must be taken into account when dots are written to the screen. Most CRT control circuits may be adjusted to compensate for these time delays.

8-1.8 Resolution

Because of the nature of the raster scan process, all graphics and characters displayed on such a monitor will be comprised of various patterns of dots produced a row at a time. These dots are called pixels, or sometimes pels (short for picture elements). The horizontal resolution of a display is dependent on the horizontal sweep speed and on the dot rate, which is determined appropriately enough by a dot clock. The dot rate is the rate with which the electron beam may be turned on and off as it is moved across the screen. The dot clock, in conjunction with the horizontal oscillator, will determine how many dots constitute a line. The number of dots that can be drawn on the screen can be approximated by dividing the dot clock frequency by the horizontal oscillator frequency.

Vertical resolution is defined as the number of lines that are displayed on the monitor. It is possible to determine the vertical resolution by dividing the horizontal oscillator frequency by the vertical oscillator frequency. For example, assuming that a hypothetical monitor has a horizontal oscillator frequency of 15,750 Hz and a vertical oscillator frequency of 60 Hz, the vertical resolution is found to be 262.5 lines. If interlaced scanning is used, then the vertical resolution will double to 525 lines; however, a complete picture, or frame, requires two periods of the vertical oscillator (two fields), as opposed to one for noninterlaced scan. Also, when interlaced scan is used, any given pixel is refreshed half as often as with noninterlaced scan (once every other field); and therefore, higher-persistence phosphors must be used in the CRT in order to avoid flickering of the display.

Example 8-1

The monochrome monitor for the IBM PC uses a dot clock frequency of 16.257 MHz and a horizontal oscillator frequency of 18.432 kHz. Ideally, what is the horizontal resolution of this monitor?

Solution

The ideal horizontal resolution of this monitor is found by dividing the dot clock frequency by the horizontal oscillator frequency.

$$\text{Horizontal resolution} = f_{\text{dot}}/f_{\text{horiz}}$$
$$= 16.257 \text{ MHz}/18.432 \text{ kHz}$$
$$= 882 \text{ pixels}$$

In actual practice, the resolution would be somewhat less than 882 pixels because of overscan and retrace time. This monitor and its associated interface and control circuitry effectively consume 162 pixels during retrace and overscan, resulting in an actual horizontal resolution of 720 pixels; that is, each scan line is composed of 720 pixels.

Example 8-2

Assuming the same conditions as in Example 8-1, if the vertical oscillator operates at a frequency of 50 Hz, what is the ideal vertical resolution of the monitor?

Solution

The vertical resolution is the number of scan lines that make up a frame. Ideally, this value is found by dividing the horizontal oscillator frequency by the vertical oscillator frequency.

$$\text{Vertical resolution} = f_{\text{horiz}}/f_{\text{vert}}$$
$$= 18.432 \text{ kHz}/50 \text{ Hz}$$
$$= 368.64 \text{ lines}$$

As was the case with horizontal resolution, the vertical resolution will be somewhat lower than the ideal, because of the vertical retrace time delay. The finite slope of the retrace portion of the vertical oscillator waveform (see Fig. 8-7) accounts for this characteristic. In actuality, this particular monitor has a true vertical resolution of 350 scan lines.

Figure 8-8 illustrates the block diagram for a circuit that could be used to interface a monitor to a computer. A large portion of the CRT control

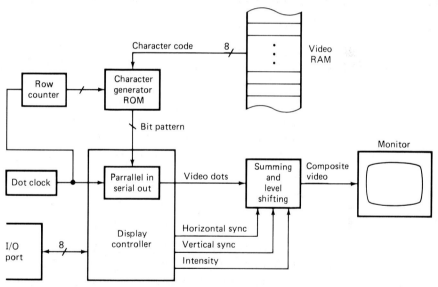

Fig. 8-8 Block diagram for a composite video interface.

task is handled by the display controller. Such devices are usually LSI chips that contain video RAM DMA circuitry, row count circuitry, and parallel to serial conversion logic. The CRT controller also controls the number of lines per field, the number of lines per character row, interlace control, and horizontal and vertical sync timing. The CRT controller is programmed via an I/O port, from which it receives initialization commands. After the controller is initialized, it usually needs no further instructions. This frees the CPU from what would be some very time-consuming display control tasks.

The circuit in Fig. 8-8 produces what is called a composite video signal; that is, all video information is contained in a single signal and transmitted over a single line. In Fig. 8-9, all of the video data is sent to the monitor

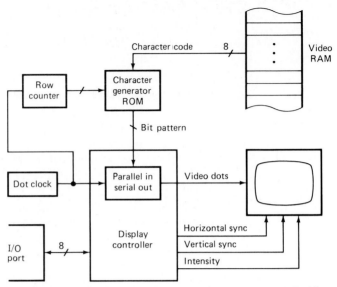

Fig. 8-9 Video display interface with separate sync and video signal lines.

over separate lines. Both approaches are used, with the composite video method generally yielding a display of slightly lower quality. Timing is very important when video displays are used, and the horizontal and vertical synchronization signals are used to keep the oscillators in the monitor running at the proper frequencies and in synchronization with the dot rate. The intensity output line is used to vary the brightness of the display.

Review Questions for Section 8-1

1. Name the two techniques by which deflection is produced in a CRT.
2. Describe the difference between normal and interlaced raster scanning.
3. Name another alternative to raster-scan-based video.
4. What are the three primary colors?
5. How does a standard color CRT differ from a monochrome unit?
6. What CRT specification is a measure of the length of time that a phosphor will continue to emit a useful amount of light after it has been excited?

8-2 VIDEO DISPLAY VARIATIONS

Section 8-1 introduced some of the basic ideas behind video displays in general. This section will present further details regarding some typical approaches to generating text or alphanumeric displays, some further information on how raster-scanned video displays operate, and some basic information on graphics displays.

8-2.1 Character-Based Displays

The characters that can be displayed on the monitor are usually stored as binary bit patterns in ROM. There are many different approaches that may be taken with respect to the way these character codes are stored and used, and a few of them will be described here.

A section of RAM is devoted entirely to storage of the character codes that are currently seen on the screen. This reserved area of memory is called the video or refresh RAM. Each byte of the video RAM contains the code for a given character position on the screen. Since the display is refreshed at relatively high speeds, the display generator circuit will usually have DMA capability so that it can update the display at these frequent intervals.

The bit patterns that represent the various letters, symbols, and numbers are stored in sequential locations in a character generator ROM (see Figs. 8-8 and 8-9). For example, the number 8 might be represented in the character ROM as shown in Fig. 8-10a embedded in an 8 × 8 array of

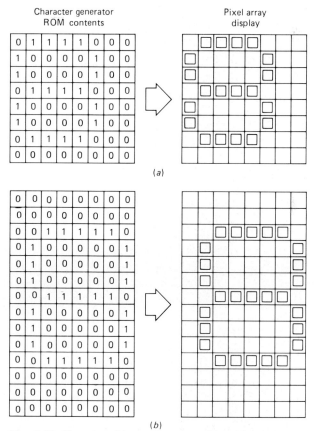

Fig. 8-10 Character bit patterns stored in video ROMs.

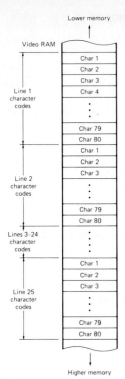

Lower memory

Video RAM

	Char 1
	Char 2
	Char 3
Line 1 character codes	Char 4
	⋮
	Char 79
	Char 80
	Char 1
	Char 2
Line 2 character codes	Char 3
	⋮
	Char 79
	Char 80
Lines 3-24 character codes	⋮
	Char 1
	Char 2
Line 25 character codes	Char 3
	⋮
	Char 79
	Char 80

Higher memory

Fig. 8-11 Typical memory map for a video RAM.

pixels, or possibly as in Fig. 8-10*b* in a 9 × 14 array. The character code read from RAM is used to point to the array of bits in the ROM that constitute a given character. A row counter is used to select which of the rows of the bit pattern array is sent to the parallel-in serial-out (PISO) shift register (see Fig. 8-8). When a key that represents a printable character is closed, the appropriate character code is generated and written to the video RAM. The location in video RAM to which the character code is loaded is designated by the position of the cursor. The cursor usually appears as a blinking box or line on the screen. Since the cursor points to a particular character location on the screen, it also indicates the video RAM location that will be written to next. In this approach, each character position is represented by a byte of RAM. In Fig. 8-10*b* we see that a byte-oriented character ROM is not wide enough to represent each row of a 9-bit-wide (pixel) character. In order to effectively create a 9-bit code for each row of a given character, all that has to be done is make the PISO register 9 bits wide, and have the LSB (the first bit shifted out) loaded with 0 when the ROM row data is loaded.

Figure 8-11 illustrates the organization of a typical video RAM, and the following steps describe the actions that occur when the display is refreshed. Assume that the first scan row of an 80-character by 25-line display is being updated.

1. The character code is read from video RAM.
2. This code is used to select the proper array of character bit patterns in the character generator ROM. A row counter is used to select the bit pattern that constitutes the row of the character that is being generated at this time. In this case, row 0 is selected, as the display is being refreshed from the very beginning.
3. The code for the next character position is read from RAM, serialized, converted to the correct levels, and displayed on the monitor.
4. Step 3 is repeated until the entire first scan line of the screen is complete, at which time horizontal retrace occurs.
5. The row counter is incremented, and the next scan line is completed. This process is repeated until the first line of character positions is finished.
6. When the first character line is complete, the row counter is reset and the character codes for the next line of characters are repeatedly sent to the character generator ROM, serialized, and displayed. This repeats until the entire screen has been refreshed.

The number of bits that make up a character code depends on the number of characters that are to be displayed. If 8 bits are used, then 256 different characters may be accessed. The number of lines per character determines how many bytes must be saved in the character ROM for each. In Fig. 8-10*a*, 8 bytes are used to store the pattern for each character, while in Fig. 8-10*b*, 14 bytes are required.

Example 8-3

A certain computer system is required to display 256 different characters embedded in 8 × 8 pixel grids. How many bytes will the character generator ROM be required to contain?

Solution

Since the characters are 8 pixels (scan lines) high, a total of 2048 bytes must be stored in the ROM. This is easily determined by multiplying the height of the characters by the number of characters to be implemented.

Example 8-4

A certain monitor is to have a display size of 80 characters by 25 lines. How many bytes of video RAM are required if the contents of four different screens are to be available for display at any time?

Solution

Assuming that each character is represented by 1 byte (the character code alone), the number of characters that can be shown on the screen at any given time is found by multiplying the number of characters per line (80) by the number of lines of text (25). This yields 2000 bytes of video RAM per screen. Obviously, the contents of four screens would require four times this amount of memory for storage, yielding 8000 bytes.

Allocating separate blocks of video RAM for storage of screen information allows the user to easily review previously entered data, and can also be used to quickly change graphic information that is being shown. This is a popular method of video storage.

In many cases, 2 bytes of video RAM must be allocated for each character that is to be displayed on the screen. This is necessary because it may be desired that various characters have particular characteristics or attributes, such as an underscore, highlighting, reverse video, or blinking. In these cases, the byte that defines how the character is to appear is called an attribute byte. Generally, the attribute byte is stored immediately following the character code in video RAM. A given attribute byte may be generated when particular key combinations are detected. Of course, the video RAM may be accessed just as any other section of RAM, and the user may change character codes and attribute bytes at his or her discretion, using assembly language or BASIC's POKE statement.

8-2.2 Graphics Displays

For applications that are mainly alphanumeric or text-related in nature, the size of the screen in characters and lines is most important. Recently, however, graphics has become a very important aspect of the computer field. The approaches to text display and graphics displays are similar in many respects, but are different enough to be studied separately.

In graphics applications, the size of the screen in pixels is the most important consideration. The greater the number of pixels, the higher the resolution. Using the data from Examples 8-1 and 8-2, it could be said that the display area of this particular monitor is 720 pixels by 350 pixels in size; but if the character generation approach discussed previously is used, the pixels are not individually controllable; that is, the display is limited to those bit patterns that are stored in the character generator ROM, and cannot be altered very easily.

Bit Mapping The display limitations just discussed can be eliminated if the pixels that constitute the display are independently addressable. This would allow the computer to be used in graphics applications as well as for text-related purposes. The inclusion of individually addressable pixels is called bit-mapped graphics. This is the most popular graphics technique in use with microcomputer systems today. In its simplest form, each pixel is controlled by a bit in the video RAM.

In terms of pixels, a typical display screen would be organized as shown by the 340 × 200 screen in Fig. 8-12. Notice that the origin of the screen is in the upper left-hand corner. This is a very commonly used organization for microcomputer systems with bit-mapped displays. The state of each pixel is determined based on the value of its associated bit in the video RAM. The screen position of a given pixel is specified in cartesian coordinates; that is, the distance of the pixel from the origin is given by a pair of numbers such as (50,10), where 50 is the x (horizontal) coordinate

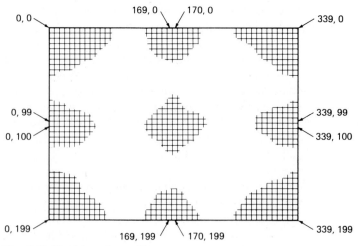

Fig. 8-12 Pixel location grid.

and 10 is the *y* (vertical) coordinate. Such coordinate systems are used quite often in high-level language graphics statements.

In terms of pixel control, a simple approach is to have each bit of the video RAM control a given pixel. This is illustrated in Fig. 8-13. Here, a

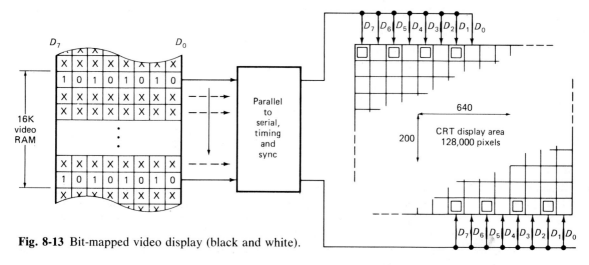

Fig. 8-13 Bit-mapped video display (black and white).

640×200 pixel display screen is controlled by a 16K byte block of video RAM. The first byte of RAM in the block controls the first 8 pixels in the first scan line, the second byte controls the second 8 pixels in the first scan line, and so on. In this way, as the raster scans across the screen and down, the contents of the RAM are loaded sequentially into the PISO register once every 8 pixels. This allows relatively simple control of the display.

The assignment of a single bit to each pixel is the most memory-efficient way of mapping the screen. If the only thing that is required is that a given pixel be turned on or off, this is the method that is used. However, if a color monitor is used, several bits must be used to control each pixel, since there are more possibilities than just on or off. Four colors could be controlled if 2 bits are assigned to each pixel. It must be considered, however, that for the same screen size in pixels as that in Fig. 8-13, the size of the video RAM would also double to 32K. This may not be practical in all cases. What is commonly done to alleviate this problem is the reduction of the horizontal resolution of the screen. If, for example, the width of the display was reduced to 340 pixels, the same 16K byte block of video RAM could be used for both the high-resolution black and white graphics mode and the lower-resolution color graphics mode. Figure 8-14 illustrates the 320×200 color graphics mode.

The main disadvantage accompanying the color graphics mode is that each pixel will be two times wider horizontally than in the high-resolution mode. This will result in "chunkier" looking displays, especially if curves are to be represented. The addition of color may more than make up for this in some applications.

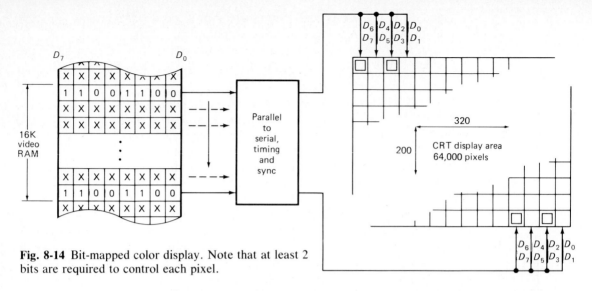

Fig. 8-14 Bit-mapped color display. Note that at least 2 bits are required to control each pixel.

Interlaced Scanning and the Graphics Screen The bit-mapping techniques that were just presented would work only if the monitor used noninterlaced scanning. That is what kept the approaches rather simple. In many systems, however, interlaced scanning may be in use. This requires a reorganization of the video RAM. You will recall that in interlaced scanning a frame is composed of an even field and an odd field. These fields are scanned sequentially, beginning with the even one. What this means is that the video RAM must be divided into two sections: one containing even field data and the other containing odd field data. Figure 8-15 illustrates the

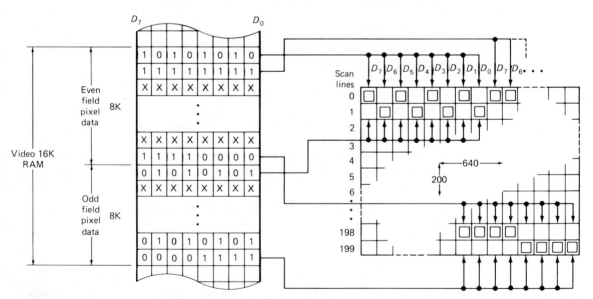

Fig. 8-15 Video RAM and pixel correspondence in an interlaced scan system. Note that even and odd field data is split into two separate sections of RAM.

operation of such a system. The first 80 bytes of video RAM contain the data for the pixels in scan line 0. These bytes will be read out sequentially at the beginning of the frame refresh, after which horizontal retrace will occur and scan line 2 will begin. The next 80 bytes of video RAM contain the data for the pixels in scan line 2 of the display. The contents of the even field block of video RAM are all sent to the monitor in this manner.

After the even field has been scanned, vertical retrace occurs and the odd field is created. From an addressing standpoint, this presents no problems, as the video RAM is still read out in a strict sequential manner. However, from a programming point of view, things get a little complicated because of the memory split. Fortunately, most microcomputer manufacturers that use this method of graphics provide routines in the operating system ROM that handle the distribution of pixel data in the video RAM. These routines are required by the high-level graphics statements, and may also be used in assembly language programs. It should also be noted that this technique would be used in interlaced scanning of non-bit-mapped displays. In such a case, the bit patterns within the character generator ROM would be split between even and odd field sections, although the video RAM would be unaffected.

Bit-Mapped Character Displays   Bit-mapped displays are well-suited to graphics applications, but are not quite so appropriate for character-based tasks. It shall be shown later that often it is quite easy to create displays of things that might not be thought easily produced, such as graphs of equations and trigonometric functions. The reason that such graphs are easy to produce is because they are described by mathematical relationships, and this is one area in which the computer excels. Alphanumeric characters, and many other visual forms, are not described by mathematical relationships. In order to create such forms on the display screen, a less elegant, brute-force approach must often be used. The technique used in many microcomputer systems that operate in a bit-mapped graphics mode is to read the bit patterns necessary to produce a given character from ROM and then load them into the video RAM in the appropriate locations. In this way, as the video RAM is read, any characters that are desired can be displayed. This is quite different than the non-bit-mapped mode of text display.

The disadvantage of bit-mapped graphics is that it requires more memory than the character generator ROM method. Consider the following example.

Example 8-5

A certain microcomputer has a monochrome display of 640 × 200 pixels in size. There are to be 256 different characters that are embedded in 8 × 8 pixel arrays. The display is also 80 characters per line by 25 lines in size. The video RAM is to be large enough to store the contents of four different display screens.

1. Using the character generator ROM approach, without bit mapping, how many bytes of character ROM and video RAM are required to implement this design?
2. Using bit-mapped graphics, how many bytes of ROM are required to store the character data and how many bytes of video RAM are required in this design?

Solution

1. With a screen size of 80 characters by 25 lines, the video RAM will require 2000 bytes per screen. Four screens yield a total of 8000 bytes of video RAM. The character generator ROM must hold the data for 256 characters that are 8 bits high. This requires 2048 bytes of ROM. A total of 10,048 bytes of the memory space must be allocated to the display.
2. In the bit-mapped mode, the ROM requirements will be the same as in part 1, 2048 bytes, because the size and number of characters have not changed. The video RAM must accommodate the data for 128,000 pixels per screen. This translates to 16,000 bytes of video RAM per screen, for a total of 64,000 bytes of video RAM. The total memory required for the bit-mapped method is 66,048 bytes of RAM.

From Example 8-5 it is obvious that in some instances, the bit-mapped technique can use up quite a bit of memory space. The advantages to bit mapping usually outweigh the disadvantages in most applications for the following reasons: Newer microprocessors can address huge amounts of memory, the cost of memory is decreasing, memory densities are increasing, custom characters can be created, and finally, the computer may be intended to be used almost exclusively for graphics applications anyway.

Review Questions for Section 8-2

1. What is the main disadvantage of bit mapping in comparison with character-generator-based display operation?
2. When interlaced scanning is used, how many fields constitute a frame?
3. What is the term given to the rate at which the display screen is updated?
4. Which display-oriented clock circuit operates at the highest speed?
5. Which display scanning method would require the higher-persistence phosphor for a given refresh rate?
6. How many scan lines constitute a frame on a standard television receiver?

8-3 GRAPHICS PROGRAMMING

Computer graphics applications have grown tremendously in recent years. Where originally computers were used largely for "number crunching" and high-speed control applications, the field has become much more diverse. Visual representations of data can make otherwise rather unremarkable collections of data yield instantly recognizable and meaningful characteristics. This is a very important aspect of computer graphics. In fact, just the presence of good graphics can make an otherwise unremarkable program (or such graphics capabilities on a given computer) a highly sought product. This section will present some of the basic techniques used in graphics programming.

8-3.1 Screen Coordinate Systems

Recently, the trend has been to integrate into high-level languages for microcomputers, graphics statements and functions that facilitate the control of bit-mapped displays. There are several reasons for this occurrence. One reason is that it makes graphics displays much easier to produce than with assembly language, which was just about the only practical alternative in the past. Of course, assembly language graphics programs usually run many times faster than equivalent high-level language programs. This is still the major advantage to working with graphics in assembly language.

Most microcomputers divide a bit-mapped display area into an array of pixels similar to that shown in Fig. 8-16. This is essentially an alternative version of Fig. 8-12. As shown in Fig. 8-16, the origin of the screen in most microcomputer systems is the upper leftmost pixel. The coordinates for any given pixel are usually specified in the form

$$(x,y)$$

where x is the horizontal displacement of the pixel from the origin and y is the vertical displacement down from the origin. When specified in this

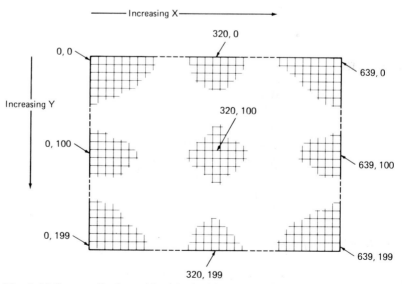

Fig. 8-16 Screen display grid with pixel locations given in physical coordinates.

manner, the pixel is located by what are called physical coordinates. Physical coordinates are fairly simple to work with; however, as used in Fig. 8-12, they can be a little inconvenient in some applications.

An alternative to the physical coordinate system is a system called world coordinates. World coordinates allow the screen to be mapped in true cartesian form; that is, the center of the screen is the origin, and there are four quadrants as shown in Fig. 8-17. An example of a screen that is laid

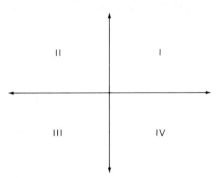

Fig. 8-17 The cartesian coordinate system.

out in world coordinates is shown in Fig. 8-18. The key points on this map are shown in color. It should be noted that it is not actually the computer itself that has the ability to use world coordinate systems, but rather, this is a feature of the programming language that is being used on that particular system. As long as the computer hardware has bit-mapping capability, either physical or world coordinate systems could be implemented, with physical coordinates being the more primitive of the two.

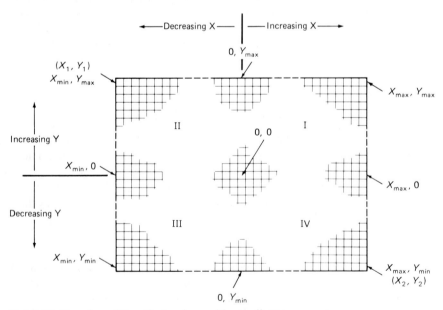

Fig. 8-18 Mapping of the display in world coordinates.

High-level languages that have provisions to use world coordinate systems usually have some provisions for scaling the x and y screen coordinate limits to any arbitrary values. These limits are set by the values of (X_1, Y_1) and (X_2, Y_2), which are shown in Fig. 8-18. These values would normally be user-definable in most cases, and the remainder of the screen would automatically be scaled in proportion to these values. For example, if $X_1 = -1$, $Y_1 = 1$, $X_2 = 1$, and $Y_2 = -1$, then the screen would be scaled as shown in Fig. 8-19a. For the values $X_1 = -5$, $Y_1 = 50$, $X_2 = 5$, and $Y_2 = -50$, the screen would be scaled as shown in Fig. 8-19b. It

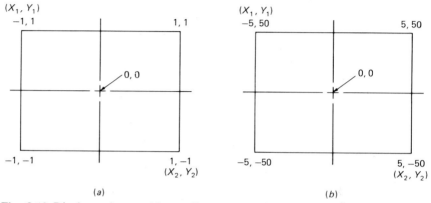

Fig. 8-19 Display using world coordinates with equal limits of 1 in the x and y directions (a) and unequally rescaled limits (b).

is important to realize that world coordinates are used mainly for the benefit of the programmer. At the machine language level, the computer still operates in the physical coordinate system. This means that when world coordinates are used, coordinate transformation must take place before an image can be mapped onto the display. The transformation is performed by routines that are part of the structure of the programming language.

8-3.2 High-Level Graphics Statements and Functions

Many dialects of BASIC that are used with microcomputers today include graphics support statements and functions. The following are typical of a few of the many possible graphics statements and commands that are often implemented. Descriptions of the actions of the commands and their attributes are also presented. The parameters that are enclosed in brackets are optional.

```
PSET (X,Y)[,C]
```

This statement is used to turn on or off the pixel located at position (X,Y). The attribute C specifies the state the pixel is to assume, where 1 = on and 0 = off. C could also represent a specific color that the pixel is to assume. If C is not specified, a default value of 1 will be assigned.

```
LINE (X1,Y1)-(X2,Y2)[,C][,B][,S]
```

This statement draws the best straight line starting at position (X1,Y1) and ending at (X2,Y2). If C = 1, then the pixels are turned on. If C is not specified, then it is assigned a value of 1 by default. B is an optional parameter that may be used that creates a box whose upper left corner is specified by (X1,Y1), while (X2,Y2) specifies the lower right corner. S represents a 16-bit value that is ANDed with the binary values of the pixels that make up the line or the box. This can be used to create dashed lines, dotted lines, and so on.

```
CIRCLE (X,Y),R[,C][,B],E][,A]
```

This statement allows circles, ellipses, and arcs to be created easily. The coordinate pair (X,Y) specifies the location of the center of the circle. R specifies the radius of the circle in the current screen coordinate system. C is a number that represents the color of the circle (if color is applicable). B represents the angle in radians, at which an arc is to begin, while E represents the angle at which the arc ends. If B and E are unspecified, a complete circle or ellipse is drawn. The parameter A specifies the aspect ratio of the circle. The aspect ratio is the ratio of the width of the display screen to the height of the screen in pixels. Ideally, a circle could be thought of as an ellipse with an aspect ratio of 1. A screen with the dimensions shown in Fig. 8-16 would produce an ellipse if an aspect ratio of 1 was used to plot a circle, because the screen (and the pixels) are not square. The aspect ratio parameter is used to form ellipses and to eliminate the distortion of circles due to screen dimension inequality. A nondistorted circle and two ellipses with different aspect ratios are shown in Fig. 8-20a, b, and c. These figures are based on the use of a display with square (on the screen, they would appear round) pixels. The actual shape of the pixels will vary from one computer to another.

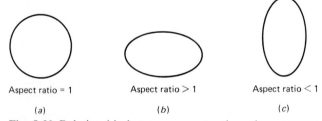

Aspect ratio = 1   Aspect ratio > 1   Aspect ratio < 1

(a)   (b)   (c)

Fig. 8-20 Relationship between aspect ratio and appearance of a circle.

```
WINDOW (X1,Y1)-(X2,Y2)
```

The WINDOW statement is used to initialize the world coordinate system for the screen, as described previously. The coordinate pair (X1,Y1) specifies the upper left corner, and (X2,Y2) specifies the lower right as shown in Fig. 8-18. The origin will be in the center of the screen.

```
SCREEN M [,C][,O][,D]
```

The SCREEN statement is used to select the type of basic display format used. For example, SCREEN 0 activates a nongraphics display mode, with the system configured for character-based use. SCREEN 1 activates a medium-resolution color graphics mode, in which the display is 320 × 200 pixels in size and is mapped as shown in Fig. 8-14. SCREEN 2 enables the high-resolution display mode, producing a display area of 640 × 200 pixels in size. The bit mapping of this screen is shown in Fig. 8-13. C is the color attribute. If C = 1, color is enabled. If C = 0, color is disabled. O is an output parameter that is used to send program output to various pages of video RAM. Depending on which screen size is in use (if different screen sizes are available), output may be sent to any one of the pages 0 through 7 in the 40-column mode, or pages 0 through 3 in the 80-column mode. The default value is normally screen page 0. The D (display) parameter is used to select which page of video RAM is visible on the screen, with a default value the same as that of [O] if omitted.

```
WIDTH N
```

The WIDTH is used to select between 40-column (N = 40) or 80-column (N = 80) modes. The SCREEN 0 mode may use either size. SCREEN 1 can use only the 40-column width. If WIDTH 80 is selected while in SCREEN 1, the SCREEN 2 mode will automatically be activated. If SCREEN 2 is active when WIDTH 40 is activated, the display will switch to SCREEN 1 mode.

8-3.3 Some Graphics Programming Applications

Some of the most useful and easily created graphics displays are those that are based on mathematical functions. Plotting in physical coordinates will be presented first, and then world coordinates will be discussed. Plotting in rectangular coordinates will be the main topic covered. Polar coordinates will also be presented, when world coordinate systems are discussed.

Plotting in Physical Coordinates   Let us begin by examining a few programming examples that demonstrate the various techniques involved in plotting functions in physical coordinates. Listing 8-1 shows a BASIC program that will plot a sinusoidal function on a 640 × 200 pixel screen, based on physical coordinates.

Listing 8-1

```
10 INPUT 'ENTER ANGLE INCREMENT SIZE (RADIANS)';I
20 INPUT ' ENTER SCALING CONSTANT' ;K
30 SCREEN 2:CLS
40 THETA = 0
50 FOR X =0 TO 639
```

Listing 8-1 (con't)

```
60 A =SIN(THETA)
70 Y = A * K = 100
80 PSET(X,Y)
90 THETA = THETA + I
100 NEXT X
```

An explanation of the program in Listing 8-1 is now in order. First of all, the user is prompted to enter values for the increment I in the angle theta, and a scaling constant K. The waveform is plotted using the PSET statement in a FOR-NEXT loop. The x-axis counter X is incremented on each pass through the loop and is used to determine the X coordinate position of the current pixel to be activated. A total of 640 loops are performed, which is also the width of the screen in pixels. This means that the full resolution of the x axis of the screen will be used. On each pass through the loop, the sine of THETA is calculated, multiplied by the scaling or proportionality constant K, and added to an offset of 100. You will recall that the maximum value that the sine function may achieve is 1. However, the screen is 200 units (pixels) high. The scaling constant is used to expand the amplitude A of SIN(THETA) to the desired value. The offset of 100 is required to center the waveform on the y axis. You will recall that in physical coordinates, the origin is in the upper left corner of the screen. The offset shifts the waveform down, correcting for the nonstandard coordinate system. THETA is incremented by I radians on each pass through the loop. Running this program with various values of I and K will result in displays that are similar to that shown in Fig. 8-21a.

Reference axes for the graph of the sine function could be added in several different ways. For example, if the lines shown in Listing 8-1a were added to the program in Listing 8-1, a display similar to that shown in Fig. 8-21b would be produced.

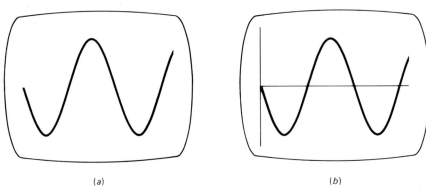

(a)   (b)

Fig. 8-21 Plot of a sinusoidal function with and without reference axes.

Listing 8-1*a*

```
41 FOR X = 0 TO 639
42 PSET(X,100)
43 NEXT X
44 FOR Y = 0 TO 199
45 PSET(0,Y)
46 NEXT Y
```

You might have noticed something peculiar about the waveforms shown in Fig. 8-21*a* and *b*. What is shown is actually representative of a $-\sin$ function; that is, these figures show inverted sine waves. This occurs because as the sine increases in the positive direction, the pixel positions being activated are moving toward the bottom of the screen. This is just the opposite of the way in which we normally plot functions, and it is due to the physical coordinate system used on the screen, with the origin (0,0) in the upper left corner. The inversion problem may easily be corrected by multiplying either A or K in line 70 by -1. This preinverts the function, providing an accurate representation. Other trigonometric functions may be plotted just as easily by substituting the desired function for SIN in line 60.

Example 8-6

Write a program that will plot a sine function $f_1(t) = \sin x$ and the square of the sine $f_2(t) = \sin^2 x$ on the 640 × 200 pixel screen. The user is to be prompted to enter the scaling factor and the phase increment. The PSET statement is to be used to plot the functions, and the LINE statement is to be used when plotting the reference axes.

Solution

Listing 8-2

```
10 SCREEN 2
20 INPUT 'ENTER SCALING FACTOR';K
30 INPUT 'ENTER INCREMENT';I
40 CLS
50 LINE (0,0) - (0,199)
60 LINE (0,100) - (639,100)
70 FOR C = 1 TO 640
80 Y1 = -K * SIN(X) + 100
90 Y2 = -K * SIN(X)^2 + 100
100 PSET(X,Y1)
110 PSET(X,Y2)
120 X = X + I
130 NEXT C
```

In this program, the scaling constant − K and y axis offset 100 have been included in the lines that calculate the values of the functions. The angle X which is being evaluated is incremented by I radians on each pass through the loop. The results produced by this program with K = 60 and I = 0.04 appear as shown in Fig. 8-22.

Ok

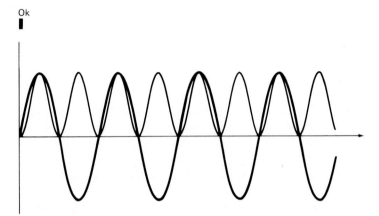

Fig. 8-22 Plot of the functions $y_1(t) = \sin x$ and $y_2(t) = \sin^2 \theta$.

Plotting complex functions using computer graphics can result in some real time savings over manual techniques. For example, summing the instantaneous amplitudes of a series of sinusoidal waveforms over an interval can yield the generation of some useful and interesting results. Tasks such as this are very time-consuming when done by hand. Fourier analysis is used to decompose a complex periodic signal into a series of harmonically related sine and/or cosine terms. For example, the actual Fourier series for an ideal square wave that steps positively at 0 time consists of an infinite number of terms, given by the formula

$$v(t) = \frac{4}{\pi}\left(V_m \sin \omega t + \frac{V_m \sin 3\omega t}{3} + \frac{V_m \sin 5\omega t}{5} + \ldots \right) \qquad \text{(Eq. 8-1)}$$

Alternatively, Eq. 8-1 can be written in the form

$$v(t) = \frac{4}{\pi} \sum_{n=1}^{n=\infty} \frac{V_m \sin n\omega t}{n} \qquad \text{(Eq. 8-1a)}$$

where $n = 1, 3, 5, 7, \ldots$.

The program in Listing 8-3 plots the sum of the first five terms of the Fourier series representation for a square wave. Performing this task manually would be extremely tedious, which makes it an ideal candidate for computerized plotting.

Listing 8-3

```
10 SCREEN 2:CLS
20 T = 0
30 LINE (0,0) - (0,199)
40 LINE (0,100) - (639,100)
50 FOR X = 0 TO 639
60 Y = SIN(T) + 1/3 * SIN(3*T)+1/5* SIN(5*T)+1/7*SIN(7*T)
   +1/9*SIN(9*T)
70 Y = -60 * Y + 100
80 PSET(X,Y)
90 T = T + .02
100 NEXT X
```

The program in Listing 8-3 would typically take about a minute to run using interpreted BASIC. Much of the lengthy run time is due to the calculations in line 60. The constant term $\dfrac{4}{\pi}$ has been omitted for simplicity, as it does not affect the shape or symmetry of the result. The display produced by this program is shown in Fig. 8-23.

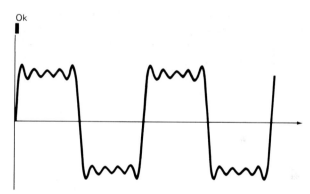

Fig. 8-23 Plot of the sum of the first five harmonics of a square wave.

The waveform could be made to more closely resemble an ideal square wave if additional terms are added to line 60. There is not room for more than about one more term on this line, so possibly the series could be broken up into two or more lines. There is, however, an approach that would require much less typing. The formula in Eq. 8-1a can be used in a less obvious way to produce the desired results. For example, if line 60 is removed from Listing 8-3 and the following lines (Listing 8-3a) are added, any number of terms may be summed to obtain the resultant waveform.

Listing 8-3*a*

```
55 FOR N = 1 TO M STEP 2
60 V = V + (1/N) * SIN(N * T)
65 NEXT N
70 Y = -60 * V + 100
95 V = 0
```

In these lines, N represents the harmonic whose amplitude is to be evaluated and M presents the highest odd harmonic to be used. Incrementing N by 2 results in only the odd values 1,3,5, . . . , of M being evaluated. Line 95 is added to clear V after each point is plotted. This must be done because the new line 60 would erroneously add the old values of V to the sum of the sine terms each time the loop is entered. It is easy to imagine the amount of typing that is saved by this technique, especially when large numbers of harmonics are to be summed.

Computerized plotting can also be used to create useful graphs. One type of graph that is commonly used in engineering and scientific work is the semilogarithmic graph. In this type of graph, one axis is linearly scaled and the second axis is scaled logarithmically. The program in Listing 8-4 will produce a two-cycle semilog graph, as shown in Fig. 8-24.

Ok

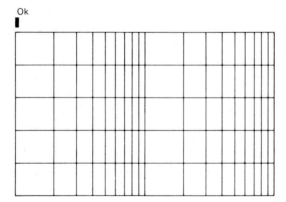

Fig. 8-24 Two cycle semi-logarithmic graph.

Listing 8-4

```
100 SCREEN 2
110 CLS
120 FOR Y = 20 TO 180 STEP 32
130 LINE(0,Y)-(639,Y)
140 NEXT Y
150 FOR K = 0 TO 638 STEP 319
160 FOR I = 1 TO 10
170 X = (LOG(I)/2.30259)*318 + K
180 LINE(X,20) - (X,180)
190 NEXT I
200 NEXT K
```

The program in Listing 8-4 operates as follows. Lines 100 and 110 activate the 640 × 200 pixel mode and clear the screen. Lines 120 through 140 form a loop that draws six equally spaced horizontal lines across the screen, each beginning at pixel position 20 and ending at pixel position 180. The horizontal lines are spaced 32 pixels apart vertically. This forms the linear scale on the graph. Lines 150 through 200 form two nested loops that create the logarithmically scaled vertical divisions. The graph is two cycles or decades wide, with each decade containing 10 vertical lines spaced proportional to the common log ($\log_{10}$) of a counter I that varies from 1 to 10. Since the computer uses natural logarithms, the formula ln $x = \log_{10} x / 2.30259$ is used to convert to common log values. The constant 318 in line 170 scales the common log to the X-axis dimensions of the screen. The variable K is used to offset the second decade of the graph to the right of the first, and to exit the program after plotting is complete. This program plots the graph very quickly, and can easily be modified to produce graphs with more than two decades. This will be left as an exercise at the end of the chapter.

Plotting in World Coordinates Using world coordinates can simplify many graphics tasks. For example, the program in Example 8-6 could be modified such that world coordinates are used. This could eliminate the need for the scaling factor. Instead, the size of the screen in the Y direction could be defined as ranging from 1 to −1. Now, when sin x = 1 or −1 at the maximums, the full Y-axis resolution would be used. Likewise, rather than varying the increment in X, the scale of the X-axis of the screen could be varied. Also, the coordinate transformation that occurs eliminates the need for multiplying the scaling constant by −1.

Using world coordinates also provides another less obvious advantage; that is, the physical size of the screen can be changed without a need for changing any scaling constants that might be used in a program. It was pointed out earlier in this chapter that on some computers, different physical screen sizes can be selected using the SCREEN statement. You will recall that SCREEN 1 activates the 320 × 200 pixel display, while SCREEN 2 activates the 640 × 200 pixel version. If physical coordinates are used, all scaling factors for the y axis coordinates must be changed if the screen size is changed. Use of world coordinates automatically scales the screen size to those dimensions that are specified in the WINDOW statement, regardless of the actual physical screen size. The aspect ratio of the screen may still cause some distortion of the plot, which can be corrected by scaling the x and y limits in the WINDOW statement accordingly. Similar to the aspect ratio of an ellipse, the aspect ratio of the screen is the ratio of the horizontal size of the screen to the vertical size, in pixels. The following example should help to illustrate the use of world coordinates.

Example 8-7

Write a program that will plot the equation $y = x^2 - 6x - 30$ in world coordinates for a screen that has a width range (on the x axis) of -20 to 20 and a vertical height range (on the y axis) of 100 to -100. The independent variable x is to be incremented from -20 to 20 in steps of 0.1. Plot the x and y reference axes such that they intersect at the origin (0,0).

Solution

Listing 8-5

```
10 SCREEN 2
20 WINDOW (-20,-100)-(20,100)
30 CLS
40 LINE (-20,0)-(20,0)
50 LINE (0,-100)-(0,100)
60 FOR X = -20 TO 20 STEP .1
70 Y = X^2 - 6*X - 30
80 PSET(X,Y)
90 NEXT X
```

An explanation of the program presented in Listing 8-5 will now be presented. As in the previous programs, SCREEN 2 (640 × 200 pixels) was chosen, although SCREEN 1 could have been used just as easily, with no further modification to the program. Line 20 scales the coordinates as specified in the statement of the problem. The actual screen width is 21 units, counting the origin, while the actual screen height is 201 units, also counting the origin. Lines 30, 40, and 50 clear the screen and plot the X and Y axes respectively. Line 60 determines the starting and ending values of X, and also the size of the increments in X. The entire range of the X axis is used for the variation of X. As X is incremented, line 70 calculates the value of Y on each pass through the loop. Line 80 is the exit point of the loop. A sample run of the program produced the display shown in Fig. 8-25. This is the familiar parabola that is studied so often in algebra courses.

The coordinate systems used thus far in this chapter have been rectangular in nature; that is, the location of a given pixel is determined using its displacement from the origin in the X and Y directions. This is the way that bit-mapped displays must be set up. However, it is often necessary to plot functions in polar coordinates. On a polar plot, the independent variable is an angle θ, while the dependent variable is the magnitude of the resultant vector r. The general form for a polar graph is shown in Fig. 8-26. This type of plot is generated by increasing θ in convenient increments,

Ok

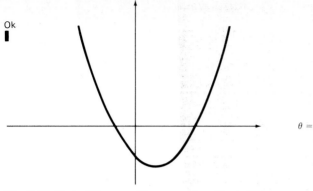

Fig. 8-25 Plot of the equation $y = x^2 - 6x - 30$.

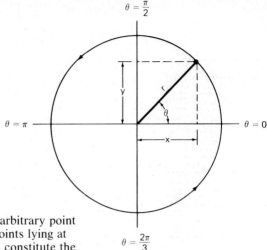

Fig. 8-26 Polar graph with an arbitrary point chosen in the unit circle (all points lying at distance $r = 1$ from the origin constitute the unit circle) for reference purposes.

calculating the magnitude of r, and plotting the resulting points at the endpoint of line r. The x and y coordinates of an arbitrary point on the colored circle are shown for reference purposes. To reiterate, the main difference between a polar plot and a linear plot is that in producing a polar plot, instead of moving continuously to the right to increase the independent variable (as when plotting the amplitude versus time characteristics of the sine), the angle is constantly increased and a counterclockwise rotation about the origin is produced. It is the distance r from the origin and the angle θ that is of interest in such a graph.

World coordinates are especially useful when polar plots of functions are desired, as the center of the screen is easily set up as the origin. In order to produce a polar plot of a function, generally the first thing that is done is the evaluation of the magnitude of r at $\theta = 0$. The angle θ is then successively incremented, and the distance r from the origin is calculated at each interval. Since the display screen is mapped using the rectangular coordinate system, the polar coordinates that are produced must first be converted into rectangular form, after which they may then be plotted on the screen. For given values of θ and r, the following equations are used to find the x and y coordinates of the point on the screen.

$$x = r \cos \theta \qquad \text{(Eq. 8-2)}$$
$$y = r \sin \theta \qquad \text{(Eq. 8-3)}$$

These equations should be familiar to most readers, as they are frequently used in the analysis of ac circuits. The program presented in Listing 8-6 will produce a polar plot based on Eqs. 8-2 and 8-3. In this case, the equation $r = 2 \cos(2\theta)$ is plotted in polar coordinates for θ varying from 0 to 2π radians.

Listing 8-6

```
10 SCREEN 2
20 PI = 3.1415926
30 WINDOW (-3,3)-(3,-3):CLS
40 LINE (0,3)-(0,-3)
50 LINE (-3,0)-(3,0)
60 FOR THETA = 0 TO 2*PI STEP PI/200
70 R = 2*COS(2*THETA)
80 X = R*COS(THETA)
90 Y = R*SIN(THETA)
95 PSET (X,Y)
100 NEXT THETA
```

The main sections of Listing 8-6 will now be discussed. Line 20 defines the value of PI for use in the incrementation of THETA. In some versions of BASIC, π is a predefined constant, and does not need to be defined. In this case, it is assumed that π must be defined explicitly. Line 30 scales the window (the screen dimensions) for a range from -3 to 3 on both the *x* and *y* axes. Lines 40 and 50 plot the *x* and *y* reference axes. In line 60, THETA is used as the counter and the independent variable, which is incremented from 0 to 200 in steps of $\pi/200$. Line 70 contains the expression to be evaluated for the dependent variable *r*. Line 80 calculates the position of the endpoint of *r* in the X direction from the origin, and line 90 calculates the Y component of the vector, while line 95 plots the points specified by X and Y. The loop is exited at line 100.

The resulting graph produced by the program in Listing 8-6 is shown in Fig. 8-27. This figure is called a four-leaved rose. The lobes (petals?) of the rose should be symmetrical; however, there is some distortion caused by the nonunity aspect ratio of the screen. This could be corrected to a

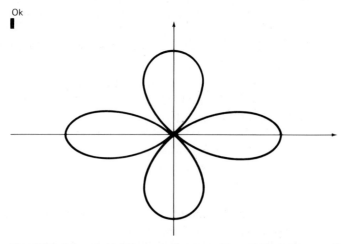

Fig. 8-27 Polar plot of the equation $r = 2(\cos 2\ \theta)$ produces a figure called a four-leaved rose. Asymmetry is due to the nonsymmetrical size of the pixels.

large extent by scaling the *y* coordinates to 4 and −4 in the WINDOW statement in line 30. Many other interesting forms can be created using polar graphing techniques. In a more practical vein, polar plots are used to describe the characteristics of closed loop systems in engineering applications. A plot called a Nyquist diagram is an example of such a graph. Antenna characteristics are also frequently described using polar graphs.

Numerical Scaling   The plots produced up to now could use a final modification to make them more useful; that is, the units on the reference axes could be scaled. In order to place numbers along the horizontal axis, we must have a statement that allows character positions to be defined. The statement that can be used in such an application is LOCATE. The LOCATE statement allows the position of the cursor to be set to any character position on the screen. The syntax for LOCATE is

```
LOCATE [line],[column],[cursor]
```

Assuming an 80-column by 25-line screen size, [line] may be any integer from 1 to 25, and [column] may have any value from 1 to 80. The [cursor] field is defined such that 1 produces a visible cursor and 0 makes the cursor invisible. In this application, the cursor does not need to be seen; therefore this field will always be set to 0.

The fields of the LOCATE statement are always determined using character positions and not pixel locations, regardless of whether physical or world coordinates are in use. The upper left corner of the screen is character position (1,1), while the lower right corner is location (25,80). This is similar to the physical coordinate system, except that the positions of the *x* and *y* axis fields are reversed.

Let us use the two-cycle semilog graph program of Listing 8-4 to demonstrate how a graph may be scaled. Let us assume that just the logarithmic portion of the graph is to be scaled such that the numbers are written on the line immediately below the graph, and the range of the graph (from left to right) is to vary from 100 to 10K. This could be used for plotting filter response, for example. The required modifications to the program are shown in Listing 8-6*a*.

Listing 8-6*a*

```
210 LOCATE 24,1,0
220 PRINT'100 200 300 400 800';
230 LOCATE 24,40,0
240 PRINT'1K 2K 3K 4K 7K 10K';
250 LOCATE 1,1,0
```

Here's how this modification works. Line 210 defines the cursor position as being located at line 24, column 1. This means that the next PRINT statement encountered will begin one line below the graph, in the first column. Line 220 prints the values of five of the vertical lines in the first cycle of the graph. The spacing between the numbers was determined experimentally; that is, a few attempts to line up various numbers were tried, until a satisfactory display was produced. Only five values were printed here, because of space limitations. Notice also that the graph cannot be scaled using a single program line. Consider that since most versions of BASIC will allow only up to 80 characters on a line, and the line number (220) and the PRINT statement take up space, the entire graph just cannot be numbered in a single line. Line 240 locates the cursor at line 24, column 40. This is the midpoint of the screen and also the location of the center of the graph. This would correspond to the 1K division of the log axis, as scaled here. Line 250 writes the remaining values for six vertical lines. Again, the character spacing was determined experimentally.

Notice that the PRINT statements in lines 220 and 240 end with semicolons (;). This was done in line 220 to cause printing to begin on the same character line on the screen when the next PRINT statement was encountered; that is, no carriage return is executed when the semicolon is used. If the colon was omitted, the characters in the PRINT statement of line 240 would be printed below those printed in line 220. The semicolon at the end of line 240 prevents the screen from scrolling up one position after that line has been printed, keeping the top of the graph visible. Finally, the LOCATE statement in line 250 results in the placement of BASIC's OK prompt and cursor at the upper left corner of the screen. If this was not done, the prompt and cursor would be written below the graph, again causing the top to scroll off the screen.

Numbering the horizontal axis of a linear graph is much easier than the log scale just considered. In the case of a linear scale, a variable could be used for the [line] field of the LOCATE statement, to which a constant can be added to position characters. It should be mentioned that if printing of characters is to be done in the area of the screen where plotting is done, the characters should be placed before the graph is plotted. This is so, because all lines and points that lie in the character line being printed will be erased by the PRINT statement.

When numbering the vertical axis of a graph, a similar technique is used, except that the character line is the LOCATE field that is varied. No specific examples of this technique will be presented here, but you may wish to experiment with it on your own.

Other Graphics Techniques Another approach to producing graphic displays uses a technique called turtle graphics. In turtle graphics, a cursor, called a turtle, is moved around the screen either by keyboard commands, through the use of a mouse, or possibly with a joystick. Often, the turtle is moved around the screen using programming statements similar to those discussed in this chapter. At the user's discretion, the turtle can leave behind it a visible trail, or it can be moved without leaving a trail. This technique is useful for producing drawings that are not mathematically defined, such as a picture of a house or a schematic diagram.

A technique called character graphics can be used to produce a few useful items such as bar charts and even rough function plots. In order to produce a bar chart, special graphics characters are written to the screen. An example of such a graphics character is a character block that turns on all of the pixels in the character position in which it is written.

In order to plot a function using character graphics, a program such as that in Listing 8-7 could be used. Here, the SPC statement is used to space asterisks a distance from the beginning of each line that is proportional to the sine of the value of a variable *x* on an 80-column screen. The problem with this approach is that the resolution of the plot is quite limited (40 or 80 positions, depending on screen size). The advantage is that no special graphics statements are needed to get a useful plot.

Listing 8-7

```
10 CLS
20 FOR X = 0 TO 5 STEP .1
30 Y = 39*SIN(X) +40
40 PRINT SPC(Y);"*"
50 NEXT X
```

Three dimensional objects can also be represented using computer graphics techniques. An example of a three dimensional plot of a sine function is presented in Fig. 8-28. In order to produce such plots, relatively complex coordinate transformations are required. A given function to be plotted is represented on three planes: the *xy* plane, the *yz* plane, and the *xz* plane. These planes and the angles at which they are oriented are described mathematically and stored in arrays in memory. The theory behind 3D plotting is beyond the scope of this book, and will not be presented in further detail.

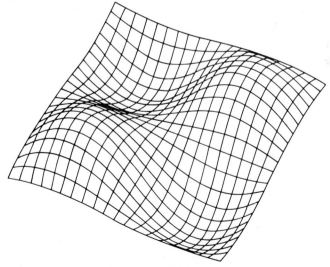

Fig. 8-28 3D plot of two sinusoidal functions.

Review Questions for Section 8-3

1. What are the two variations of rectangular coordinate systems that are used with bit-mapped displays?
2. Using physical coordinates, where is the origin of the display screen located?
3. What is the function of a scaling constant?
4. Which coordinate system would be used to plot the amplitude versus phase characteristics of a sinusoidal function?
5. What is the aspect ratio of a display screen?
6. Why does inversion of functions that are plotted in the physical coordinate systems occur, unless corrective action is taken?

SUMMARY

This chapter has introduced some of the ideas behind the hardware and programming aspects of display control and graphics. Most microcomputer displays are based upon the raster-scanned CRT. Using this method, a picture is formed by modulating the intensity of an electron beam that is continuously swept across and down the face of the CRT. There are two methods of raster scanning that are used: interlaced and noninterlaced. In the interlaced method, a complete picture is formed by two passes of the electron beam down the screen.

A section of memory is reserved for storage of character codes or pixel data. This is called the video RAM. Character-based displays read their pixel bit patterns from a character generator ROM. The video RAM is used to store the character codes that select various bit patterns in the character ROM. In graphics-based displays, the screen image is contained in the video RAM itself. This allows greater control over the form of the information that is shown on the screen. A CRT controller is usually used to produce the necessary timing and control signals for the monitor. The CRT controller is also responsible for controlling the access to the video RAM for the display interfacing circuitry.

Graphics images are formed by turning on and off various pixels on the screen. At the machine language level, this is done by writing bytes into the video RAM. Many versions of BASIC used today have graphics statements and functions that can be used in programs. There are two coordinate systems used with bit-mapped displays: physical coordinates and world coordinates. Physical coordinates are those that are used by the display control circuitry, and are determined by the size of the screen in pixels. World coordinates are user-defined, and effectively allow the screen to be scaled to arbitrary sizes.

CHAPTER QUESTIONS

8-1. What is the purpose of the constant 2.30259 in the program of Listing 8-4?

8-2. In the program of Listing 8-6, why is the value 2 used as the value that terminates the FOR-NEXT loop?

8-3. Name one disadvantage of bit-mapped graphics as opposed to character graphics.

8-4. What is the advantage of using a CRT controller to coordinate screen refresh operations?

8-5. What is a field?

8-6. When is a field effectively the same as a frame?

8-7. A certain application requires a character generator ROM that will contain the bit patterns for 128 characters. Each character is to consist of an array of 8 pixels wide by 12 pixels high. How many bytes must be contained in the ROM for these characters?

8-8. What are the two methods of causing the deflection of the electron beam in a CRT?

8-9. How can one quickly tell the difference between a conventional three-gun color CRT and a single-gun CRT?

8-10. At what point in a color CRT do the red, green and blue electron beams converge?

CHAPTER PROBLEMS

8-11. A certain monochrome monitor has a screen size of 720 pixels horizontally by 350 pixels vertically. If each character displayed occupies a 9×14 grid of pixels as in Fig. 8-7b, how many characters can be shown in a line and how many lines of characters can be viewed at one time?

8-12. A certain system has a dot rate of 6.4 MHz. If the horizontal oscillator runs at a frequency such that a line is scanned in 50 μs, what is the horizontal size of the screen in pixels? (Assume that overscan and retrace time are negligible.)

8-13. A certain computer that uses bit-mapped graphics has a screen size of 1000×1000 pixels. If the screen can display 50 lines, with each line containing 100 characters, what is the size of the grid (in pixels) in which a given character is formed?

8-14. Referring to Problem 8-12, if the characters are embedded in grids that are 8 pixels wide, how many columns wide is the screen?

8-15. A dot clock operating at 16 MHz drives an eight-stage PISO shift register. What is the dot rate at the serial output?

8-16. Modify the program in Listing 8-4 such that a four-cycle semilog graph is produced.

8-17. The transfer characteristics of a silicon diode are approximated by the equation

$$I = I_s e^{V_F/V_T}$$

where I_S is the saturation current, V_F is the voltage drop across the diode, V_T is a constant equal to 0.026 V, and e is the base of the natural logarithms. Write a program that will plot the shape of this curve for forward drops across the diode that range from 0 to 0.7 V. Assume $I_S = 20$ pA. Use the full horizontal resolution of the 640 × 200 pixel screen. Scale the vertical axis such that the bottom of the screen represents 0 mA and the top of the screen represents 50 mA. Use the physical coordinate system.

8-18. The equation $r = 1 - 2 \sin \theta$ produces a figure called a limacon when plotted in polar coordinates. Write a program that will plot this equation on a screen of range -2 to 2 on the x axis and 3 to -3 on the y axis.

8-19. A certain complex waveform is described by the equation

$$A(t) = k\left(\sin \theta t + \frac{1}{2}\sin 2\,\omega t + \frac{1}{3}\sin 3\,\omega t + \frac{1}{4}\sin 4\,\omega t \right)$$

Write a program that will plot this function on the 640 × 200 pixel screen in physical coordinates. The program is to prompt the user for a scaling factor K, ω, and the time t increment value.

8-20. Repeat Question 8-18 with the equation $r = 1 + \cos \theta$.

DATA COMMUNICATIONS AND NETWORKING

The area of data communications plays a significant role in the overall study of modern computer systems operation. Simply stated, data communication is the transference of data among the various devices that constitute a system. Typical components that may be included in such systems are microcomputers, mainframe computers, dumb terminals, line printers, mass storage devices, and intelligent instrumentation, just to name a few.

In the most general of terms, all communication systems require the following three physical elements: a transmitter, a transmission medium, and a receiver. No one part is more important than the others. Of course, the data or information to be transmitted, and its structure, is also of critical importance in the overall study of such systems.

The topics that are covered in this chapter include the various formats used to represent digital data and how the conversions from one format to another are implemented. The physical characteristics of the data transmission medium and the options that are available will be discussed, along with some commonly used data communication protocols and error-checking/correcting methods. In particular, the operation and construction of modems and data communication standards will be presented as well as an introduction of the basic operation and characteristics of a representative local area network.

9-1   LOGICAL REPRESENTATION OF DATA

This section will provide an introduction to some of the more popular formats used for the representation of data, in particular the ASCII code. The concepts of parallel and serial data transmission will also be discussed.

9-1.1 Data and Information

Often, the terms data and information are used synonymously. While this generally presents no problem in most situations, the two do not mean the same thing. Therefore, before proceeding, let us make a clear distinction between data and information. In terms of a digital system, data is any group of bits that is moved, manipulated, or operated on in some way. A given block of data (normally a byte in length for most microcomputers) does not necessarily have any specific meaning. Information, however, is data that conveys or represents some specific meaning. The specific information or meaning that a given piece of data carries depends on the coding system that is applied to it.

9-1.2 Standard Data Codes

There are many different codes that are used to represent information. Probably the most widely used code in the field of data communications is the American Standard Code for Information Interchange (ASCII) code. ASCII is a 7-bit alphanumeric code that represents alphabetic characters, numbers, punctuation marks, various symbols, and control codes. Figure 9-1 shows the construction of the ASCII code. The 3 most significant bits, b_7, b_6, and b_5, of a given character are designated at the top of the rows, while the 4 least significant bits, b_4, b_3, b_2, and b_1, are listed in the left-hand column. In order to determine the ASCII code for a given character, the character of interest is located on the chart, and the bit patterns that

ASCII Codes

b4 b3 b2 b1	b7 0 b6 0 b5 0	0 0 1	0 1 0	0 1 1	1 0 0	1 0 1	1 1 0	1 1 1
0 0 0 0	NUL	DLE	SP	Ø	'	P	@	p
0 0 0 1	SON	DC1	!	1	A	Q	a	q
0 0 1 0	STX	DC2	''	2	B	R	b	r
0 0 1 1	ETX	DC3	#	3	C	S	c	s
0 1 0 0	EOT	DC4	$	4	D	T	d	t
0 1 0 1	ENQ	NAK	%	5	E	U	e	u
0 1 1 0	ACK	SYN	&	6	F	V	f	v
0 1 1 1	BEL	ETB	'	7	G	W	g	w
1 0 0 0	BS	CAN	(	8	H	X	h	x
1 0 0 1	HT	EM	)	9	I	Y	i	y
1 0 1 0	LF	SS	*	:	J	Z	j	z
1 0 1 1	VT	ESC	+	;	K	[	k	{
1 1 0 0	FF	FS	,	<	L	~	l	⌐
1 1 0 1	CR	GS	_	=	M	]	m	}
1 1 1 0	SO	RS	.	>	N	∧	n		
1 1 1 1	SI	US	/	?	O	—	o	DEL

Fig. 9-1 ASCII code conversion table.

intersect at that location form its code. For example, the ASCII code for uppercase *H* is found to be 1001000, or 48_{16}.

Notice that the 4 least significant bits of the codes for the digits 0 through 9 are the correct binary (actually BCD) equivalents of these numbers. If a computer was to perform arithmetic operations on numerical data that is in ASCII form, the 3 MSBs could be masked off, leaving the binary representation of each digit. Some additional processing is required to produce the standard binary representation for numbers that are described by more than one ASCII code. This is not a great problem, however, as many CPUs have BCD arithmetic capability.

The control codes in the ASCII code do not represent printable characters, but rather are used to indicate status or initiate some action. For example, if the control code for *BEL* was sent from a microcomputer, it would cause the bell (or its equivalent) to sound on a terminal, while the code for *LF* would cause a line feed to occur if it was sent to a printer. Quite often, a large portion of the ASCII control codes are not implemented.

Example 9-1

If the following BASIC statement was executed, what would be the result?

```
PRINT ASC(S)
```

Solution

The ASC function returns the decimal representation of the ASCII code of the argument (in this case, S). In this example, 83 would be returned and printed on the screen.

Example 9-2

What is the result of the execution of the following BASIC statement?

```
PRINT CHR$(92)
```

Solution

The CHR$ function works just the opposite of the ASC function; that is, its execution results in the character that is represented by the argument to be returned. In this case, the character ~ would be printed.

Although ASCII code has been standardized, not all microcomputers and peripheral devices interpret all of the codes the same way. This is especially true of the control codes. In order to determine the exact interpretation of the ASCII code used by a given machine, one must review the technical literature for that machine.

A few other codes that are not used nearly as often with microcomputers are the extended binary-coded decimal information code (EBCDIC) and the Hollerith code. EBCDIC is an 8-bit code developed by IBM for use with its equipment (with the IBM PC being a notable exception). Hollerith code is a 12-bit code used to represent data on punched cards. This form of data entry is rarely used in microcomputer applications.

An explanation of some of the terms used in relation to data communications is also appropriate at this time. Generally, a word is taken to mean a group of bits that represent a single entity of information. For example, the 7-bit ASCII code for a given character is often referred to as a word, or a code word, even though it does not represent an actual word. If one is working with EBCDIC, then a given code word is 8 bits long. Do not confuse this interpretation with that used to describe operand lengths in relation to the 8088 CPU, for example, where a word means an operand that is 2 bytes long. In this chapter, a word will be interpreted as meaning a group of bits that represents a character or other piece of information that is implemented in a given coding scheme.

Review Questions for Section 9-1

1. Explain the difference between data and information.
2. How long is an ASCII code word?
3. How would the ASCII code be classified, as opposed to BCD for example?
4. What term is applied to ASCII codes that do not represent printable characters?
5. What is the ASCII code representation for the letter q?

9-2 PARALLEL AND SERIAL DATA COMMUNICATION

Data that is to be transmitted from one point to another may be organized in either a parallel or serial format. Each format has certain inherent advantages and disadvantages associated with it. Generally speaking, parallel data transmission results in a greater transfer of data in a given time. Serial transmission methods can also attain high data transfer rates, but the reduction in the required number of conductors is the most important characteristic in relation to parallel transfer.

9-2.1 Parallel Data Transfer

The microprocessor data bus architecture studied earlier could be considered representative of a parallel data communication channel. The data bus is used to carry data that is sent to and from the 8088, a byte at a time. It is possible to consider the data bus to be an 8-bit communication channel that could be shared among over 1 million distinct memory locations and 65,536 I/O ports. Of course, the address and control buses are an intimate part of this structure, which increases the total number of lines incorporated in the communication/control system to well over 28. This is an acceptable number of lines considering the relatively short physical distances over which data is sent. Also, in general, such a large number of data and control lines also implies very high speed data transfer, which, of course, is one of the hallmarks of modern computers. Timing required to coordinate the movement of data from one place to another is provided by individual control lines such as $\overline{\text{MWTC}}$ and $\overline{\text{MRDC}}$.

It is more than likely that if a computer was to be used in a parallel data communication system, the 8 bits that are available at a given I/O port would be used as a starting point to form a communication channel that is isolated from the computer's bus system.

As previously stated, one of the primary advantages to transmitting data in a parallel manner (possibly 8 bits at a time) is speed. In general, with all things being equal, it would take seven times as long to send the equivalent of an ASCII character from one place to another 1 bit at a time as it would to send all 7 bits simultaneously, over seven or possibly eight data lines. In most cases, additional control lines would be required for purposes such as handshaking and polling. These extra lines contribute to cabling costs, but are usually necessary when a practical system is considered.

9-2.2 Serial Data Transfer

If one is to consider the parallel transmission of data, a major problem soon arises. Using ASCII code as an example, when the 7 code bits must be sent over a long distance, such as across town or across the country, the cost of the multiple transmission lines quickly becomes excessive. Add to this several control lines, and the cost of wiring quickly gets out of hand. It would be much more economical to transmit the data 1 bit at a time over a single data line than over seven or more individual ones. When data is transmitted 1 bit at a time over a single channel, it is referred to as being in serial format.

Data sent to an output port of a computer can be converted from parallel to serial form using a parallel-in serial-out (PISO) shift register at the transmitting end of the channel. Conversely, the serial data stream may be converted to parallel form using a serial-in parallel-out (SIPO) shift register at the receiving end. Of course, additional circuitry is required to control and time the data conversion process, but normally the lower cost of the cabling requirements for serial transfer more than makes up for this added complexity.

Synchronous Serial Data Transfer The problem with serial data transmission is that the devices at the sending and receiving ends of the channel must somehow be synchronized with one another. Synchronization may be achieved by sending a common clock signal over a second transmission line. Whenever a master clock signal is used to derive timing at both ends

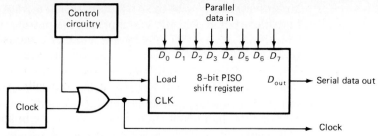

Fig. 9-2 Parallel to serial conversion using a shift register.

of the channel, we have what is called synchronous transmission. Figure 9-2 shows a simple circuit that could be used to transmit synchronous data. In this circuit, the control circuitry would load data into the shift register, and then gate the clock on. In this way, both the clock and the data stream would be sent at the same time. At the receiving end of the channel(Fig. 9-3), the clock is used to shift the serial data into a SIPO

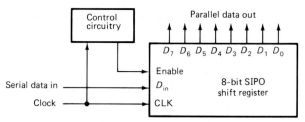

Fig. 9-3 Serial to parallel conversion using a shift register.

shift register. The control circuitry at the receiver would be used to detect the end of the code word, at which time it would disable the serial input of the shift register and enable the parallel outputs, causing transfer of data to a parallel input port.

The main problem with this form of synchronous data transmission is that two lines are required, and although this is a substantial improvement over parallel transmission, it is still possible to further reduce the number of transmission channels to one. One way of providing this line reduction is to eliminate the necessity for a common clock. This is done in asynchronous transmission, which will be covered shortly. In a more frequently used version of synchronous data transfer, the separate clock line is not required; but instead, special data encoding techniques are used that allow the receiver to extract the exact transmitter clock frequency and phase from the incoming data stream. This type of synchronous data transmission is usually used for high-speed (up to 10 Mbits/s) data communications applications. One of the more popular data communication networking schemes that uses synchronous transmission will be discussed in Sec. 9-4.

Asynchronous Data Transfer The term asynchronous implies that data may be transmitted at irregular intervals, and that the clocks of the receiving and transmitting ends of the system are not necessarily exactly synchronized with one another (not operating at exactly the same frequency and phase). These are typical characteristics of asynchronous data communication systems. The overall system may be considered asynchronous; however, the receiving and transmitting ends are coordinated with the addition of extra bits in each code word; that is, typically, start and stop bits are added to each code word that is transmitted. These bits are used to inform the receiver that a code word is about to come in and, possibly, when the code word has ended. For example, if 8-bit code words are to be sent asynchronously, they might be represented as shown in Fig. 9-4. In this

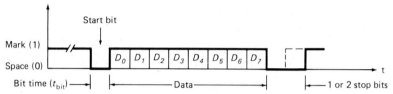

Fig. 9-4 Possible format for asynchronous serial data transmission.

case, the transmission line is held in what is called the marking condition when no data is being sent. In data communications, the condition that represents a logical 1 in the transmission channel is called a mark. The condition that represents logical 0 is called a space. It is common practice to leave an asynchronous channel in the mark state when it is inactive.

The circuit shown in Fig. 9-5 could be used to transmit asynchronous serial data as described by Fig. 9-4. The control circuitry would be used

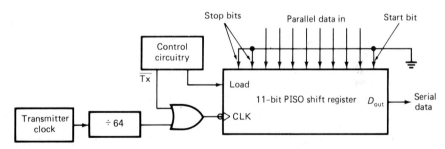

Fig. 9-5 Circuit for transmitting data asynchronously.

to load the desired data word, plus the start and stop bits, into the PISO register under processor control. The transmitter clock in this circuit operates at 64 times the baud rate for the transmission of a given data word. The baud rate is the reciprocal of the time duration during which a given bit is present on the transmission channel, which in this case is also the rate at which bits are shifted out of the PISO register. This time interval is called the bit time t_{bit}.

Example 9-3

The clock in Fig. 9-5 operates at a frequency of 7.04 kHz. Determine the baud rate (Bd) and bit time for a transmitted code word.

Solution

The clock signal is divided by 64, producing a frequency of 110 Hz. This signal is applied to the clock input of the PISO shift register. An analysis of basic shift register circuitry shows that one shift will occur on each triggering edge of the clock signal (the negative edge in this example). Therefore, each bit will be present at the output of the register for 9.09 ms (the bit time), which corresponds to a baud rate of 110. This is a commonly used baud rate in low-speed applications.

In reference to Fig. 9-4, it can be seen that the transmission of a code word is preceded by driving the channel to the space (logic low) state for 1 bit time. This is called a start bit. This bit is used at the receiving end of the channel to initialize the receiver circuitry. In an asynchronous system, the transmitter and receiver clocks operate at approximately the same frequency and phase. They are not phase-locked to one another as might be the case in synchronous transmission. One possible approach to a circuit that will receive asynchronous data is shown in Fig. 9-6. This circuit is designed to work with serial data that is transmitted by the circuit in Fig. 9-5, using the data format shown in Fig. 9-4.

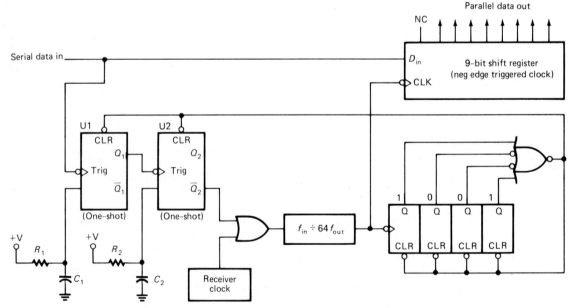

Fig. 9-6 Asynchronous data receiving circuitry.

The actual operating details of Fig. 9-6 will now be presented. Assume that the circuit in Fig. 9-5 is transmitting a code word at 110 Bd. Once again, it is important to realize that when the channel is inactive, or idling, it is held in the mark state. Now, when the input of the receiver is driven to logic low (space) by the reception of the start bit, one-shot U1 is triggered by this falling edge. The values of R_1 and C_1 are chosen such that the Q output of U1 goes high for 1-bit time interval (t_{bit} = 9.09 ms for 110 Bd). When the Q output of U1 falls to logic 0, one-shot U2 is triggered. The values of R_2 and C_2 are chosen such that Q of U2 would normally be driven low for slightly longer than 9 bit-time intervals (say about 9.9 or 10 × t_{bit}). For the time that U2 is triggered, the receiver clock f = 7.04 kHz is gated into a divide by 64 counter, which in turn drives the SIPO shift register. A timing diagram for this circuit is shown in Fig. 9-6. Notice that the clock signal f_{out} applied to the shift register causes data bits to be shifted in at approximately the middle of a given bit time interval (data is shifted in on falling edges of f_{out}). This is the key to the elimination of the need for a synchronizing clock signal; that is, even if the transmitter and receiver clocks differ slightly in phase and frequency, these differences are reduced by a factor of 64, because of the frequency divider stages used in both ends. This means that the data bits may be shifted out, displaced slightly in time in either direction, relative to the falling edges of f_{out}, without loss of data. Although the receiver has been designed to capture 8-bit data words, a 9-bit shift register is used. In order to understand why the 9-bit shift register is used, let us consider how the circuit determines when it has captured the last data bit in a word. At the output of the divide by 64 counter, a 4-bit counter is decoded such that it clears itself and the one-shots after nine shifts (see Fig. 9-7). This ensures that if the last data bit was a logic 1, it has had time to make the transition from high to low, without retriggering U1 and initiating a false receive shift sequence. As a consequence of this action, the first stop bit will also be shifted into the SIPO register. If an 8-bit register was used, the first data bit that was received would be shifted out and lost. Instead, the stop bit that is shifted in is just ignored.

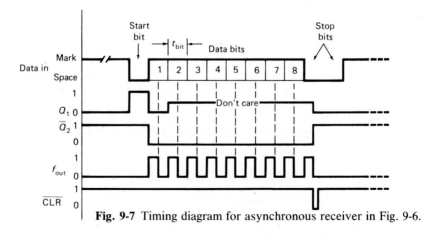

Fig. 9-7 Timing diagram for asynchronous receiver in Fig. 9-6.

Normally, it is necessary for devices at both ends of a channel to have the ability to both send and receive data. This means that both transmit and receive circuitry would be required at both ends of the communication channel. Complete transmit/receive circuits are available in LSI form. These devices are called universal asynchronous receiver-transmitters (UARTs). Generally, these devices contain all of the control, shift register, and clock circuitry required for data communication. Most UARTs may also be programmed to operate at any of several different baud rates, with options for using different code word lengths and different numbers of start and stop bits.

9-2.3 Baud Rate and Data Rate

It is now appropriate to distinguish between the terms baud rate and data rate. The baud rate is a measure of the reciprocal of the time that a given bit (data, stop, start, or other bit) is present in the transmission channel. At 110 Bd, assuming that a given bit can only assume one of two levels, a maximum of 110 bits can be sent in 1 s. The data rate is related only to the rate at which data bits are transmitted. The start and stop bits are not considered when determining the data rate because they do not add to the information content of the signal (this is also the case for error detection bits, if applicable). Using the system just described in Fig. 9-5, a given code word is 8 bits long, and each code word is bracketed by a total of 3 start and stop bits. When clocking out bits at a rate of 110 bits/s, if 3 out of every 11 bits do not represent information, the data rate is found by multiplying the baud rate by the number of bits/code word divided by the total bits/word, including start and stop bits (8/11). This yields a data rate of 80 bits/s.

Example 9-4

A certain asynchronous data transmission system uses 7-bit code words, bracketed by 2 stop bits and 1 start bit. If the data is transmitted at 3200 Bd, how many characters can be transmitted in 1 s?

Solution

At a rate of 3200 Bd, 3200 bits are transmitted per second. Seven out of every ten bits are data; therefore, the data rate is 2240 bits/s. The number of characters transmitted per second is found by dividing the data rate by the number of bits per character. This yields 320 characters/s.

Review Questions for Section 9-2

1. In general, what is the main advantage of parallel data transfer over serial?

2. What type of data transfer requires a master clock for timing at both the transmitting and receiving ends of a channel?
3. In Fig. 9-5, how many stages are required in the counter that performs the divide by 64 function?
4. Define baud rate in terms of bit time.
5. In general, will the data rate of a communication system be higher, lower, or the same as the baud rate?
6. Which form of serial data communication is normally used for high-speed applications?

9-3 DATA TRANSMISSION: MODULATION, DEMODULATION, AND MODEMS

Up to this point, we have been concerned with the representation of data in the form of binary numbers or, more specifically, in the form of two different logic levels. The signal levels used to represent the data up to this point have not been stated explicitly, but most of us would tend to think in terms of TTL voltage levels, as would be the case at the inputs and outputs of the control circuits and shift registers used to serialize the data. This is perfectly acceptable when working within the confines of the computer itself. However, TTL voltage levels are generally unacceptable when data transmission over a distance of more than a few feet is considered. It is therefore appropriate that we now discuss the actual methods used in the conversion of data from logic levels to forms that are more suitable for long-distance transmission.

9-3.1 Modulation

Nearly everyone is familiar with amplitude and frequency modulation to some extent. These methods of modulation are used extensively in radio and television broadcasting applications. In this form, the signals are essentially analog in nature. However, these same techniques can be used to transmit digital data from one location to another as well.

Amplitude modulation is not used very often in data communication systems because of its poor noise rejection characteristics. Just as normal AM radio broadcasts are more susceptible to most sources of noise than FM, the same is true when digital data is considered. For this reason, we shall concentrate on frequency modulation in this section.

As stated earlier, data is generally sent in a serial manner when long distances are to be covered. One communication system that is readily available for long-distance data communications is the telephone system. The most obvious point of access to the phone system is at the point where a standard telephone would be connected. Since residential phone lines are designed primarily to carry audio (analog) information, they are limited in high-frequency response to about 3 kHz. This means that high-speed data communication is not feasible over these lines. As a consequence, the asynchronous receive/transmit techniques discussed earlier are usually employed. At the other extreme, it is not possible to transmit dc voltage levels over the telephone system either. This eliminates the possibility of sending data in bit level forms. What all of this means is that the stream of serial data that is produced at the output of the PISO register must be converted into a form that is compatible with the analog phone system. One of the most common ways to transmit digital data over such a system is to use a modem (modulator/demodulator). When transmitting data, most modems shift the operating frequency of an oscillator from one value for logic low inputs to another for logic high inputs. This is called frequency shift keying (FSK). A block diagram for a microcomputer-controlled FSK circuit is shown in Fig. 9-8. Internally, this circuit would

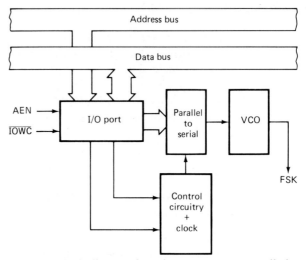

Fig. 9-8 Block diagram for microcomputer-controlled transmission of FSK serial data.

be similar to that of Fig. 9-5, with the main difference being the addition of a voltage-controlled oscillator (VCO). Two frequencies that are commonly used to represent digital data are 1200 Hz for a mark (logic high) and 2200 Hz for a space (logic low). The response of the VCO to a serial bit stream (Fig. 9-9a) is shown in Fig. 9-9b.

Figure 9-9c illustrates another method that is used to transmit digital data over an analog channel. This is called phase shift keying (PSK). In PSK modulation, whenever the input changes logic levels, the output of an oscillator is phase-shifted by 180 degrees. It is these phase reversals that are detected at the receiving end of the channel.

Some modems are designed for direct connection to the telephone lines, while some require an acoustic coupler to interface to the telephone system. An acoustic coupler is just a device into which the handset of the telephone is placed. Inside the coupler are a microphone to pick up the incoming signal and a speaker from which the FSK data is coupled to the handset microphone. The direct connect method is much more popular today, as it allows for automatic dialing and answering. Direct coupling is also more reliable because of the all-electronic nature of the connection.

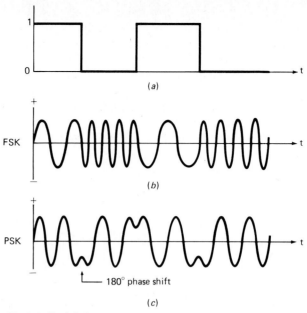

Fig 9-9 Serial data (*a*) and the resulting FSK (*b*) and PSK (*c*) output waveforms.

9-3.2 Demodulation

At the receiving end of the communication channel, the frequency or phase modulated signals must be reconverted (demodulated) into logic levels that are compatible with the digital circuitry used to process the data. FSK data can be demodulated rather easily using many different circuit design approaches, several of which will now be presented.

Phase-Locked Loop Demodulation Phase-locked loops (PLLs) are used frequently in nearly all areas of electronic communication. They are especially useful in the demodulation of serial data. The details of the operation of PLLs are beyond the scope of this text, but a few simple PLL-based demodulation circuits will be described, as they are not too difficult to understand if the PLL is treated essentially as a black box.

One possible FSK demodulation circuit is shown in Fig. 9-10. In this approach, two 567-tone decoders are used to detect the presence of the mark and space frequencies. Tone decoders are actually specially designed phase-locked loop circuits that will detect the presence of a signal within a narrow frequency range and produce a digital output that indicates whether or not that particular frequency is present. When detection occurs, the PLL is said to be in phase lock. The digital outputs of the tone decoder are decoded by additional logic to reproduce the original data that was transmitted.

Here is a brief description of how the 567-tone decoders in the demodulator operate. We will limit our discussion to U1 in Fig. 9-10, as both

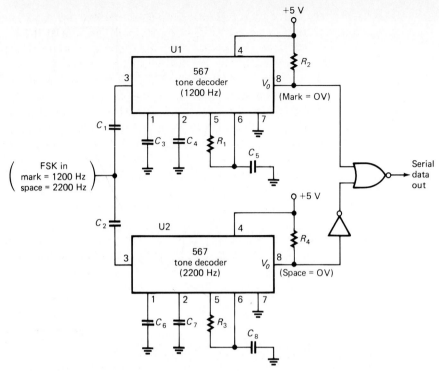

Fig. 9-10 FSK demodulator based on phase-locked loop tone decoders.

halves of the circuit are similar. First, the frequency of an internal oscillator is set to run at approximately the same frequency that is to be detected, using R_1 and C_5 and the equation

$$f_o = 1/R_1C_5 \qquad \text{(Eq. 9-1)}$$

Capacitor C_3 is used to set the capture range (the range of frequencies about f_o that the PLL will detect) according to the equation

$$\text{Capture range (Hz)} = 1070\sqrt{\frac{V_{in}}{f_oC_4}} \qquad \text{(Eq. 9-2)}$$

where C_4 is in μF.

The actual capture range bandwidth required would depend on how much deviation from the intended frequency of a mark or space is expected. Typically this would be around 10 or 20 Hz. The amplitude of the input signal also must be known to accurately determine the capture range of the PLL. The V_{in} factor in Eq. 9-2 is an rms value.

Pin 8 of the 567 is an open-collector-type output, and as such it requires a pull-up resistor to properly drive TTL logic devices. Generally, this resistor is around 10k in value. When the correct frequency is detected and locked onto by the 567, this output is pulled to ground. The NOR gate is used to decode the outputs of the two 567s and produce a stream of bits that are the same as was originally present at the input to the modulator. The bit stream would then be fed into a circuit similar to the one that was presented in Fig. 9-6 for parallel conversion.

Phase-locked loops can also be used to demodulate PSK data transmissions. In one approach, a PLL-based circuit would be designed to track the carrier frequency produced by the modulator. Now, when the phase of the carrier reverses on a logic level change, the PLL would momentarily lose lock, producing a pulse at its lock status output. A digital circuit would then decode these pulses and produce a bit stream that was the same as the original input. The design of the digital circuitry required to reconstruct the bit stream would be more complex than that of the FSK demodulator, and will not be presented here.

One-Shot FSK Demodulation One-shots can also be used to demodulate FSK serial data. The circuit in Fig. 9-11 can be used to extract the data bits

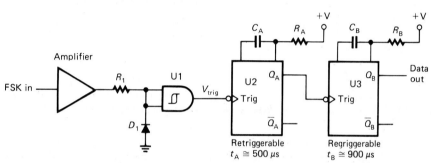

Fig. 9-11 One-shot based FSK demodulator.

from the 1200- to 2200-Hz FSK signals that were used with the PLL demodulator. Refer to the timing diagram shown in Fig. 9-12 during the

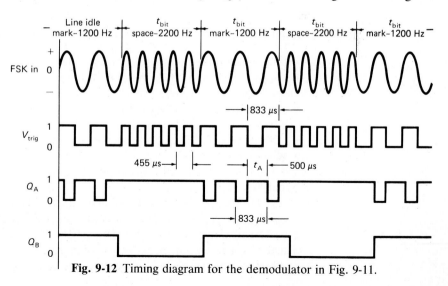

Fig. 9-12 Timing diagram for the demodulator in Fig. 9-11.

following circuit description. The FSK signal is amplified and the negative going portions are clipped off by the amplifier and D_1. Schmitt trigger U1 squares up the signal and ensures that it is TTL-compatible. This signal is used to trigger one-shot U2. You will recall that when the line is idle, it is in the mark (1200-Hz) state. Components C_a and R_a are chosen such that U2 has a time constant tA of about 500 μs. This means that while the line is marking, U2 will time out in between falling edges of V_{trig}. When U2 times out, it triggers U3, causing Q_B to be held high. This occurs because U3 is set up for a time delay of 900 μs. In other words, as long as the channel is marking, U3 will be retriggered because Q_A will fall from logic 1 to logic 0 once every 833 μs, which is shorter than the time constant of U3 (900 μs). Now, when the line is in the space condition (2200 Hz), one-shot U2 is retriggered before it has a chance to time out, which causes its output Q_A to remain high. Once Q_A is high for longer than 900 μs, one-shot U3 will time out, causing its output Q_B to drop to logic 0. Using this approach, maximum transmission rates of about 300 Bd are possible. The circuit could operate unreliably at higher baud rates, because less than four cycles of the 1200 Hz mark signal would be available for capture and conversion by the demodulator and the serial to parallel conversion circuitry that would follow. You will recall that some margin for error must be included because the transmitter and receiver clocks are not synchronized. If higher baud rates were required, the mark and space frequencies could be increased. Of course, this would require modification of the one-shots' time constants.

9-3.3 Data Communication Systems

So far, the circuits and signal formats that are encountered in data communication applications have been covered as more or less isolated topics. Let us now tie together the information that has already been presented.

Three possible variations used in long-distance data communication are shown in Fig. 9-13a, b and c. Let us consider the transmission channel to be the lines supplied in the telephone system. The main difference between the approaches shown is the type of modem that is used in each. The equipment that generates, processes and displays the data is called data terminal equipment (DTE). Computers and monitors are the DTEs in most systems. Modems are referred to as data communication equipment (DCE). If a telephone and acoustic coupler are used, they are also considered to be part of the DCE.

Actually, in Fig 9-13a, true modems are not even used. The term UmodemE implies both modulation and demodulation capabilities in both DCEs. Each end of this system is designed to either send or receive data, but not both. This is known as simplex data communication. An example of such a system would be a stock market ticker tape receiver.

In Fig. 9-13b, half duplex data communication is used. In the half duplex mode, the DCE at each end can either send or receive data, but cannot

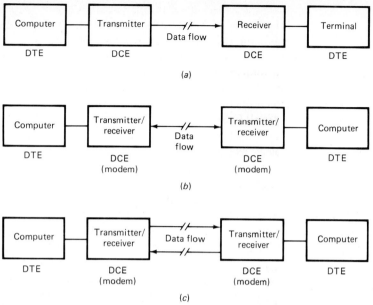

Fig. 9-13 Simplex (*a*), half duplex (*b*) and full duplex (*c*) data communication systems.

do both simultaneously. This mode of operation is very popular, because it is relatively easy to implement.

Full duplex transmission is employed in Fig. 9-13*c*. Full duplex means that data can be sent and received simultaneously by DCEs at both ends of the channel. Although two separate channels are shown, this is not always necessary. Sometimes the mark and space frequencies used by the DCEs at the opposite ends of the line may be staggered. For example, the mark frequency for the left-hand modem may be 1200 Hz, while that of the modem on the right is 2200 Hz. The space frequencies would also be different for each of the DCEs. This is a form of frequency domain multiplexing.

9-3.4 The DCE-DTE Interface

Many modems conform to a standardized interface specification called RS-232-C. This standard defines all control, data transfer, and connector pin assignments used between the DCE (typically a modem) and the DTE (terminal or computer). From a physical standpoint, a 25-pin connector (DB-25) is used to connect the DCE and DTE. The DB-25 connector and its pin assignments are presented in Fig. 9-14*a* and *b*. Normally, most of the control lines specified in the standard are not used, as not all systems require their use. Those lines that are typically used are shown in the block diagram of Fig. 9-15. In this system, an RS-232-C interface is used to control a modem at each end of the telephone connection.

Pin	Name	EIA RS-232-C designation	Function
1	–	AA	Protective ground
2	TxD	BA	Transmitted data
3	RxD	BB	Received data
4	$\overline{\text{RTS}}$	CA	Request to send
5	$\overline{\text{CTS}}$	CB	Clear to send
6	$\overline{\text{DSR}}$	CC	Data set ready
7	GND	AB	Signal GND/common RTN
8	$\overline{\text{CD}}$	CF	RCVD line sig. detector
9	–	–	Reserved for testing
10	–	–	Reserved for testing
11	–	–	Unassigned
12	–	SCF	Secondary received line signal detector
13	–	SCB	Secondary clear to send
14	–	SBA	Secondary transmitted data
15	–	DB	Transmitter signal element timing
16	–	SBB	Secondary received data
17	–	DD	Receiver signal element timing
18	–	–	Unassigned
19	–	SCA	Secondary request to send
20	$\overline{\text{DTR}}$	CD	Data terminal ready
21	–	CG	Signal quality detector
22	–	CE	Ring indicator
23	–	CH/CI	Data signal rate selector
24	–	DA	Transmit signal element timing
25	–	–	Unassigned

(a)

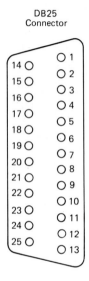

DB25 Connector

(b)

Fig. 9-14 RS-232-C line definitions (a) and standard DB25 connector (b).

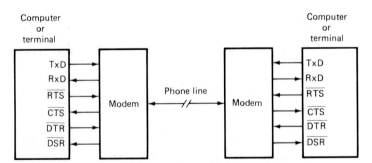

Fig. 9-15 Commonly used RS-232-C data and control lines.

Often, for short-distance communications purposes, the RS-232-C interface can be used without resorting to the use of a modem. A typical connection is shown in Fig. 9-16. Notice that each line is connected not

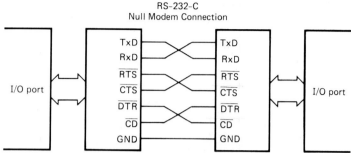

Fig. 9-16 RS-232-C null modem connections.

to the point with the same designation but rather to its complementary line. This type of connection is required by some RS-232 devices, and is called a null modem connection. Special null modem connectors are available that provide this line swapping interconnection.

The RS-232-C signal levels are shown in Fig. 9-17. The shaded areas represent valid logic levels. Any voltage between -3 and -15 V is

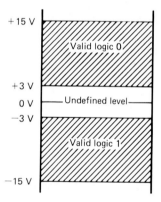

Fig. 9-17 Voltage levels defining valid and invalid states on RS-232-C lines.

considered to be a valid logic high (mark) level. Similarly, any voltage between $+3$ and $+15$ V is a valid logic low (space). The range from $+3$ to -3 V is undefined. When no data is being transmitted, the $T \times D$ line is held in the logic high state.

Review Questions for Section 9-3

1. What is meant by the terms mark and space?
2. What state does the output of a modem usually assume when it is idle (no data is being transmitted)?
3. What is the difference between a DCE and a DTE?

4. What mode of operation is said to be in use if devices at both ends of a communication channel can transmit and receive data simultaneously?
5. Why is it necessary to use FSK or PSK to transmit digital data over the telephone system?
6. In Fig. 9-10, what is the function of R_2?
7. In Fig. 9-11, what is the purpose of D_1? the Schmitt trigger?

9-4   SHORT RANGE DATA COMMUNICATIONS

There are circumstances where there are alternatives to the use of modem and long-distance telephone-line-based FSK and PSK data communications. For example, the main disadvantage of the residential telephone system in data communication applications is the low bandwidth. Special leased line services are provided by telephone companies for higher data transmission capability on dedicated data transmission lines. Rates of 50K bits/s and higher are possible on such systems, but this is only really considered when high-volume long-distance data communication is required. Often, the distances involved in a data communication system are short enough that dedicated networks become a practical alternative. For example, all of the microcomputers in an office building could be linked to form a network. Networking has become increasingly important in recent years, as microcomputers have become a common business tool.

The RS-232-C method discussed previously is often used for short-range data communication. This section will begin with an examination of some commonly used network structures. In addition, a few other data communication interfaces will be discussed.

9-4.1   Ethernet

Ethernet is what is referred to as a local area network (LAN). Developed by Xerox Corporation, Ethernet has become one of the most popular microcomputer networking systems used today. In the Ethernet network, serial data is transferred synchronously at a rate of 10 Mbits/s over a coaxial cable. Such extremely high transmission rates imply sophisticated control circuitry, and indeed, this is the case. Fortunately, the Ethernet system has been supported by major IC manufacturers, such as Intel, which produces an Ethernet serial interface chip, the 82501.

The transmission medium of the Ethernet system is a coaxial cable. Coaxial cable is used to provide a high degree of noise immunity and minimal radiation loss. Ten million bits/s is quite a high frequency in itself, and the rapid rise and fall times of the pulses that make up the data on the transmission line will produce much noise at higher harmonics. This would cause severe interference with other communication equipment if the shielding provided by coaxial cable was not present.

Equipment is interfaced to the main coaxial cable via transceivers. A transceiver performs the parallel to serial and serial to parallel data conversion required by a given device. The transceivers connected to the coaxial cable can be spaced a minimum distance of 2.5 apart from one another. The maximum distance allowed for a single Ethernet line is 500; however, repeaters may be inserted at the ends of the lines to extend the maximum distance to 2500. Repeaters are circuits that pick up the transmitted signal at the end of the cable, clean it up, and retransmit it down the rest of the line. The point at which a transceiver is connected to the Ethernet coaxial cable is called a node. There may be up to 1000 nodes on a single network. A typical Ethernet system is illustrated in Fig. 9-18.

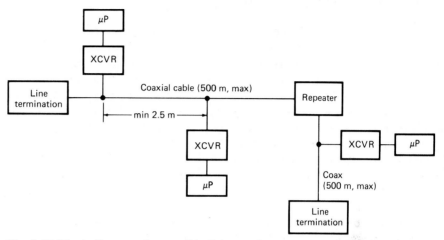

Fig. 9-18 Block diagram of a possible Ethernet local area network (LAN).

The data and control bits that make up a given message packet are called a frame. A frame is divided into five fields, as shown in Fig. 9-19. Each field is in turn divided into 8-bit groups called octets. Transmission begins with the sending of 64 bits that are referred to as a preamble. The preamble is used to notify other devices on the system that transmission is about to begin. The frame begins with a 6-octet-long destination specification. This activates the transceiver that is intended as the destination of the data. The transceiver that is sending the data then identifies itself with a 6-octet-long source address. Next, a 2-octet-type field is sent, followed by the actual data. The length of the data field may vary from 46 to 1500 octets in length. The last field sent is called the frame check sequence. This is a cyclic redundancy code block that is used for error detection purposes. Error detection will be discussed later in this chapter.

9-4.2   IEEE-488 GPIB

Not all data communication applications require the extreme transmission speeds possible with LANs such as Ethernet. Most electronic equipment manufacturers produce instruments that can be interfaced to a microcomputer for automatic data logging and control purposes. The most commonly used instrument interfacing standard is the IEEE-488 general purpose interface bus (GPIB) standard, originally developed by Hewlett-Packard.

The GPIB is a parallel data communication and control bus, in which all signals are TTL-compatible and active-low. A list of the line assignments

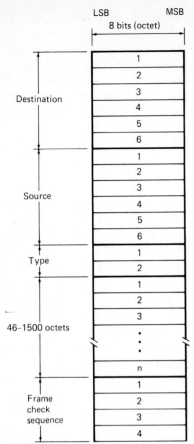

Fig. 9-19 Composition of a transmission frame in the Ethernet system.

IEEE–488 GPIB
Pin Assignments

Pin	IEEE-488 designation	Function
1	DI/01	Data in/out
2	DI/02	Data in/out
3	DI/03	Data in/out
4	DI/04	Data in/out
5	EOI	End or identify
6	DAV	Data valid
7	NRFD	Not ready for data
8	NDAC	No data accepted
9	IFC	Interface clear
10	SRQ	Service request
11	ATN	Attention
12	Shield	Shield
13	DI/05	Data in/out
14	DI/06	Data in/out
15	DI/07	Data in/out
16	DI/08	Data in/out
17	REN	Remote enable
18	GND	Ground
19	GND	Ground
20	GND	Ground
21	GND	Ground
22	GND	Ground
23	GND	Ground
24	Logic GND	Logic ground

(a)

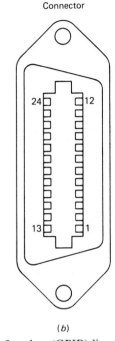

Connector

(b)

Fig. 9-20 IEEE-488 general purpose interface bus (GPIB) line definitions (*a*) and standard connector (*b*).

and an illustration of the standard 24-pin GPIB connector are shown in Fig. 9-20*a* and *b*.

A device that is connected to the GPIB is designated as either a controller, a talker, a listener, or a talker/listener. The controller is typically a microcomputer that is responsible for controlling the other devices on the bus. Multiple controllers may be connected to the bus; however, only one controller may be active at any given time. Figure 9-21 shows a typical

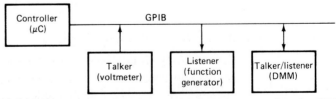

Fig. 9-21 Structure of an instrumentation system using the GPIB.

GPIB configuration. Devices of limited flexibility are usually designated as talkers (a single-range digital voltmeter) or listeners (a signal generator). A digital multimeter would have to be able to talk (send data to the controller) and listen (change functions on command). Brief descriptions of the various GPIB lines are presented below.

Data lines

DIO1 – DIO8: Data, address, and control words are multiplexed onto these eight lines.

Control lines

ATN: Asserted to activate listener whose address is on the bus.

IFC: Used by the controller to initialize the devices that are connected to the bus.

SRQ: Driven low by a device requesting service.

REN: Issued by the controller. Causes the listening device that was addressed to disregard its front panel control settings.

EOI: If asserted by a talker, this signal indicates the end of a multiple byte transfer. If asserted by a controller, it represents a polling operation (used with ATN).

Handshaking Lines

DAV: Asserted by the controller. Indicates that a control byte has been placed on the bus.

NRFD: Asserted by an active listener to prevent new data or control bytes from being placed on the bus.

NADC: Asserted by the listener. Indicates that the last byte placed on the bus has not yet been accepted.

Each device connected to the controller via the GPIB has a fixed address that is hard-wired into its GPIB interface. This address may usually be changed using switches or jumpers. The IEEE-488 standard is very comprehensive and covers almost all possible device configurations and conditions that could occur on the bus. Data rates as high as 1 Mbits/s can be achieved using the GPIB interface. Several major IC manufacturers produce GPIB support ICs, which simplify the interfacing process.

9-4.3 The RS-449 Data Communication Standard

Another DCE to DTE serial interfacing standard is RS-449. This standard is not used nearly as often in microcomputer-based systems, and is only presented for the sake of completeness. The line designations and connector outline for RS-449 are shown in Fig. 9-22a and b.

Pin	EIA RS-449 designation	Function		Pin	EIA RS-449 designation	Function
1	—	Shield		20	RC	Receive ground
2	SI	Signaling rate indicator		21	-	Unassigned
3	—	Unassigned		22	$\overline{SD}$	Send data
4	$\overline{SD}$	Send data		23	ST	Send timing
5	ST	Send timing		24	$\overline{RD}$	Receive data
6	$\overline{RD}$	Receive data		25	RS	Request to send
7	$\overline{RS}$	Request to send		26	RT	Receive timing
8	RT	Receive timing		27	$\overline{CS}$	Clear to send
9	$\overline{CS}$	Clear to send		28	$\overline{IS}$	Terminal in service
10	$\overline{LL}$	Local loopback		29	$\overline{DM}$	Data mode
11	$\overline{DM}$	Data mode		30	$\overline{TR}$	Terminal ready
12	$\overline{TR}$	Terminal ready		31	$\overline{RR}$	Receiver ready
13	$\overline{RR}$	Receiver ready		32	$\overline{SS}$	Select standby
14	$\overline{RL}$	Remote loopback		33	$\overline{SQ}$	Signal quality
15	$\overline{IC}$	Incoming call		34	$\overline{NS}$	New signal
16	$\overline{SF}$	Select frequency		35	TT	Terminal timing
17	TT	Terminal timing		36	$\overline{SB}$	Standby indicator
18	$\overline{TM}$	Test mode		37	SC	Send common
19	SG	Signal ground				

(a)

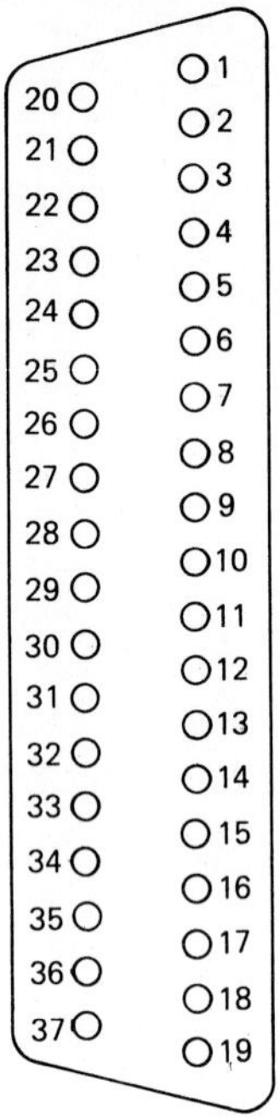

(b)

Fig. 9-22 RS-449 line definitions (*a*) and standard DB37 connector (*b*).

9-4.4 The Centronics Parallel Interface

The Centronics parallel interface is one of the most widely used methods of connecting microcomputers to peripheral devices such as printers. The various Centronics line designations and connector outline are shown in Fig. 9-23*a* and *b*. Notice that many of the signal lines have corresponding return lines. The return lines are basically the same as ground returns.

When the computer is ready to send a character code to the printer, it first places the code on the data lines. Next, the STROBE line is asserted. If the character code was accepted, the printer will drive the ACKNOWL-EDGE line low, indicating that the character has been received. If the printer cannot accept any input, it will assert the BUSY signal. This line is monitored by the computer to determine whether or not it should send data to the printer. Many printers contain a section of RAM that is dedicated to the temporary storage of incoming data. This allows the computer to dump a long sequence of characters to the printer, without having to wait for the relatively slow process of printing to occur in between data transfers. This type of memory is called a buffer. Many manufacturers also produce printer buffers that contain large amounts of memory. These buffers are inserted between the computer's output port and the printer. The idea behind buffering is to relieve the computer of the task of constantly polling the printer to determine whether more

Centronics Parallel
Interface
Pin Assignments

Signal pin	Return pin	Signal name
1	19	Strobe
2	20	Data 1
3	21	Data 2
4	22	Data 3
5	23	Data 4
6	24	Data 5
7	25	Data 6
8	26	Data 7
9	27	Data 8
10	28	Acknowledge
11	29	Busy
12	N/A	Paper end
13	N/A	Select
14	N/A	Undef'd.
15	N/A	Undef'd.
16	N/A	0 V
17	N/A	0 V
18	N/A	+5 V
19 ↕ 30	N/A ↕ N/A	Gnd ↕ Gnd
31	N/A	Input prime
32	N/A	Fault
33	N/A	Undef'd.
34	N/A	Undef'd.
35	N/A	Undef'd.
36	N/A	Undef'd.

(a)

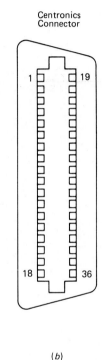

Centronics
Connector

(b)

Fig. 9-23 Centronics interface line definitions (*a*) and standard connector (*b*).

character data can be sent. This increases system throughput, especially when large amounts of printing are to be done.

9-4.5 Current Loops

In nearly every system considered thus far, the state of any given bit present in the transmission channel has been defined in terms of voltage. The exception is when FSK and PSK modulation techniques are used, because then the frequency or phase of the modulated signal is the key to its logical interpretation. However, once the FSK or PSK signal has been demodulated, a link such as RS-232 or RS-449 is used to transfer the data to the DTE, and both of these methods define logic states in terms of voltage. Voltage sources are easy to implement, and their outputs are easy to monitor. This is why most often logic levels are defined by voltages. However, problems can occur when voltage levels are to be sent over distances of greater than 100 ft or so. The problem is that in order to prevent loading of the voltage source, the receivers should have high input impedances. This in turn makes the transmission line very susceptible to noise induced by stray electromagnetic fields. Also, in order to prevent attenuation of the logic signals being sent, the line resistance must be kept very low. These considerations, plus the fact that the cables employed must contain multiple conductors (making them somewhat expensive for long runs), have led to the use of current loops.

A current loop is a closed loop of wire that is driven by a controlled current source. One possible configuration that would allow communication between two computers via a current loop is shown in Fig. 9-24. Here,

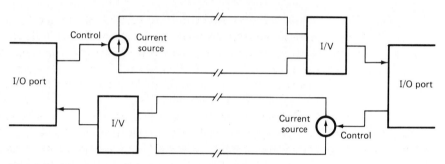

Fig. 9-24 Data transmission over current loops.

the logic levels that are to be sent from one end to the other are defined in terms of current levels. For example, logic low may be represented by 0 mA, while logic high is 20 mA. The received current is converted into the proper voltage level by an I/V converter at the receiving end. Of course, in order to keep cabling costs down, data is sent in serial form.

The main advantage of the current loop is that the I/V receiver that closes the loop is a low input impedance device. This reduces sensitivity to induced noise on the loop. Also, since the transmitter is a current source, the resistance of the loop is normally not too critical. Consider that the output voltage produced by the current source can assume any value (within limits) required to force 20 mA to flow through the loop in the logic high state.

One possible circuit that can be used as a voltage-controlled current source is shown in Fig. 9-25. Basically, the circuit works as follows. The output of a TTL gate (the digital input V_{in}) drives the noninverting input of a differential amplifier. Transistors Q_1 and Q_2 provide the high-current drive required by the current loop. The end of resistor R_6 that is connected to the emitters of Q_1 and Q_2 is used to provide voltage feedback to the inverting input of the diff amp. The other side of R_5 provides voltage feedback to the noninverting input of the diff amp. The circuit operates such that if the TTL gate's output is low, transistors Q_1 and Q_2 are driven into cutoff. This results in 0 current flow through R_5, and therefore, no current flow through the loop. This is required by the diff amp in order to

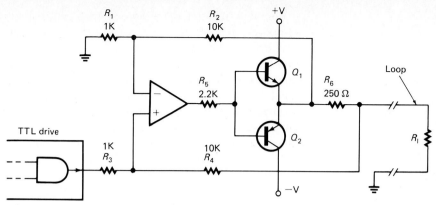

Fig. 9-25 Current loop driver (V/I converter).

maintain approximately 0 differential voltage between the inverting and noninverting terminals. If the output of the TTL gate is high, a differential voltage will appear between the inverting and noninverting inputs of the op amp, and Q_1 and Q_2 will be driven by the diff amp such that the voltage drop across R_5 is equal to V_{in} (the output of the TTL gate). With $R_5 = 250\ \Omega$, a current of 20 mA will be forced through the loop. This forces the voltage differential between the inputs of the diff amp to approximately 0. The diff amp provides a large amount of negative feedback, which tends to hold the loop current at a constant level for a given value of V_{in}.

A possible design for the I/V converter needed at the receiver end of the current loop is shown in Fig. 9-26. Here, a 100 Ω resistor is used to

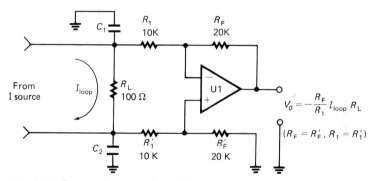

$$V_O = -\frac{R_F}{R_1} I_{loop} R_L$$

$$(R_F = R'_F,\ R_1 = R'_1)$$

Fig. 9-26 Current loop receiver (I/V converter).

terminate the loop. Capacitors C_1 and C_2 are used to filter any induced ac voltage to ground. Basically, when current is forced into the loop, R_L produces a voltage drop that is sensed by differential amplifier U1. For a given gain, the output of the diff amp will be proportional to $I_{loop}R_L$. Since loop current is constant at a given logic state, V_O should also be constant. When no current is forced in the loop, no voltage drop is developed across R_L and the output of the diff amp is 0 V. The output of the diff amp could be conditioned such that it is compatible with the logic devices in the receiver.

You will recall from Chap. 6 that often it is desirable to have the computer electrically isolated from the outside world. Optoisolators can provide this type of protection when used at the ends of the current loop data link. As an added benefit, it is relatively easy to convert the current levels carried by the loop into digitally compatible voltage levels using widely available optoisolators that are designed specifically for this purpose.

Current loops are commonly encountered in industrial settings, where cable runs are long (sometimes over 1000 ft) and high noise is the normal state of affairs. Analog transducers that monitor process control factors under the control of a computer are frequently connected to A/D and D/A circuitry via current loops.

9-4.6 Short-Haul Modems

In some small-scale data communications applications, none of the previously mentioned techniques can be used effectively. For example, consider a situation in which a smart terminal located at one end of a college campus is to be interfaced to a mainframe located at the other end of the campus. The distance between the terminal and the computer may be too great for practical use of a current loop. Let us also assume that this terminal is to be used mainly for graphics applications, which work most effectively at very high data rates. The necessity for high-speed data transfer precludes the use of a modem that utilizes the existing telephone system of the campus. From the alternatives covered so far, we are left with few choices. One would be to set up a network such as Ethernet. The problem here is that Ethernet is relatively expensive, and is not justifiable for such a small-scale system. In such a case, one very practical alternative would be to use a short-haul modem.

The principles behind the operation of a short-haul modem are basically the same as those of a standard modem; that is, the data to be transmitted is serialized and sent to a modulator. The modulator transmits the data over a dedicated transmission line to the modem at the receiving end. The short-haul modem is more effective than a current loop over long distances, because the high-frequency modulated signal (most likely FSK) will not be attenuated as dramatically. Very long current loop runs would require very heavy gauge wire to keep resistances within acceptable limits. Also, once again, it is not a voltage or current level that is being used to represent data, but the frequency of the signal. This provides a high degree of noise immunity.

9-4.7 Fiber Optic Data Communications

In recent years, fiber optic data communication has become a major technology. In fiber optics, a stream of serial data is used to modulate the intensity of a light source. The output of this light source is coupled to a fiber optic cable, which acts as the transmission medium. At the receiving end, a device such as a photodiode or phototransistor is used to convert the modulated light it receives into an electrical signal.

The main advantage of fiber optics is the tremendous data rate that can be achieved. Consider the FSK modulation technique presented earlier in this chapter. It can easily be deduced, looking at Fig. 9-12, that if one were to attempt to shift the oscillation frequency at a rate greater than that of the mark frequency, that all logic high bits would be lost. This is also similar to the problem of aliasing that occurs in time-sampled systems. What this all boils down to is that information cannot be sent at a rate that is greater than ½ of the frequency of the carrier. This fact is related to the Nyquist sampling theorem that was discussed in the section on A/D conversion in Chap. 7. Taking this into consideration, a typical infrared light source used in fiber optic applications that emits light at a frequency of around 10^{14} Hz could allow data transmission rates in the gigabits/s range. The primary limiting factor is the rate at which the light source can be turned on and off, and the response time of the light detectors used in the system.

One possible configuration for a simple fiber optic data communication system (simplex) is shown in Fig. 9-27. In order to take advantage of the

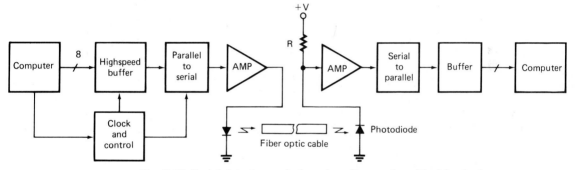

Fig. 9-27 Serial data transmission via a fiber optic cable (simplex).

high transmission speeds possible, the data to be transmitted is loaded into a high-speed buffer. The data is then shifted out and used to turn a laser diode on and off. Laser diodes can be turned on and off in very short times (<1 ns); therefore, data can be transmitted at very high rates. At the receiver, the pulses of light are converted into an electrical signal and processed as required for use by the computer.

Aside from the high data rates that fiber optic data links allow, there are several other advantages that are also important. First, since the data carrier is light, electromagnetic interference (in the normal sense of the word) is eliminated. It is easy to shield the cable from external light, which would be the only type of external electromagnetic energy that could induce noise in the cable. Another advantage is that a single fiber can carry thousands of separate data channels. The various data sources can be time domain multiplexed together at very high rates, without significantly affecting the useful data rate of any given channel, because of the extremely high transmission bandwidth. Time domain multiplexing is the sharing of a common transmission line by several devices, where each device is allotted a certain time interval in which to access the line. This can save money and weight when compared to multiple wire cables that are now required.

Fiber optics is a growing field, and new developments are announced all the time. Currently, fiber optics are used mainly by the telephone company. However, fiber optic data communication equipment is also in use in small-scale data communication networks at the present time. In military applications, fiber optic data links have been used to replace the wiring in the avionics equipment in many aircraft. The result is a substantial weight savings and higher noise immunity, when compared to conventional wiring methods.

Review Questions for Section 9-4

1. What type of data transmission is used on the Ethernet system?
2. What is the fundamental message unit called in an Ethernet system?
3. What are the designations given to devices that are connected to an IEEE-488 GPIB?
4. Over which GPIB lines are device addresses transmitted?
5. Is the GPIB designed for parallel or serial data transfer?
6. What form of data transmission is used with a short-haul modem?

9-5   DATA ENCODING

Data can be encoded using a number of different methods. Prior to this section, data encoding has not really been discussed. Consider the serial data format that was presented in Fig. 9-4. Most of us would assume that if the data field of this word was 10011101, for example, the resulting voltage waveform produced would appear something like that shown in Fig. 9-28 (TTL levels have been used, and the start and stop bits have

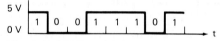

Fig. 9-28 NRZ serial data stream.

been omitted). This is indeed a valid possibility, and it is called nonreturn to zero (NRZ) encoding.

9-5.1   Nonreturn to Zero Encoding

The term NRZ comes from the fact that during times in which the serial data is high for more than 1 consecutive bit time, the output of the DCE that is driving the communication channel also remains constantly high.

NRZ is relatively easy to produce, as it is the natural form for the bits coming out of a shift register. Because it is easy to produce, NRZ encoding is usually used whenever possible. Most asynchronous communication devices use the NRZ format. A variation on NRZ encoding is called bipolar NRZ, or NRZ-B. In bipolar NRZ, the signal states assumed for logic high and low are positive and negative voltage levels. The bipolar NRZ equivalent to Fig. 9-28 is shown in Fig. 9-29. Bipolar NRZ has the advantage of producing higher average signal power levels than unipolar NRZ at a given peak to peak pulse amplitude level.

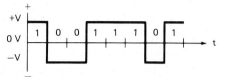

Fig. 9-29 Bipolar NRZ serial data stream.

9-5.2 Return to Zero Encoding

Return to zero (RZ) encoding is an alternative that provides significant advantages over either NRZ or NRZ-B encoding. The main feature of RZ encoding is that the pulse that represents logic high will always return to zero before the transmission of the next bit. Figure 9-30 illustrates RZ

Fig. 9-30 RZ encoded serial data.

encoding for the code word 10011101. Unlike NRZ encoding, under certain conditions, the transmitter clock frequency can be extracted from an RZ encoded signal. This requires the use of what is called bitstuffing. Basically, logic 1s are stuffed into certain positions in the bit stream, producing predictable (periodic) pulse edges in the data stream. The transmitter clock frequency can be easily determined based on these regular intervals. At the receiver, the extra bits are removed from the data. This makes synchronous communication possible without a dedicated clock line.

The disadvantage of RZ encoding as compared to NRZ is that for a given data rate, RZ requires a greater channel bandwidth. This occurs because there are more high to low and low to high transitions in a given period of time. If the channel bandwidth is not high enough, severe distortion of the signal will occur (loss of high frequency signal components).

9-5.3 Manchester Encoding

Manchester or biphase encoding is another technique that is used in synchronous data communications applications. The important feature of Manchester encoding is that the transmitter clock frequency is easily extracted from the signal. Usually, phase-locked loop circuitry is used to provide clock regeneration. Figure 9-31 shows the Manchester encoded

Fig. 9-31 Manchester or biphase data encoding.

waveform that would be produced, again, using the bit sequence 10011101. In Manchester encoding, it is the edges of the signal, and not the levels, that are used to indicate whether a given bit is logic high or low. A high to low (falling or negative-going) transition indicates logic high, while a low to high (positive or rising) edge indicates logic low. As with RZ encoding, Manchester encoding requires higher channel bandwidth for a given data rate, when compared to NRZ.

All of the data encoding methods reviewed in this section are shown in Fig. 9-32. It is easy to see why Manchester and RZ encoding techniques require higher channel bandwidths, based on this illustration.

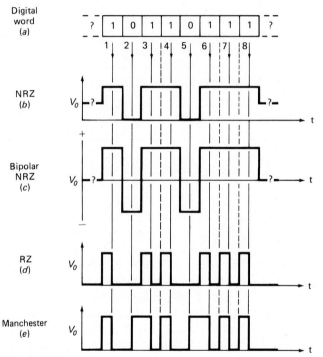

Fig. 9-32 Examples of various data encoding methods applied to a serial bit stream.

9-5.4 Pulse Modulation

Pulse trains can also be used to carry analog, as well as digital, information. Although the pulse modulation methods to be presented are normally not used to convey digital data, they are encountered in some computer-based data acquisition and telemetry applications. This being the case, brief descriptions of these transmission formats will be presented.

The waveform in Fig. 9-33a, represents a sinusoidal signal that is to be used as the input to several different pulse modulation circuits. Figure 9-33b shows the output of a pulse amplitude modulation (PAM) circuit. This particular form of PAM is called flat-topped PAM, and basically, the

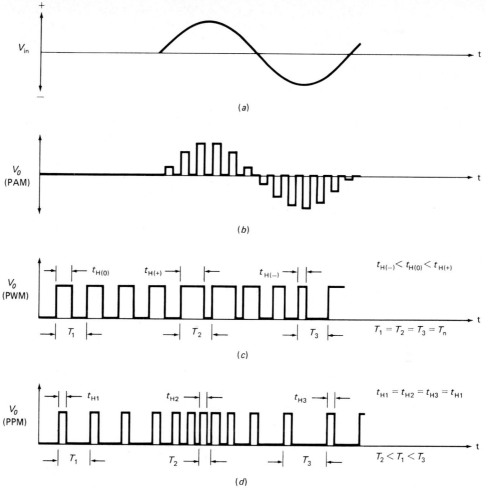

Fig. 9-33 Pulse modulation waveforms produced in response to a sinusoidal input.

resultant signal is a series of fixed duration samples whose amplitude is proportional to the amplitude of the analog input signal. This type of signal could possibly be used to drive the input of an A/D converter that is interfaced to a port of a computer.

Figure 9-33c illustrates the response of a pulse width modulator (PWM) circuit to V_{in}. In this particular example, the duty cycle of the output is proportional to the amplitude of the input signal. Notice that the spacing between rising edges T_n is constant, while the pulse high time t_{hn} varies with V_{in}. This signal could be demodulated by accumulating a count while the pulse is high. This count would be proportional to the amplitude of V_{in} at the sample point.

The final form of pulse modulation to be presented is called pulse position modulation (Fig. 9-33d). In this form of modulation, the pulse duration t_{hn}) is constant, while the spacing in between pulses T_n is proportional to the amplitude of V_{in}. Again, the amplitude of V_{in} could be determined by using counters, or possibly with a frequency to voltage (F/V) converter. The output of the F/V converter could then be used to drive an A/D converter.

Review Questions for Section 9-5

1. What is the advantage of NRZ-B over unipolar NRZ?
2. Why is bit stuffing used in conjunction with RZ encoding?
3. What is another name for Manchester encoding?
4. How is the presence of a logic 1 represented in a Manchester encoded data stream?
5. What is the main advantage of NRZ encoding over both Manchester and RZ decoding?
6. Which form of pulse modulation is used least frequently?

9-6   ERROR DETECTION AND CORRECTION

In order for data that is sent between various devices and locations to be of any practical use, it must be error-free. Unlike the human brain, most electronic devices cannot tolerate the corruption of data being sent to it. People can readily infer meanings and intentions based on previous information, surrounding letters and words, and various other subtle cues, while machines can't (not yet anyway). For example, if when reading an article on electronics, a person comes upon a misspelled word, such as *fuze*, often the misspelling may go unnoticed. It is obvious that what was meant was the word *fuse*. This occurs because we tend to analyze the whole word or statement as a single entity of information. We do not usually analyze each individual character used to make up a given word. Also, fuze and fuse are phonetically similar, which also makes the misspelling less noticeable. Machines, on the other hand, are far less tolerant of such errors. A lost bit can effectively turn an entire stream of data into garbage, when supplied to a computer.

In order to ensure the integrity of data that is sent from and received by digital devices, various error detection and error correction techniques have been developed. In this section, several of these methods will be discussed. Since error detection is essential to error correction, let us now examine a few commonly used error detection methods.

9-6.1   Parity Checking

Parity checking should be quite familiar to you at this point. You will recall that parity checking was discussed in Chap. 5, as one method by which the correct operation of memory devices could be verified as they are accessed. For the sake of completeness, a quick review of parity generation and detection will now be presented.

The addition of a parity bit to a data word allows the detection of a change of state in any single bit position at the receiving end of the channel. This parity bit is used to produce either an even number of 1s in the data word (even parity) or an odd number of 1s in the data word (odd parity). Simple exclusive OR (XOR) gates can be used to generate either type of parity. The logic diagram for a parity generator is shown in Fig. 9-34. If the inverter is included in this circuit, then odd parity is produced, while if it is omitted, then even parity is generated. In either case, the parity bit is produced for a 7-bit word. This circuit could be used to add a parity bit to an ASCII character, producing an 8-bit code word.

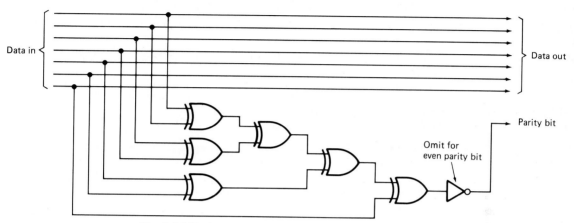

Fig. 9-34 Parity generator for 8-bit data words.

Parity checkers are basically the same as parity generators. For example, if the circuit of Fig. 9-34 is used to add an even parity bit to an ASCII character, the parity checker of Fig. 9-35 could be used to indicate whether or not a bit has somehow changed states during transmission (parity error), by producing a logic 1 at its output. Actually, if an odd number of bits change states, the parity checker will produce a logic high output, indicating an erroneous input; while if an even number of bits have changed states, no parity error occurs and the data is accepted as correct. This is the main

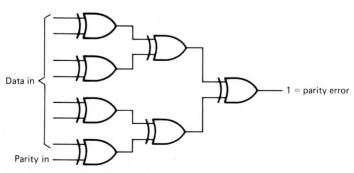

Fig. 9-35 Parity checker for 8-bit data plus an ninth parity bit.

weakness associated with simple parity generation and detection. Also, the inclusion of a single parity bit in a block of data is not sufficient to determine which bit(s) have changed states. Measures taken to overcome these problems will be covered next.

Example 9-5

The ASCII code representation for the character "=" is sent to an even parity generator. What logic state will be produced at the output of the parity generator?

Solution

The binary representation for "=" in ASCII code is 0111101. Since this word contains five 1s, the parity generator will produce logic 1 at its output, resulting in an even number of 1s.

9-6.2 Cyclic Redundancy Checking

One of the more popular error detection techniques in use is cyclic redundancy checking (CRC). CRC is what is referred to as a recursive code. In a recursive code, the state of a given bit is dependent on the states of the preceding bits. This means that multiple errors can be detected with relative ease, because a change of 1 or possibly more bits will almost always result in a code word that could not exist unless bits were lost. When using CRC, several extra bits are generated, based on the original code word and a special code word called a generator polynomial. These bits are added to a shifted version of the original data bits in the code word or block. At the outset, in order to implement CRC coding, a quantity called a generator polynomial is selected. The generator polynomial is used as a key for encoding and decoding the data at both the sending and receiving ends of the channel. The generator polynomial is really nothing more than a particular pattern of bits that is usually expressed in polynomial form. For example, a commonly used generator polynomial is

$$G(x) = x^{16} + x^{15} + x^5 + 1$$

This is equivalent to 11000000000010001_2, and it is used as the basis of modifications that are to be performed on the data that is to be transmitted. Let us use a shorter generator polynomial to keep the arithmetic manipulations somewhat simpler in the upcoming discussion. Arbitrarily, the generator polynomial

$$G(x) = x^4 + x^2 + 1$$

will be assumed to be used at the sending and receiving ends of our data communication system. In order to apply $G(x)$ to the transmission of a message (in this case, an ASCII character will be the message), the following steps are performed. First, the group of bits that constitutes the data or information to be transmitted is expressed in polynomial form, and is denoted as $M(x)$. For example, if the ASCII code for the character G (1000111) was to be sent using CRC techniques, the polynomial that represents this 7-bit code would be written

$$M(x) = x^6 + x^2 + x + 1$$

where the bit positions that contain 1s are assigned the weight, in exponential notation, of their respective positions. Note that $x = x^1$ and $1 = x^0$.

With the character expressed as a message polynomial $M(x)$, it is then multiplied by the degree of the generator polynomial $G(x)$. The degree of any polynomial is equal to the highest exponent with a nonzero coefficient. In this case, the degree of our $G(x)$ is 4. Multiplying $M(x)$ by the degree of $G(x)$ is accomplished by adding 4 to the exponents of the terms in $M(x)$, which is also the same as shifting the polynomial $M(x)$ to the left by 4 places. We shall designate the shifted polynomial as $M(x)x^4$. Writing the shifted polynomial, we obtain

$$M(x)x^4 = x^{10} + x^6 + x^5 + x^4$$

The next step in the transmission process is to divide the shifted polynomial by the generator polynomial. This process is shown below. This division will result in a quotient polynomial $Q(x)$ and a remainder polynomial $R(x)$.

$$
\begin{array}{r}
x^6 + x^4 + x^2 + x + 1 \quad \longleftarrow Q(x) \\
G(x) \longrightarrow x^4 + x^2 + 1 \overline{)\, x^{10} + \qquad\qquad x^6 + x^5 + x^4 } \quad \longleftarrow M(x)x^4 \\
\underline{x^{10} + \qquad x^8 + x^6} \\
x^8 + \qquad x^5 + x^4 \\
\underline{x^8 + x^6 + \qquad x^4} \\
x^6 + x^5 \\
\underline{x^6 + \qquad x^4 + \qquad x^2} \\
x^5 + x^4 + \qquad x^2 \\
\underline{x^5 + \qquad x^3 + \qquad x^1} \\
x^4 + x^3 + x^2 + x^1 \\
\underline{x^4 + \qquad x^2 + \qquad 1} \\
x^3 + \qquad x^1 + 1 \quad \longleftarrow R(x)
\end{array}
$$

From the division just presented, the quotient $Q(x)$ is discarded and the remainder $R(x)$ is added to the shifted polynomial to produce the transmitted polynomial $T(x)$. In symbols, this operation is expressed as

$$T(x) = M(x)x^4 + R(x)$$

Using the values obtained above, we get

$$T(x) = (x^{10} + x^6 + x^5 + x^4) + (x^3 + x + 1)$$

The parentheses can be removed for clarity, producing

$$T(x) = x^{10} + x^6 + x^5 + x^4 + x^3 + x + 1$$

which, in binary form (what would actually be transmitted), appears as

$$T(x) = 10001111011$$

The transmitted polynomial $T(x)$ is now sent to the receiver. At the receiver, $T(x)$ is once again divided by the generator polynomial $G(x)$. If no bits have been lost, the division will produce a remainder of 0. However, if one or more bits have been lost, a nonzero remainder will be produced. Let us divide $T(x)$ by $G(x)$ and verify that no remainder is produced, when no bits in $T(x)$ are lost.

$$
\require{enclose}
\begin{array}{r}
x^6 + x^4 + x^2 + x^1 + 1 \qquad \longleftarrow Q(x) = M(x) \\[2pt]
G(x) \longrightarrow x^4 + x^2 + 1 \enclose{longdiv}{x^{10} + x^6 + x^5 + x^4 + x^3 + x^2 + x^1 + 1} \quad \longleftarrow T(x)
\end{array}
$$

During the process of dividing $T(x)$ by $G(x)$, the quotient produced is the original code word $G(x)$ that formed the original message. The main advantage of CRC coding is that multiple errors can be detected with high reliability (generally >99 percent confidence of error detection for multiple bit errors, with judicious selection of the generator polynomial), whereas with simple parity checking, there is a 50-50 chance that multiple errors will go undetected. The reason that this characteristic is important is based on the assumption that if 1 bit is lost, there is a very good chance that several other successive bits were also lost. This is called an error burst. CRC coding is often used to verify the validity of data that is stored and retrieved from magnetic tape and disks, and to verify the validity of data in conventional data communication applications.

The disadvantage of using CRC coding, or any other error-checking method that adds extra bits to the data stream, is that code efficiency is reduced. In effect, the check bits contain redundant information that results in a smaller amount of information conveyed in a given period of time.

Cyclic redundancy coding can also be used in data encryption applications. If very long code blocks and generator polynomials are used, the resulting data stream is virtually impossible to decode (decrypt) without knowledge of the original generator polynomial. The generator polynomial provides the key to deciphering the message.

9-6.3 The Hamming Code

The result of an analysis (of the bit groups or words that make up a given code system) that determines the minimum number of bits that must be lost (changed) such that one code word will change to another is referred to as the Hamming distance of that code. If ASCII code is used as an example, it is easy to see that changing just 1 bit will result in the representation of a different character. For example, if the first bit of the ASCII code for A (1000001) is lost (changed to 0), then the resulting code word (0000001) would be interpreted as representing the control character SOH (start of heading). Since a change in identity does in fact occur, when a single bit is altered, it can be said that ASCII code has a Hamming distance of 1. Such changes in identity would occur in almost all code systems for a single bit loss, because most code systems have a Hamming distance of 1. Increasing the Hamming distance of a code makes it possible to detect and correct errors that occur during transmission, which is the whole idea behind the use of Hamming code.

To emphasize the usefulness of the Hamming code, consider that a single parity bit added to a code word would indicate only that an error has occurred if a single bit was lost; it would not indicate which bit has been affected. This means that the entire word must be retransmitted. It will be shown that the use of Hamming code techniques allows for the detection and correction of the errors that may occur during transmission, if extra parity bits are added to each code word (a series of code words taken as a single block could also be used). The additional parity bits increase the Hamming distance of the code, thereby allowing for error correction.

The technique to be shown here will allow for the correction of the loss of a single bit (either data or parity) in a 7-bit code word (ASCII code will be used). The parity bits are generated based on the composition of groups of bits within the original code word.

In order to implement the Hamming technique in a code that represents characters composed of words of N bits in length, parity bits will be inserted in bit positions 1, 2, 4, 8, . . . , n of the original code word, such that n is less than or equal to the number of bits N in each code word. This method will allow the correction of single-bit errors. For example, using ASCII code words, parity bits would be added such that the final code word for a given character would be constructed as shown below, where P_1, P_2, and P_3 represent the parity bits inserted in positions 1, 2, and 4 of the original ASCII character, and b_1 through b_7 represent the bits that make up the original ASCII character.

Bit position	1	2	3	4	5	6	7	8	9	10
Bit contents	P_1	b_1	P_2	b_2	b_3	P_3	b_4	b_5	b_6	b_7

If longer code words were to be used, such as with EBCDIC (8 bits per code word), then a fourth parity bit would be placed in position 11, with the eighth bit of the EBCDIC word entered in position 12.

Sticking with ASCII, and using even parity, the states of the parity bits in positions 1, 2, 4, and 8 are determined as follows.

P_1: Even parity for bits in positions b_1, b_3, b_5, and b_7 of the original code word.

P_2: Even parity for bits in positions b_2, b_3, b_6, and b_7 of the original code word.

P_3: Even parity for bits in positions b_4, b_5, b_6, and b_7 of the original code word.

The pattern that is developing is fairly obvious; that is, P_1 is the parity bit for every other bit of the original code word, beginning with the first bit b_1. P_2 is the parity bit for every other pair, starting at bit b_2 of the code word. P_3 is the parity bit for every other group of 4 bits, starting with bit b_4 of the code word. If a given code word was longer than 7 bits, then a fourth parity bit P_4 would be required for every other group of 8 bits, beginning with bit 8 of the code word. Again, since ASCII is a 7-bit code, only 3 parity bits are required for correction of a single-bit error.

Let us now determine the states of the parity bits that would be added to the ASCII code for the character A. First, the ASCII code for A is 1000001. Writing this down with parity bits added yields

Bit position	1	2	3	4	5	6	7	8	9	10
Contents	P_1	1	P_2	0	0	P_3	0	0	0	1

The states of the parity bits are determined using the groupings explained previously, yielding $P_1 = 0$, $P_2 = 1$, $P_3 = 1$. Combining these bits, the 10-bit code for A is

Bit positions	1	2	3	4	5	6	7	8	9	10
Contents	0	1	1	0	0	1	0	0	0	1

Let us now examine how the Hamming code allows an error bit to be detected. Assume that the previously determined 10-bit representation for A is sent to a receiver, and the bit in position 10 has been altered somehow, resulting in the reception of the following data word.

Bit positions	1	2	3	4	5	6	7	8	9	10
Received bits	0	1	1	0	0	1	0	0	0	0

At the receiver, the parity bits are extracted from positions 1, 3, and 6, and what is assumed to be the original ASCII code word is reassembled. This results in the following code word and parity bits.

Received parity bits $P_3 = 1, P_2 = 1, P_1 = 0$
Received code word   1000000

Now, the same procedure used to generate the original parity bits is used on the received code word (not including the parity bits that are received). This results in the generation of the 3 new parity bits.

Parity bits generated from received code word:

$P_3 = 0, P_2 = 0, P_1 = 1$

These 3 parity bits are XORed with their counterparts from the received word as follows.

	P_3	P_2	P_1
Received parity bits	1	1	0
New parity bits	0	0	1
Result of XOR	1	1	1

The value of the resulting 3-bit number (the P_3 column is the MSB 1 × 2^2, and the P_1 column is the LSB 1 × 2^0) gives the position of the bit in the original code word that has been lost. In this case, the procedure indicates that bit 7 of the code word must be complemented, and indeed, this is the bit that is in error. Notice that if the received code word was not altered during transmission, the parity bits produced at the receiver would match those that were transmitted, which would indicate that the data was error-free; that is, the result of XORing the parity bits would be 0, and there is no 0th bit position.

The Hamming error correction method is fairly difficult to implement. It is also, however, quite effective, which makes it an error correction method worth gaining some familiarity with. Once again, the disadvantage of using the Hamming code is a reduction of coding efficiency. The most efficient codes have a Hamming distance of 1; however, they are also the most susceptible to errors.

Review Questions For Section 9-6

1. What types of errors are not detected using simple parity checking?
2. What is the parity of the code word 10001101?
3. What is the term applied to the polynomial that is used to create a unique output from a CRC, based on a given input word?
4. By what is the original data polynomial multiplied when CRC error checking is to be used?
5. What is the degree of the polynomial $x^5 + x^2 + x + 1$?
6. What does the Hamming distance of a code word indicate?

SUMMARY

Communication between computers and various other devices depends on the reliable transmission of data. Data may be transferred in either parallel or serial formats. Parallel transfer is generally faster, while serial techniques are less costly. Most short-range data communication, such as between a microcomputer and a printer, is done using parallel data and control lines. The RS-232-C, the RS-422, and the Centronics parallel interface standards are a few of the most frequently encountered short-range data communications methods in use.

Serial data transfer is used when longer distances must be covered. If the telephone system is to be used, then modems are required at each end of the channel. Modems translate a stream of serial data into a form that is suitable for transmission over the telephone system. Usually, FSK or PSK modulation is used in these applications. Phase-locked loops or one-shots may be used to demodulate the transmitted data. Serial to parallel and parallel to serial conversion and timing are provided by DCEs (data communication equipment) at each end of the channel. The equipment that processes the recovered data is referred to as DTE (data terminal equipment). Serial data may also be transmitted over current loops or with short-haul modems. These devices provide an alternative to the use of the telephone system.

Error detection may be provided by generating a parity bit for each transmitted code word. Cyclic redundancy checking is also used to provide more reliable error detection. Errors may also be corrected using Hamming code techniques. Such error detection and correction techniques make data communications very reliable, but they also reduce code efficiency.

CHAPTER QUESTIONS

9-1. What is the advantage of NRZ-B over unipolar NRZ?

9-2. Why is bit stuffing used in conjunction with RZ encoding?

9-3. What is another term applied to Manchester encoding?

9-4. How is the presence of a logic high bit represented when Manchester encoding is used?

9-5. State one advantage of NRZ encoding over Manchester and RZ.

9-6. Which form of pulse modulation is used least often? Why?

9-7. When will a single parity bit check indicate the reception of correct data even though bits were lost?

9-8. What is the parity of the bit sequence 00000000?

9-9. What term is applied to the situation where several consecutive bits in a data stream are lost?

9-10. How many bits are used to represent a character in EBCDIC?

9-11. What is the term used to describe the technique in which a single transmission line is used by different transmitters and receivers at different times?

9-12. In an asynchronous data communication system, why is it common practice to shift bits from the serial data stream into the receiver at approximately the middle of each bit-time interval?

9-13. What LSI device is designed to provide both serial transmit and receive functions for a DCE device?

9-14. What is the term applied to the technique that allows two or more devices to use the same transmission line at the same time?

9-15. Which error-checking technique has applications in the field of cryptography?

CHAPTER PROBLEMS

9-16. Refer to Fig. 9-5. At what frequency must the clock operate to result in a baud rate of 3600?

9-17. Refer to Fig. 9-10. What logic level will be produced at the output of the NOR gate if U1 is phase-locked and U2 is not? What logic level would be produced if neither U1 nor U2 is in phase lock?

9-18. The data rate of a certain asynchronous transmission is specified as 3309.1 bits/s. What is the baud rate if ASCII characters with 1 parity bit, 1 start bit, and 2 stop bits are transmitted?

9-19. What is the degree of the generator polynomial $G(x) = x^4 + x + 1$?

9-20. Write the resulting polynomial if $x^4 + x^3 + 1$ is multiplied by the degree of $G(x)$ in Problem 9-19.

9-21. What is the baud rate of a serial data stream where $t_{bit} = 312.5$ μs.?

9-22. Assume that the generator polynomial $G(x) = x^5 + x^3 + x$ is used to create a CRC code for the transmission of the message polynomial for the ASCII character 8. Determine the transmitted polynomial $T(x)$ that would result.

9-23. A certain character consists of 7 data bits plus 1 start bit, 3 parity bits, and 2 stop bits. If this character is sent at a rate of 9600 Bd, determine the data rate.

9-24. From Problem 9-22, determine the remainder polynomial that would be produced if the MSB of $T(x)$ was lost during transmission.

9-25. Determine the Hamming code word that would be produced for the ASCII code for the letter W.

9-26. Determine the Hamming code word that would be produced for the ASCII code for the letter X.

9-27. From Fig. 9-10, determine the values required for C_5, C_4, C_8, and C_7 based on the following conditions: $V_{in} = 0.5 \ V_{rms}$, $f_{mark} = 1200$ Hz $\pm$ 20 Hz, $f_{space} = 2200$ Hz $\pm$ 20 Hz. Assume $R_1 = 6.8$K , $R_3 = 4.7$K.

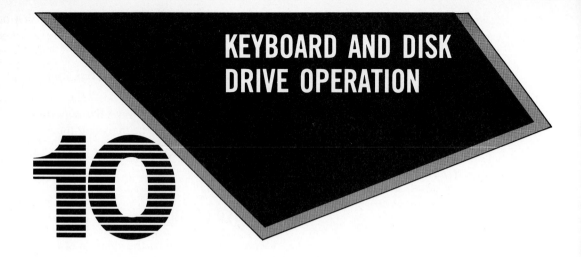

KEYBOARD AND DISK DRIVE OPERATION

Although the microprocessor and its associated control, memory, timing, and interfacing circuitry are essential building blocks of the microcomputer, it is the addition of the various peripheral devices that makes the microcomputer a truly useful tool. The basics of the video display, which is usually the primary output device of a microcomputer, and some graphics programming applications have been covered already. In this chapter, two other nearly indispensable peripheral devices and their operation will be discussed, namely the keyboard and the disk drive. Many of the techniques and ideas relating to I/O interfacing, data communication, and linear circuit operation are involved in the study of these peripheral devices. In particular, the disk drive encompasses a wide range of electronic design techniques. This chapter will introduce the reader to some of the commonly used circuit designs employed in keyboard and disk drive circuitry.

10-1 KEYBOARD OPERATION

In general, the keyboard is the most commonly used input device of the computer. As in the case of the video display, the keyboard is usually considered as being practically an integral part of the microcomputer system, and indeed, this is literally the case with some microcomputers. There are several different approaches by which a keyboard can be interfaced to a microcomputer, and there are also several different ways by which keyboards may be decoded and designed electrically and mechanically. This section will present a few of the more commonly encountered approaches to keyboard design and interfacing.

10-1.1 Switch Matrix Scanning and Encoding

Most keyboards consist of a group of switches arranged in a rectangular matrix. In such a switch matrix, the closure of a given switch produces a unique bit pattern to be produced on the circuit's output lines. This bit pattern may then be read by the CPU and processed or interpreted and acted upon as required. Since the transfer of data via the human to computer interface that is provided by the keyboard is a relatively low-speed process, most keyboards are designed for interrupt-driven operation. This allows the CPU to service the keyboard only when necessary (which is normally an infrequent occurrence), and also allows the keyboard to be ignored if so desired.

One possible arrangement that could be used for an interrupt-driven hexadecimal numeric keypad is shown in Fig. 10-1. The operation of this

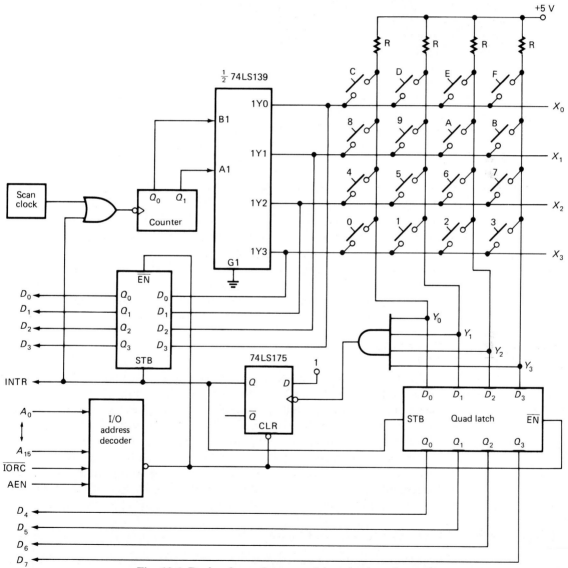

Fig. 10-1 Design for an interrupt-driven keyboard encoder.

circuit as it might be used in an 8088-based system will be discussed. Assume that a programmable interrupt controller (PIC) is used to process interrupts. This simplifies the actual keyboard circuitry because the actions required to produce the interrupt acknowledge ($\overline{\text{INTA}}$) and interrupt type number responses are handled by the PIC.

Let us first examine the operation of Fig. 10-1 when none of the keys are being pressed. First, lines Y_0, Y_1, Y_2, and Y_3 are pulled high by the pull-up resistors. These four lines are connected to the data inputs of a quad latch and also a four-input AND gate. As long as Y_0 through Y_3 remain high, because no switch has been closed, the Q output of the D flip-flop will remain low (it would have been cleared at the outset, possibly during system initialization), gating the scan clock signal into a two-stage binary counter. The term *scan clock* is derived based on the fact that as the clock operates, each of the row lines X_0 through X_3 is pulled low and then returned high, one after another, by the 74LS139 1 of 4 decoder. The scan clock may be an actual part of the keyboard circuit, or it may be derived from the CPU and its associated circuitry. The output of the 74LS139 in response to the binary counter that drives it is shown in Fig. 10-2. It can readily be determined that as long as no switch has been

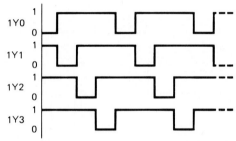

Fig. 10-2 Timing diagram for the output of the 1 of 4 decoder in Fig. 10-1.

closed, the rows of the matrix are continually scanned. It should also be clear that the two quad latches will strobe in data from the keyboard only if the D flip-flop's Q output is high.

Let us now assume that switch 5 has been pressed. When the scan clock causes line X_2 (1Y2 of the 74LS139) to be pulled low, the output of the AND gate will go low, clocking logic 1 onto the Q output of the D flip-flop. This level disables the scan clock, strobes the states of lines Y_0 through Y_3 and X_0 through X_3 into the quad latches, and initiates an interrupt request. Since we are assuming that a PIC is being used, we need not be concerned about interrupt handling at this time. When the keyboard service routine is entered, the contents of the X and Y latches will be read. When this occurs, the output of the keyboard address decoder is driven low, enabling the outputs of the latches; while at the same time the inputs of the latches are disabled, the D flip-flop is cleared, and the scan clock is gated to the counter. After the keyboard read cycle has ended, the output of the address decoder returns high, and the outputs of the latches are tristated. Now, since the 5 key was pressed, lines X_2 and Y_1 would have been low when the latches were strobed, while the remainder of the keyboard matrix lines would be high. On the basis of these conditions, the byte that would be read by the service routine would be 11011101 (DD_{16}). This value could be translated into the numerical value of the key that is pressed in software, possibly using the XLAT instruction and a translation table. Pressing any of the remainder of the keys will also produce a unique output byte, which could be decoded in a similar manner.

Figure 10-1 is a relatively complex circuit, and there are many other possible variations that could be used in the design of the circuit. For example, rather than latching the states of the outputs of the 74LS139, the output of the counter could be monitored. This would reduce the number of latches required by two and increase the efficiency of the circuit. Consider that if the counter size was increased by two more stages, and all four lines were monitored, then 16 rows of switches could be monitored for a total of 64 keys. This possibility is illustrated in Fig. 10-3. This circuit

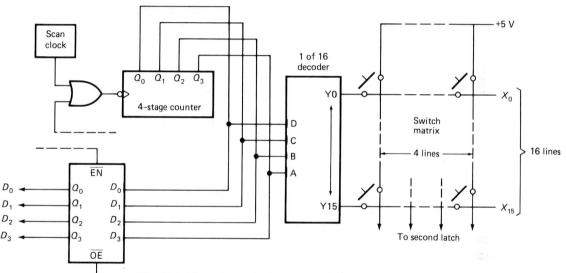

Fig. 10-3 Encoding the output of the binary counter enables 4 lines to carry data for 16 switch lines.

is 25 percent efficient in terms of utilizing all 8 bits of the data bus to represent a given key (this does not include the use of shifted characters, which would increase coding efficiency).

Although the decoding approach used in Fig. 10-1 is very inefficient (6.25 percent efficient to be precise), it does have one interesting feature; that is, it is very easy to detect certain multiple key closures with this circuit. It can readily be seen by the nature of the circuit that when a single key is pressed, 2 and only 2 bits will be high when the row and column line states are strobed into the latches. Assume, for example, that both keys 0 and 4 were pressed at the same time. This would inhibit the scan clock and generate an interrupt request; however, the byte that will be sent to the service routine would be 11101100 (EC_{16}). The lookup or translation table would contain no such value, and therefore the service routine would determine that invalid data was entered (two keys are pressed), and the appropriate action would be taken. There is another way (other than scanning the lookup table for a match) in which the closure of two keys simultaneously in the circuit of Fig. 10-1 could be detected quite easily with a minimum of programming. This will be left as a problem at the end of the chapter.

10-1.2 Switch Debouncing

Quite often, whenever contact is made between the contacts of a switch, there is a short interval (possibly of about 1 or 2 ms) during which the contacts will open and close, or bounce. Figure 10-4 illustrates a typical

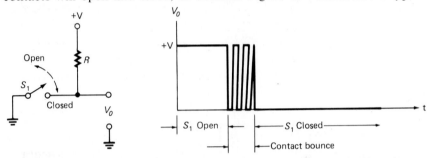

Fig. 10-4 Waveform produced by the bouncing of the SPST switch when thrown to the closed position.

switch circuit and the waveform produced by switch bounce. Many readers have no doubt encountered the results of contact bounce when their calculator keyboards have begun to wear out. A common example may be when a certain key is pressed once and 5 or 6 digits flash onto the display. This is the result of contact bounce. Because digital circuits respond with such extreme speed, there is a chance that the multiple contacts or transitions could be interpreted as a series of valid key presses in one system, while perhaps in another system the state of the switch might be sampled during the time interval in which it has bounced from the desired state. In either case, switch bounce can cause trouble.

Hardware Switch Debouncing   There are several ways in which contact bounce may be eliminated. One possible method uses a latch configured as shown in Fig. 10-5a. As seen in the waveforms in Fig. 10-5b, once the latch has been set or cleared, it will remain in that state regardless of contact bounce (bouncing on the contact occurs between t_1 and t_2). It is very unlikely that the switch will bounce all the way from one contact to the other, and any bouncing that does occur places the latch in the quiescent or no-change state. The disadvantage to this technique is the requirement for a single pole double throw (SPDT) switch, which would be more expensive than a simpler SPST switch (also sometimes referred to as a class A switch), which would commonly be found on a keyboard.

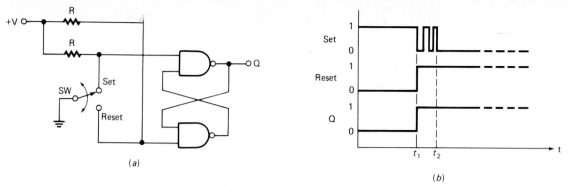

Fig. 10-5 An RS latch used to debounce SPDT switches (a) and the waveforms produced when switch is thrown (b).

A second method of switch debouncing that may be used with SPST switches is presented in Fig. 10-6a and b. This approach uses a one-shot to eliminate false transitions. If a nonretriggerable one-shot is used, the time-out period of the one-shot is chosen such that it is somewhat longer than the maximum expected duration of the contact bounce interval. This

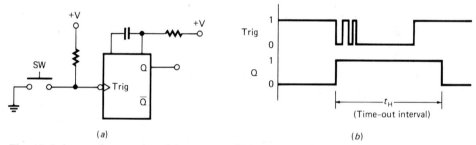

Fig. 10-6 A one-shot used to debounce an SPST push-button switch (a) produces the waveforms shown in (b).

means that when the switch is closed, the one-shot is triggered only once and the contact bounce (undesired triggers) is ignored. By the time the one-shot has timed out, the switch state is stable, or possibly the switch has been released. A retriggerable one-shot could also be used with little difference in circuit operation. This type of debouncing would typically be used in a system where the output of the one-shot is responded to or sampled immediately and only once during the time-out interval. This means that if the switch or key is held closed, it is responded to only one time, and that is during the time interval when the one-shot is triggered. The switch must be released and pressed again in order to retrigger the one-shot and produce a second closure event.

In a computer keyboard-type application, it would probably be desirable that if the key is held down for an extended period of time, this condition be interpreted as multiple key closures (automatic repeat). Such a response would require the use of a retriggerable one-shot with a gated clock (trigger) input or some similar circuit. One possible way of implementing this function is shown in Fig. 10-7. In this circuit, as long as the switch is

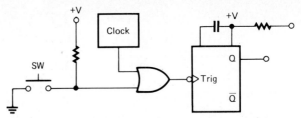

Fig. 10-7 Using the switch to gate a clock signal to a one-shot allows a constant level to be maintained.

closed, a clock signal is applied to the trigger input of the one-shot. The clock continually retriggers the one-shot, producing a constant high output at Q. Of course, the effects of contact bounce are also eliminated, which is the whole purpose of using the circuit.

The addition of extra hardware for switch debouncing adds to the complexity and expense of the system, and therefore is often undesirable. Bounceless switches can be obtained, which eliminate the necessity for the extra debouncing circuitry; but these switches are more expensive than standard switches, and they may start to bounce anyway after frequent and heavy use.

Software Switch Debouncing Switch bounce can be eliminated using programming techniques as well as hardware. For example, let us assume that in a certain microcomputer when a key is pressed and the keyboard service routine is initiated, there is the possibility that the contacts could be in the process of bouncing, and an invalid state is in existence when key status is read. This could lead to erroneous data being passed to the CPU. However, the keyboard service routine could be written such that each time it is invoked, the output of the keyboard is read after a time delay that allows contact bounce to cease. This method is usually used in less expensive systems.

10-1.3   Switch Construction and Operation

Most readers will visualize switches as operating by forcing two or more contacts into physical contact when a given switch is activated or closed. Indeed, these types of switches were used in the preceding discussion because they are so familiar. However, there are other alternatives to physical contact switches that are commonly used in electronic equipment. Switches that do not require contact to be made or broken physically are usually more reliable than their strictly mechanical counterparts, because of the elimination of contact wear and the reduced possibility of contact contamination.

Capacitive Switches One of the more popular types of switches employed in keyboard applications is the capacitive switch. Figure 10-8 illustrates one possible construction for such a switch. Basically, the idea behind the action of the capacitive switch is that when it is depressed, the plates of

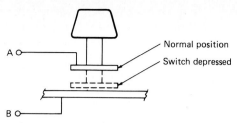

Fig. 10-8 Construction of a capacitive push-button switch.

a capacitor are brought closer together. This produces an increase in capacitance, as can be determined using Eq. 10-1.

$$C = \epsilon\frac{A}{d}$$ (Eq. 10-1)

where A = plate area, d = plate separation, and ϵ = the permittivity of the dielectric separating the plates.

The pressing of a capacitive switch could be detected by using the switch capacitance to change the frequency of an oscillator, where one frequency is produced when the switch is in the normal position and a second (usually lower) frequency is generated when the switch is pressed. The problem with this approach would be the necessity for several oscillators and the corresponding tone decoding circuitry.

A second method of detecting capacitive switch activity works in a slightly different manner. From basic electrical theory, capacitance can also be defined by the equation

$$C = Q/V$$ (Eq. 10-2)

where Q is the charge on the capacitor in coulombs and V is the voltage across the capacitor. Equations 10-1 and 10-2 can be combined to produce the equation

$$V = \frac{Qd}{\epsilon A}$$ (Eq. 10-3)

Basically, Eq. 10-3 says that given a charged capacitor, if the distance between the plates is decreased, the voltage across the capacitor will also decrease. Such a voltage change could be detected by what is called a sense amplifier, and then converted into a logic level. Releasing the key returns the plates to their original spacing, causing the voltage to return to its original value.

Hall Effect Switches   Recently, Hall effect devices have been used in keyboard switch applications. A Hall effect device could be described as a magnetically controlled semiconductor switch. Basically, a Hall effect device operates such that when no magnetic field is applied, current will flow through the device rather easily. However, if a magnetic field is applied to the device perpendicular to the direction of current flow, the resistance of the device increases. A strong enough field will completely block all current flow. The advantage of a Hall effect switch over a mechanical switch is analogous to that of a transistor over a relay. The construction of a possible Hall effect switch is shown in Fig. 10-9a and b.

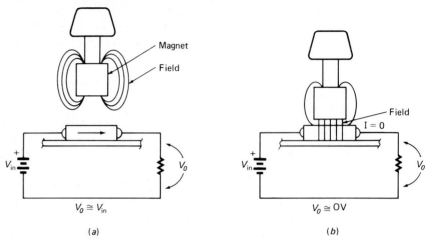

Fig. 10-9 Illustration of the operation of a Hall effect-type push-button switch.

Optoelectronic Switches The last type of switch to be discussed in this section is the optoelectronic switch. As shown in Fig. 10-10, when the key is not

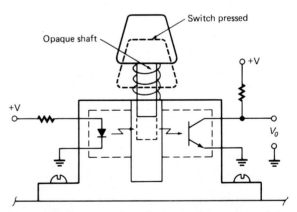

Fig. 10-10 Cross section of an optoelectronic push-button switch.

pressed, light emitted from a LED illuminates the junction of a phototransistor, which is driven into conduction, producing a low value of V_O. Depressing the key places an opaque surface in between the LED and the phototransistor, blocking the light. Under these conditions, the transistor will go into cutoff, producing a high value of V_O. This type of optical detection is used very frequently in many electronic and electromechanical systems.

Final Comments on Switches   In the cases of the capacitive, Hall effect, and optoelectronic switches, it is usually necessary to use switches that exhibit a snap action when they are pressed or released; that is, when a key is pressed, the part of the switch that causes the electrical change should move rapidly to the desired position once a trip position is reached. This prevents the switch from being in an invalid state, halfway between open and closed, for a long period of time. This is a form of hysteresis, and it helps the switch to function more reliably. Most keyboards that use key switches with such hysteresis produce a click when any of the keys are pressed or released.

10-1.4   Additional Keyboard Interfacing Methods

There are many ways in which a keyboard can be interfaced to a microcomputer. Largely, the approach taken depends on the size, the sophistication, and, to some extent, the intended cost of the microcomputer.

The Keyboard Side of the System   In systems where the keyboard is an integral part of the microcomputer (the keyboard is not removable), it is common to have many parallel data and control lines interconnecting the keyboard and the CPU board. For example, the circuit in Fig. 10-11 might be used to form a 64-key keyboard. This circuit operates in a manner similar to that of Fig. 10-1, with modifications made as described for Fig. 10-3. Some of the other required circuitry has been left out for the sake of clarity, but the circuit in Fig. 10-11 is essentially complete. The key point to notice is that there are eight keyboard data lines and a key closure signal line that must be sent to the CPU and/or its interfacing circuitry. Of course, the keyboard would also require at least one control line coming from the

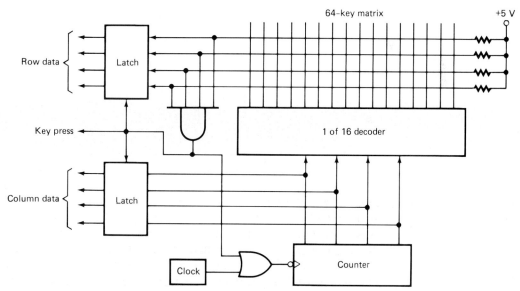

Fig. 10-11 Block diagram of a circuit used to encode a 64 key matrix.

CPU and power and ground lines. This produces a total of 11 lines between the keyboard and the CPU. If the keyboard is an integral part of the computer, then perhaps the latches, counter, decoder, and other parts of the keyboard interface could be mounted on the motherboard. Indeed, this is what is done in many microcomputers where the keyboard and motherboard are part of the same box. In this approach, using the keyboard matrix of Fig. 10-11, a 20-conductor ribbon cable would be used to connect the row and column lines to the CPU board.

Most newer, more powerful microcomputers are rather large and heavy, and therefore it is more practical to attach the keyboard to the main CPU board via a coiled cord. In such a case, it is best to keep the number of conductors in the cord to a minimum. Looking at Fig. 10-11, it can be determined that about the only way to accomplish this task is to send the keyboard row and column data to the CPU in serial format. Many manufacturers now use keyboards that contain their own CPU for control, decoding, and communication (with the main CPU) purposes. A block diagram for such a keyboard that might be used in conjunction with Fig. 10-11 is shown in Fig. 10-12. Notice that the number of lines connecting the keyboard and the computer is reduced significantly. In circuits like that of Fig. 10-12, the CPU used to control the keyboard circuitry may

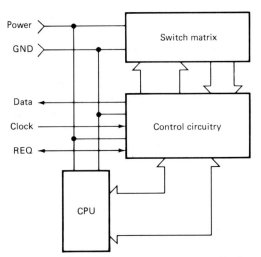

Fig. 10-12 Block diagram of keyboard circuit with a dedicated CPU, using serial data transfer.

also have access to its own ROM which contains a control program that runs and decodes the keyboard. The REQ line shown in Fig. 10-12 could be used by the computer to read the current state of the keyboard, or it could be used by the keyboard control CPU to cause the computer to accept a character. The dedicated keyboard CPU is also responsible for interpreting shifted characters, detecting invalid multiple key closures, and software-based switch debouncing tasks, thus further reducing the work load on the main system processor.

The CPU Side of the System   At the main CPU side of the system, the serial data must be converted to parallel form before a keystroke can be acted upon or interpreted. This conversion would usually be done using shift registers and timing (a clock) generated either on the main CPU board or from the keyboard itself. Since the keyboard is physically close to the computer, a separate clock line would be used to synchronize the system, simplifying the serial data transfer process. This being the case, simple NRZ encoding could also be used as the format of the serial data stream.

Another feature that is often included in the receiving side of the system is a keyboard buffer. You will recall the statement that on the average, the keyboard requires little attention from the CPU. While this is true, there may be times when the CPU is just too busy to read input from the keyboard. During these times it would be advantageous if there was some way to retain information entered via the keyboard. This is exactly what the keyboard buffer does. Rather than having the CPU read and interpret each keystroke as it enters, the data is written into a small section of memory for future use, much as the instruction queue of the 8088 CPU holds instruction opcodes. This allows keystrokes to accumulate, rather than be lost. Keyboard buffers are usually small in size, storing around 10 bytes or so, but this is enough space for most circumstances.

Review Questions for Section 10-1

1. What method of I/O control is usually used in keyboard interfacing applications?
2. How are switches usually arranged on a keyboard?
3. What is the term given to undesired opening and closing of switch contacts when switch position is changed?
4. What is another term applied to describe an SPST switch?
5. What are the advantages of capacitive, Hall effect, and optical switches over their mechanical counterparts?
6. What type of one-shot should be used for the circuit shown in Fig. 10-7 to operate properly?

10-2   DISK DRIVES

Although not necessarily an essential part of the microcomputer system, the addition of one or more disk drives increases the utility and power of the microcomputer dramatically. Rapid access and high storage density are the main advantages gained with the addition of a disk drive.

The operation and circuitry of the typical disk drive is a rather complex topic, as elements of digital circuitry, serial data encoding, and linear circuitry are intimately involved with one another. This section will present the main ideas behind the operation of disk drives, primarily from the aspect of commonly encountered drive circuitry and data representation and storage formats.

10-2.1 Data Recording Techniques

Data is represented by selectively orienting the magnetic domains of an iron-oxide coating on the surface of a disk. Prior to the recording of data, the magnetic domains in this disk film are essentially randomly oriented to one another as illustrated in Fig. 10-13. Because of this random

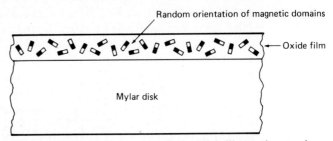

Fig. 10-13 Cross section of a floppy disk illustrating random orientation of magnetic domains in oxide coating.

orientation, the magnetic fields produced by the domains tend to produce a uniform, very low strength magnetic field over the surface of the disk. Data is written to the disk by applying a magnetic field to a small area of the disk, as the disk is rotated. The field is produced by supplying current to a small coil in a recording or write head that contacts the disk surface. The magnetic field produced by the head forces the domains of the disk surface to align themselves along the axis of the applied field, as shown in Fig. 10-14. The direction of the current flow through the head, which represents 1s and 0s, determines the orientation of the domains of the

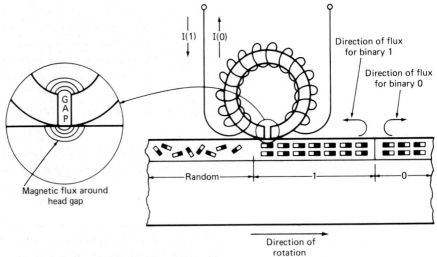

Fig. 10-14 Current flow through the coil causes alignment of the magnetic domains in the disk's oxide coating.

magnetic film. A small gap in the section of the head core that contacts the disk causes the generated flux to be concentrated at the surface of the disk. Normally, this gap is filled with a nonmagnetic material, such as glass or ceramic.

During a disk read operation, no external current is supplied to the head. As the disk rotates beneath the head, each time the domains of opposite direction are encountered, as in movement from a 1 to a 0 or vice versa, a voltage pulse is produced in the head coil. The polarity of the pulse depends on the alignment of the domains that are encountered. These pulses are then processed and converted into levels that are compatible with the computer's digital circuitry. It should be readily apparent that the data written to and read from the disk is serial in nature. This means that much work has to be done on the data that is to be written to or read from the disk. These techniques will be discussed next.

Disk Data Representation   You will recall from the previous discussions on data communication that it is most convenient to obtain serial data directly from a digital circuit in nonreturn to zero (NRZ) form. NRZ is produced naturally when data is output from a parallel-in serial-out shift register. Unfortunately, NRZ data is not compatible with the magnetic recording techniques employed with disk storage. The main reason for this incompatibility is because a coil will not produce an induced voltage when it is moved parallel relative to a field of magnetic flux. In Fig. 10-14 it can be seen that the only time a current will be induced in the head (in a read operation) is when a transition from 1 to 0 or from 0 to 1 is encountered. During the time intervals when the head is passing over a given bit area, the motion of the head is parallel to the magnetic flux, and no voltage is induced. This could lead to problems in that if a long series of 1s or 0s is encountered, synchronization between the interfacing circuitry and the data stream that is read from the disk could be lost.

There are basically two solutions to this problem. One would be to record a clock signal onto a track of the disk for synchronization purposes. The second alternative, which is normally used in microcomputer disk drive applications, is to encode the data that is written to the disk using a data encoding technique from which clock synchronization information can be derived.

Let us arbitrarily assume that the bit sequence 10111000011 is to be written to a disk. The NRZ representation for this stream of bits is shown as the top waveform in Fig. 10-15a. Notice that there are very few

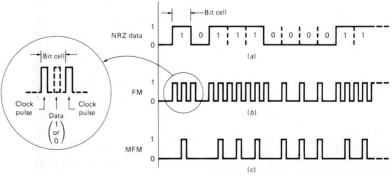

Fig. 10-15 An NRZ data stream (a) and equivalent FM (b) and MFM (c) waveforms.

transitions from which synchronization can be derived, and for the most part, the transitions occur at random intervals, depending on the data that is represented. The middle waveform illustrates the frequency modulation (FM) representation for this bit sequence. In FM, each data bit is enclosed between two high pulses. The time interval from rising edge to rising edge of these pulses is called a bit cell. If a 1 is to be stored, a pulse will be written inside this interval, while the absence of a pulse represents logic 0. Using the FM encoding technique, the synchronization signal will always be available for disk read operations.

A second method called modified FM (MFM) is illustrated in the bottom waveform in Fig. 10-15b. The logic behind the MFM waveform is less obvious than in FM, but here is the idea behind it. In MFM, the data bit is written in the center of each bit cell. A clock bit is written at the beginning of a given bit cell only if no high bit (a low is represented by the lack of a high bit in a cell) was written in the preceding cell and the next cell will not contain a data high bit.

The advantage of MFM over FM can be inferred directly from Fig. 10-15c. Assuming that both the FM and MFM waveforms are scaled in the same time units, it is seen that on the average, fewer transitions need to be detected to read or write in MFM in a given time interval. This is important, because the read-write head and the magnetic film on the disk have limited bandwidths; that is, one can align the domains in the disk only so fast, with a given recording field intensity, and the high-frequency response of the head will also be limited. Keeping these considerations in mind, one can infer that it should be possible to record data at a higher density using MFM as opposed to FM, and this is the case. Generally, FM is used on systems that use single-density disks, while MFM is used in double-density systems. In the MFM (double-density) approach, the bit cell time duration is half that of the FM (single-density) method. Assuming equal disk rotation speeds, the MFM technique will allow twice as many bits to be stored in a given length of disk space as FM, with about the same bandwidth. The disadvantage of MFM is that the circuitry required to encode and decode the data is more complex.

Disk Data Organization   Some of the details of disk organization were presented in Chap. 1. We will now expand on that information and look at a representative disk structure. You will recall that disks are divided into tracks (sometimes called cylinders), which in turn are divided into sectors. The index hole provides the master reference by which the first sector of each track is located. Let us assume that our system divides each disk into 39 tracks, and each track is divided into 8 sectors, as shown in Fig. 10-16a. If each sector contains 512 bytes, then the disk can store 159,744 bytes on a side. A double-sided disk could store twice as many bytes (319,488). However, not all of this space can be used to store programs or data.

Some disk space must be allocated for organization purposes. Figure 10-16b shows one possible organization of a disk. The first two tracks of

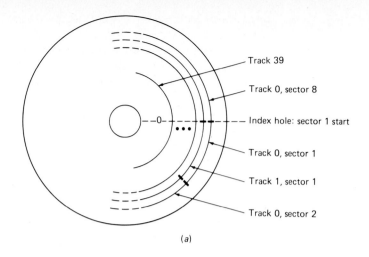

(a)

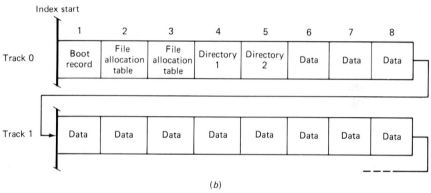

(b)

Fig. 10-16 Soft-sectored disk organization (*a*) and possible sector use allocations (*b*).

the disk are shown, represented in a linear manner. The first sector of track 0 contains a boot record. The boot record is used when the system is booted-up; that is, the boot record contains a short program that causes the correct routines in the operating system to be executed for loading the disk-based operating system (DOS). The ROM-based operating system would be responsible for initiating the activation of the boot record (if a disk is in the drive) on system reset.

In the structure depicted in Fig 10-16*b*, sectors 2 and 3 are reserved for a file allocation table. This part of the disk is used to store data relating to how much space is available for and has been taken up by files on the disk, and where such space is located. The directories are used to hold the name and extension of each of the files on the disk. There may also be other specifications relating to the types of files that are present, but these aspects of disk organization will not be covered in this text. Keep in mind that there are many different disk organization schemes, depending on the system being used. This kind of information can usually be found in the technical manuals written for a given system.

10-2.2 Circuit Operation

Now that some background information on disk data storage and organization has been presented, the hardware aspect of disk drives will be discussed. The typical disk drive is composed of several major subsections, as illustrated in Fig. 10-17. The primary digital sections are contained in

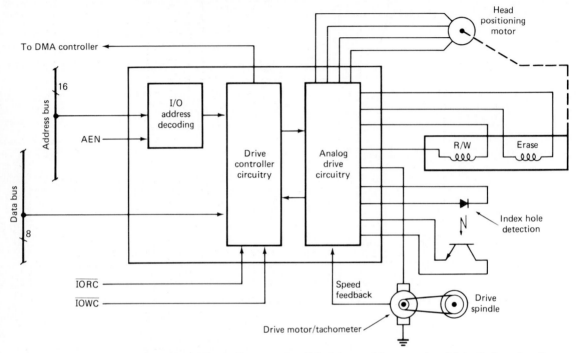

Fig. 10-17 Block diagram of a disk drive and its associated interfacing circuits.

the I/O address decoding section and the drive controller circuitry. These sections are responsible for interpreting commands supplied by the CPU and coordinating data transfer to and from the disk. The analog drive circuitry provides conditioning of the signals that represent data written to and read from the disk, and controlling of the disk rotational velocity and head positioning. Typical approaches used to implement each of these functions will now be presented.

Drive Controller Circuitry Disk drive control is a complex task. To this end, the current trend is to use microprocessors or VLSI disk controllers to handle much of the work involved in disk control activities. A representative disk controller is the Intel 8272A. The internal block diagram for this device is shown in Fig. 10-18. The 8272A is housed in a 40-pin DIP.

The 8272A is similar to a microprocessor in many respects, and is also a rather complex device. The disk controller is addressed as an I/O device by the CPU for programming and status determination purposes. Although it is not possible to present a detailed discussion of the operation of the

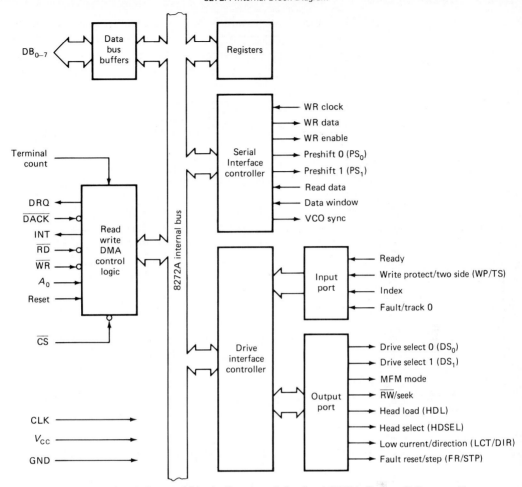

Fig. 10-18 Internal block diagram of the Intel 8272A floppy disk controller (FDC). (Courtesy of Intel Corporation.)

8272A here, basically, the 8272A operates in one of two modes: read/write ($\overline{\text{RD}}/\overline{\text{WR}}$) or seek. In the seek mode, the disk controller is positioning the head over the desired track, and awaiting the sensing of the disk index hole. After the correct head position has been set, a disk read or write operation may begin. The functions of the various pins of the 8272A will now be presented.

DB_{0-7}	These are bidirectional lines used for the transfer of data to and from memory and disk, and the main CPU and the disk controller.
$\overline{\text{CS}}$	Active low input. Enables $\overline{\text{RD}}$ and $\overline{\text{WR}}$ inputs.
$A_0, \overline{\text{RD}}, \overline{\text{WR}}$	These inputs are driven by the main CPU to read the status of, and supply instruction to, the 8272A. They are encoded as shown in Fig. 10-19.

8272A A_0, $\overline{RD}$, $\overline{WR}$ Decoding

A_0	$\overline{RD}$	$\overline{WR}$	Function
0	0	1	Read main status register
0	1	0	Illegal
0	0	0	Illegal
1	0	0	Illegal
1	0	1	Read from data register
1	1	0	Write into data register

Fig. 10-19 Decoding of the 8272A control inputs. (Courtesy of Intel Corporation.)

DRQ	Active high output. Used to initiate a DMA transfer for read or write operations.
$\overline{DACK}$	Active low input. Driven low by DMA controller during DMA transfers.
TC	Terminal count; active high input. High indicates end of DMA transfer.
INT	Active high output. Signals interrupt request.
CLOCK	Clock input.
$\overline{WR}$ CLK	Read/write clock input. Used to determine bit cell duration during disk write.
VCO SYNC	Used to disable the voltage-controlled oscillator of a phase-locked loop when low. The PLL is discussed later in this section.
DATA WINDOW	Input supplied by PLL. Indicates bit cell time duration during disk read.
$\overline{WR}$ DATA	Serial data (and clock information) bits written to disk.
$\overline{WR}$ ENABLE	Enables disk write circuitry.
$\overline{RD}$ DATA	Serial data input from disk read operation.
$PS_{0,1}$	Used for timing compensation of data bits during write operations.
READY	Active high input. Sent by drive circuit to indicate to system CPU that drive is ready for read or write operation.
INDEX	Active high input. Supplied by index hole detection circuitry. Indicates start of first sector on track.
HDL	Active high output. Causes head to contact disk surface.
$\overline{RW}$/SEEK	High indicates seek mode selected. Low indicates selection of read/write mode.
LCT/DIR	Used to lower head current for inner track writing in $\overline{RD}/\overline{WR}$ mode. Controls direction of head movement in seek mode.
FR/STP	In $\overline{RD}/\overline{WR}$ mode, it resets fault flip-flop. In seek mode, it supplies step pulses to head positioning motor.

WP/TS	Active high input. In $\overline{RD}/\overline{WR}$ mode, signal supplied by write protects notch sensing circuitry. In seek mode, used to indicate double- or single-sided disk.
HDSEL	Selects head (side 0 or side 1) when reading or writing to a two-sided disk.
$DS_{0,1}$	Used to select drive 0 or drive 1 in a dual drive system.
FLT/TRK0	Used to signal a drive fault in $\overline{RD}/\overline{WR}$ mode. Track 0 detection input in seek mode.
MFM MODE	Tied high for MFM operation, low for FM operation.

The pin descriptions presented above indicate that although the disk controller does simplify drive circuitry greatly, much more circuitry is required to produce a practical disk drive. In particular, there is a need for a relatively large amount of analog or linear circuitry to control the various motors and process the data and timing stream produced during read and write operations. The functions of many of the 8272A's pins should become more clearly understood after the operation of the remaining sections of the disk drive control and signal processing circuitry are covered.

Drive Motor Speed Regulation One of the first requirements of the analog circuitry employed in many disk drives is to control the drive motor such that a constant rotational speed is produced. As usual, there are many different approaches that are used to meet this requirement. In any case, in order to maintain constant speed under varying load conditions, some type of feedback that is related to motor speed is required for extreme stability. A classical analog servomechanism is one design possibility that allows very stable speed regulation. The block diagram in Fig. 10-20 illustrates such a system.

Let us assume that a simple permanent magnet field dc motor is used to rotate the disk. Here's how the servo works. When switch $\overline{S_1}$ is placed in the RUN position, a reference voltage is applied to one input of an

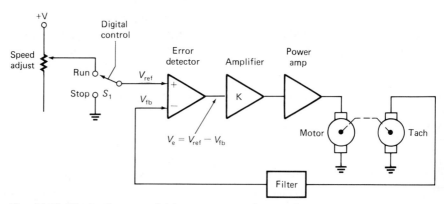

Fig. 10-20 Block diagram of drive motor speed control servo.

error detector (differential amplifier), while the output of a tachometer that is mechanically coupled to the drive motor is applied to the other. Initially, the motor is not running, and hence the output of a tachometer is 0. The error detector senses the difference between the reference voltage and the tachometer feedback and produces an output voltage that is proportional to this difference. The error signal is amplified and applied to the motor, which begins rotating. As the motor rotates faster, the tachometer output increases until it is equal to the applied reference voltage. At this point the error voltage is at a minimum and the desired speed is attained. If the load on the motor should increase (load will vary from one disk to another, and also as the head contacts the disk at various places), the motor will tend to slow down. This reduces the tachometer output voltage, resulting in a large error signal, which in turn causes greater drive to be applied to the motor. In this way, a nearly constant disk rotational velocity is maintained. When the switch is in the STOP position, the motor will also stop. The speed may be adjusted by changing the reference voltage via the speed adjustment potentiometer.

An alternative to the voltage-feedback servo is a phase-locked-loop-based servo. The block diagram of Fig. 10-21 illustrates such a system. In

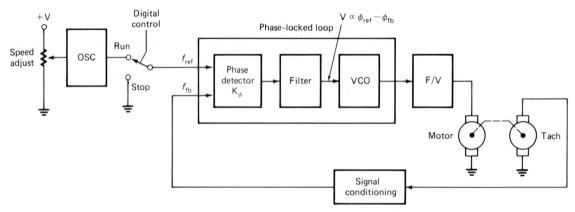

Fig. 10-21 Block diagram of a PLL-based servo for drive motor speed control.

this case, rather than sensing the difference between reference and feedback voltages, the phase difference between a reference oscillator and a signal, whose frequency is proportional to motor speed, is used. In Fig. 10-21, the tachometer produces an ac output signal. The frequency of this signal is proportional to motor speed. The PLL operates such that when the frequencies of f_{ref} and f_{fb} are equal, a voltage-controlled oscillator (VCO) runs at a fixed frequency. This frequency is converted into a voltage which drives the motor. When the motor is running at the correct speed, the tachometer frequency and the clock frequency will be equal, with a very slight phase difference existing. This is shown in Fig. 10-22a. Like the servo in Fig. 10-20, when the load on the motor increases, it tends to slow down. This results in a frequency deviation away from that of the reference oscillator. The difference in frequency also produces a difference in phase

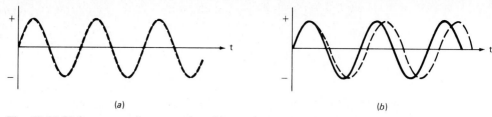

Fig. 10-22 Voltage waveforms produced by tachometer and PLL reference oscillator when motor speed is correct (*a*) and when motor speed is slightly low (*b*).

between the two signals, as shown in Fig. 10-22*b*. The phase shift is detected and converted into an increased drive to the motor, which compensates for the increased load.

One of the advantages of using the PLL-based servo is that even though a very small change in tachometer frequency may occur (so small that it is nearly unnoticeable), the phase shift between the reference signal and the tachometer signal will increase with time, eventually causing correction. Also, if the reference oscillator is synchronized with the system clock, frequency drift, caused by temperature changes or by slight changes in clock frequencies encountered when a disk is used in different computers, will tend to be canceled out.

It should be pointed out that some disk controllers (the 8272A, for example) use phase-locked loops to synchronize data transfer during disk read operations (clock extraction). This means that one may encounter two or more PLL circuits within a given disk drive system, each there for a different purpose.

Often, the tachometer used to provide motor speed feedback is an integral part of the motor itself. The drive hub or spindle is usually coupled to the motor with a rubberized fabric belt. This is shown in Fig. 10-23.

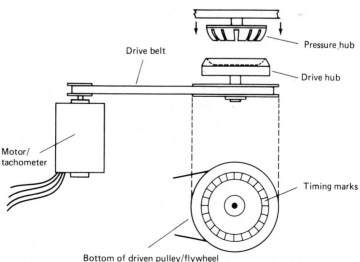

Fig. 10-23 Typical mechanical drive linkage.

The pressure hub is forced down into the disk hole when the door to the drive is closed. Usually, the bottom of the driven pulley will have timing marks placed on it. These are used to adjust the speed of the drive with either a 50- or 60-Hz light source. A similar method is used on many stereo turntables. The timing marks are illuminated by the proper light source while the drive motor is in operation. When the marks appear to be stationary, the drive is operating at the correct speed.

On some disk drives, optical timing similar to that of Fig. 10-23 is used to produce motor-speed feedback information, instead of a tachometer. In such cases, a photodetector is used to sense the marks. Magnetic devices, such as Hall effect sensors, are also used in some designs. Regardless of the actual type of transducer used to provide feedback for control purposes, most drive-speed regulation circuits will operate very similar to the servos that were presented in this section. As usual, the actual details will vary from one manufacturer to another.

Head Positioning: Stepper Motors   Once the disk is rotating at the correct speed, generally, the read-write (and erase) head must be positioned at the desired track. Most often, head positioning is accomplished using a stepper motor. A stepper motor is a motor that does not rotate in a continuous manner, but rather rotates a fixed angular increment at a time. There are a number of different types of stepper motors available, and each has its own advantages and disadvantages. Two types of permanent magnet rotor stepper motors will be discussed here. But first, one might ask why stepper motors are used as opposed to, say, a standard PM dc motor, as in the case of the disk drive motor. The main reasons are that stepper motors are less expensive to use than equivalent servomotor-based systems and continuous rotation is not required. The requirement for continuous rotation of the disk, however, eliminates the use of a stepper motor in that area of the disk drive.

A cutaway view of a stepper motor and its schematic symbol are shown in Fig. 10-24a and b. This particular motor is referred to as a bipolar

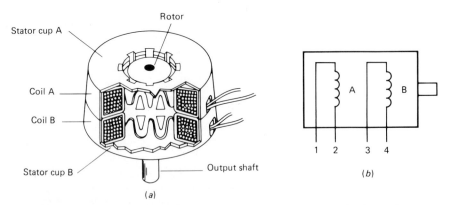

Fig. 10-24 Cutaway view of a bipolar, PM stepper motor (*a*) and schematic symbol (*b*).

stepper motor. Two coils are wound around the upper and lower halves of the motor's stator. The stator surrounds a rotor that contains specifically aligned permanent magnets. The size of a step is determined by the number of magnets and stator poles used in the construction of the motor. Typical step sizes are 18, 15, and 7.5 degrees. Stepper motors also exhibit a holding torque when the rotor is not moving. This helps to keep the motor stationary, once the final position has been attained.

Figure 10-25a illustrates the drive circuitry required to operate a bipolar stepper motor from a digital circuit. Figure 10-25b shows the logic levels required to produce rotation in a given direction. For the first step, inputs A and C are driven high, while B and D are low. This turns on transistor pairs Q_1 through Q_4 and Q_5 through Q_8. Using conventional current flow,

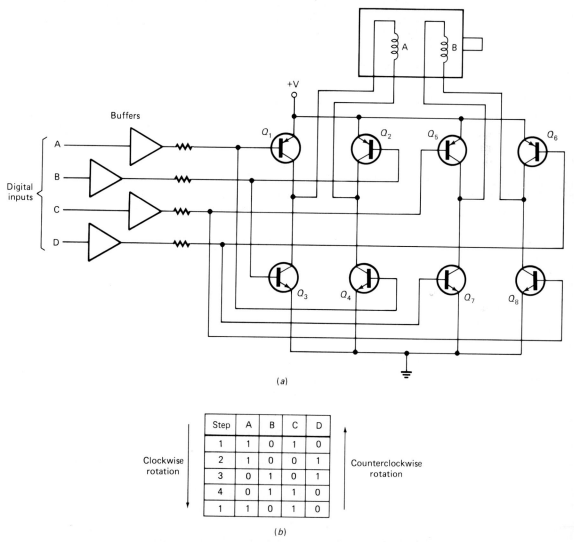

(a)

Step	A	B	C	D
1	1	0	1	0
2	1	0	0	1
3	0	1	0	1
4	0	1	1	0
1	1	0	1	0

Clockwise rotation

Counterclockwise rotation

(b)

Fig. 10-25 Bipolar stepper motor drive circuit (a) and step sequence table (b).

current will flow from the top of both coils A and B to ground. This causes the rotor to move one increment. On the second step, input C is driven low and input D is driven high. This reverses the direction of current flow through coil B, causing another increment of the rotor position. The remainder of the sequence listed in Fig. 10-25b is repeated as required to bring the motor to the correct position. Reversing the order of the applied input levels causes the motor to step in the opposite (counterclockwise) direction.

The disadvantage of the circuit in Fig. 10-25 is that many transistors are required to control the motor. Also, it is possible that when moving from one step to another, the wrong transistors will be conducting for a short period of time. For example, when going from Step 2 to Step 3, both Q_1 and Q_3 may be on, causing a high current drain on the power supply and overstressing the driver transistors. Avoiding this situation adds to the complexity of the digital circuit or possibly to the software routines used to produce the drive signals.

An alternative to the bipolar stepper motor is the unipolar stepper motor. Such a motor is presented in Fig. 10-26a. The difference between this

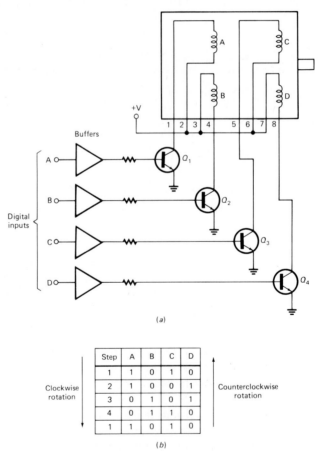

(a)

Step	A	B	C	D
1	1	0	1	0
2	1	0	0	1
3	0	1	0	1
4	0	1	1	0
1	1	0	1	0

Clockwise rotation

Counterclockwise rotation

(b)

Fig. 10-26 Unipolar stepper motor drive circuit (a) and step sequence table (b).

motor and that of Fig. 10-25 is that there are two coils wound on each stator half. The use of two coils on each stator cup eliminates the need for the more complex bipolar driver circuit, hence reducing the number of transistors needed to drive the motor. Also, should some overlap of step pulses occur, no shorting of the power supply to ground directly through transistors will occur. The step sequence shown in Fig. 10-26b is the same as that of the bipolar stepper motor.

In a practical circuit, each of the coils of a stepper motor would have a diode connected across it. These diodes are sometimes called freewheeling diodes. The diodes in Fig. 10-27 are shown as they would be connected

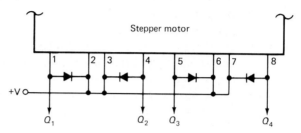

Fig. 10-27 Placement of freewheeling diodes across stator coils.

to the unipolar stepper motor. The function of the diodes is to reduce the EMF that is induced in a given coil when its driver transistor is abruptly cut off by providing a low impedance path of conduction. Without the diodes, such induced voltages could reach very high levels, possibly destroying the driver transistors.

The stepper motor in Fig. 10-26 could be connected to 4 bits of a latched output port, as shown in Fig. 10-28. In this example, the 8088s AL register

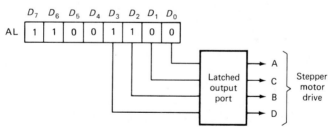

Fig. 10-28 Latched output port for generation of stepper motor drive signals.

is used to supply the desired bit patterns to the port. Notice how the outputs of the port are connected to the drive circuit. This "scrambling" of the connections was done to allow the contents of the AL register to be rotated to cause movement of the motor. Register rotation is very easy to implement, as opposed to, say, using a lookup table that contains the step patterns. Initially loading AL with 0011 0011 (33_{16}) and then repeatedly rotating to the right will produce clockwise rotation of the motor. Rotation to the left will cause counterclockwise rotation. The AL contents that

AL contents

	D_7	D_6	D_5	D_4	D_3	D_2	D_1	D_0		
1	0	0	1	1	0	0	1	1	(33_{16})	← Initial contents
ROR										
2	1	0	0	1	1	0	0	1	(99_{16})	
ROR										
3	1	1	0	0	1	1	0	0	(CC_{16})	
ROR										
4	0	1	1	0	0	1	1	0	(66_{16})	
ROR										
1	0	0	1	1	0	0	1	1	(33_{16})	

Fig. 10-29 The sequence of the AL register contents as the step pulses are applied to the motor.

occur during the clockwise rotation sequence are shown in Fig. 10-29. The timing diagram in Fig. 10-30 illustrates the waveforms that would be present at the inputs to the motor drive circuit during this operation.

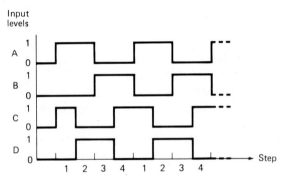

Fig. 10-30 Timing diagram illustrating the sequence of the logic levels applied to the motor drive circuit.

Since the position of a stepper motor's rotor is predictable, it can be used for very accurate position control. This is why stepper motors are used so often to move the read-write head in disk drives. A commonly used head positioning arrangement employs a stepper motor–driven lead screw. Stepper motors are available in which when the rotor turns, a threaded shaft is moved linearly along the axis of the rotor. This is shown in Fig. 10-31. Generally, the disk controller is responsible for providing the control pulses to the head positioning motor. Note that if a disk controller such as the 8272A is used, step commands produced by the chip will consist of a series of pulses on a single line (see Fig. 10-18). In order to drive the stepper motor, this pulse train would be applied to a digital circuit such as a recirculating shift register.

Index Hole Detection Once the read-write head has been positioned over the desired track, the disk controller must determine where the various sectors are on that track. The index hole of a soft-sectored disk provides the disk

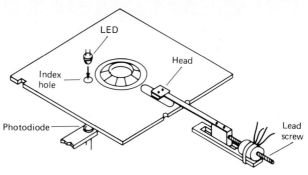

Fig. 10-31 Stepper motor–driven lead screw positioning of the head over the disk.

controller with a signal that indicates the start of the first sector on each track. Index hole detection can be provided by a very simple circuit consisting of a LED and a phototransistor or photodiode. The physical placement of these devices was shown in Fig. 10-31. In Fig. 10-32a, the

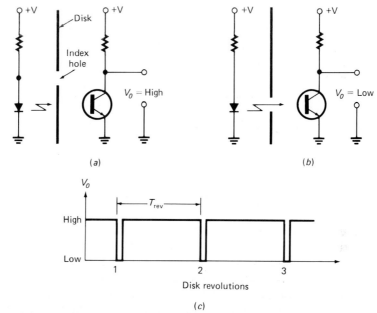

Fig. 10-32 Index hole detection circuitry (a), (b) and pulse waveform produced by disk rotation (c).

detector circuit is shown with its output response for the times when the disk is blocking the emission of the LED. In this case, the phototransistor is in cutoff, and V_O is at a maximum. Figure 10-32b shows the detection of the index hole, which causes saturation of the phototransistor and a low value of V_O. For a continuously spinning disk, the waveform shown in Fig. 10-32c would be produced. The negative-going pulses would be sent to the drive controller to signal the start of the first sector on a given track.

Read and Write Circuitry Now that the head has been positioned over the correct track and the correct sector has been located (the seek phase of operation is complete), either a read or a write operation may be performed. The circuit in Fig. 10-33 is representative of that which is found in many disk drives. Refer to this circuit during the following discussions.

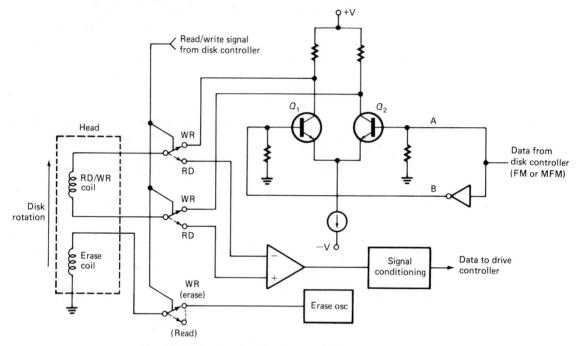

Fig. 10-33 Read-write circuit organization.

Reading the Disk Assuming that the disk is rotating, the drive controller will send a signal to the $\overline{RD}/\overline{WR}$ switches, placing them in the read position. As the disk rotates beneath the read-write head, the changes in orientation of the magnetic flux at the disk surface will induce voltage across the $\overline{RD}/\overline{WR}$ coil. You will recall that when FM or MFM encoding techniques are used, the transitions in logic state (flux polarity) or lack thereof are used to represent 1s and 0s. The voltages produced by the coil are very low in amplitude (in the mV range); and therefore they are applied to a differential amplifier in order to increase their amplitude. After amplification, the signal is squared-up and made compatible with the logic used in the drive controller. Many disk drives rely on a PLL to extract timing information from the conditioned data stream. This signal is then used to synchronize the reading of the data.

As the data is read from the disk, it is converted from FM or MFM format into NRZ serial format. This NRZ data is then converted into parallel form and sent to the main system bus a byte at a time. Often, the data is loaded directly into memory in a DMA transfer. Reading and transfer continue until the end of the file is reached or a specific number of bytes have been read. Special code sequences are used to signify the end of a file, and the drive controller monitors the incoming data for these codes and, upon detection, terminates the read operation.

The Write Operation   Again, assuming that the desired track and sector have been located, the disk write operation may begin. First the drive controller sends a signal to the switches, placing them in the write position. This connects the $\overline{RD/WR}$ coil to the output of a differential amplifier, shown as Q_1, Q_2, and associated circuitry. At the same time, the erase oscillator is gated to the erase coil in the head. As the disk passes below the erase coil, the applied ac signal scrambles the magnetic domains into random orientation with one another. If this preerase step was not performed, then during the writing of new data, some of the domains that were oriented in a previous write operation might not be realigned completely (because of magnetic hysteresis), possibly causing errors in the newly recorded data.

Once the disk has passed beneath the erase head, it encounters the read-write head. The bases of Q_1 and Q_2 are driven to opposite logic levels when a given bit is sent to the head. For example, let us assume that when a logic 1 is sent from the drive controller, input A is driven high and input B is driven low. Conversely, for a logic low, A is driven low and B is driven high. This means that when logic 1 is sent to the head, Q_2 will saturate and Q_1 will cut off. This results in current flow (conventional) from the bottom of the $\overline{RD/WR}$ coil to the top. When logic 0 is sent to the head, Q_1 and Q_2 switch states and current flows from the top of the coil to the bottom. As the disk moves below the head, the domains in the oxide film will tend to align with the direction of the field applied by the head (refer to Fig. 10-14). When the desired amount of data has been written to the disk, the write process is terminated.

10-2.3   General Disk and Disk Drive Care

There are many conflicting opinions concerning the cleaning of disk drive read-write heads. Many manufacturers produce high-quality head-cleaning supplies, and the recommendations for cleaning intervals vary greatly from one manufacturer to another. It is the author's feeling that in general, the read-write head(s) should be cleaned only when necessary; that is, if disk errors begin to occur after a disk drive has seen extensive service, then cleaning the heads is in order. Some disk cleaning packages state that the heads should be cleaned after every use. This is more than likely a way to get the consumer to buy disk-cleaning devices more frequently, and is not good practice, as the cleaning process does tend to cause some head wear.

It is possible that what appears to be a faulty disk drive or a bad disk is just the manifestation of a buildup of oxide particles on the read, causing unreliable operation. A cleaning will usually fix this problem. The lining of the floppy disk jacket is designed to collect any loose oxide and dust particles; and therefore, the heads should not become "dirty" for quite a long time. Of course, if the computer has been operated in an environment in which there is a lot of smoke or dust in the air, then cleaning will be required more often than usual. Using a disk whose magnetic surface has been touched can quickly lead to problems, as oils from the skin that get on the disk will build up and adhere to the head. Commercially available head-cleaning disks will effectively remove these deposits. In short, it is best to apply some common sense, and eventually, with experience, one will be able to determine when the drive heads should be cleaned.

Head alignment can also be performed using special alignment disks. These disks have accurately located fixed bit patterns written on them, which are used to trim the head position. Special software routines are used to cause the drive to perform different functions for long periods of time, during which adjustments are made. Generally, standard test equipment, special test fixtures, and technical data relating to a given system are required to perform many of these operations.

Disk rotational speed adjustments can usually be made rather easily, using the timing marks on the drive flywheel. The 60 Hz line voltage provides an accurate frequency reference from which speed calibration can be derived.

Review Questions for Section 10-2

1. What is the term applied to the time window during which a given bit is present in FM or MFM data encoding?
2. How are the magnetic domains of the disk surface coating caused to align properly when writing to the disk?
3. During what phase of disk operation is the erase head activated?
4. Which I/O method is usually used in order to provide high-speed data transfer between memory and disk?
5. What is the term for the force that causes a stepper motor (when deenergized, or energized but not being supplied with step pulses) to tend to remain in a fixed position?

SUMMARY

This chapter has dealt with two practically essential components of the typical microcomputer system: the keyboard and the disk drive. The circuits embodied in these sections of the computer encompass many different aspects of electronic design. Keyboards are constructed around a matrix of switches. The switches are continuously scanned and then encoded when a switch is closed. Interrupt I/O is usually used to allow more efficient CPU operation. The keyboard switches may be debounced using hardware or software techniques. Often, nonmechanical contact switches are used for greater reliability.

Disk drives are usually controlled by dedicated VLSI devices called disk controllers. The disk controller coordinates the activities of the various sections of the drive mechanism and its associated electronics. Circuits encountered in disk drives include phase-locked loops, differential amplifiers, servomechanisms, stepper motors, optoelectronic devices, and various digital circuit configurations. The servo is usually used to control disk rotational speed, while stepper motors control head positioning. Data is encoded on the disk in a self-clocking format, which is usually either FM or MFM encoding. Disk read operations derive timing synchronization from the data stream using phase-locked loops. The index hole is detected by optical means and is used to produce pulses that mark the start of the sectors on the disk.

CHAPTER QUESTIONS

10-1. What do we call the section of memory that is reserved for storing keystrokes prior to processing by the main system CPU?

10-2. How can the number of data lines connecting the keyboard to the computer be reduced?

10-3. What advantage does the circuit in Fig. 10-7 have over that in Fig. 10-6?

10-4. How can the main system CPU be relieved of much of the burden of monitoring and controlling the keyboard?

10-5. Why do many switches used in keyboard construction have snap action?

10-6. What is the term applied to the snap action of a switch?

10-7. What are the two common data encoding techniques used for disk data storage?

10-8. Why is a differential amplifier required to send data to the read-write head in Fig. 10-33? (Hint: Consider that the applied digital signal varies from 0 to +5 V.)

10-9. Why are diodes connected across the stator windings of stepper motors?

10-10. Name two types of PM rotor stepper motors.

10-11. What is the function of the index hole on a soft-sectored floppy disk?

10-12. Which data encoding technique is used most often for double-density recording on disk?

10-13. What are the two general modes of operation that a disk drive will engage in?

10-14. What is the function of a servo in a disk drive application?

10-15. Why is NRZ data encoding not used to store data on disks?

10-16. What is the advantage of MFM over FM in disk data storage?

CHAPTER PROBLEMS

10-17. Refer to Fig. 10-7. What relationship between the clock period and the one-shot's time out period must exist if the one-shot is to be retriggered continuously while the switch is held closed?

10-18. In reference to the circuit in Fig. 10-1, if the CPU reads a byte from the latches, what is a simple software method for determining whether two keys have been pressed simultaneously?

10-19. In Fig. 10-1, how can the outputs of the latches be enabled by the CPU?

10-20. In Fig. 10-1, if the *A* key is pressed, what will be the binary and hex contents of the latches?

10-21. In Fig. 10-1, if the scan clock operates at a frequency of 1 kHz, how often will a given row be activated by the 74LS139?

10-22. Why is an OR gate used to inhibit the scan clock in Fig. 10-1? What modifications would be necessary to use an AND gate instead?

10-23. Sketch the FM and MFM waveforms that would be produced in response to the NRZ waveform in Fig. 10-34.

Fig. 10-34 NRZ waveform for Problem 10-23.

10-24. Refer to Fig. 10-32*c*. If a disk rotates at 300 rpm, what is the period of the pulse T_{rev}?

10-25. Assume that the stepper motor in Fig. 10-26*a* is connected to a latched port at I/O address FF00. Write the mnemonics for an 8088 program that will cause the motor to rotate in the clockwise direction. The program must include a delay that executes F000 times before every step, except for the very first one.

10-26. What sequence is represented by the bit stream in Fig. 10-35?

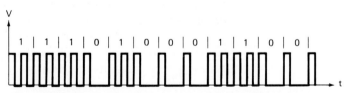

Fig. 10-35 FM encoded data waveform for Problem 10-26.

TROUBLESHOOTING TECHNIQUES AND EQUIPMENT

11

In general, today's microcomputers and the components used in their construction are very reliable, often providing years of trouble-free service. However, there is always a chance that at some point in time, one or more components in the system will fail. Often, the source of trouble can be tracked down with little difficulty, using a minimal amount of test equipment, or possibly none. In other cases, the solution to a problem may require the use of sophisticated digital and analog test equipment. This chapter is intended to provide a brief introduction to some of the troubleshooting techniques that are commonly used to isolate and correct problems that develop in microcomputer systems. To this end, the general principles behind the use and operation of commonly used digital test equipment will be presented. A section covering some of the more commonly encountered power supply circuits will also be presented, as the power supply is just as much an essential part of the computer system as the CPU.

11-1   PRELIMINARY TESTING

There are a few simple checks that should be made whenever a microcomputer or one of its associated peripheral devices is not operating correctly. For the most part, these preliminary steps are self evident, commonsense procedures.

One of the first things that should be done is to note the symptoms that are caused by the problem. It is also quite helpful to write down any odd behavior that may have preceded the breakdown, if possible. If the computer was being used by someone else at the time of failure, such information should be gathered from that person.

11-1.1 Mechanically Related Problems

Considering the microcomputer and its peripherals as a whole, the most likely sources for problems (other than operator errors) are those sections that are mechanical in nature. This includes gear trains, linkages and sockets, and connectors of all sorts. Let us first consider what can go wrong with sockets and connectors. Assuming that the system has been set up correctly and has until recently been operating properly, one of the first areas that could become a problem source is the system interconnecting cables. Cables are often subjected to harsh treatment, such as being pulled on and twisted. This can result in broken wires and bent connectors. If such a problem is suspected, it is a good idea to check the continuity of each conductor within the cable. Defective cables should be repaired or replaced. The contacts in the cable connectors may also become oxidized or contaminated with some foreign material, resulting in a high-resistance connection. The most common cause for this occurrence is improper handling of the connector. Touching the contacts will result in a film of oil and salts being transferred to them. The oil acts as an insulator, and the salts are somewhat corrosive to the metal contacts; therefore they should be removed as soon as possible. Contact cleaners are available that will remove these oils. Circuit boards with edge connectors can also experience this problem, and likewise should not be handled improperly.

Integrated circuits are usually either soldered or socket mounted on circuit boards. Socket mounting is advantageous when replacement of a device may be required, but it can also be a potential problem source. Poor contact between the IC pins and the socket contacts can result from contamination of the socket contacts, or from the IC not being seated properly. Even a properly seated IC may eventually begin to work loose from the socket for various reasons, such as vibration or thermal expansion. Reseating the IC will usually correct such a problem. Components that are soldered directly to a circuit board are usually more reliable, but are more difficult to remove and replace.

11-1.2 General Electronic Problem Sources

Problems that are purely electrical in nature will usually be caused by failed semiconductor (active) components. Although semiconductor devices are extremely reliable, they are generally not as reliable as passive components such as resistors and capacitors. What this basically means is that if a component failure is suspected, it will more than likely be an integrated circuit or transistor that has failed. The main reason for this situation is that these devices are more easily damaged by voltage, current, and temperature excesses.

Environmental and electrical conditions that exceed the maximum allowable specifications for a given device may cause catastrophic failure or may degrade the performance level of the device below acceptable limits. It is usually much easier to locate a device that has undergone a catastrophic failure as opposed to a performance degradation, especially if the device shows obvious signs of failure such as cracking and charring. A device whose performance has degraded may work fine sometimes or most of the time, while failing at other times. It is often very difficult to correct such intermittent types of problems. Many times, a device will malfunction only when it heats up to a certain temperature. For example, if a computer consistently operates just fine for a short time and then suddenly breaks down, there is a good chance that some device is failing when the operating temperature rises to a certain level. In these cases, spraying the suspect component(s) with electronic coolant will often isolate the defective device, which would then be replaced.

Many microcomputers have an internal fan that circulates room air over the circuits. Blocked vent openings can lead to overheating of the computer and eventual device failure. It is important to determine whether such conditions exist where the computer is located, and to take the necessary corrective action.

11-1.3   Service Information

The information presented in the preceding paragraphs provides a useful starting point for troubleshooting a microcomputer and its peripheral devices. In order to correct many problems, however, complete technical information for the equipment being tested must be available. All but the most obvious problems require detailed information, such as logic diagrams, schematics, and timing diagrams. Productive troubleshooting without this data is practically impossible in many instances. Service information may be supplied by the manufacturer of the system, or it may have to be purchased from a third-party source. Service literature will normally list all important test points, and may also include descriptions of circuit operation and step-by-step troubleshooting procedures.

It is also a good idea to have on hand various data books that detail the pin designations and operation of specific devices, such as digital and linear integrated circuits. Knowing the operation of the individual ICs is an immense help when a problem has been narrowed down to a few components.

11-1.4   Fault Isolation

After checking the more obvious system interconnections, and if the problem has not been found or corrected, one must resort to more sophisticated test procedures. One of the first steps in the troubleshooting process is to determine which section or sections of the system could produce the problem that is being encountered; that is, in order to limit the number of devices to examine and test, one must be able to logically deduce which section or sections of the system could be responsible for the symptoms that are present. For example, Fig. 11-1 shows the block diagram for a typical microcomputer system. Let us assume that the system was functioning properly for several months; but then one day when it was turned on, it would not boot-up the DOS, although the drive

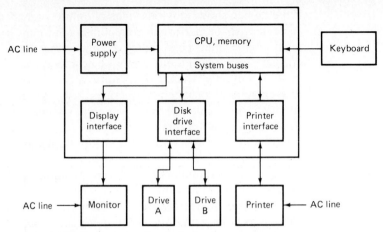

Fig. 11-1 Block diagram of a typical microcomputer system.

A activity light came on. After some further examination it was found (by looking in the drive door) that the drive A motor did indeed operate when the system attempted to boot-up, and that the ROM-based BASIC interpreter would function properly after boot-up failed.

On the basis of the information presented above, it would seem that the problem could be either in drive A, in the disk interface circuitry, or possibly on the CPU board, but which one? Since there are two disk drives in the system, it is convenient to swap the positions of the two drives. If, after the swap, the system boots-up properly, then the circuitry in drive A itself is at fault. However, if this technique does not work, then the problem lies either in the drive interface or on the CPU board. The important thing to note at this point is that the number of possible candidates for the problem has been reduced significantly. At this point, one would probably suspect the drive interface card, especially if the other peripherals were still functioning normally. Consider that if the problem was in the circuitry that drives the data or address buses, to which the drive interface is connected, then the other peripherals (and possibly the entire system) would probably not function. Swapping the drive interface card with a known good unit would be the quickest way of answering this question.

Assuming that replacing the drive interface board has corrected the problem, it is possible to use the information that was previously gathered to determine which section of the drive interface board is defective. A possible block diagram for the disk drive controller is shown in Fig. 11-2. Since the motor was turning when a disk read was initiated (when the computer attempted to boot-up), we know that the motor control section is working. This would tend to point to one of the data read circuits of the interface as the offending circuit. The problem has now been narrowed down to a handful (or less) of ICs. It would be difficult to determine exactly which section of the data read-related circuitry was defective without using more advanced test procedures.

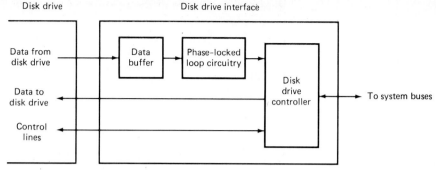

Fig. 11-2 Block diagram of disk drive interface.

In the field, one often does not have the time to delve much deeper than board-level troubleshooting. The defective circuit board is usually replaced and serviced at a later date, at which time the individual circuit boards would be analyzed at the component level. Quite often, special test fixtures are required to perform the component-level testing.

Remembering a few simple rules can help make troubleshooting a quick and efficient process. The first thing to do is eliminate the most obvious problem possibilities, such as cabling and power connections, and gather as much information relating to the problem as possible. The next step is to try to determine which section or sections of the system in general could possibly cause the problem. If the suspect section is located on a circuit board, that board may be replaced to ensure that it is the source of the problem. At this point, one would then troubleshoot the defective circuit board. This is a basically commonsense approach to troubleshooting, and it will yield acceptable results in most cases. Of course, one must have a general idea of how the various sections and subsections in the system interact in order to apply such methods.

Review Questions for Section 11-1

1. In general, which parts in a microcomputer system will tend to be least reliable?
2. Rather than arbitrarily replacing components, what should the technician do first?
3. Generally speaking, what are the two kinds of failure that a component can experience?
4. Which method of component mounting is most reliable?
5. Why are sockets used to mount some ICs?

11-2 DIGITAL TEST EQUIPMENT FUNDAMENTALS

The sources of many problems that develop in microcomputer systems can be determined without the use of sophisticated test equipment. However, there is always the possibility that particularly stubborn problems will require intensive use of such equipment. This section will discuss the fundamental principles of the operation and use of commonly used digital test equipment.

11-2.1 The Logic Probe

The logic probe is to digital circuit testing what the VOM is to linear circuit testing. The typical logic probe will have three LED indicators, as shown in Fig. 11-3, the states of which represent the conditions that exist at a

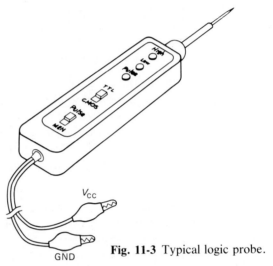

Fig. 11-3 Typical logic probe.

particular circuit node. The logic probe receives its power from the circuit under test; that is, leads are provided that are connected to ground and V_{CC}, which is usually +5 V. A node that is acting as an open circuit (floating) will result in all indicators turned off. The presence of valid logic 1 or valid logic 0 states is indicated by the lighting of the HIGH or LOW LEDs respectively. Since the indicators will turn on only when valid states are present, the user need not be concerned with interpreting absolute voltage values, as would be necessary if a VOM was used.

Most logic probes will also include a switch that is used to select between TTL and CMOS modes. These two families of logic devices have different logic threshold levels. The probe will automatically adjust its threshold levels when the switch is set for one family or the other. The ranges of valid logic levels for LS TTL devices are $V_{OH} = +2.7$ to +5 V and $V_{OL} = 0$ to 0.5 V. CMOS devices may be operated at supply voltages ranging from 3 to 18 V. The exact valid logic thresholds for a given CMOS device are dependent on the supply voltage value. If the logic probe is powered from the CMOS supply, and it is set to the CMOS mode, it will automatically adjust its threshold levels accordingly.

One of the most useful features of the logic probe is its ability to indicate the presence of single pulses (and glitches) and pulse trains. Some fundamental characteristics of pulse trains can also be determined very easily using the logic probe. For example, a typical logic probe display interpretation legend is presented in Fig. 11-4. A square wave that is lower

Input condition	LED response		
	High	Low	Pulse
Open circuit (floating)	○	○	○
Logic low (0)	○	◉	○
Logic high (1)	◉	○	○
Square wave f < 1 MHz	◉	◉	☀
Square wave f > 1 MHz	○	○	☀
High duty cycle pulse train	◉	○	☀
Low duty cycle pulse train	○	◉	☀

○ LED off

◉ LED on

☀ Blinking LED

Fig. 11-4 Interpretation of the logic probe indicator LEDs.

than 1 MHz in frequency will cause the PULSE indicator to flash at about a 2-Hz rate, while both the HIGH and LOW indicators appear to be on continuously. This occurs because a square wave has a 50 percent duty cycle, which causes the HIGH and LOW indicators to be turned on for equal lengths of time. Square waves that are higher than 1 MHz result in continuous flashing of the PULSE LED, while the HIGH and LOW indicators remain unlit.

Pulse trains that have a high duty cycle will cause the PULSE indicator to flash while the HIGH LED appears to remain on. Low duty cycle pulse trains activate the LOW LED and the PULSE indicator. Information such as this cannot be attained using a standard VOM or DMM.

The heart of the pulse indicator circuitry in the logic probe is a pulse stretcher. A pulse stretcher can be constructed using one shots, as shown in Fig. 11-5. The necessity for the pulse stretcher is based on the fact that a pulse of very short duration would make the logic level indicators blink so quickly that the pulse would not be detectable by the human eye. As

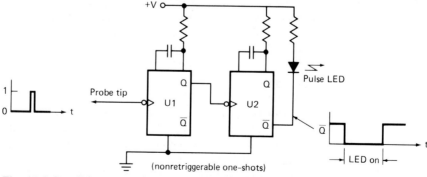

Fig. 11-5 Possible design for a pulse stretcher.

shown in Fig. 11-5, a short pulse will trigger U1, which after timing out will in turn trigger U2, causing the LED to light up for an easily visible time interval. Nonretriggered one-shots will produce a series of flashes from the LED if a continuous pulse train is applied to the input. The duty cycle of the pulse train will determine which of the logic level indicators appears to remain lit.

Most logic probes also include a switch that enables a pulse memory feature. This is usually a latch that captures the pulse event and holds the pulse LED on. Pulse storage is useful if a line is being monitored for the occurrence of infrequent pulses, where it is not possible to continuously watch the pulse indicator. Logic probes have quite an advantage over most oscilloscopes when it comes to detecting transient pulses and glitches in a circuit, because such pulses will usually not be visible on the scope display. Oscilloscopes require repetitive signals in order to produce a stable display, even though the pulse amplitude is high enough to trigger the sweep.

11-2.2 Logic Pulsers

Logic pulsers are used to stimulate the inputs to digital devices. Typical logic pulsers are very similar to logic probes in appearance, as can be seen in Fig. 11-6. Like the logic probe, the logic pulser will usually derive its

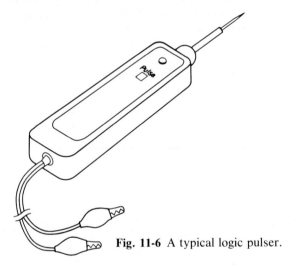

Fig. 11-6 A typical logic pulser.

power from the supply that is powering the circuit under test. Basically, when the pulser is connected to a circuit node, its internal circuitry senses the logic level that is present; and when the pulse switch is depressed, a short duration pulse of the opposite logic level with respect to the node being probed is generated. The probe output driver circuitry is designed so that the pulse will overpower the output of the gate that is currently driving the node. Since the pulse is of very short duration (typically around 100 μs), no damage will occur to the active gate outputs that are being driven. Most logic pulsers will produce a pulse train if the trigger button is held down for longer than about a second. This feature is useful for simulating a clock signal in sequential logic circuits. Prior to the advent of the logic pulser, an IC would have had to be removed from the circuit, or proper in-circuit input levels would have to be established in order to perform such testing.

The logic probe is usually used in conjunction with the logic pulser to monitor the response of the circuit output to the applied pulse. Figure 11-7 illustrates a typical application.

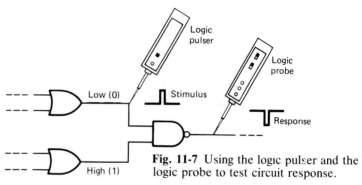

Fig. 11-7 Using the logic pulser and the logic probe to test circuit response.

11-2.3 Signature Analysis

The main idea behind signature analysis is to synchronously capture a sequence of events at a circuit node and generate a unique code, called a signature. The signature is an alphanumeric code that is determined by the events that have occurred at the test point during the sample interval. An instrument called a signature analyzer is used to perform this test. A simplified logic diagram for a signature analyzer is shown in Fig. 11-8.

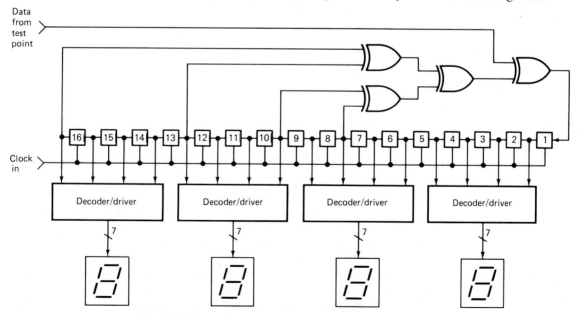

Fig. 11-8 Block diagram for a signature analyzer.

The heart of the signature analyzer is a 16 stage shift register, with feedback derived from XORing the outputs of stages 7, 9, 12, and 13 with the logic level that is present at the circuit test node. This special feedback connection forms what is called a pseudorandom sequence generator (PRSG). These types of circuits are also used to generate CRC codes in data communication applications. Shift registers are synchronous circuits, and the clock signal used to drive the PRSG is taken from the circuit under test, in order to synchronize shifting with the occurrence of events at the test node. Start and stop inputs are also included in the signature analyzer, but are not shown in Fig. 11-8 for clarity. The start and stop inputs are connected to points in the circuit under test that are designed or designated specifically for signature analysis testing applications. After the test period has ended, the outputs of each stage in the shift register are gated to decoder drivers that produce the signature for the node. The resulting output is then compared with the signature for the same node that was developed for a known good circuit. The signature display output will be a four-character alphanumeric code, composed of the characters 0, 1, 2, 3, 4, 5, 6, 7, 8, 9, A, C, F, H, P, and U. Using the signature analysis troubleshooting method, one can progress through a circuit until a mismatch in signatures occurs. The device or devices that are connected to that node would then be the prime suspect(s).

The main advantage of signature analysis is that the signature analyzer itself is relatively small, easy-to-use, and reliable. It can be shown that signature analyzers will detect an error at a test node over 99.99 percent of the time. One of the disadvantages of signature analysis is the requirement for a special signature testing operation mode that can be activated in the circuit under test; that is, most systems must have been designed to work with a signature analyzer in order to use this troubleshooting technique. Also, equipment that is in the process of development is not compatible with signature analysis troubleshooting because frequent circuit modifications that will affect the signature are usually made quite often.

11-2.4   Logic Analyzers

The logic analyzer is one of the most powerful and versatile pieces of digital test equipment available today. The function of the logic analyzer is to display state information that has been gathered from several different points in a system. In some respects, the logic analyzer is similar to an oscilloscope. The fundamental difference between the two instruments is that the oscilloscope provides a graphical view of signals in the time domain (amplitude as a function of time), while the logic analyzer allows one to view signals in what is called the data domain. As a further comparison, consider that the spectrum analyzer gives the operator a look at a signal in the frequency domain (amplitude as a function of frequency). In the frequency and time domains, both the amplitude and time or frequency are continuous. In the data domain, discrete logic levels are represented as a function of discrete events, such as the falling or rising transitions of a clock signal.

Data can be displayed in a number of different manners on the logic analyzer. For example, Fig. 11-9 shows a photograph of a microprocessor-controlled logic analyzer that is displaying data in hex, binart, and octal forms. This form of display is produced when the instrument is operated in what is called the parallel state mode. Probably the more familiar display

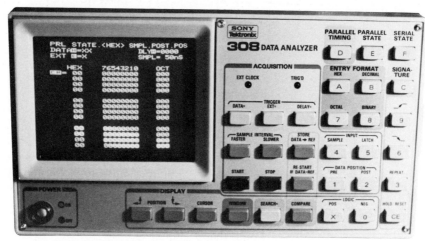

Fig. 11-9 A logic analyzer operating in the parallel state display mode.

to most readers is the timing diagram. An example of a timing diagram that might be displayed by a logic analyzer is shown in Fig. 11-10. The clock waveform is normally not displayed by the analyzer, and is presented for reference purposes.

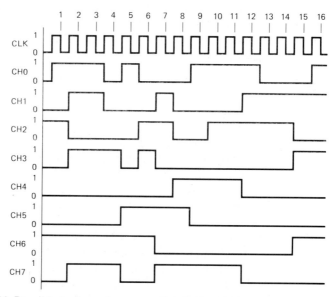

Fig. 11-10 Possible logic analyzer parallel timing display. Note that the clock (color) is usually not shown.

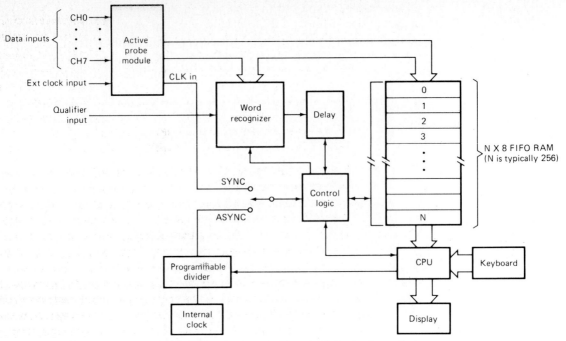

Fig. 11-11 Simplified block diagram for a logic analyzer.

A simplified block diagram for a logic analyzer is shown in Fig. 11-11. In this example, eight lines are used to provide input to an active probe. The probe provides high-impedance buffering, to prevent loading of the test points, and threshold level sensing. The clock input can be used to synchronize sampling of the data inputs with the clock of the circuit under test. A switch is set to choose between synchronous and asynchronous sampling modes. In the asynchronous mode an internal clock sets the rate at which data samples are taken. The user can select between sampling on either the falling or the rising edge of the clock. Each edge that occurs (either synchronously or asynchronously) causes the data present at the probe to be shifted into an 8-bit-wide n-bit-deep first-in first-out (FIFO) block of RAM. Each successive sample taken is pushed into the RAM, causing all earlier samples to be shoved deeper into the memory. Samples that are shifted past the nth memory location are lost.

Although the operator can initiate and stop sampling with the push of a button, usually, a word recognition feature, qualifier, or both are used to stop the data sampling process. The qualifier input may be programmed to trigger either the beginning or the end of the sample sequence when the point to which it is connected in the circuit goes either low (0) or high (1). The qualifier input may also be ignored by the analyzer by programming it as a don't care (X) input. Word recognition is a very powerful feature of the logic analyzer that may be used alone or in conjunction with the qualifier input to terminate or initiate a sample run. Here's how word recognition works. The operator enters an 8-bit word (in hex, binary, octal, or decimal, depending on the features of the particular logic analyzer in use) into the word recognizer section of the instrument, and then initiates a sample run. As words are clocked into the analyzer, they are compared to the user-supplied trigger word. When a match occurs, sampling may be terminated or started. The choice between having the trigger event either start or stop sampling is made prior to sampling, when the operator selects either pretrigger or posttrigger sample storage, respectively. This feature allows the operator to effectively watch for the occurrence of important events in the system that either are initiated by the recognized word, or themselves cause the recognized word (trigger event) to occur. Word recognition may be bypassed by programming all bits in the reference word to don't care states, or selected data bits may be set to don't care states. For example, if the data trigger word is entered in binary as 1100XXXX, the qualifier is programmed as X, and sample acquisition is started in the pre-trigger mode, then the first time that $CH_7 = 1$, $CH_6 = 1$, $CH_5 = 0$, and $CH_4 = 0$, the logic analyzer will terminate the sample run. If posttriggering was used, then sampling would begin when 1100XXXX was detected, and it would end when the sample storage memory was full (1100XXX would be shifted to the last location).

As far as the choice between pretriggering and posttriggering is concerned, it may be unknown to the operator whether the conditions that exist before or after word recognition and qualifier triggering are of importance. Often the data on both sides of the trigger is important and must be analyzed. If this is the case, a delay can be used to stop or start the reading of data an arbitrary number of samples after the trigger conditions have been recognized. This allows conditions that have occurred prior to and after the trigger event to be examined simultaneously. Using Fig. 11-10 as an example, let us assume that the analyzer has been set to take samples on the falling edge of the clock signal. The successive falling clock edges are numbered in the timing diagram. Sampling is performed on the falling edges of the clock because due to the nature of the circuit under test, the data test points may be in the process of changing states on the rising clock edges. Sampling on the falling edges of the system clock (in the synchronous mode) gives the data time to settle before being read, preventing any ambiguity. If posttriggering with no delay was used, the qualifier was a don't care state, and the word recognizer was programmed to trigger on the detection of 10010001 (CH7 is the MSB), then the user would start the sample run manually. When the analyzer reads 10010001 (at sample 8), then n consecutive samples, including those present at clock edge 8, would be stored in the memory. This action is illustrated in Fig. 11-12a. You will recall that n is the number of words in the memory (a word is 8 bits wide in this analyzer). Using pretriggering, for these same conditions, the analyzer would be enabled by the operator. When the word 10010001 was detected, sampling would be discontinued. This is illustrated in Fig. 11-12b. The difference between these two options is that in pretriggering, samples occurring after triggering (including the trigger word) are stored, while in posttriggering, the samples gathered prior to and including the trigger word are stored.

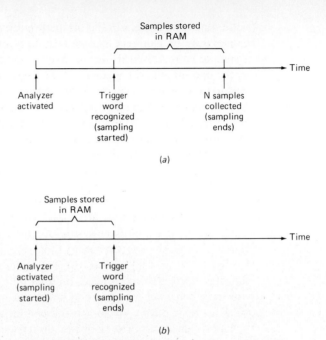

(a)

(b)

Fig. 11-12 Representation of sampling intervals for posttriggering (a) and pretriggering (b).

Thus far, logic analyzer operation in the synchronous clocking mode has been assumed. Synchronous clocking is usually the more convenient mode of operation to use. There may be times when it is advantageous to use asynchronous clocking, however. For example, consider a case where it is suspected that a glitch is occurring on one of the test points that is being monitored. This is shown in Fig. 11-13a. Glitches can be sources of much trouble and frustration in digital circuits. Again, assuming that system state changes occur on the rising edges of the system clock, we would most likely use falling edge triggering in the logic analyzer, if the synchronous mode was used. Notice, however, that in Fig. 11-13a the glitch on line A has ceased to exist when the clock falls. If the glitch is not present on the falling edge of the clock, it will not be captured and stored by the logic analyzer, producing the display in Fig. 11-13b.

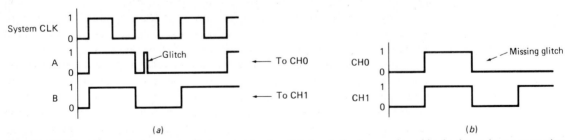

(a)

(b)

Fig. 11-13 Waveforms that are actually present in circuit (a) and display produced by logic analyzer operating in the synchronous mode, falling edge triggered (b).

In the synchronous mode, the logic analyzer is almost ideally suited to capturing synchronous events. Glitches and other unwanted state changes may occur at random points in time relative to the clock of the circuit being monitored. This means that they are not synchronous events. In order to capture such occurrences, the logic analyzer is operated in the asynchronous mode (see Fig. 11-11). When sampling data asynchronously, the internal clock is operated at a high rate relative to the rate at which the test points will change states. A representative illustration comparing the asynchronous clock and the circuit waveforms is shown in Fig. 11-14a. The resulting logic analyzer display is shown in Fig. 11-14b. Notice

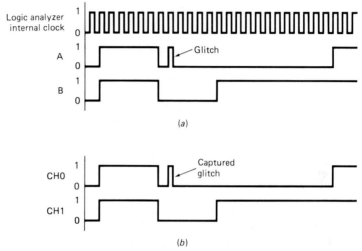

Fig. 11-14 Circuit waveforms and logic analyzer internal clock (a) and resulting logic analyzer display (b).

that the glitch was captured because it caused line A to be high during a sample interval. Asynchronous sampling can also be used to detect changes in state that occur on the wrong clock edge. For example, in Fig. 11-10, all lines can change states only on rising edges. If a line was erroneously changing states on a falling edge, it might appear normal in synchronous sampling. Using asynchronous sampling, the clock can be monitored along with the data, which allows the mistimed state change to be viewed.

The disadvantage of using asynchronous sampling is that since the internal clock must operate at very high speeds relative to the changes in incoming data or system clock, very few state transitions will be captured in a given sample run. The ability to display glitches and illegally timed transitions, however, more than makes up for this problem.

There are usually many more variations available on most logic analyzers. For example, a series of sample words can be stored in one memory block and compared to those that are collected at a later time. In this way, comparisons between the two sets of samples can be made easily and the differing samples may even appear highlighted on the display. Logic analyzers are available that can be set up to monitor serial data channels such as RS-232, as well as perform the functions already presented. Also, many can be used as signature analyzers. These options add greatly to the flexibility of this versatile piece of test equipment.

11-2.5 In-Circuit Emulation

In-circuit emulation is a method that is frequently used to test the operation of microprocessor-controlled systems. In this test method, the CPU is removed from the circuit and the remaining support circuitry is controlled by a computer that acts like (emulates) the original CPU. The advantage of using a computer to simulate the CPU is that the engineer is given a much higher degree of control over system operation.

11-2.6 Software Troubleshooting Techniques

An aspect of the troubleshooting and testing process used in computer applications that has not been mentioned yet in this chapter is that of software troubleshooting. A good diagnostic program can sometimes be as useful as a logic analyzer in finding circuit faults. For example, a program that does nothing other than loop repeatedly can be used to generate repetitive patterns that can be viewed on a logic analyzer or signature analyzer. Ports can easily be tested using software and a logic probe, as was done in the accompanying *Laboratory Manual*.

Because of the power and usefulness of software test routines, many microcomputers include self-test routines that are invoked when the system is first turned on. Such programs may test the system RAM, peripheral device operation, power supply operation, and many other sections of the system. Any errors that are detected may be listed on the display, as an aid to troubleshooting. Very sophisticated diagnostic programs are available that will report on sections and even individual ICs that have failed or are not operating at top efficiency.

Once one has obtained some familiarity with a given microcomputer, its operation, and its peripheral devices, custom programs can be created to aid in the troubleshooting process. Generally, assembly language is used to create these programs because of the speed and high degree of control over the system that it allows. At this point in time, the reader should be able to create such programs with little trouble, especially if he or she has access to system repair data, memory maps, and other related information.

Section 11-2 Review Questions

1. How is the presence of a floating node indicated by a logic probe?
2. Why is the standard oscilloscope not a good choice of equipment for detecting glitches?
3. What is a signature?
4. When using a logic analyzer, what mode of operation allows data to be displayed in binary form?
5. What instrument is used to apply a stimulus to a test node?

Although the majority of the circuitry that is used in computer applications is digital in nature, there are usually a few nondigital circuits that are also incorporated in the system. Probably the most obvious nondigital circuitry is found in the power supply sections of the computer and the peripheral devices. Other sections that may contain a large number of linear circuits, aside from power supplies, are the disk drives and monitors; and to a certain extent, the operation of these two types of circuits has already been presented. It would be impossible to examine all of the possible linear circuits that could be encountered in a computer system in this text, but the operation of a few representative power supply designs will be presented.

11-3.1 Power Supply Operation

A microcomputer power supply must produce several stable sources of dc voltage for system operation. Commonly used voltages are $+5$ V, ± 21 V, ± 5 V and $+22$ V. There are basically two types of power supplies used to produce these voltages: linear and switching power supplies. The reader should be familiar with the operation of typical linear power supplies, but a brief review of this information will be presented.

Linear Power Supplies   The term linear power supply is derived from the fact that linear voltage regulators are used in the design. A supply that provides a source of $+5$ V regulated and ± 51 V unregulated is shown in Fig. 11-15. The main sections of bipolar in the supply are the line filter, power transformer, bridge rectifier, and filter capacitors. The bipolar supply would normally be used to power sections of the system that contain linear circuits, such as op amps, D/A and A/D converters, and stepper motors.

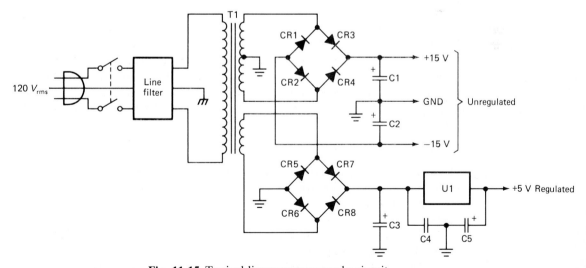

Fig. 11-15 Typical linear power supply circuit.

It may also be used to provide voltage for certain logic devices that require both positive and negative voltages.

The regulated section of the power supply is used to provide a very stable voltage for the majority of the logic devices in the system. Since typically there are many logic devices in the system, the 5-V supply must be designed to provide tight regulation under very heavy loads (often much greater than 10 A). This means that the filter capacitor C_3 must be very large and that the regulator must also be a high-power device. Typical filter capacitor values in such circuits may range from 10,000 to over 50,000 μF, and as such, these capacitors tend to be rather large. The regulator must be able to dissipate large amounts of power and will usually be mounted on a large heat sink.

In order to understand why linear regulators require such large heat sinks, consider the regulator shown in Fig. 11-16, in which the load is the

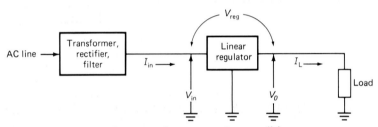

Fig. 11-16 Linear voltage regulator operating conditions.

logic circuitry that is being powered. Let us assume that this is a 5-V regulator ($V_O = 5$ V) and that $I_{in} = I_L = 10$ A. If $V_{in} = 10$ V, then the regulator voltage drop V_{reg} is 5 V. The power dissipated by the regulator is the product of V_{reg} and I_{in}. Using this information, we calculate the power dissipation of the regulator as follows.

$$
\begin{aligned}
P_{reg} &= V_{reg}I_{in} \\
&= 5\text{ V} \times 10\text{ A} \\
&= 50\text{ W}
\end{aligned}
\qquad \text{(Eq. 11-1)}
$$

The power dissipated by the load is found in a similar manner.

$$
\begin{aligned}
P_L &= V_O I_L \\
&= 5\ V \times 10\text{ A} \\
&= 50\text{ W}
\end{aligned}
\qquad \text{(Eq. 11-2)}
$$

The total power dissipation of the circuit (assuming negligible transformer and rectifier losses) is 100 W. In this particular circuit, only 50 percent of the total power dissipation, the power that is dissipated by the logic circuits, is doing any useful work. The remaining 50 percent is wasted as heat by the regulator.

Because the linear-regulator-based high-current supply requires large amounts of capacitance and heat sink area, it will tend to be large and heavy. This is to be avoided if at all possible.

In some systems, rather than have one large, expensive high-power regulator supply voltage for the entire microcomputer, several smaller regulators are distributed throughout the system. This is called distributed regulation, and is illustrated in Fig. 11-17. There are several advantages

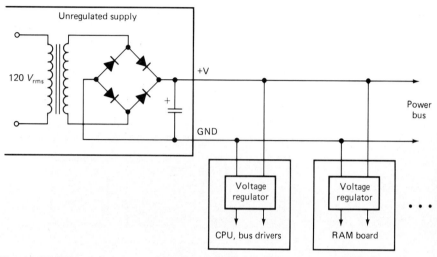

Fig. 11-17 Voltage regulator placement in a system using distributed regulation.

to this regulation approach. First, voltage drops along the main power bus lines will be less bothersome because each circuit board carries its own regulator. The regulator will also provide a high degree of isolation from one section of the system to another. This isolation reduces the likelihood of switching transients in one section affecting another. One final advantage of distributed regulation is that the smaller regulators are much less expensive than one large high-power regulator.

When troubleshooting linear power supplies, the VOM or DMM is the most useful test instrument to use. The most common problem that will develop in a linear power supply is failure of the voltage regulator. If a power supply failure is suspected, the best thing to do first is disconnect it from the computer circuitry and test it under no-load conditions. Sometimes, a short in the circuit being powered will cause the regulator to overheat and shut down. Testing under no-load conditions will usually indicate if the problem is actually in the power supply or in some other section of the computer.

The oscilloscope can be used to check for excessive ripple in the filtered output. High values of ripple may indicate that the supply is being overloaded, a filter capacitor is becoming leaky, or one or more diodes in the rectifier have failed. Again, disconnecting the supply from the computer circuit will reduce the number of possible problem sources to those in the supply itself, if the problem persists.

In general, devices that have shorted out will become very hot when the computer is turned on. With a little experience, the technician can locate such components just by feeling them.

Switching Power Supplies   Because of the inefficiency, high power dissipation, and large size of linear power supplies, the current trend is to use switching power supplies in many microcomputer systems. There are several advantages that can be realized by using a switching supply, but in order to understand them better, let us examine the circuit shown in Fig. 11-18.

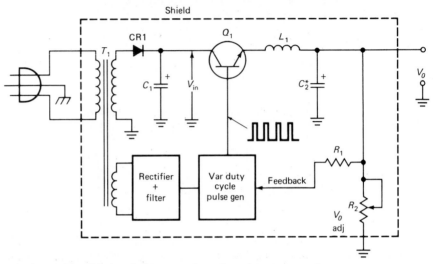

Fig. 11-18 Simplified switching regulator-based power supply.

This circuit is representative of many switching supplies in use. The transformer T_1 has two secondaries. The bottom secondary winding is used to form a low-power dc supply for regulator control purposes. The top secondary winding is used to provide the main voltage source from which the regulated output is derived. Usually, this secondary will produce a rather high voltage (50 to 100 V). The output of the top secondary is rectified and filtered by C_1. Transistor Q_1 is switched on and off at a high frequency by the variable duty cycle oscillator.

Inductor L_1 and capacitor C_2 form the filter circuit for the output of the supply. The inductor is used because the dc voltage produced at its right side, and applied to C_2, is proportional to the average value of the voltage produced at the emitter of Q_1. You will recall that without an inductor, the filter capacitor would tend to charge to the peak value of the incoming pulsating dc. The idea here is that the average voltage level at the emitter of Q_1 is proportional to the duty cycle of the base drive signal. The higher the duty cycle, the higher V_O will be. The actual value of V_O is sampled via R_1 and R_2 and applied to a duty cycle control input on the pulse generator. In this way, changes in V_O will be sensed and compensated for either by increasing or decreasing the duty cycle of the base drive signal. Figure 11-19a and b illustrates this concept, where V_M is the peak or maximum voltage produced at the emitter of the transistor.

Because the transistor is operated in either cutoff or saturation, its average power dissipation is rather low. Let us consider a situation where V_{in} is 50 V and V_O is 5 V and the pulse generator operates at a constant

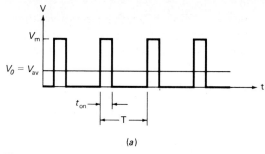 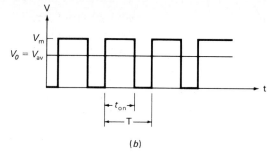

Fig. 11-19 Low-duty cycle waveform and average dc level (*a*) and higher-duty cycle with average dc level (*b*).

frequency of 50 kHZ (not uncommon). The relationship between V_O and V_{in} is given by the equation

$$V_O = (t_{ON}/T)V_M \qquad \text{(Eq. 11-3)}$$

where t_{on}/T is the duty cycle and $V_M = V_{in}$ (to a close approximation).

Using Eq. 11-3, it can be shown that the required duty cycle that will produce $V_O = 5$ V is 0.1 (10 percent). This means that on the average, Q_1 will be in saturation for 10 percent of the time, and it will be in cutoff for 90 percent of the time. When in saturation, a typical transistor will drop about 0.5 V from collector to emitter; that is, $V_{ce(sat)} = 0.5$ V, while carrying maximum current. In cutoff, transistor conduction is practically 0, and $V_{ce} = V_{in}$. Assuming that the transistor supplies 10 A ($I_{c(sat)}$) to the circuit being powered when it is in saturation, the transistor power dissipation is found as follows.

$$
\begin{aligned}
P_{sat} &= V_{ce(sat)} I_{c(sat)} \\
&= 0.5 \text{ V x } 10 \text{ A} \qquad \text{(Eq. 11-4)} \\
&= 5 \text{ W}
\end{aligned}
$$

In cutoff, transistor power dissipation is very low, and will be considered negligible. The average power dissipation of the transistor may now be approximated as follows.

$$
\begin{aligned}
P_{avg} &= P_{sat}(t_h/T) \\
&= 5 \text{ W x } 0.1 \qquad \text{(Eq. 11-5)} \\
&= 500 \text{ mW}
\end{aligned}
$$

The preceding analysis points out one of the major advantages of the switching regulator over the linear regulator: high efficiency. Notice how low the average power dissipation of the switching transistor Q_1 is in comparison to the linear regulator that was previously discussed. Switching supplies can easily exceed 90 percent efficiency.

Another advantage that can be realized using a switching regulator is a significant reduction in the size of the required filter capacitors. The main function of a filter capacitor is to reduce ripple (ripple is an ac component that is present in the dc output) in the dc output of the supply. The amount of capacitance required to maintain a given amount of ripple is inversely proportional to the frequency of the ripple component. For a standard linear power supply, using a full wave rectifier driven by the 60 Hz ac line, the ripple frequency is 120 Hz. Compare this with the ripple frequency of 50 kHz that is encountered in Fig. 11-18. This means that C_2 can be relatively low in value (usually around 8000 to 10,000 µF). Sometimes, rather than use one large filter capacitor (C_2 in Fig. 11-18), several smaller capacitors of around 1000 µF are placed in parallel with one another. This is done because very large capacitors do not behave ideally at the high frequencies that are common in switching supplies.

The net effect of using a switching supply is that for a given power rating, the switching supply will be much more efficient and smaller and lighter than an equivalent linearly regulated supply. There are, however, a few disadvantages that are associated with switching supplies. First of all, because very high currents are being switched on and off at a rapid rate, powerful high frequency noise will be produced by the supply. This noise can interfere with nearby equipment and possibly even the logic circuits that are being powered. Such noise necessitates the use of electromagnetic shielding around the power supply.

One other disadvantage of switching power supplies is that they are much more complex than linear supplies. This means that the chances of something going wrong are increased, and the troubleshooting process will usually take a much longer time.

The same general rules that apply to the testing of linear supplies apply to the testing of switching supplies. The oscilloscope is required much more often when testing switching supplies because of the oscillator circuits that are included in the circuitry. The service data for a given supply will usually include waveforms and voltage levels that should exist at various test points. These are used to adjust and troubleshoot the circuit.

11-3.2 Line Filtering

As seen in Fig. 11-15, most computer power supplies will include a filter circuit on their ac line input. Such filters serve two purposes. First, they prevent high-frequency noise that may be present on the ac line from being coupled into the computer circuitry. Second, the filter prevents computer-generated noise from being coupled to the ac line, and possibly interfering with other equipment. A typical line filter circuit is shown in Fig. 11-20.

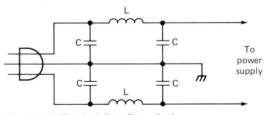

Fig. 11-20 Typical line filter design.

This filter is basically two low-pass pifilters (one for each line) that shunt high-frequency noise to ground. This type of filter is very effective at reducing high-frequency noise to negligible levels.

Computer circuits are also easily damaged by line transients. For example, during a lightning storm, a strike on a power line can easily produce a voltage spike of several thousand volts. If coupled into the computer, many circuits could be destroyed. In order to prevent this occurrence, surge suppressors are used to condition the ac line at the point where the computer is connected. A surge suppressor is usually constructed from devices called varistors. A varistor is a device that exhibits nondestructive breakdown when its rated breakdown voltage is exceeded. Most varistors are made of silicon carbide. A surge suppressor that is used on the 120 V rms ac line will typically have a breakdown voltage of around 180 V. Connecting two varistors to the line as shown in Fig. 11-21 will short transient voltage spikes to ground before they have a chance to damage the computer.

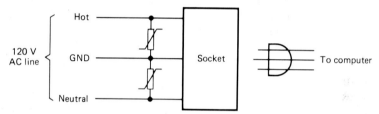

Fig. 11-21 Placement of varistors for line transient protection.

Section 11-3 Review Questions

1. Why are line filters used in computer power supplies?
2. What would be indicated by an oscilloscope if a filter capacitor was to become leaky?
3. Which type of regulated power supply is most efficient?
4. Why are high switching frequencies used in switching power supplies?
5. What is the ripple frequency associated with a power supply that uses a full wave rectifier connected to the 60 Hz line?
6. Why are regulators sometimes distributed around various sections of a system rather than using one regulator at the power supply?

SUMMARY

This chapter has presented an overview of commonly encountered digital test equipment, test procedures, and power supply circuit operations. Logic probes, logic pulsers, signature analyzers, and logic analyzers are used very often to troubleshoot computer circuits. The logic probe provides a visual indication of activity at a test point, while a logic pulser is used to stimulate test points so that a response can be evaluated. The signature analyzer provides a method by which coded representations of test node activity can be compared to a reference code. A mismatch in signatures indicates a fault in the circuit at that point. Logic analyzers allow the operator to view the logic states of several different lines simultaneously. Word recognition can be used to trigger the start or end of a sample interval. Samples may be taken synchronously or asynchronously. Circuit emulation is another testing technique in which the CPU is simulated by a computer. This approach allows a high degree of flexibility and complete control over the actions of the system under test.

Computer power supplies are used to produce the dc voltages required by the various sections in the system. Power supplies may be either regulated or unregulated. Regulators may be either linear or switching types. Switching regulators are more efficient, but are more complex and relatively noisy. Standard analog test equipment—such as VOMs, DMMs, and oscilloscopes—is usually used to troubleshoot the power supply section of a computer.

CHAPTER QUESTIONS

11-1. What is a common cause of contact oxidation?

11-2. If the output of an LS TTL gate was measured with a DMM and found to be $+2.2$ V, what could you conclude about the gate?

11-3. What is the term that is used to describe a short-lived pulse?

11-4. What is the duty cycle of an ideal square wave?

11-5. What is the main factor that will determine the valid logic threshold values for a CMOS gate?

11-6. Why must nonretriggerable one-shots be used in the circuit of Fig. 11-5?

11-7. Why is the oscilloscope not the most effective piece of equipment to use when hunting for glitches?

11-8. What is an application for the logic pulser when it produces a continuous pulse train?

11-9. What is a signature?

11-10. State two positive features that are associated with the signature analyzer.

11-11. Why aren't signature analyzers used very often during the development of prototype equipment?

11-12. What mode of operation allows glitches to be viewed with the logic analyzer?

11-13. In the most general of respects, what is the difference between the time domain and the data domain?

11-14. What mode of operation allows the states of test points to be viewed in binary form on a logic analyzer?

11-15. From what is sample timing derived when a logic analyzer is used in the synchronous mode?

11-16. What type of triggering is used to store samples that occur prior to the trigger event?

11-17. What type of triggering is used to cause the storage of data that was sampled both before and after a trigger event?

CHAPTER PROBLEMS

11-18. Assuming maximum coding efficiency, how many unique codes could be produced by the signature analyzer in Fig. 11-8?

11-19. Describe the response that would be produced by a logic probe if it was connected to a test node that produced the timing diagram in Fig. 11-22.

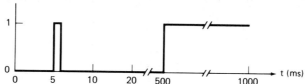

Fig. 11-22 Timing waveform for Problem 11-19.

11-20. Four points in a computer circuit produce the waveforms shown in Fig. 11-23 (in the time domain). Sketch the display that would be produced by a logic analyzer that was operated synchronously, if rising edge triggering was used. (*Note:* The system clock is shown for reference purposes.)

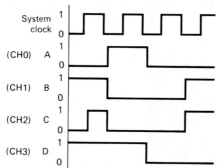

Fig. 11-23 Timing waveforms for Problem 11-20.

11-21. Repeat Problem 11-20, assuming that asynchronous sampling, where the internal clock frequency is much higher than the system clock, is used.

11-22. Refer to Fig. 11-16. If $I_{in} = I_l = 15$ A, $V_{in} = 12$ V, and $V_O = 5$ V, determine P_l, P_{reg}, and the regulator efficiency.

11-23. In Fig. 11-19a, if $V_M = 40$ V, and $T = 40$ µs, what duty cycle is required to produce $V_{AV} = 5$ V?

11-24. What would be the frequency of the ripple component in the output of a switching supply that produced the waveform described in Problem 11-23?

APPENDIX A: 8088 Instruction Set Summary

DATA TRANSFER

MOV = Move:	76543210	76543210	76543210
Register/memory to/from register	100010 d w	mod reg r/m	
Immediate to register/memory	1100011 w	mod 0 0 0 r/m	data
		data if w = 1	
Immediate to register	1011 w reg	data	data if w = 1
Memory to accumulator	1010000 w	addr-low	addr-high
Accumulator to memory	1010001 w	addr-low	addr-high
Register/memory to segment register	10001110	mod 0 reg r/m	
Segment register to register/memory	10001100	mod 0 reg r/m	

PUSH = Push:		
Register/memory	11111111	mod 1 1 0 r/m
Register	01010 reg	
Segment register	000 reg 110	

POP = Pop:		
Register/memory	10001111	mod 0 0 0 r/m
Register	01011 reg	
Segment register	000 reg 111	

XCHG = Exchange:		
Register/memory with register	1000011 w	mod reg r/m
Register with accumulator	10010 reg	

IN = Input from:		
Fixed port	1110010 w	port
Variable port	1110110 w	

OUT = Output to:		
Fixed port	1110011 w	port
Variable port	1110111 w	

XLAT = Translate byte to AL	11010111	
LEA = Load EA to register	10001101	mod reg r/m
LDS = Load pointer to DS	11000101	mod reg r/m
LES = Load pointer to ES	11000100	mod reg r/m
LAHF = Load AH with flags	10011111	
SAHF = Store AH into flags	10011110	
PUSHF = Push flags	10011100	
POPF = Pop flags	10011101	

ARITHMETIC

ADD = Add:	76543210	76543210	76543210
Reg./memory with register to either	000000 d w	mod reg r/m	
Immediate to register/memory	100000 s w	mod 0 0 0 r/m	data
		data if s:w = 01	
Immediate to accumulator	0000010 w	data	data if w = 1

ADC = Add with carry:			
Reg./memory with register to either	000100 d w	mod reg r/m	
Immediate to register/memory	100000 s w	mod 0 1 0 r/m	data
		data if s:w = 01	
Immediate to accumulator	0001010 w	data	data if w = 1

INC = Increment:		
Register/memory	1111111 w	mod 0 0 0 r/m
Register	01000 reg	

AAA = ASCII adjust for add	00110111	
DAA = Decimal adjust for add	00100111	

SUB = Subtract:	76543210	76543210	76543210
Reg./memory and register to either	001010 d w	mod reg r/m	
Immediate from register/memory	100000 s w	mod 1 0 1 r/m	data
		data if s:w = 01	
Immediate from accumulator	0010110 w	data	data if w = 1

SBB = Subtract with borrow			
Reg./memory and register to either	000110 d w	mod reg r/m	
Immediate from register/memory	100000 s w	mod 0 1 1 r/m	data
		data if s:w = 01	
Immediate from accumulator	0001110 w	data	data if w = 1

DEC = Decrement:		
Register/memory	1111111 w	mod 0 0 1 r/m
Register	01001 reg	

NEG = Change sign	1111011 w	mod 0 1 1 r/m

CMP = Compare:	76543210	76543210	76543210
Register/memory and register	001110 d w	mod reg r/m	
Immediate with register/memory	100000 s w	mod 1 1 1 r/m	data
		data if s:w = 01	
Immediate with accumulator	0011110 w	data	data if w = 1

AAS = ASCII adjust for subtract	00111111	
DAS = Decimal adjust for subtract	00101111	
MUL = Multiply (unsigned)	1111011 w	mod 1 0 0 r/m
IMUL = Integer multiply (signed)	1111011 w	mod 1 0 1 r/m
AAM = ASCII adjust for multiply	11010100	00001010
DIV = Divide (unsigned)	1111011 w	mod 1 1 0 r/m
IDIV = Integer divide (signed)	1111011 w	mod 1 1 1 r/m
AAD = ASCII adjust for divide	11010101	00001010
CBW = Convert byte to word	10011000	
CWD = Convert word to double word	10011001	

LOGIC

	76543210	76543210	76543210
NOT = Invert	1111011 w	mod 0 1 0 r/m	
SHL/SAL = Shift logical/arithmetic left	110100 v w	mod 1 0 0 r/m	
SHR = Shift logical right	110100 v w	mod 1 0 1 r/m	
SAR = Shift arithmetic right	110100 v w	mod 1 1 1 r/m	
ROL = Rotate left	110100 v w	mod 0 0 0 r/m	
ROR = Rotate right	110100 v w	mod 0 0 1 r/m	
RCL = Rotate through carry flag left	110100 v w	mod 0 1 0 r/m	
RCR = Rotate through carry right	110100 v w	mod 0 1 1 r/m	

AND = And:			
Reg./memory and register to either	001000 d w	mod reg r/m	
Immediate to register/memory	1000000 w	mod 1 0 0 r/m	data
		data if w = 1	
Immediate to accumulator	0010010 w	data	data if w = 1

TEST = And functions to flags, no result:			
Register/memory and register	1000010 w	mod reg r/m	
Immediate data and register/memory	1111011 w	mod 0 0 0 r/m	data
		data if w = 01	
Immediate data and accumulator	1010100 w	data	data if w = 1

Mnemonics © Intel, 1978 (Courtesy of Intel Corporation.)

OR = Or:

		76543210 76543210 76543210		
Reg./memory and register to either		000010dw	mod reg r/m	
Immediate to register/memory		1000000w	mod 0 0 1 r/m	data
			data if w=01	
Immediate to accumulator		0000110w	data	data if w=1

XOR = Exclusive or:

Reg./memory and register to either		001100dw	mod reg r/m	
Immediate to register/memory		1000000w	mod 1 1 0 r/m	data
			data if w=01	
Immediate to accumulator		0011010w	data	data if w=1

STRING MANIPULATION

REP = Repeat	1111001z
MOVS = Move byte/word	1010010w
CMPS = Compare byte/word	1010011w
SCAS = Scan byte/word	1010111w
LODS = Load byte/wd to AL/AX	1010110w
STOS = Store byte/wd from AL/A	1010101w

CONTROL TRANSFER

CALL = Call:

Direct within segment		11101000	disp-low	disp-high
Indirect within segment		11111111	mod 0 1 0 r/m	
Direct intersegment		10011010	offset-low	offset-high
			seg-low	seg-high
Indirect intersegment		11111111	mod 0 1 1 r/m	

JMP = Unconditional Jump:

Direct within segment		11101001	disp-low	disp-high
Direct within segment-short		11101011	disp	
Indirect within segment		11111111	mod 1 0 0 r/m	
Direct intersegment		11101010	offset-low	offset-high
			seg-low	seg-high
Indirect intersegment		11111111	mod 1 0 1 r/m	

RET = Return from CALL:

Within segment		11000011	
Within seg. adding immed. to SP		11000010	data-low	data-high
Intersegment		11001011	
Intersegment, adding immediate to SP		11001010	data-low	data-high

		76543210 76543210 76543210	
JE/JZ = Jump of equal/zero		01110100	disp
JL/JNGE = Jump on less/not greater or equal		01111100	disp
JLE/JNG = Jump on less or equal/not greater		01111110	disp
JB/JNAE = Jump on below/not above or equal		01110010	disp
JBE/JNA = Jump on below or equal/ not above		01110110	disp
JP/JPE = Jump on parity/parity even		01111010	disp
JO = Jump on overflow		01110000	disp
JS = Jump on sign		01111000	disp
JNE/JNZ = Jump on not equal/not zero		01110101	disp
JNL/JGE = Jump on not less/greater or equal		01111101	disp
JNLE/JG = Jump on not less or equal/ greater		01111111	disp
JNB/JAE = Jump on not below/above or equal		01110011	disp
JNBE/JA = Jump on not below or equal/above		01110111	disp
JNP/JPO = Jump on not par/par odd		01111011	disp
JNO = Jump on not overflow		01110001	disp
JNS = Jump on not sign		01111001	disp
LOOP = Loop CX times		11100010	disp
LOOPZ/LOOPE = Loop while zero/equal		11100001	disp
LOOPNZ/LOOPNE = Loop while not zero/equal		11100000	disp
JCXZ = Jump on CX zero		11100011	disp

INT = Interrupt:

Type specified		11001101	type
Type 3		11001100	

INTO = Interrupt on overflow		11001110
IRET = Interrupt return		11001111

PROCESSOR CONTROL

CLC = Clear carry		11111000	
CMC = Complement carry		11110101	
STC = Set carry		11111001	
CLD = Clear direction		11111100	
STD = Set direction		11111101	
CLI = Clear interrupt		11111010	
STI = Set interrupt		11111011	
HLT = Halt		11110100	
WAIT = Wait		10011011	
ESC = Escape (to external device)		11011xxx	mod x x x r/m
LOCK = Bus lock prefix		11110000	

Notes:

AL = 8-bit accumulator
AX = 16-bit accumulator
CX = Count register
DS = Data segment
ES = Extra segment
Above/below refers to unsigned value.
Greater = more positve
Less = less positive (more negative) signed values
if d = 1 then "to" reg; if d = 0 then "from" reg
if w = 1 then word instruction; if w = 0 then byte instruction

if mod = 11 then r/m is treated as a REG field
if mod = 00 then DISP = 0*, disp-low and disp-high are absent
if mod = 01 then DISP = disp-low sign-extended to 16-bits, disp-high is absent
if mod = 10 then DISP = disp-high: disp-low
if r/m = 000 then EA = (BX) + (SI) + DISP
if r/m = 001 then EA = (BX) + (DI) + DISP
if r/m = 010 then EA = (BP) + (SI) + DISP
if r/m = 011 then EA = (BP) + (DI) + DISP
if r/m = 100 then EA = (SI) + DISP
if r/m = 101 then EA = (DI) + DISP
if r/m = 110 then EA = (BP) + DISP except if mod = 00 and
  r/m = 110 then EA = disp-high: disp-low.
if r/m = 111 then EA = (BX) + DISP
DISP follows second byte of instruction (before data if required)

if s:w = 01 then 16 bits of immediate data form the operand
if s:w = 11 then an immediate data byte is sign extended to
  form the 16-bit operand
if v = 0 then "count" = 1; if v = 1 then "count" in (CL)
x = don't care
z is used for string primitives for comparison with ZF FLAG

SEGMENT OVERRIDE PREFIX

0 0 1	reg	1 1 0		

REG is assigned according to the following table:

16-Bit (w = 1)	8-Bit (w = 0)	Segment
000 AX	000 AL	00 ES
001 CX	001 CL	01 CS
010 DX	010 DL	10 SS
011 BX	011 BL	11 DS
100 SP	100 AH	
101 BP	101 CH	
110 SI	110 DH	
111 DI	111 BH	

Instructions which reference the flag register file as a 16-bit object use the symbol FLAGS to represent the file:

FLAGS = X:X:X:X:(OF):(DF):(IF):(TF):(SF):
  (ZF):X:(AF):X:(PF):X:(CF)

Mnemonics © Intel, 1978 (Courtesy of Intel Corporation.)

CHAPTER 1

Questions

1-1. I/O (input/output) ports.

1-3. Low bandwidth.

1-5. Serially.

1-7. No. Yes, a selectric is a formed character device.

1-9. The data bus.

Problems

1-11. Approximately 900 Bd.

1-13. Approximately 9600 Bd.

1-15. 1024 (1K) bytes/sector.

CHAPTER 2

Questions

2-1. 20 bits.

2-3. AX (AL,AH), BX (BL,BH), CX (CL,CH), DX (DL,DH).

2-5. A string must be stored in contiguous memory locations.

2-7. ASCII Adjust for Add (AAA) instruction.

2-9. The base pointer (BP).

Problems

```
2-11.   MOV SP,[BP]      1000 1011  (8B)
                         0110 0110  (66)
                         0000 0000  (00)

2-13.   POP [A5C0]       1000 1111  (8F)
                         0000 0110  (06)
                         1100 0000  (C0)
                         1010 0101  (A5)

2-15.   XCHG BP,AX       1001 0101  (95)

2-17.   CMP AL,XX        1100 0011  (C3)
                         XXXX XXXX  (XX)
```

CHAPTER 3

Questions

3-1. Code segment.

3-3. A file is a contiguous block of data that is stored on disk.

3-5. Macro.

3-7. Pointers are enclosed in brackets [pointer].

3-9. The brackets indicate that the contents of SI point to the operand address in the current data segment.

Problems

3-11. XCHG DI,AX.

3-13. ADD CH,AL.

3-15. SF will be set.

3-17. $3D40_{16}$.

3-19.
```
XXXX:0100 MOV AX,C000
XXXX:0103 MOV ES,AX
XXXX:0105 MOV AX,AB00
XXXX:0108 MOV SS,AX
XXXX:010A MOV AX,0000
XXXX:010D MOV DS,AX
```

3-21.
```
XXXX:0100 MOV DX,0000
XXXX:0103 IN AL,DX
XXXX:0104 CMP AL,00
XXXX:0106 JZ 0103
XXXX:0108 OUT [10],AL
XXXX:010A CMP DX,0009
XXXX:010D JE 0100
XXXX:010F INC DX
XXXX:JMP 0103
```

3-23. $162C_{16}$.

CHAPTER 4

Questions

4-1. ALE.

4-3. RESET must be held high for four (4) clock cycles.

4-5. $FFFF0_{16}$.

4-7. DMA.

4-9. $\overline{\text{IORC}}$, $\overline{\text{IOWC}}$, and $\overline{\text{AIOWC}}$.

4-11. Handshaking signals.

Problems

4-13. $t_H = 69.18$ ns, $t_L = 140.46$ ns.

4-15. $\overline{\text{CS}} = 0$, $\overline{\text{WE}} = 0$.

4-17. $\overline{\text{CS}} = 1$, $\overline{\text{WE}} = 0$ and $\overline{\text{CS}} = 1$, $\overline{\text{WE}} = 1$.

4-19. 14.31 MHz.

4-21. 7.85 μs.

CHAPTER 5

Questions

5-1. Flip-flops.

5-3. Serial memories.

5-5. Burst refresh.

5-7. Power dissipation is too high, and too many transistors are required per cell.

5-9. Once every 2 ms.

Problems

5-11. 89.6 μs.

5-13. 2%.

5-15. No. Memory contents are not destroyed when locations are read.

5-17. See the figure below.

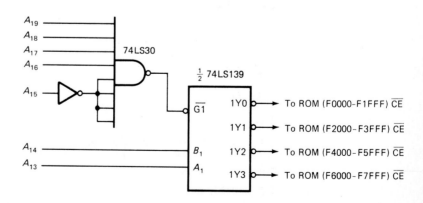

5-19. See the figure below.

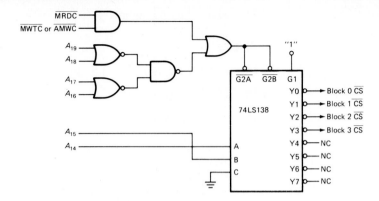

CHAPTER 6

Questions

6-1. Programmed I/O is the simplest approach, but it would waste much time. A better approach would be to have a timer generate an interrupt at fixed intervals. This would be more complex from the hardware side, but more efficient from a CPU time standpoint.

6-3. Polled I/O.

6-5. AEN is used to disable I/O ports during DMA operations.

6-7. 64K (65,536).

6-9. Disk drives and magnetic tape storage units.

6-11. Interrupt-driven I/O.

6-13. The IF flag must be set.

6-15. In the AEOI mode, the IS (In Service) register of the 8255A is automatically reset on the trailing edge of the second INTA pulse. The most significant IS flag that is set will be cleared.

6-17. Mode 2.

Problems

6-19. See the figure below.

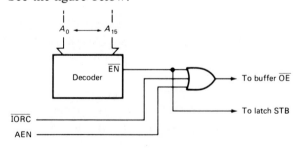

6-21. See the figure below.

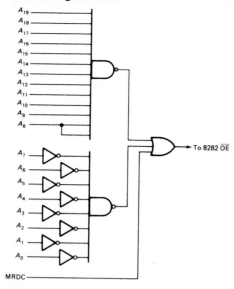

6-23. See the figure below.

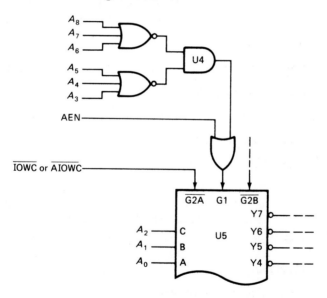

6-25. $S_7 = 0$, $S_6 = 0$, $S_5 = 1$, $S_4 = 0$, $S_3 = 1$, $S_2 = 1$, $S_1 = 0$, $S_0 = 1$.

6-27. OCW3:

A_0	D_7	D_6	D_5	D_4	D_3	D_2	D_1	D_0
0	0	0	0	0	1	0	1	1

6-29. Mode definition control word

D_7	D_6	D_5	D_4	D_3	D_2	D_1	D_0
1	0	0	0	1	0	0	1

CHAPTER 7

Questions

7-1. Aliasing error.

7-3. Offset error (positive) and nonlinearity error.

7-5. EOC can be used to initiate an interrupt request, or it may be polled.

7-7. Gain error.

7-9. Wide resistor value ranges are necessary and poor temperature tracking characteristics.

7-11. Zero offset compensation.

Problems

7-13. 2.48 V.

7-15. 4.5 V.

7-17. A coupling capacitor could be placed in series with the output of the D/A converter.

7-19. 10 stages.

7-21. 5 bits.

7-23. 63 comparators.

7-25. 10.625 V.

CHAPTER 8

Questions

8-1. Conversion constant for natural log to common ($\log_{10}$) log.

8-3. Bit mapped graphics are less memory efficient.

8-5. A field is a sequence of scan lines that is produced during one CRT vertical deflection period.

8-7. 1,536 bytes of ROM are required (use a 2048×8 ROM).

8-9. Conventional color CRTs have circular phosphors, while trinitron types have rectangular phosphors.

Problems

8-11. 80 characters/line, 25 lines.

8-13. Character grid size = 10 pixels horiz. by 20 pixels vert.

8-15. Dot rate = 0.125 μs. This is the period of time in which a given dot (pixel) is drawn on the CRT.

8-17.
```
10 REM **** SET HIGH RES AND CLEAR SCREEN ***
20 SCREEN 2: CLS
30 REM **** X IS THE HORIZ. POSITION COUNTER
35 REM
40 FOR X = 0 TO 639
45 REM
50 REM **** SHOCKLEY'S EQUATION ****
55 REM
60 I = 20E-12 * EXP(VF/0.026)
65 REM
70 REM **** SCALE Y-AXIS FOR 50 mA AT TOP **
75 Y = -4000 * I + 199
80 REM
85 REM **** PLOT I vs V ****
90 REM
100 PSET(X,Y),1
105 REM
110 REM **** INCREMENT VF BY 0.7/640 ****
115 REM
120 VF = VF + 1.0955E-3
125 REM
130 NEXT X
```

8-19.
```
10 REM **** PLOT FUNCTION ****
20 SCREEN 2
30 INPUT "ENTER TIME INCREMENT (SECONDS)"; T
40 INPUT "ENTER RADIAN FREQUENCY (OMEGA)"; W
50 INPUT "ENTER SCALING FACTOR"; K
60 CLS
70 FOR X = 0 TO 639
80 A = K*(SIN(W*T)+1/2*SIN(2*W*T)+1/
   3*SIN(3*W*T)+1/4*SIN(4*W*T)
90 Y = -A + 100
100 PSET(X,Y),1
110 NEXT X
```

CHAPTER 9

Questions

9-1. Higher average signal power levels.

9-3. Bi-phase.

9-5. Simpler to produce.

9-7. When an even number of bits are lost.

9-9. Burst error.

9-11. 8 bits.

9-13. A UART.

9-15. Cyclic redundancy coding.

Problems

9-17. Logic high. Logic low.

9-19. Degree = 4.

9-21. 3200 Bd.

9-23. 5600 bits/s.

9-25.
$$
\begin{array}{cccccccc}
 & b_1 & b_2 & b_3 & b_4 & b_5 & b_6 & b_7 \\
\text{ASCII ``W''} = & 1 & 1 & 1 & 0 & 1 & 0 & 1
\end{array}
$$

$$
\begin{array}{rl}
\text{Hamming code word} = & P_1\ b_1\ P_2\ b_2\ b_3\ P_3\ b_4\ b_5\ b_6\ b_7 \\
= & 0\ \ 1\ \ 1\ \ 1\ \ 1\ \ 0\ \ 0\ \ 1\ \ 0\ \ 1
\end{array}
$$

9-27.

$C_5 = 1/f_{MARK}R_1$
$\quad = 1/1200 \times 6800$
$\quad = 0.123\ \mu F$

$C_8 = 1/f_{SPACE}R_3$
$\quad = 1/2200 \times 4700$
$\quad = 0.097\ \mu F$

$C_4 = V_{in}/[f_{MARK}(CR/1070)^2]$
$\quad = 0.5/[1200 \times (40/1070)^2]$
$\quad = 0.298\ \mu F$

Where CR is the capture range in Hz.

$C_7 = V_{in}/[f_{SPACE}(CR/1070)^2]\ (\mu F)$
$\quad = 0.5/[2200 \times (40/1070)^2]$
$\quad = 0.163\ \mu F$

CHAPTER 10

Questions

10-1. Buffer.

10-3. Holding the key results in a constant Q output, useful for implementing automatic keystroke repeat.

10-5. To prevent illegal half-closed states.

10-7. FM and MFM.

10-9. To suppress induced EMF during field collapse.

10-11. Used to provide a signal that marks the start of the first sectors on each track.

10-13. Seek and read/write.

10-15. Clock synchronization cannot be derived from NRZ.

Problems

10-17. The clock period must be shorter than the time constant of the one-shot.

10-19. Latch outputs are enabled by reading the keyboard port.

10-21. Each row is scanned once every 3 ms.

10-23. See the figure below.

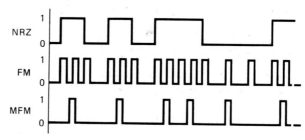

10-25.

```
0100      MOV AL,33
0102      MOV DX,FF00
0105      MOV CX,F000
0108      OUT DX,AL
010A      ROR AL,1
010C      LOOP 010C
010E      JMP  0105
```

CHAPTER 11

Questions

11-1. Improper handling of mating surfaces.

11-3. Glitch or transient.

11-5. Supply voltage.

11-7. Requires a repetitive signal to lock on to. Also, glitches vanish so rapidly that they are hard to see on the display even when they cause triggering.

11-9. A four-character code that represents the sequence of events at a test point.

11-11. Circuit and test program modifications would change the signature, making it useless.

11-13. The time domain is continuous while the data domain is defined by discrete, discontinuous events.

11-15. The system clock.

11-17. Delayed triggering.

Problems

11-19. From $t = 0$ to 500 ms, the LOW indicator would be on. After $t = 500$ ms, the HIGH indicator would be on. The pulse indicator would blink on from $t = 6$ ms to about 506 ms (this assumes negative triggering of pulse-stretching circuitry).

11-21. See the figure below.

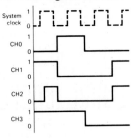

11-23. $t = 5 \, \mu s$

Index

Serial
    data transfer, 323–329
    memory, 149
Serial-in serial-out (SISO) shift register, 169
Servo, 381–383
Settling time, 248–249
74LS139, 181
74LS243, 120
74LS373, 196, 198
SF (*see* Sign flag)
Shadow mask, 284
SHL/SAL instruction, 64–65
SHR instruction, 64–65
Short-haul modem, 346
Sign flag (SF), 52
Signature analysis, 403–404
Simplex, 334
SISO (*see* Serial-in serial-out shift register)
Software interrupt, 80
Source code, 88
Space, 325, 330
Stack, 29, 78
Start bit, 326
Status codes, 103–104
STC instruction, 81
STD instruction, 81
STDS instruction, 66, 68–69
Step size, 247
Stepper motor, 384–388
STI instruction, 81
Streaming tape, 18
String, 66
Successive approximation register (SAR), 269
Summing converter, 250–253
Switching regulator, 414–416
Synchronous data transfer, 323–324
System unit, 3

TEST instruction, 63–64
Thyristor, 234–235
Track, 376–377
Transfer function
    A/D, 262–263

Transfer function (continued)
    D/A, 246
Trap flag (TF), 52
Triac, 234
Tristate, 118–119
Turtle graphics, 314
2112 RAM (*see* Random access memory)
2176 RAM (*see* Random access memory)
Two-pass assembler, 89

U (unassemble command), 91
UART (*see* Universal asynchronous receiver-transmitters)
Ultraviolet (UV) radiation, 167–168
Universal asynchronous receiver-transmitters (UART), 328

v field, 64, 93
Vector, 78–79
Vectored interrupt, 78, 207
Video RAM (*see* Random access memory)

W (write command), 105–106
w field, 31
WAIT instruction, 81, 113
WIDTH statement, 303
WINDOW statement, 302
WORD PTR, 66, 93
Word recognizer, 406–407
World coordinates, 300–301, 309–314

XCHG instruction, 47–49
XOR instruction, 63–64

Zero flag (ZF), 52
ZF flag (*see* Zero flag)